AF673493

NCERT SOLUTIONS

with Chapterwise **Study Notes**

PHYSICS 11th

Fully Updated as per Latest NCERT Textbook

NCERT SOLUTIONS

with Chapterwise **Study Notes**

PHYSICS 11th

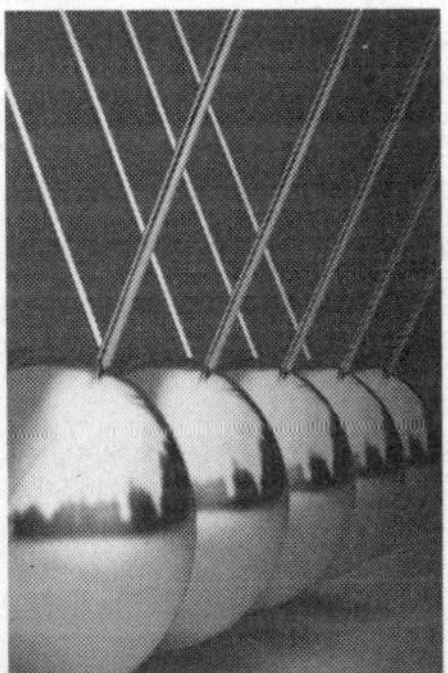

Author

Dr Sanjeev Varshney

Mukesh Kumar

Including Selected Questions of DIKSHA

arihant

SUCCESS AND NOTHING LESS

arihant
SUCCESS AND NOTHING LESS

ARIHANT PRAKASHAN (Series), MEERUT

All Rights Reserved

© Publisher

No part of this publication may be re-produced, stored in a retrieval system or by any means, electronic, mechanical, photocopying, recording, scanning, web or otherwise without the written permission of the publisher. Arihant has obtained all the information in this book from the sources believed to be reliable and true. However, Arihant or its editors or authors or illustrators don't take any responsibility for the absolute accuracy of any information published and the damage or loss suffered thereupon.

All disputes subject to Meerut (UP) jurisdiction only.

卐 Administrative & Production Offices

Regd. Office

'Ramchhaya' 4577/15, Agarwal Road, Darya Ganj, New Delhi -110002
Tele: 011- 47630600, 43518550

卐 Head Office

Kalindi, TP Nagar, Meerut (UP) - 250002
Tel: 0121-7156203, 7156204

卐 Sales & Support Offices

Agra, Ahmedabad, Bengaluru, Bareilly, Chennai, Delhi, Guwahati, Hyderabad, Jaipur, Jhansi, Kolkata, Lucknow, Nagpur & Pune.

卐 **PRICE** ₹275.00

卐 **PO No. :** TXT-59-T070752-4-26

Published by Arihant Publications (India) Ltd.

For further information about the books published by Arihant, log on to www.arihantbooks.com or e-mail at info@arihantbooks.com

Follow us on

Preface

Feeling the immense importance and value of NCERT books, we are presenting this book, having the **NCERT Exercises Solutions**. For the overall benefit of the students we have made this book unique in such a way that it presents not only solutions but also detailed explanations. Through these detailed and through explanations, students can learn the concepts which will enhance their thinking and learning abilities.

We have introduced some Additional Features with the solutions which are given below:

- **Explanatory Solutions** Along with the solutions to questions we have given all the points that tell how to approach to solve a problem. Here we have tried to cover all those loopholes which may lead to confusion. All formulae and hints are discussed in full detail.
- Also included **Thinking Process** and **Mistake Alert** to understanding 'How to solve question' and points of mistakes.
- **Note** We have provided notes also to solutions in which special points are mentioned which are of great value for the students.

Apart from all those who helped in the compilation of this book a special note of thanks to all. With the hope that this book will be of great help to the students, we wish great success to our readers.

Dr Sanjeev Varshney
Mukesh Kumar

Contents

Units and Measurements

CHAPTER 01

Important Points

01 Measurement The comparison of any physical quantity with its standard unit is called measurement.

02 International System of Units (SI) This system of units contains 7 fundamental units and 2 supplementary units.

03 Fundamental Units

S. No.	Fundamental quantity	Fundamental unit	Symbol
1.	Length	metre	m
2.	Mass	kilogram	kg
3.	Time	second	s
4.	Electric current	ampere	A
5.	Temperature	kelvin	K
6.	Luminous intensity	candela	Cd
7.	Amount of substance	mole	mol

04 Supplementary Units

(i) Radian (rad) $\rightarrow$ unit of plane angle

(ii) Steradian (sr) $\rightarrow$ unit of solid angle

05 Few Other Units of Length, Mass, Time and other quantities

Astronomical Unit (AU) = 1.496×10^{11} m

Light year (ly) = 9.46×10^{15}m

Parallactic second (par sec) = 3.084×10^{16}m

Pound = 0.4536 kg , Slug = 14.59 kg

Atomic mass unit (u) = 1.66×10^{-27}kg

Shake = 10^{-8} s , Barn = 10^{-28}m^2

06 Significant figures in a measured value of a physical quantity are the digits that are known reliably plus the first uncertain digit.

07 In addition or subtraction, the final result should retain the same number of decimal places as the number with the least number of decimal places.

Example Add the 436.32 g , 227.2g and 0.301 g with due to regards to significant figures.

$\therefore$ We have 436.32 g + 227.2g + 0.301 g $\Rightarrow$ 663.82 g

But answer should be reported to one decimal places.

So, final answer will be 663.89 g.

08 In multiplication or division, the final result should retain the same number of significant figures as the number with the least significant figures.

Example Density $= \dfrac{\text{Mass}}{\text{Volume}} = \dfrac{4.237}{2.51}$ (4 significant figures)

(3 significant figures)

$= 1.687251$

Final result $= 1.69\ \text{g/cm}^3$ (rounded to 3 significant figures)

09 Rounding off uncertain digits is a method used in computation involving approximate numbers to reduce them to a specified number of significant figures. This is done by removing insignificant digits based on standard rules.

- It the digit to be dropped is more than 5, increase the preceding digit by 1.
- If the digit to be dropped is less than 5, leave the preceding digit unchanged.
- If the digit to be dropped is exactly 5, then

(i) Preceding digit is left unchanged if it is even.

(ii) Preceding digit is raised by one; if it is odd.

Example

(i) Round off 2.745 to three significant figures.

- The digit to be dropped is 5.
- The preceding digit is 4 (even), so it remains unchanged.
- Result 2.745 (becomes 2.74 on rounding off)

(ii) Round off 2.735 to three significant figures.
- The digit to be droped is 5.
- The preceding digit is 3 (odd), so it is increased by 1.
- Result 2.735 (becomes 2.74 on rounding off).

10 The difference in the true value and the measured value of a quantity is called error of measurement.

11 Absolute error = True value – Measured value

12 **Mean Absolute Error** The arithmetic mean of the magnitudes of absolute errors is called mean absolute error.

If $\Delta a_1, \Delta a_2, \ldots\ldots, \Delta a_n$ are absolute errors in n measurements then mean absolute error

$$\Delta a_m = \frac{|\Delta a_1| + |\Delta a_2| + \ldots. + |\Delta a_n|}{n}$$

13 **Relative Error or Fractional Error** The ratio of mean absolute error to the mean value is called relative or fractional error.

Relative or fractional error $(\delta_a) = \dfrac{\Delta a_m}{a_m}$

14 **Percentage Error** Relative or fractional error, represented in percentage is called percentage error.

$$\text{Percentage error} = \frac{\Delta a_m}{a_m} \times 100\%$$

15 **Propagation of Error**

(i) **Error in Sum or Difference** Maximum absolute error in sum or difference of two quantities is equal to sum of the absolute errors in the individual quantities.
If $x = a + b$ or $x = a - b$ then, $\Delta x = \pm (\Delta a + \Delta b)$

(ii) **Error in a Product or Division** Maximum fractional error in a product or division of quantities is equal to sum of the fractional errors in the individual quantities.

If $x = a \times b$ or $x = a / b$, then $\dfrac{\Delta x}{x} = \pm \left(\dfrac{\Delta a}{a} + \dfrac{\Delta b}{b} \right)$

(iii) If $x = a^n / b^m$ and absolute errors in a and b are $\pm \Delta a$ and $\pm \Delta b$, then maximum fractional error is given by

$$\frac{\Delta x}{x} = \pm \left(n\frac{\Delta a}{a} + m\frac{\Delta b}{b} \right)$$

16 Dimensions Dimensions of any physical quantity are those powers which are raised on fundamental units to express the unit of that physical quantity.

17 Principle of Homogeneity of Dimensions Only those physical quantities can be added or subtracted which have same dimensions.

18 Applications of Dimensions

(i) To check the correctness of any physical equation.

(ii) To convert any physical quantity from one system of units to another system of units.

$$n_1 u_1 = n_2 u_2$$

where n_1, n_2 are the magnitudes and u_1, u_2 are the units of physical quantity in two different systems of units.

(iii) To establish the relation among various physical quantities.

Exercises

Question 1 Fill in the blanks

(a) The volume of a cube of side 1 cm is equal to ...... m^3.

(b) The surface area of a solid cylinder of radius 2.0 cm and height 10.0 cm is equal to ...... $(mm)^2$.

(c) A vehicle moving with a speed of 18 km/h covers ...... m in 1s.

(d) The relative density of lead is 11.3. Its density is ...... g/cm^3 or ...... kg/m^3.

Sol.

(a) The volume of a cube of side 1 cm is given by, $V = (1\text{ cm})^3$

or $$V = (10^{-2}\text{ m})^3 = 10^{-6}\text{ m}^3$$

(b) The surface area of a solid cylinder of radius r and height h is given by

$$A = \text{Area of two caps} + \text{Curved surface area}$$
$$= 2\pi r^2 + 2\pi rh = 2\pi r(r + h)$$

Here, $r = 2\text{ cm} = 20\text{ mm}, h = 10\text{ cm} = 100\text{ mm}$

∴ Surface area of the solid cylinder

$$A = 2 \times \frac{22}{7} \times 20(20 + 100)\,(\text{mm})^2 = \frac{880}{7} \times 120\text{ mm}^2$$
$$= 15085\text{ mm}^2 = 1.5085 \times 10^4\text{ mm}^2$$
$$= 1.5 \times 10^4\text{ mm}^2$$

(c) Here, speed of the vehicle $v = 18\ \text{km/h} = \dfrac{18 \times 1000}{3600} = 5\ \text{m/s}$

$$\text{Distance} = \text{Speed} \times \text{Time}$$

$\therefore$ Distance travelled in 1 s, $x = vt = 5 \times 1 = 5\ \text{m}$

Note If speed is in 'm/s' then time should be in 'second' and if speed in 'km/h' then time should be in 'hour'.

Quick Solution

$$\text{Distance} = \text{Speed} \times \text{time}$$
$$= 18\ \text{km/h} \times \frac{10}{18}\ \text{h} = 0.005\ \text{km} = 5\ \text{m}$$

(d) Relative density of lead = 11.3

Density of water = $1\ \text{g/cm}^3$

We know that relative density of lead = $\dfrac{\text{Density of lead}}{\text{Density of water}}$

$\therefore$ Density of lead = Relative density of lead × Density of water

$$= 11.3 \times (1\ \text{g/cm}^3) = 11.3\ \text{g/cm}^3$$

Density of water in SI system = $10^3\ \text{kg/m}^3$

$\therefore$ Density of lead = $11.3 \times 10^3\ \text{kg/m}^3$

$$= 1.13 \times 10^4\ \text{kg/m}^3$$

Mistake Alert Students take formula of relative density as

$$\text{Relative density} = \frac{\text{Density of water}}{\text{Density of material}}$$

While the correct one is, Relative density $= \dfrac{\text{Density of material}}{\text{Density of water}}$

Question 2 Fill in the blanks by suitable conversion of units.

(a) $1\ \text{kg-m}^2/\text{s}^2$ ...... $\text{g-cm}^2/\text{s}^2$

(b) 1 m = ... ly (light year)

(c) $3.0\ \text{m/s}^2$ = ... km/h^2

(d) $G = 6.67 \times 10^{-11}\ \text{N-m}^2/\text{kg}^2$ = ... $\text{cm}^3/\text{s}^2\cdot\text{g}$

Sol.

(a) $1\ \text{kg-m}^2/\text{s}^2 = 1(10^3\text{g})(10^2\ \text{cm})^2/\text{s}^2$

$(\because 1\ \text{kg} = 1000\ \text{g} = 10^3\ \text{g},\ 1\ \text{m} = 100\ \text{cm} = 10^2\ \text{cm})$

$$= 10^3 \times 10^4\ \text{g-cm}^2/\text{s}^2 = 10^7\ \text{g-cm}^2/\text{s}^2$$

(b) We know that 1 light year (ly) = 9.46×10^{15} m

$$\therefore \quad 1\ \text{m} = \frac{1}{9.46 \times 10^{15}}\ \text{ly} = 1.057 \times 10^{-16}\ \text{ly}$$

(c) $3.0\ \text{m/s}^2 = 3 \times 10^{-3}\text{km} \times \left(\frac{1}{60 \times 60}\text{h}\right)^{-2}$

$(\because 1\ \text{km} = 1000\ \text{m} \therefore 1\ \text{m} = 10^{-3}\ \text{km},\ 1\text{h} = 60 \times 60\ \text{s} \therefore 1\ \text{s} = \frac{1}{60 \times 60}\text{h})$

$= 3 \times 10^{-3} \times (3600)^2\ \text{km/h}^2 = 3.888 \times 10^4\ \text{km/h}^2 = 3.9 \times 10^4\ \text{km/h}^2$

(d) $G = 6.67 \times 10^{-11}\text{N-m}^2/\text{kg}^2$

$= 6.67 \times 10^{-11}(10^5\ \text{dyne})(10^2\ \text{cm})^2(10^3\text{g})^{-2}$ $(\because 1\ \text{Newton} = 10^5\ \text{dyne})$

$= 6.67 \times 10^{-11} \times 10^5 \times 10^4 \times 10^{-6}\ \text{dyne-cm}^2/\text{g}^2$

$= 6.67 \times 10^{-8}\ (\text{g-cm/s}^2)\ \text{cm}^2/\text{g}^2 = 6.67 \times 10^{-8}\text{cm}^3/\text{g-s}^2$

Question 3 A calorie is a unit of heat or energy and it equals about 4.2 J, where $1\ \text{J} = 1\ \text{kg-m}^2/\text{s}^2$. Suppose we employ a system of units in which the unit of mass equals α kg, the unit of length is β m, the unit of time is γ s. Show that a calorie has a magnitude $4.2\ \alpha^{-1}\beta^{-2}\gamma^2$ in terms of new units.

Sol. The dimensional formula of energy = $[ML^2T^{-2}]$

Let M_1, L_1, T_1 and M_2, L_2, T_2 are the units of mass, length and time in given two systems.

$\therefore \quad M_1 = 1\text{kg}, M_2 = \alpha\,\text{kg}, L_1 = 1\,\text{m}, L_2 = \beta\,\text{m}, T_1 = 1\ \text{s}, T_2 = \gamma\ \text{s}$

For any physical quantity, the product of its magnitude and unit is always constant (i.e. principle of homogeneity).

$\therefore \quad n_1 u_1 = n_2 u_2$

or $\quad n_2 = n_1 \frac{u_1}{u_2}$

$$= 4.2\left[\frac{M_1}{M_2}\right] \times \left[\frac{L_1}{L_2}\right]^2 \times \left[\frac{T_1}{T_2}\right]^{-2} = 4.2\left[\frac{1}{\alpha}\text{kg}\right] \times \left[\frac{1}{\beta}\text{m}\right]^2 \times \left[\frac{1}{\gamma}\text{s}\right]^{-2}$$

$n_2 = 4.2\alpha^{-1}\beta^{-2}\gamma^2$ new unit

$\therefore \quad 1\ \text{cal} = 4.2\alpha^{-1}\beta^{-2}\gamma^2$ new unit **Hence Proved.**

Question 4 Explain the statement clearly "To call a dimensional quantity 'large' or 'small' is meaningless without specifying a standard for comparison." In view of this, reframe the following statements wherever necessary :

(a) Atoms are very small objects.

(b) A jet plane moves with great speed.

(c) The mass of Jupiter is very large.

(d) The air inside this room contains a large number of molecules.

(e) A proton is much more massive than an electron.

(f) The speed of sound is much smaller than the speed of light.

Sol. The statement is true. Any dimensional physical quantity can be called large or small by specifying a standard for comparison.

For example, the mass of a boy is 40 kg, which is very small in comparison to the mass of the earth (6×10^{24} kg) but very large in comparison to the mass of an electron (9.1×10^{-31} kg).

(a) The size of an atom is very small in comparison to the size of a sugar cube.
(b) A jet plane moves faster than a superfast train.
(c) The mass of Jupiter is very large as compared to the mass of Uranus.
(d) The air inside this room contains large number of molecules than in one mole of air.
(e) The statement is already correct.
(f) The statement is already correct.

Question 5 A new unit of length is chosen such that the speed of light in vacuum is unity. What is the distance between the sun and the earth in terms of the new unit, if light takes 8 min and 20 s to cover this distance?

Sol. The speed of light in vacuum (c) = 1 (new unit of length s^{-1})

Time taken by light to reach the earth

$$t = 8 \text{ min} + 20 \text{ s} = (8 \times 60 + 20) \text{ s} = 500 \text{ s}$$

$\therefore$ Distance between the sun and the earth = Speed of light × Time

$$x = c \times t$$
$$= 1 (\text{new unit of length s}^{-1}) \times 500 \text{ s}$$
$$= 500 \text{ new unit of length}$$

Mistake Alert Student might try to use traditional unit like meter or kilometer.

Question 6 Which of the following is the most precise device for measuring length?

(a) A vernier callipers with 20 divisions on the sliding scale.
(b) A screw gauge of pitch 1 mm and 100 divisions on the circular scale.
(c) An optical instrument that can measure length to within a wavelength of light?

Sol. The instrument whose least count is minimum, is called the most precise device.

(a) Number of divisions on vernier scale = 20

Main Scale Division (MSD) = 1 mm

As 20 divisions on vernier scale will be equal to the 19 divisions on main scale.

$\therefore$ Vernier Scale Division (VSD) $= \frac{19}{20}$ MSD

Least count of varnier callipers = 1 MSD – 1 VSD

$$= 1\,\text{MSD} - \frac{19}{20}\,\text{MSD} = \frac{1}{20}\,\text{MSD}$$

$$= \frac{1}{20}\,\text{mm} = \frac{1}{200}\,\text{cm} = 0.005\,\text{cm}$$

(b) Pitch of screw guage = 1 mm

Number of divisions on circular scale = 100

$$\text{Least count of screw guage} = \frac{\text{Pitch}}{\text{Number of divisions on circular scale}}$$

$$= \frac{1}{100}\,\text{mm} = \frac{1}{1000}\,\text{cm}$$

$$= 0.001\,\text{cm}$$

(c) Wavelength of light $(\lambda) \approx 10^{-7}$ m $= 10^{-5}$ cm $= 0.00001$ cm

$\therefore$ As the given optical instrument can measure length to within a wavelength of light, therefore least count of the given optical instrument

= Wavelength of light

= 0.00001 cm

The least count is minimum for the given optical instrument. Therefore, the given optical instrument is the most precise.

Question 7 A student measures the thickness of a human hair by looking at it through a microscope of magnification 100. He makes 20 observations and finds that the average width of the hair in the field of view of the microscope is 3.5 mm. What is the estimate on the thickness of hair?

◎ ***Thinking Process*** Magnification is the process of enlarging an object's apparent size. In microscopy it is achieved by using lenses that bend light ray to form a larger image.

Sol. Magnification of microscope = 100

Observed width of the hair = 3.5 mm

Estimate on the thickness of hair is given by

$$\text{Magnification} = \frac{\text{Observed width}}{\text{Real width}}$$

or

$$\text{Real width} = \frac{\text{Observed width}}{\text{Magnification}} = \frac{3.5}{100}$$

$$= 0.035\,\text{mm}$$

Question 8 Answer the following

(a) You are given a thread and a meter scale. How will you estimate the diameter of the thread?

(b) A screw gauge has a pitch of 1.0 mm and 200 divisions on the circular scale. Do you think, it is possible to increase the accuracy of the screw gauge arbitrarily by increasing the number of divisions on the circular scale?

(c) The mean diameter of a thin brass rod is to be measured by vernier callipers. Why is a set of 100 measurements of the diameter expected to yield a more reliable estimate than a set of 5 measurements only?

Sol.

(a) The diameter of a thread is so small that it cannot be measured using a metre scale. To measure the diameter of the thread, we wound a number of turns of the thread on the metre scale so that the turns are closely touching one another but not overlapping.

Count the number of turns (n) and measure the length (l) of the coiled thread using the metre scale.

$$\text{Diameter of thread} = \frac{\text{Length of coiled thread } (l)}{\text{Number of turns } (n)}$$

(b) Yes, the accuracy of the screw guage can be increased by increasing the number of divisions on the circular scale as the least count of the screw gauge is given by

$$\text{Least count} = \frac{\text{Pitch}}{\text{Number of divisions on circular scale}}$$

From the formula it is clear that by increasing the number of divisions on circular scale. Least count can be decreased, hence the accuracy will increase.

It is possible theoretically but practically it may not be possible because it is difficult to take the reading precisely as the resolution of human eye is not so high.

(c) The mean diameter of a thin brass rod measured by a vernier calliper from a set of 100 measurements is more reliable than the diameter obtained from a set of 5 measurements because the probability of making a positive random error is equal to the probability of making a negative random error.

Therefore, in a large number of measurements these errors cancel each other and we get more reliable value. It also makes arithmetic mean closer to true value.

Question 9 The photograph of a house occupies an area of 1.75 cm^2 on a 35 mm slide. The slide is projected on to a screen and the area of the house on the screen is 1.55 m^2. What is the linear magnification of the projector-screen arrangement.

Sol. Area of object $= 1.75\ \text{cm}^2 = 1.75 \times 10^{-4}\text{m}^2$

Area of image $= 1.55\ \text{m}^2$

$$\therefore \text{Areal magnification} = \frac{\text{Area of image}}{\text{Area of object}}$$

$$= \frac{1.55}{1.75 \times 10^{-4}} \approx 8857$$

$$\text{Linear magnification} = \sqrt{\text{Areal magnification}}$$

$$= \sqrt{8857} = 94.1$$

Mistake Alert Student take formula of Areal magnification as,

$$\text{Areal magnification} = \frac{\text{Area of object}}{\text{Area of image}}$$

While correct one is, Areal magnification $= \dfrac{\text{Area of image}}{\text{Area of object}}$.

Question 10 State the number of significant figures in the following:

(a) 0.007 m^2 (b) 2.64×10^{24} kg (c) 0.2370 g/cm^3

(d) 6.320 J (e) 6.032 N/m^2 (f) 0.0006032 m^2

Sol. The number of significant figures in the given quantities are given below.

(a) In 0.007, the number of significant figure is 1.
Because in a number less than 1, the zero's on the right of the decimal point but to the left of the first non-zero digit are not significant.

(b) In 2.64×10^{24}, the number of significant figures is 3.
Because all non-zero digits are significant, power of 10 is not taken in significant figure.

(c) In 0.2370, the number of significant figures is 4, as all non-zero digit left to decimal and trailing zero are significant because zero between two non-zero digits is significant.

(d) In 6.320, the number of significant figures is 4 because all zero to the right of the last non-zero digit after the decimal point are significant.

(e) In 6.032, the number of significant figures is 4 (reason is same as in part 'c').

(f) In 0.0006032, the number of significant figures is 4 (reason is same as in part 'a').

Mistake Alert Students do not consider 0 after decimal as significant figure in case of 0.2370 and 6.320 while they are significant.

Question 11 The length, breadth and thickness of a rectangular sheet of metal are 4.234 m, 1.005 m and 2.01 cm respectively. Give the area and volume of the sheet to correct significant figures.

Sol. Given, length $(l) = 4.234$ m

breadth $(b) = 1.005$ m

thickness $(t) = 2.01$ cm $= 0.0201$ m

$$\text{Area of sheet } (A) = 2(l \times b + b \times t + t \times l)$$
$$= 2[(4.234 \times 1.005) + (1.005 \times 0.0201) + (0.0201 \times 4.234)]$$
$$= 2 \times 4.3604739$$
$$= 8.7209478 \text{ m}^2$$

As thickness has least number of significant figures 3, therefore rounding-off area up to three significant figures, we get

Area of sheet $(A) = 8.72 \text{ m}^2$

Volume of sheet $(V) = l \times b \times t$

$$= 4.234 \times 1.005 \times 0.0201 = 0.0855289$$

Rounding-off up to three significant figures, we get

Volume of the sheet $= 0.0855 \text{ m}^3$

Note If different values of a same quantity are given in different units, then first of all convert them in same units without changing the number of significant figures.

Question 12 The mass of a box measured by a grocer's balance is 2.3 kg. Two gold pieces of masses 20.15 g and 20.17 g are added to the box. What is (a) the total mass of the box, (b) the difference in the mass of the pieces to correct significant figures?

Sol. Given, mass of the box $(m) = 2.3$ kg

Mass of first gold piece $(m_1) = 20.15 \text{ g} = 20.15 \times 10^{-3} \text{ kg} = 0.02015$ kg

Mass of second gold piece $(m_2) = 20.17 \text{ g} = 20.17 \times 10^{-3} \text{ kg} = 0.02017$ kg

(a) Total mass of the box $(M) = m + m_1 + m_2$

$$= 2.3 + 0.02015 + 0.02017$$
$$= 2.34032 \text{ kg}$$

As the mass of the box has least decimal place *i.e.*, one decimal place, therefore total mass of the box can have only one decimal place.

Rounding-off the total mass of the box up to one decimal place, we get

Total mass of the box $(M) = 2.3$ kg

(b) Difference in masses of gold pieces $(\Delta m) = m_2 - m_1$

$$= 20.17 - 20.15 = 0.02 \text{ g}$$

(The masses of two gold pieces has two decimal places, therefore it is correct up to two places of decimal.)

Question 13 A famous relation in physics relates 'moving mass' m to the 'rest mass' m_0 of a particle in terms of its speed v and speed of light c. (This relation first arose as a consequence of special relativity due to Albert Einstein). A boy recalls the relation almost correctly but forgets where to put the constant c. He writes $m = \frac{m_0}{(1-v^2)^{1/2}}$.

Guess, where to put the missing c?

Sol. The relation written by the boy $m = \frac{m_0}{(1-v^2)^{1/2}}$.

According to the principle of homogeneity of dimensions, the dimensions on either side of a relation must be same *i.e.*, the powers of M, L, T on either side of a relation must be same.

Dimension of m is equal to the dimension of m_0, therefore the denominator $(1-v^2)^{1/2}$ should be dimensionless. In denominator 1 is dimensionless but factor v^2 is not dimensionless. To make it dimensionless we have to divide it by the same physical quantity with same power, therefore it should be v^2/c^2, to become dimensionless.

Hence, the correct relation should be $m = \frac{m_0}{\left(1-\frac{v^2}{c^2}\right)^{1/2}}$

Question 14 The unit of length convenient on the atomic scale is known as an angstrom and is denoted by Å. (1 Å $= 10^{-10}$ m). The size of the hydrogen atom is about 0.5 Å. What is the total atomic volume in m^3 of a mole of hydrogen atoms?

◎ ***Thinking Process*** Total volume for a mole of atoms Multiply the single atom's volume by Avogadro's number.

Sol. Radius of hydrogen atom $(r) = 0.5$ Å $= 0.5 \times 10^{-10}$ m

Volume of each hydrogen atom $(V) = \frac{4}{3}\pi r^3$

$$= \frac{4}{3} \times 3.14 \times (0.5 \times 10^{-10})^3$$

$$= 5.234 \times 10^{-31} m^3$$

Number of atoms in one mole of hydrogen = Avogadro number (N)

$$= 6.023 \times 10^{23}$$

$\therefore$ Atomic volume of 1 mole of hydrogen atoms (V')

= Volume of a hydrogen atom × Number of atoms

$$V' = V \times N$$

$$= 5.236 \times 10^{-31} \times 6.023 \times 10^{23} m^3$$

$$= 3.152 \times 10^{-7} m^3 = 3 \times 10^{-7} m^3$$

Question 15 One mole of an ideal gas at standard temperature and pressure occupies 22.4 L (molar volume). What is the ratio of molar volume to the atomic volume of a mole of hydrogen? (Take the size of hydrogen molecule to be about 1 Å.) Why is this ratio so large?

Sol. Given, molar volume of one mole of hydrogen

$$= 22.4\ \text{L} = 22.4 \times 10^{-3}\ \text{m}^3$$

Diameter of hydrogen molecule $(d) = 1\ \text{Å} = 10^{-10}$ m

$$\therefore \text{ Radius of hydrogen molecule } (r) = \frac{d}{2} = \frac{10^{-10}}{2}$$

$$= 0.5 \times 10^{-10}\ \text{m}$$

$$\text{Volume of one molecule of hydrogen} = \frac{4}{3}\pi r^3$$

$$= \frac{4}{3} \times 3.14 \times (0.5 \times 10^{-10})^3$$

$$= 5.234 \times 10^{-31}\ \text{m}^3$$

Number of molecules in one mole of hydrogen = Avogadro number (N)

$$= 6.023 \times 10^{23}$$

$\therefore$ Atomic volume of one mole of hydrogen

= Number of molecules in one mole of hydrogen × Volume of one molecule of hydrogen

$$= 6.023 \times 10^{23} \times 5.234 \times 10^{-31}$$

$$= 3.152 \times 10^{-7}\ \text{m}^3$$

$$\therefore \quad \frac{\text{Molar volume}}{\text{Atomic volume}} = \frac{22.4 \times 10^{-3}}{3.154 \times 10^{-7}} = 7.1 \times 10^4$$

This ratio is very large, which shows that the inter molecular separation in a gas is much larger than the size of a molecule.

Question 16 Explain this common observation clearly—If you look out of the window of a fast moving train the nearby trees, houses etc., seem to move rapidly in a direction opposite to the train's motion, but the distant, objects (hill tops, the moon, the stars etc.,) seem to be stationary. (In fact, since you are aware that you are moving, these distant objects seem to move with you.)

Sol. Nearby objects tree, houses, etc show greater angular displacement in our field of vision as the train moves, making them appear to move faster in the opposite direction. Distant objects hill tops, the moon, the stars, etc Show very little angular displacement, so they seems stationary or move with us. This is an effect of relative motion.

Question 17 The sun is a hot plasma (ionized matter) with its inner core at a temperature exceeding 10^7 K and its outer surface at a temperature of about 6000 K. At these high temperatures, no substance remains in a solid or liquid phase. In what range do you expect the mass density of the sun to be, in the range of densities of solids and liquids or gases? Check if your guess is correct from the following data :
Mass of the sun $= 2.0 \times 10^{30}$ kg and radius of the sun $= 7.0 \times 10^8$ m.

Sol. Given, mass of the sun $(M) = 2.0 \times 10^{30}$ kg

Radius of the sun $(R) = 7.0 \times 10^8$ m

$$\text{Density of the sun} = \frac{\text{Mass of the sun } (M)}{\text{Volume of the sun } (V)} \quad \left[\because \text{Density} = \frac{\text{Mass}}{\text{Volume}}\right]$$

$$\rho = \frac{M}{\frac{4}{3}\pi R^3} = \frac{3}{4}\frac{M}{\pi R^3}$$

$$= \frac{3 \times 2.0 \times 10^{30}}{4 \times 3.14 \times (7.0 \times 10^8)^3}$$

$$= \frac{3 \times 10^{30}}{6.28 \times 343 \times 10^{24}}$$

$$= 1.392 \times 10^3$$

$$\approx 1.4 \times 10^3 \text{ kg/m}^3$$

This density is of the order of density of solids and liquids and not of gases.

The temperature of inner core of the sun is 10^7 K while the temperature of the outer layers is nearly 6000 K. At so high temperature no matter can exist in its solid or liquid state.

Every matter is highly ionised and present as a mixture of nucleus, free electrons and ions which is called plasma. The density of plasma is so high due to inward gravitational attraction on outer layers due to inner layers of the sun.

DIKSHA APP Questions

Multiple Choice Questions

Q.1 Percentage error in mass and momentum are 2% and 4% respectively. Maximum possible percentage error in the measurement of kinetic energy is

(a) 6% (b) 8%

(c) 10% (d) 9%

Sol. (c) $KE = \frac{p^2}{2m}$

$$\%\text{error in KE} = 2 \times \%\text{error in } p + 1 \times \%\text{error in } m$$
$$= 2 \times 4\% + 1 \times 2\%$$
$$= 10\%$$

Q.2 What are the dimensions of a and b in the relation $F = a\sqrt{x} + bt^2$, where F is force, x is distance and t is time

(a) $[ML^{1/2}T^{-2}]$, $[MLT^{-4}]$ (b) $[ML^{-1/2}T^{-2}]$, $[MLT^{4}]$

(c) $[ML^{3/2}T^{-2}]$, $[ML^2T^{-4}]$ (d) $[ML^{-3/2}T^{-2}]$, $[ML^{-2}T^{-4}]$

Sol. (a) $[F] = [MLT^{-2}]$

$$[x] = [L]$$
$$[t] = [T]$$
$$[a] = \left[\frac{F}{\sqrt{x}}\right] = \frac{[MLT^{-2}]}{[L^{1/2}]} = [ML^{1/2}T^{-2}]$$

(b) $\left[\frac{F}{t^2}\right] = \frac{[MLT^{-2}]}{[T^2]} = [MLT^{-4}]$

Short Answer Type

Q.1 (a) If energy (E), velocity (v) and time (T) are chosen at fundamental quantities, what will be the dimensional formula of force ?

(b) If the unit of force, energy and velocity are 10 N, 100 J and 5 m/s respectively. Find the units of mass, length and time.

Sol. (a) Given, $F = \frac{E}{V.T}$

Dimensional formula

$$[F] = \frac{[E]}{[V]\cdot[T]} = [E][V]^{-1}[T]^{-1}$$

(b) The dimensional formula of

force $= [MLT^{-2}] = 10\,N$ ... (i)

Energy $= [ML^2T^{-2}] = 100\,J$ ... (ii)

Velocity $= [LT^{-1}] = 5\,m/s$ ... (iii)

Dividing equation (ii) by Eq. (i) we have

$$[L] = \frac{100\,J}{10\,N} = \frac{100\,Nm}{10\,N} = 10\,m$$

Substituting the unit of [L] in Eq. (ii), we have

$$[T^{-1}] = \frac{5\,m/s}{[L]} = \frac{5\,m/s}{10\,m}$$

$$[T] = \frac{10\,m}{5\,m/s} = 2\,s$$

Substituting the unit of [L] and [T] in Eq. (i), we have

$$[M] = \frac{10\,N}{[L]\,[T^{-2}]} = 10\,N\,\frac{4\,s^2}{10\,m} = 4\,kg$$

Q.2 A represents radiation pressure, *c* represents is speed of light and *q* represents the radiation energy per second per unit area per unit time, then calculate non-zero integers such that $p^x q^y c^z$ is dimensionless.

Sol. Given, $p = [ML^{-1}T^{-2}]$

$$q = [MT^{-3}]$$

$$c = [LT^{-1}]$$

$$[M^0L^0T^0] = [ML^{-1}T^{-2}]^x\,[MT^{-3}]^y\,[LT^{-1}]^z$$

Comparing the power of M, L, T in both sides

$$x + y = 0 \quad \text{...(i)}$$

$$-x + z = 0 \quad \text{...(ii)}$$

$$-2 - 3y - z = 0 \quad \text{...(iii)}$$

Solving equations, (i), (ii) and (iii), we get

$$x = 1, y = -1, z = 1$$

Motion in a Straight Line

CHAPTER 02

Important Points

01 **Rest** An object is said to be at rest, if it does not change its position with respect to its surroundings with time.

02 **Motion** An object is said to be in motion, if it changes its position with respect to it s surroundings with time.

03 Rest and motion are relative states. It means an object can be at rest with respect to one object but can be in motion with respect to another object at the same time.

04 **Point Mass Object** An object can be considered as a point mass, if the distance travelled by it is very large in comparison to its own dimensions.

05 **Distance or Total Path Length** Total length of the path transversed by an object during motion is called distance or total path length. It is a scalar quantity. It cannot be negative or zero but can be positive only.

06 **Displacement** The shortest distance between the initial and final positions of any object is called its displacement. It is a vector quantity. It can be positive, negative or zero.

07 **Speed** The speed of any object is the ratio of distance travelled by it to the time taken.

$$\text{Speed} = \frac{\text{Distance travelled}}{\text{Time taken}}$$

Its unit is m/s and it is a scalar quantity.

08 **Uniform Speed** An object is said to be moving with a uniform speed, if it covers equal distances in equal intervals of time, no matter how small these time intervals may be.

09 **Variable or Non-uniform Speed** An object is said to be moving with a variable or non-uniform speed, if it covers unequal distances in equal intervals of time, however small these time intervals may be.

10 **Velocity** The velocity of an object is the ratio of its displacement to the time taken.

$$\text{Velocity} = \frac{\text{Displacement}}{\text{Time taken}}$$

Its unit is m/s and it is a vector quantity.

11 **Uniform Velocity** An object is said to be moving with a uniform velocity, if it undergoes equal displacements in equal intervals of time, however small these time intervals may be.

12 **Variable or Non-uniform Velocity** An object is said to be moving with a variable or non-uniform velocity, if it undergoes unequal displacements in equal intervals of time, however small these time intervals may be.

13 The slope of position-time graph represents the velocity.

14 **Relative Velocity** The relative velocity of object A with respect to object B is defined as the time rate of change of relative position of object A with respect to object B.

15 If two objects A and B are moving with velocities $\mathbf{v}_A$ and $\mathbf{v}_B$ then, relative velocity of object A with respect to object B is given by

$$\mathbf{v}_{AB} = \mathbf{v}_A - \mathbf{v}_B$$

(i) If both objects are moving in the same direction, then

$$v_{AB} = v_A - v_B$$

(ii) If both objects are moving in opposite directions, then

$$v_{AB} = v_A + v_B$$

(iii) If both objects are moving in directions making an angle θ, then

$$v_{AB} = \sqrt{v_A^2 + v_B^2 - 2v_A v_B \cos\theta}$$

16 **Acceleration** The rate of change of velocity with respect to time is called acceleration.

$$\text{Acceleration}\,(a) = \frac{\text{Change in velocity}}{\text{Time interval}}$$

Its unit is m/s^2 and it is a vector quantity.

17 Instantaneous Acceleration Instantaneous acceleration of an object is the first derivative of velocity with respect time at a given instant.

$$a = \frac{dv}{dt} = \frac{d^2x}{dt^2}$$

18 Equations of uniformly accelerated motion

(i) $v = u + at$

(ii) $s = ut + \frac{1}{2}at^2$

(iii) $v^2 = u^2 + 2as$

(iv) $S_n = u + \frac{a}{2}(2n - 1)$

19 Slope of velocity-time graph represents acceleration.

20 Area under velocity-time graph is equal to the displacement.

Exercises

Question 1 In which of the following examples of motion, can the body be considered approximately a point object?

(a) A railway carriage moving without jerks between two stations.

(b) A monkey sitting on the top of a man cycling smoothly on a circular track.

(c) A spinning cricket ball that turns sharply on hitting the ground.

(d) A tumbling beaker that has slipped-off the edge of a table.

Sol. Any object can be considered as a point object if the distance travelled by it is very large in comparison to its dimensions.

(a) A railway carriage is moving without jerks between two stations because the distance between stations is much greater than the size of the railway carriage. Therefore railway carriage can be taken as a point object.

(b) A monkey sitting on the top of a man cycling smoothly on a circular track. Man along with monkey is cycling smoothly which indicates that the distance travelled by the man is very large, therefore monkey can be taken as a point object.

In points (c) and (d) the distance travelled is not so large therefore, spinning cricket ball and a tumbling beaker cannot be taken as a point object.

Question 2 The position-time (x-t) graphs for two children A and B returning from their school O to their homes P and Q respectively are shown in below figure. Choose the correct entries in the brackets below.

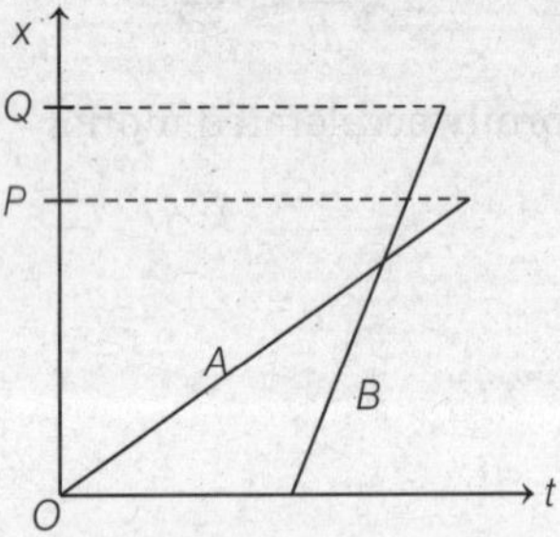

(a) (A/B) lives closer to the school than (B/A)

(b) (A/B) starts from school earlier than (B/A)

(c) (A/B) walks faster than (B/A)

(d) A and B reach home at the (same/different) time.

(e) (A/B) overtakes (B/A) on the road (once/twice).

Sol.

(a) Draw normals on graphs from points P and Q. It is clear that $OQ > OP$. Therefore, child A lives closer to the school than child B.

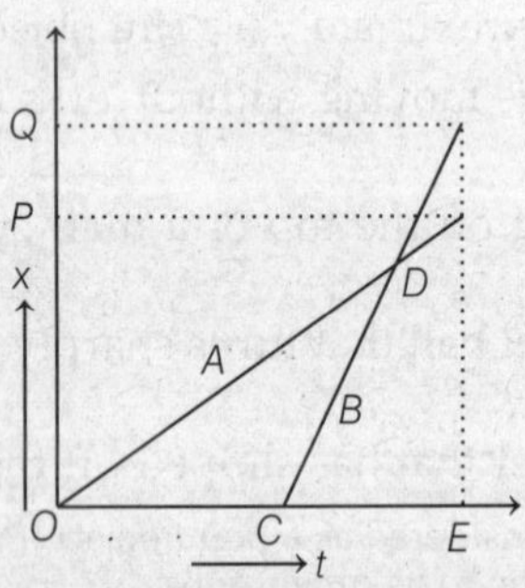

(b) Child A starts from school at time $t = 0$ (because its graph starts from origin) while child B starts from school at time $t = OC$. Therefore child A starts from school earlier than B.

(c) The slope of distance-time graph represents the speed. More the slope of the graph, more will be the speed. As the slope of the x-t graph of B is higher than the slope of the x-t graph of A, therefore child B walks faster than child A.

(d) Corresponding to points *P* and *Q*, the value of *t* from *x*-*t* graphs for children *A* and *B* is same *i.e.*, *OE*. Therefore, children *A* and *B* will reach their homes *P* and *Q* at the same time.

(e) *x*-*t* graphs for children *A* and *B* intersect each other at a point *D*. Child *B* starts later but reaches home at the same time as that of child *A*, therefore child *B* overtake child *A* on the road once.

Question 3 A woman starts from her home at 9.00 AM, walks with a speed of 5 km/h on a straight road up to her office 2.5 km away, stays at the office up to 5.00 PM and returns home by an auto with a speed of 25 km/h. Choose suitable scales and plot the *x*-*t* graph of her motion.

Sol. **Scale chosen**

Time on *X*-axis, 1 division = 1h

Distance on *Y*-axis, 1 division = 0.5 km

Woman starts at 9.00 AM *i.e.*, at 9.00 AM the distance covered in zero.

Distance of her office from home $(x) = 2.5$ km

Speed of the woman when she goes from her home to her office

$$(v_1) = 5 \text{ km/h}$$

$$\therefore \text{Time taken to reach the office } (t_1) = \frac{\text{Distance}}{\text{Speed}} = \frac{x}{v_1}$$

$$= \frac{2.5}{5} = \frac{1}{2} \text{ h} = 30 \text{ min}$$

Time of arival at office = (9.00 AM) + (30 min)

= 9.30 AM

i.e., at 9.30 AM the distance covered will be 2.5 km.

This part of journey is represented in graph by *OA*.

Woman stay at office from 9.30 AM to 5.00 PM, therefore she is stationary at that time *i.e.*, there is no change in distance only time is changing, so the graph for this portion will be a line parallel to time axis. This part of journey is represented in graph by *AB*.

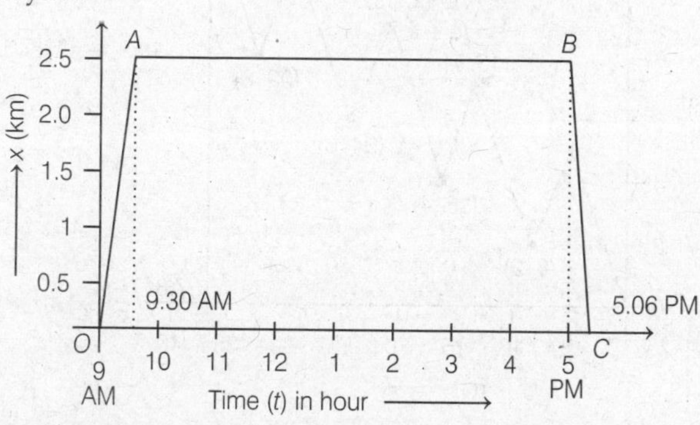

Speed of the woman when the return home by an auto $(v_2) = 25$ km/h

$\therefore$ Time taken by the woman to reach her home from office

$$t_2 = \frac{\text{Distance}}{\text{Speed}} = \frac{x}{v_2} = \frac{2.5}{25} = \frac{1}{10}\text{ h}$$

$$= \frac{60}{10}\text{ min} = 6\text{ min} \qquad (\because 1\text{ h} = 60\text{ min})$$

She leaves the office at 5.00 PM and takes 6 min to reach home. Therefore, she reaches her home at 5.06 PM at this time the distance is zero.
This part of journey is represented in graph by *BC*.

Mistake Alert Student can make mistake in plotting the graph and also misrepresent the direction of motion.

Question 4 A drunkard walking in a narrow lane takes 5 steps forward and 3 steps backward, followed again by 5 steps forward and 3 steps backward and so on. Each step is 1 m long and requires 1s. Plot the *x*-*t* graph of his motion. Determine graphically and otherwise how long the drunkard takes to fall in a pit 13 m away from the start.

Sol. The *x*-*t* graph of the drunkard is shown in figure.
Length of each step = 1 m taken along *Y*-axis.
Time taken for each step = 1 s taken along *X*-axis.
Drunkard takes 5 steps forward and 3 steps backward.
Time taken in 8 steps = 8 s
For the graph

X	5 m	5 − 3 = 2 m	2 + 5 = 7 m	7 − 3 = 4 m ...
Y	5 s	8 s	8 + 5 = 13 s	13 + 3 = 16 s ...

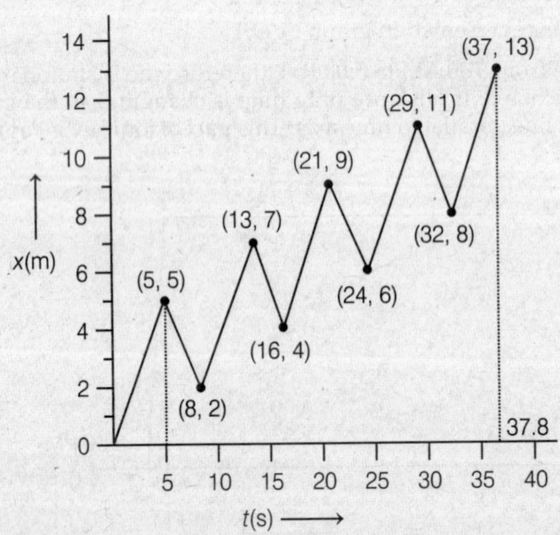

As drunkard takes 5 steps forward and 3 steps backward, therefore he moves 5 m forward and 3 m backward.

∴ Distance travelled in 8 s in 8 steps = 5 − 3 = 2 m

Distance travelled in 16 s in 16 steps = 2 × 2 = 4 m

Distance travelled in 24 s in 24 steps = 2 × 3 = 6 m

Distance travelled in 32 s in 32 steps = 2 × 4 = 8 m

Distance travelled in next 5 s in next 5 steps taken in forward direction = 5 m

∴ Total distance travelled in (32 + 5 =) 37 s in 37 steps = 8 + 5 = 13 m

Distance of the pit from the starting point = 13 m

Therefore, drunkard will fall in the pit in 37 s.

Question 5 A car moving along a straight highway with speed of 126 km/h is brought to a stop within a distance of 200 m. What is the retardation of the car (assumed uniform) and how long does it take for the car to stop?

Sol. Initial velocity of the car (u) = 126 km/h

$$= 126 \times \frac{5}{18} \text{ m/s} \qquad \left(\because 1 \text{ km/h} = \frac{5}{18} \text{ m/s}\right)$$

$$= 35 \text{ m/s}$$

Final velocity of the car (v) = 0

Distance travelled (s) = 200 m

From equation of motion, $v^2 = u^2 + 2as$

or
$$a = \frac{v^2 - u^2}{2s}$$

$$= \frac{0 - (35)^2}{2 \times 200}$$

$$= -3.06 \text{ m/s}^2$$

∴ Retardation of the car = − 3.06 m/s²

From equation of motion, $v = u + at$

or
$$t = \frac{v - u}{a}$$

$$= \frac{(0 - 35)}{(-49/16)}$$

$$= 11.4 \text{ s}$$

∴ Car will stop after 11.4 s.

Question 6 A player throws a ball upwards with an initial speed of 29.4 m/s.

(a) What is the direction of acceleration during the upward motion of the ball?

(b) What are the velocity and acceleration of the ball at the highest point of its motion?

(c) Choose the $x = 0$ m and $t_0 = 0$ s to be the location and time of the ball at its highest point, vertically downward direction to the positive direction of X-axis and give the signs of position, velocity and acceleration of the ball during its upward and downward motion.

(d) To what height does the ball rise and after how long does the ball return to the player's hand? (Take, $g = 9.8 \text{ m/s}^2$ and neglect air resistance.)

Sol.

(a) The ball is moving under the effect of gravity and therefore the direction of acceleration is vertically downward i.e. in the direction of acceleration due to gravity.

(b) At the highest point of its motion velocity is zero and acceleration is equal to the acceleration due to gravity (9.8 m/s^2).

(c) **During upward motion**

Sign of position is negative.
Sign of velocity is negative.
Sign of acceleration is positive.

During downward motion

Sign of position is positive.
Sign of velocity is positive.
Sign of acceleration is positive.

(d) Let the ball rises upto maximum height h.

nitial velocity of ball $(u) = -29.4$ m/s

$$g = 9.8 \text{ m/s}^2$$

Final velocity at maximum height $(v) = 0$

Using equation of motion, $v^2 - u^2 = 2gh$

$$0 - (-29.4)^2 = 2 \times 9.8 \times h$$

or $$h = \frac{29.4 \times 29.4}{2 \times 9.8}$$

$\Rightarrow$ $$h = 44.1 \text{ m}$$

Again using equation of motion, $v = u - gt$

$$0 = 29.4 - 9.8t$$

or $$t = \frac{29.4}{9.8} = 3\text{ s}$$

Time of ascent is always equal to the time of descent.

$\therefore$ Total time after which the ball returns to the player's hand

$$= 2t = 2 \times 3 = 6\text{ s}$$

Mistake Alert Student can use incorrect sign convention for position velocity (v) and acceleration (a).

Question 7 Read each statement below carefully and state with reasons and examples, if it is true or false. A particle in one-dimensional motion

(a) with zero speed at an instant may have non-zero acceleration at that instant.

(b) with zero speed may have non-zero velocity.

(c) with constant speed, must have zero acceleration.

(d) with positive value of acceleration must be speeding up.

Sol.

(a) True, if an object is thrown vertically upward then, at the highest point its speed is zero but its acceleration is equal to the acceleration due to gravity in downward direction.

(b) False, because velocity is defined as speed in a given direction. If speed is zero then magnitude of velocity is zero and hence velocity is also zero.

(c) True, if a particle is moving with a constant speed along a straight line then its velocity is also constant and hence its acceleration is zero.

(d) False, if we take vertically downward direction as positive, then a ball thrown vertically upward, slower down in speed while acceleration is positive.

True, if ball is freely falling downward under gravity, then acceleration is positive and ball is speeding up.

Hence, the answer of this statement depends upon the choice of instant of time taken as origin.

Question 8 A ball is dropped from a height of 90 m on a floor. At each collision with the floor, the ball loses one-tenth of its speed. Plot the speed-time graph of its motion between $t = 0$ to 12 s.

Sol. Initial velocity of the ball (u) = 0

Height of the point from where the ball is dropped, $h = 90$ m

Acceleration $g = 9.8\text{ m/s}^2$

Using equation of motion $v^2 = u^2 + 2gh$

$$v^2 = (0)^2 + 2 \times 9.8 \times 90$$

($\because$ Ball is dropped from rest so initial velocity is zero)

$$v = \sqrt{2 \times 9.8 \times 90} = \sqrt{2 \times 49 \times 2 \times 9} = 42 \text{ m/s}$$

i.e. where $u = 0, t = 0$

Using equation of motion, $h = ut_1 + \frac{1}{2}gt_1^2$

$$90 = 0 \times t_1 + \frac{1}{2} \times 9.8 \times t_1^2$$

or $t_1 = \sqrt{\frac{2 \times 90}{9.8}} = \frac{30}{7} = 4.28 \text{ s}$

When $u = 42 \text{ m/s}, t = 4.28 \text{ s}.$

After striking on floor the ball loses 10% of its speed.

$\therefore$ Velocity of first rebounce $(v_2) = v - \frac{v}{10}$

($\because$ At each collision the ball loses one-tenth of its speed)

$$= \frac{9v}{10} = \frac{9}{10} \times 42 = 37.8 \text{ m/s}$$

If ball rebounces upto height h', then again using equation of motion

$$(0)^2 = (37.8)^2 - 2 \times 9.8 \times h'$$

or $h' = \frac{37.8 \times 37.8}{2 \times 9.8} = 72.9 \text{ m}$

Time taken $t_2 = \sqrt{\frac{2h'}{g}} = \sqrt{\frac{2 \times 72.9}{9.8}} = 3.857$

When $u = 37.8 \text{ m/s}, t = 3.857 \text{ s}$

Total time = 4.28 + 3.857 = 8.137

The ball will take further 3.857 s to fall (at time of descent = time of ascent) back to floor, where its velocity before striking the ground will be 37.8 m/s.

Velocity of the ball after striking the floor $= 37.8 - \frac{37.8}{10} = 34.02 \text{ m/s}$

Total time elapsed before upward motion = 4.28 + 3.857 + 3.857

$$= 11.994 \text{ s} \approx 12 \text{ s}$$

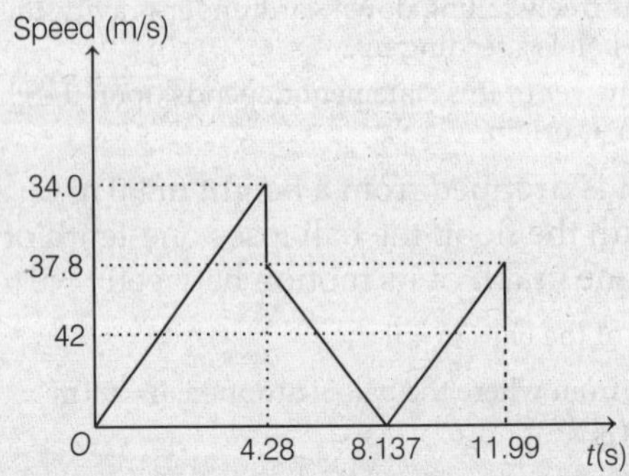

Therefore, the ball will rise only once after striking on floor between time interval $t = 0$ s to $t = 12$ s and the speed-time graph is shown in above figure.

Question 9 Explain clearly with examples, the distinction between the following.

(a) Magnitude of displacement (sometimes called distance) over an interval of time and the total length of path covered by a particle over the same interval.

(b) Magnitude of average velocity over an interval of time and the average speed over the same interval. [Average speed of a particle over an interval of time is defined as the total path length divided by the time interval.]

Show in both (a) and (b) that the second quantity is either greater than or equal to the first. When is the equality sign true?

[For simplicity, consider one-dimensional motion only.]

Sol.

(a) The magnitude of displacement of a particle is equal to the shortest distance between the initial and final positions in a given time interval while the total length of path covered by the particle is the length of the path actually traversed by it.

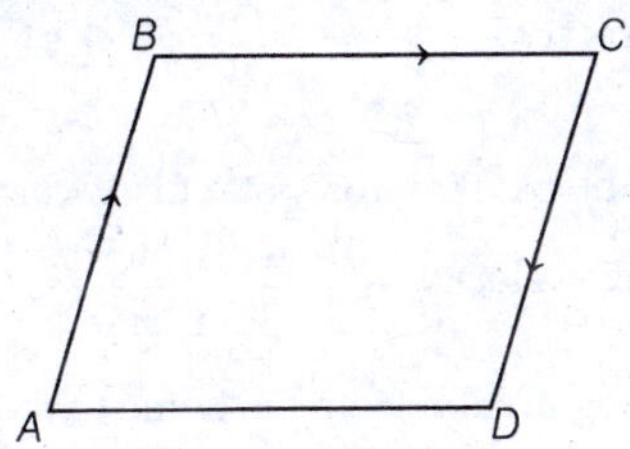

If a particle starts its motion from point A and goes from A to B, then B to C and then goes from C to D.

Displacement of the particle = distance AD

Total length of path = Distance AB + Distance BC + Distance CD

Therefore, in one-dimensional motion displacement is either equal or less than the total length of the path covered by a particle in a given time interval.

(b) Average velocity is equal to the ratio of the total displacement to the total time taken.

$$\therefore \text{ Magnitude of average velocity} = \frac{\text{Displacement}}{\text{Total time}}$$

$$= \frac{AD}{t}$$

Average speed is equal to the ratio of the total distance travelled to the total time taken.

$$\therefore \quad \text{Average speed} = \frac{\text{Total distance}}{\text{Total time}} = \frac{AB + BC + CD}{t}$$

Therefore, in one-dimensional motion magnitude of average velocity either equal or less than the average speed over an interval of time.

Both quantities in part (a) and part (b) are equal if the object moves in a straight line.

Question 10 A man walks on a straight road from his home to a market 2.5 km away with a speed of 5 km/h. Finding the market closed, he instantly turns and walks back home with a speed of 7.5 km/h. What is the

(a) magnitude of average velocity?

(b) average speed of the man over the following interval of time?
(i) 0 to 30 min (ii) 0 to 50 min (iii) 0 to 40 min

Note You will appreciate from the exercise why it is better to define average speed as total path length divided by time and not as magnitude of average velocity. You would not like to tell the tired man on his return home that his average speed was zero.

Sol.

(a) As man return his home, therefore total displacement of the man = 0

$$\therefore \quad \text{Average velocity} = \frac{\text{Total displacement}}{\text{Total time}} = 0$$

(b) Speed of man during motion from his home to the market $(v_1) = 5 \text{ km/h}$.
Speed of man during motion from market his home $(v_2) = 7.5 \text{ km/h}$
Distance between his home and market $(x) = 2.5 \text{ km}$

(i) **Taking time interval 0 to 30 min**

Time taken by man to reach the market $t_1 = \frac{x}{v_1} = \frac{2.5}{5}$

$$= \frac{1}{2} = 30 \text{ min}$$

Hence, the man moves from his home to the market in $t = 0$ to 30 min

$$\therefore \quad \text{Average velocity} = \frac{\text{Total displacement}}{\text{Total time}} = \frac{2.5}{\frac{1}{2}} = 5.0 \text{ km/h}$$

$$\text{Average speed} = \frac{\text{Total distance}}{\text{Total time}} = \frac{2.5}{\frac{1}{2}} = 5.0 \text{ km/h}$$

(ii) **Taking time interval 0 to 50 min**

Time taken by man in returning to his home from the market

$$t_2 = \frac{x}{v_2} = \frac{2.5}{7.5}$$

$$= \frac{1}{3} \text{ h}$$

$$= 20 \text{ min}$$

$\therefore$ Total time of journey $(T) = t_1 + t_2 = 30 + 20$

$$= 50 \text{ min}$$

$\therefore$ Total displacement = 0 (as man return to its initial position)

$\therefore$ Average velocity $= \frac{\text{Total displacement}}{\text{Total time}} = 0$

Total distance = 2.5 + 2.5 = 5.0 km

$\therefore$ Average speed $= \frac{\text{Total distance}}{\text{Total time}} = \frac{5.0}{50/60}$ km/h

$$= 6 \text{ km/h}$$

(iii) **Taking time interval 0 to 40 min**

First 30 min is used to reach the market.

$\therefore$ Time of return journey $(t_3) = 40 - 30 = 10$ min

Distance travelled in 10 min $= v_2 \times t_3$

$$= 7.5 \times \frac{10}{60} \text{ km}$$

$$= 1.25 \text{ km}$$

Total displacement = 2.5 − 1.25

$$= 1.25 \text{ km}$$

$\therefore$ Average velocity $= \frac{\text{Total displacement}}{\text{Total time}}$

$$= \frac{1.25}{(40/60)}$$

$$= 1.875 \text{ km/h}$$

Total distance travelled = 2.5 + 1.25 = 3.75 km

$\therefore$ Average speed $= \frac{\text{Total distance}}{\text{Total time}}$

$$= \frac{3.75}{\frac{40}{60}} = 5.625 \text{ km/h}$$

Mistake Alert Student get confuse between average speed and average velocity. Average speed is total distance divided by total time while average velocity is total displacement divided by total time.

Question 11 In 9 and 10 we have carefully distinguished between average speed and magnitude of average velocity. No such distinction is necessary when we consider instantaneous speed and magnitude of velocity. The instantaneous speed is always equal to the magnitude of instantaneous velocity. Why?

Sol. Instantaneous velocity is defined as the velocity at a particular instant of time, while the instantaneous speed is the limiting value of the average speed *i.e.*, first derivative of the distance with respect to time at that instant of time $\left(\frac{dx}{dt}\right)$.

When time interval is very small then magnitude of displacement is equal to the distance travelled and therefore magnitude of instantaneous velocity is just equal to the instantaneous speed.

Question 12 Look at the graphs (a) to (d) carefully and state with reasons, which of these cannot possibly represent one-dimensional motion of a particle.

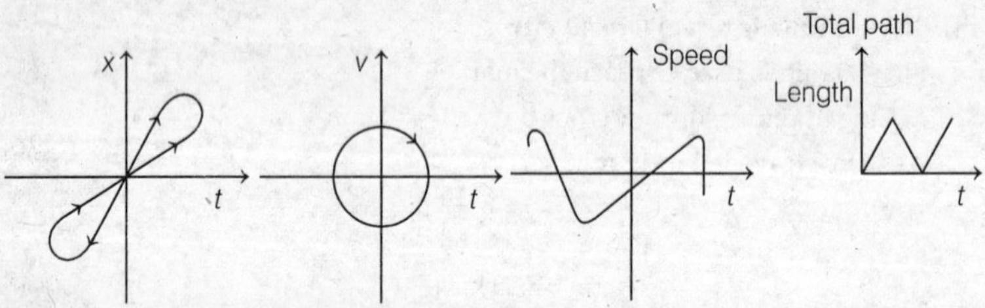

(a) (b) (c) (d)

Sol.

(a) No, graph (a) is not representing one-dimensional motion of a particle, because graph shows two different positions of the particle at same instant of time. (At time t_1 particle is at position P and Q and at time t_2 particle is at position R and S), which is not possible.

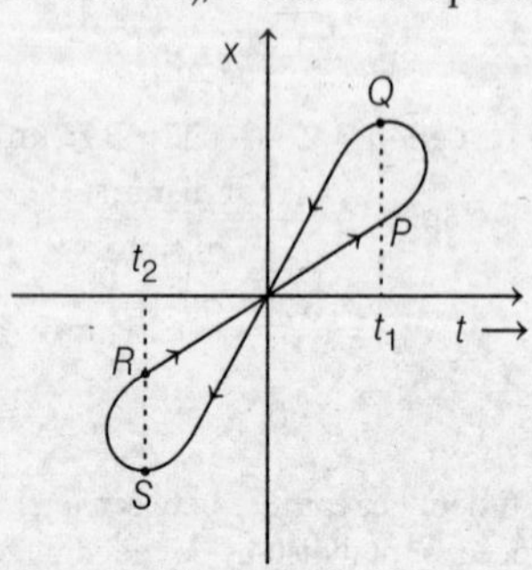

(a)

(b) No, graph (b) cannot represent one-dimensional motion of a particle, because graph shows one positive velocity (v_1) and another negative velocity ($-v_2$) of the particle at the same instant of time (t_1) which is not possible.

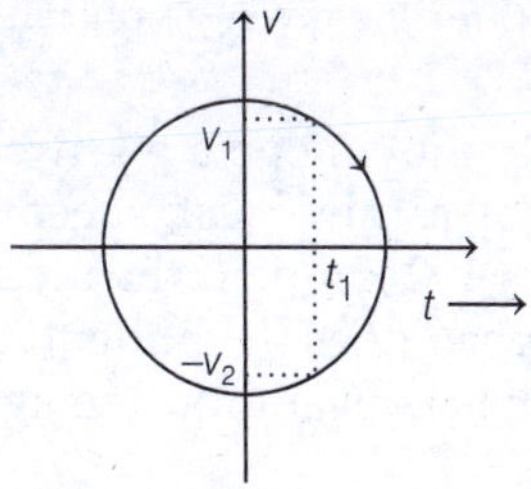

(b)

(c) No, graph (c) cannot represent one-dimensional motion of a particle, because graph shows negative speed of the particle while speed cannot be negative.

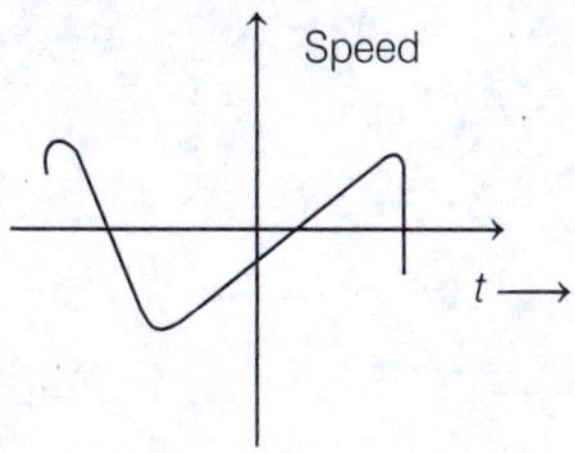

(c)

(d) No, graph (d) cannot represent one-dimensional motion of a particle, because graph shows that total path length increases from time $t = 0$ to $t = t_1$, but decreases from $t = t_1$ to $t = t_2$. But total path length of a moving particle can never decrease with time.

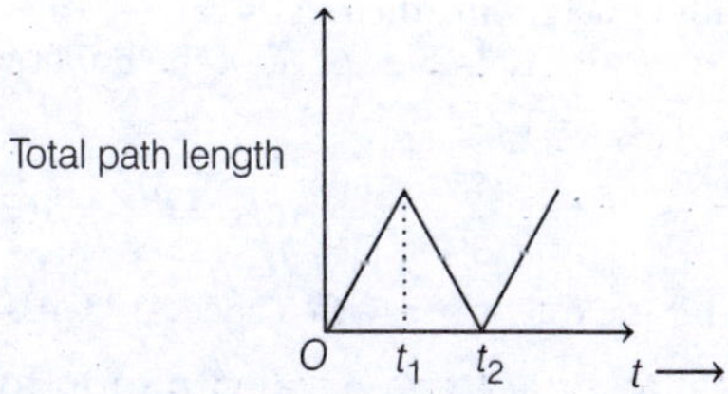

(d)

Question 13 Figure shows the x-t plot of one-dimensional motion of a particle. Is it correct to say from the graph that the particle moves in a straight line for $t < 0$ and on a parabolic path for $t > 0$? If not, suggest a suitable physical context for this graph.

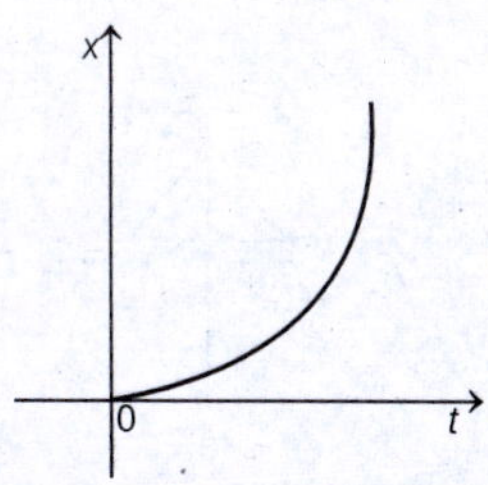

Sol. No, it is not correct to say from the graph that the particle moves in a straight line for $t < 0$ and on a parabolic path for $t > 0$, because x-t graph does not represent the trajectory of the path followed by the particle. The graph shows that the particle is at $x = 0$ at $t = 0$ and after then x is increasing with time t.

Context A suitable context for the given graph can be the motion of a freely falling particle under gravity.

Question 14 A police van moving on a highway with a speed of 30 km/h fires a bullet at a thief's car speeding away in the same direction with a speed of 192 km/h . If the muzzle speed of the bullet is 150 m/s, with what speed does the bullet hit the thief's car? (Note Obtain that speed which is relevant for damaging the thief's car.)

◎ ***Thinking Process*** First find the effective speed as bullet along with police van then find the final speed of bullet relative to the speed of thief's car.

Sol. Speed of police van (v_P) = 30 km/h

$$= 30 \times \frac{5}{18} \text{ m/s} \qquad \left(\because 1 \text{ km/s} = \frac{5}{18} \text{ m/s}\right)$$

$$= \frac{25}{3} \text{ m/s}$$

Speed of thief's car (v_T) = 192 km/h

$$= 192 \times \frac{5}{18} \text{ m/s} = \frac{160}{3} \text{ m/s}$$

Muzzle speed of bullet (v_B) = 150 m/s

The bullet is sharing the speed of the police van, therefore effective speed of the bullet

$$v_B' = v_B + v_P$$

$$= 150 + \frac{25}{3} = \frac{475}{3} \text{ m/s}$$

Speed of the bullet with which it hits the thief's car

= Relative speed of the bullet w.r.t. thief's car (v_{BT})

$$v_{BT} = v_B' - v_T$$

$$= \left(\frac{475}{3} - \frac{160}{3}\right) \text{m/s} = \frac{315}{3} = 105 \text{ m/s}$$

Therefore, bullet will hit the thief's car with a speed 105 m/s.

Question 15 Suggest a suitable physical situation for each of the following graphs

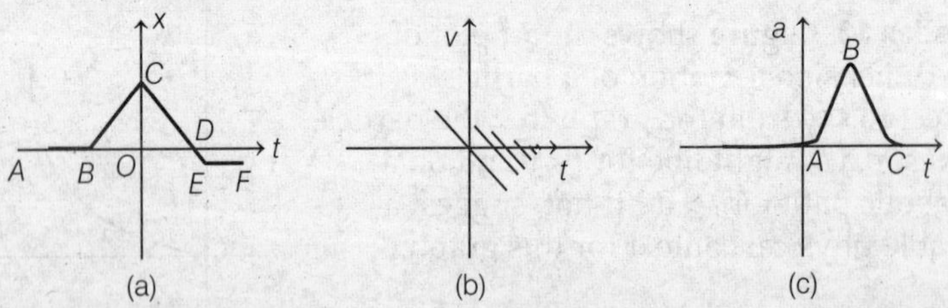

Sol.

(a) AB part of x-t graph shows $x = 0$ *i.e.*, body is at rest, part BC represent that x increases with t with a constant speed (as slope of x-t graph represents the speed), attains a maximum value at C and then x decreases with t and becomes zero of point D and then increases in opposite direction upto point E and then attains a constant values, which is represented by part EF.

This physical situation is obtained when a ball which is at rest on the smooth floor of a room is kicked. It strikes the wall and rebounces back with a reduced speed as slope of part CD is less than the slope of part BC. When ball strikes the opposite wall it comes at rest.

(b) The graph shows that the velocity changes sign again and again and every time it loses some of its speed. This situation is obtained when a ball is thrown up with some initial velocity. During upward motion its speed decreases and becomes zero at highest point, then it returns back and falls freely under gravity. On striking the ground, it rebounds with a reduced speed each time.

(c) The graph shows that the acceleration is zero initially, it means body is moving with constant velocity. Its acceleration increases for a short interval of time and then decreases to zero and then again body starts to move with a constant velocity.

This situation is obtained when a cricket ball moving with a constant velocity hits a bat for a short interval of time for which it accelerates.

Question 16 Figure gives the x-t plot of a particle executing one-dimensional simple harmonic motion (You will learn about this motion in more details in chapter 14). Give the signs of position, velocity and acceleration variables of the particle at $t = 0.3$ s, 1.2 s, -1.2 s.

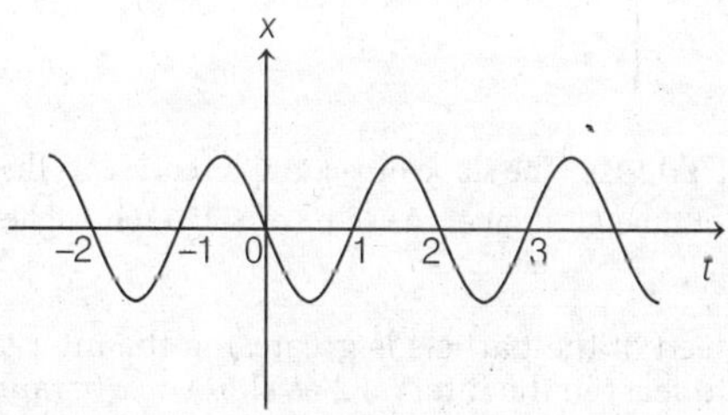

◎ ***Thinking Process*** In SHM, the acceleration $a = -\omega^2 x$ *i.e.*, acceleration is directly proportional to the displacement and opposite in direction.

Sol. In simple harmonic motion, the acceleration is given by

$$a = -\omega^2 x \qquad \text{...(i)}$$

where, x is the displacement, ω is the angular frequency and negative sign shows that the direction of acceleration is opposite to the direction of displacement.

The velocity is given by $v = \frac{dx}{dt}$ = Slope of x-t graph ...(ii)

(a) At time $t = 0.3$ s, x is negative and slope of x-t graph is negative, therefore position and velocity of the particle is negative but according to Eq. (i) acceleration is positive.

(b) At time $t = 1.2$ s, x is positive and slope of x-t graph is positive, therefore position and velocity of the particle is positive but according to Eq. (i) acceleration is negative.

(c) At time $t = -1.2$ s, x and t both are negative, therefore position of the particle is negative. As x and t both are negative therefore from Eq. (ii) velocity is positive and according to Eq. (i) acceleration is positive.

Question 17 The following figure gives the x-t plot of a particle in one-dimensional motion. Three different equal intervals of time are shown. In which interval is the average speed greatest and in which is the least? Give the sign of average velocity for each interval.

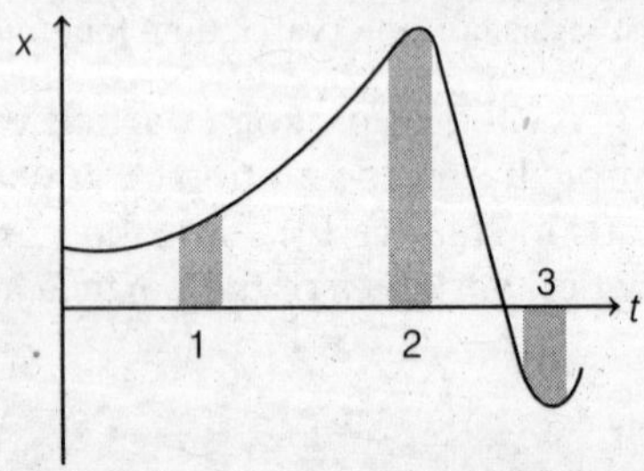

◎ *Thinking Process* The slope of x- t graph represents the average speed in that interval of time *i.e.*, higher the slope of x- t graph, higher is the average speed.

Sol. The average speed of the particle is greatest in the interval 3 as slope of x-t graph is greatest and least in the interval 2 as slope of x-t graph is least there.

Slope of x-t graph is positive for interval 1 and 2 and negative for interval 3, therefore average speed is positive for internal 1 and 2 but negative for interval 3.

Question 18 Following figure gives a speed-time graph of a particle in motion along a constant direction. Three equal intervals of time are shown. In which interval is the average acceleration greatest in magnitude? In which interval is the average speed greatest? Choosing the positive direction as the constant direction of motion give the signs of v and a in the three intervals. What are the accelerations at the points A, B, C and D?

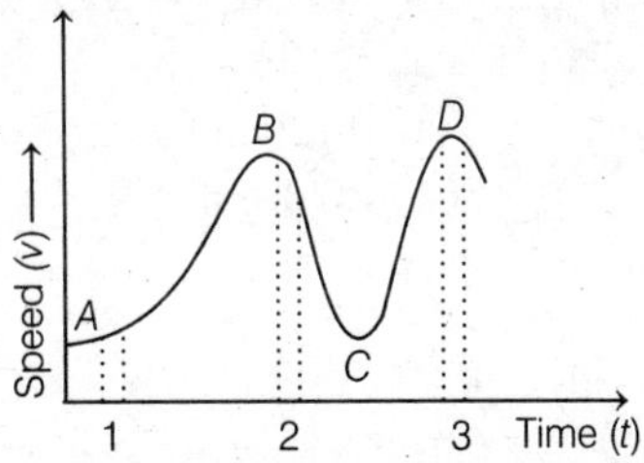

◎ ***Thinking Process*** The slope of v- t graph represents the acceleration *i.e.*, higher the slope of v- t graph, higher the acceleration.

Sol. The slope of v-t graph is highest for interval 2 therefore, magnitude of average acceleration is greatest for interval 2.

Average speed is greatest for interval 3, as peak D corresponds to maximum value on speed axis.

In interval 1, speed > 0, therefore speed is positive slope of v-t graph is also positive, therefore acceleration is also positive.

In interval 2, speed > 0, therefore speed is positive. Slope of v-t graph is negative, therefore acceleration is negative.

In interval 3, speed > 0, therefore speed is positive. Slope of v-t graph is zero, as tangent at this point is parallel to time axis. Hence, acceleration is zero.

At point A, B, C and D graph is parallel to time axis, therefore slope of v-t graph is zero and here acceleration is zero at all four points.

DIKSHA APP Questions

☐ Multiple Choice Questions

Q.1 A bus is moving with a speed of 10m/s on a straight road. A scooterist wishes to overtake the bus in 100 s. If the bus is at a distance of 1 km from the scooterist with what speed should the scooterist chase the bus?

(a) 10 m/s (b) 20 m/s
(c) 40 m/s (d) 25 m/s

Sol. (b) Let v be the velocity of the scooter the distance between the scooter and bus = 1000 m

The velocity of the bus = 10m/s

Time taken to overtake = 100 s

Relative velocity of the scooter with respect to the bus = $(v_s - 10)$

$$\therefore \quad \frac{1000}{(v_s - 10)} = 100 \text{ s}$$

$$\Rightarrow \quad v_s = 20 \text{ m/s}$$

Q.2 A car, moving with speed of 50 km/hr, can be stopped by brakes after at 6 m. If the same car is moving at a speed of 100 km/hr, the minimum stopping distance is

(a) 12 m (b) 18 m
(c) 24 m (d) 6 m

Sol. (c) Speed of the car when stopping distance is 6 m is given as

$$u_1 = 50 \text{ km/hr}$$

Let, $u_2 = 100$ km/hr

Now, $v^2 = u^2 - 2as$

$$\Rightarrow \quad 0 = u^2 - 2as$$

$$\Rightarrow \quad s = \frac{u^2}{2a} \Rightarrow s \propto u^2$$

(a is constant and negative as considering retardation)

$$\therefore \quad \frac{s_2}{s_1} = \frac{u_2^2}{u_1^2} = \frac{100^2}{50^2}$$

$$\Rightarrow \quad s_2 = 4s_1 = 4 \times 6 = 24 \text{ m}$$

Q.3 If a body loses half of its velocity on penetrating 3 cm in a wooden block then how much will it penetrate more before coming to rest.

(a) 1 cm (b) 2 cm (c) 3 cm (d) 4 cm

Sol. (a) In first case

$$v = \frac{u}{2}, s = 3 \text{ cm}$$

As $$v^2 - u^2 = 2as$$

$$\therefore \quad \left(\frac{u}{2}\right)^2 - u^2 = 2a \times 3$$

$$a = \frac{-u^2}{8}$$

In second case

$$v = 0, u = \frac{u}{2}, a = \frac{-u^2}{8}$$

$$\therefore \quad 0^2 - \left(\frac{u}{2}\right)^2 = 2\left(-\frac{u^2}{8}\right)s$$

$$s = 1 \text{ cm}$$

□ Short Answer Type

Q.1 An electron travelling with a speed of 5×10^3 m/s passes through an electric field with an acceleration of 10^{12} ms^{-2}.

(a) How long will it take for the electron to double its speed?

(b) What will be the distance covered by the electron in this time ?

Sol. (a) $v = 5 \times 10^3$ m/s

$$a = 10^{12} \text{ m/s}^2$$

let consider initial velocity = u

Final velocity = 2 u

Using equation of motion

$$v = u + at$$

$$t = \frac{v - u}{a} \Rightarrow t = \frac{2u - u}{a}$$

$$t = \frac{u}{a} = \frac{5 \times 10^3}{10^{12}} = 5 \times 10^{-9} \text{ s}$$

(b) $v^2 - u^2 = 2as$

$$s = \frac{v^2 - u^2}{2a}$$

$$= \frac{(2u)^2 - u^2}{2a} = \frac{3u^2}{2a}$$

$$= \frac{3 \times (5 \times 10^3)^2}{10^{12}} = 7.5 \times 10^{-5} \text{ m}$$

Q.2 A rocket is fired vertically from the ground with a resultant vertical acceleration of 10 m/s^2. The fuel is finished in 1 minute and it continues to move up. What is the maximum height reached?

Sol. Height covered in 1 min

$$S_1 = ut + \frac{gt^2}{2} = 0 + \frac{1}{2} \times 10 \times (60)^2 = 18000 \text{ m}$$

Velocity attained after 1 min

$$v = u + at = 0 + 10 \times 60 = 600 \text{ m/s}$$

After the fuel is finished, $u = 600$ m/s, $v = 0$

$$v^2 - u^2 = 2gs$$

$$\Rightarrow \quad 0 - (600)^2 = 2 \times (-9.8) \times S_2$$

$$S_2 = \frac{(600)^2}{2 \times 9.8} = 18367.3 \text{ m}$$

Maximum height reached

$$S_1 + S_2 = 18000 \text{ m} + 18367.3 \text{ m}$$

$$= 36.4 \text{ km}$$

Motion in a Plane

CHAPTER 03

Important Points

01 **Scalars** Those physical quantities which require only magnitude but no direction for their complete representation, are called scalars. For example, distance, speed, pressure and density etc.

02 **Vectors** Those physical quantities which require magnitude as well as direction for their complete representation and follows the laws of vector addition, are called vectors. For example, displacement, velocity, acceleration, force and momentum etc.

03 **Equal Vectors** Two vectors having equal magnitude and same direction are called equal vectors.

04 **Negative Vectors** Two vectors of equal magnitude but opposite in directions are called negative vectors of each other.

05 **Collinear Vectors** Those vectors which are acting along parallel straight lines in same or opposite directions are called collinear vectors.

06 **Coplanar Vectors** Those vector which are acting in the same plane are called coplanar vectors.

07 **Zero Vector or Null Vector** A vector whose magnitude is zero but the direction is uncertain is called a zero vector or null vector.

08 **Unit Vector** A unit vector of any given vector **A** is a vector of unit magnitude in the same direction of the given vector. It is denoted by $\hat{\mathbf{A}}$ and given by $\hat{\mathbf{A}} = \dfrac{\mathbf{A}}{|\mathbf{A}|}$

09 **Triangle Law of Vector Addition** If two vectors acting on a particle at the same time are represented in magnitude and direction by the two sides of a triangle taken in one order, then their resultant vector is represented in magnitude and direction by the third side of the triangle taken in the opposite order.

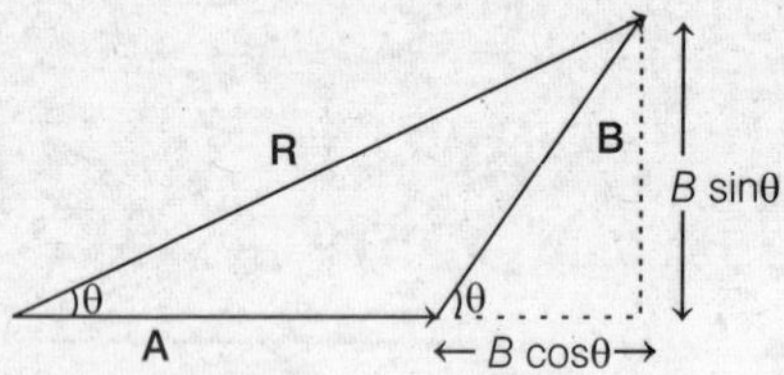

If two vectors **A** and **B** are acting at a particle at the same time, making an angle θ, then their resultant **R** is given by

$$R = \sqrt{A^2 + B^2 + 2AB\cos\theta}$$

and $$\tan\beta = \frac{B\sin\theta}{A + B\cos\theta}$$

10 **Parallelogram Law of Vector Addition** If two vectors acting on a particle at the same time are represented in magnitude and direction by the two adjacent sides of a parallelogram drawn from a point, then their resultant vector is represented in magnitude and direction by the diagonal of the parallelogram drawn from the same point.

11 Vector addition is commutative *i.e.,*

$$\mathbf{A} + \mathbf{B} = \mathbf{B} + \mathbf{A}$$

12 Vector addition is associative *i.e.,*

$$(\mathbf{A} + \mathbf{B}) + \mathbf{C} = \mathbf{A} + (\mathbf{B} + \mathbf{C})$$

13 **Rectangular Component of a Vector in a Plane**

If a vector **A** is inclined at an angle θ, from X-axis then,

Its component along X-axis is $A_x = A\cos\theta$

Its component along Y-axis is

$$A_y = A\sin\theta$$

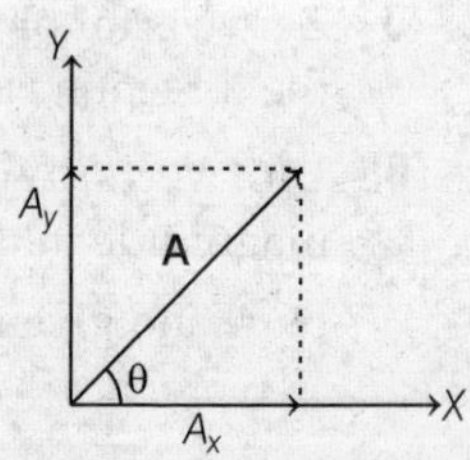

The magnitude of vector A

$$A = \sqrt{A_x^2 + A_y^2}$$

and Direction of vector A $\tan\theta = \dfrac{A_y}{A_x}$

14 Scalar Product (or dot product) of Two Vectors Scalar product of two vectors is equal to the product of their magnitudes and the cosine of angle between them.

$$\mathbf{A} \cdot \mathbf{B} = AB\cos\theta$$

15 Properties of Scalar Product

(i) Scalar product is commutative *i.e.,*

$$\mathbf{A} \cdot \mathbf{B} = \mathbf{B} \cdot \mathbf{A}$$

(ii) Scalar product is distributive *i.e,*

$$\mathbf{A} \cdot (\mathbf{B} + \mathbf{C}) = \mathbf{A} \cdot \mathbf{B} + \mathbf{A} \cdot \mathbf{C}$$

(iii) Scalar product of two normal vectors is zero.

i.e., $$\mathbf{A} \cdot \mathbf{B} = AB\cos 90° = 0$$

(iv) Scalar product of two parallel vectors is equal to the product of their magnitudes *i.e.,*

$$\mathbf{A} \cdot \mathbf{B} = AB\cos 0° = AB$$

(v) For unit vector

$$\hat{\mathbf{i}} \cdot \hat{\mathbf{i}} = \hat{\mathbf{j}} \cdot \hat{\mathbf{j}} = \hat{\mathbf{k}} \cdot \hat{\mathbf{k}} = 1 \text{ and } \hat{\mathbf{i}} \cdot \hat{\mathbf{j}} = \hat{\mathbf{j}} \cdot \hat{\mathbf{k}} = \hat{\mathbf{k}} \cdot \hat{\mathbf{i}} = 0$$

16 Vector or Cross Product of Two Vectors Cross product of two vectors is equal to the product of their magnitudes and sine of the angle between them.

$$\mathbf{A} \times \mathbf{B} = AB\sin\theta\, \hat{\mathbf{n}}$$

where, $\hat{\mathbf{n}}$ is a unit vector perpendicular to the plane containing **A** and **B**.

17 If $\mathbf{A} = A_x\hat{\mathbf{i}} + A_y\hat{\mathbf{j}} + A_z\hat{\mathbf{k}}$ and $\mathbf{B} = B_x\hat{\mathbf{i}} + B_y\hat{\mathbf{j}} + B_z\hat{\mathbf{k}}$

then, $$\mathbf{A} \times \mathbf{B} = \begin{vmatrix} \hat{\mathbf{i}} & \hat{\mathbf{j}} & \hat{\mathbf{k}} \\ A_x & A_y & A_z \\ B_x & B_y & B_z \end{vmatrix}$$

18 The path of a projectile is parabolic.

19 For angular projection,

Time of flight $T = \dfrac{2u\sin\theta}{g}$

Maximum height $H = \dfrac{u^2\sin^2\theta}{2g}$

Horizontal range $R = \dfrac{u^2\sin 2\theta}{g}$

20 Horizontal range is maximum when angle of projection is 45°.

21 Angular displacement $(\Delta\theta) = \dfrac{\Delta s}{r}$

Its unit is radian.

22 Angular v elocity $(\omega) = \dfrac{d\theta}{dt}$

Average angular velocity $\omega_{av} = \dfrac{2\pi}{T} = 2\pi n$

where, T is time period and n is frequency. Its unit is rad/s.

23 Relation between linear velocity and angular velocity

$$v = r\omega$$

24 Centripetal acceleration $(a_c) = \dfrac{v^2}{r} = r\omega^2$

Its direction is always towards the centre of the circular path.

Exercises

Question 1 State for each of the following physical quantities, if it is a scalar or a vector :
Volume, mass, speed, acceleration, density, number of moles, velocity, angular frequency, displacement, angular velocity.

Sol. Scalar quantities Volume, mass, speed, density, number of moles and angular frequency.

Vector quantities Acceleration, velocity, displacement and angular velocity.

Question 2 Pick out the two scalar quantities in the following list :

Force, angular momentum, work, current, linear momentum electric field, average velocity, magnetic moment, reaction as per Newton's third law, relative velocity.

Sol. Work and current are scalar quantities.

Question 3 Pick out the only vector quantity in the following list :
Temperature, pressure, impulse, time, power, total path, length, energy, gravitational potential, coefficient of friction, charge.

Sol. Impulse is only a vector quantity in the given quantities.

Question 4 State with reasons, whether the following algebraic operations with scalar and vector physical quantities are meaningful

(a) Adding any two scalars.

(b) Adding a scalar to a vector of the same dimensions.

(c) Multiplying any vector by any scalar.

(d) Multiplying any two scalars.

(e) Adding any two vectors.

(f) Adding a component of a vector to the same vector.

◎ **Thinking Process** Two vectors of same dimensions can be added or subtracted. Similarly, two scalars of same dimensions can be added or subtracted.

Sol.

(a) No, adding any two scalar is not meaningful because only the scalars of same dimensions *i.e.,* having same unit can be added.

(b) No, adding a scalar to a vector of the same dimensions is not meaningful because a scalar cannot be added to a vector.

(c) Yes, multiplying any vector by any scalar is meaningful. When a vector is multiplied by a scalar we get a vector, whose magnitude is equal to the product of magnitude of vector and the scalar and direction remains the same as the direction of the given vector.

e.g., A body of mass 4 kg is moving with a velocity 20 m/s towards east then, product of velocity and mass gives the momentum of the body, which is also a vector quantity.

$$\mathbf{p} = m\mathbf{v} = 4 \text{ kg} \times (20 \text{ m/s}) \text{ (east)} = 80 \text{ kg-m/s, east}$$

(d) Yes, multiplying any two scalars is meaningful. Density ρ and volume V both are scalar quantities. When density is multiplies by volume, then we get $\rho \times V = m$, mass of the body, which is a scalar quantity.

(e) No, adding any two vectors is not meaningful because only vectors of same dimensions *i.e.,* having same unit and nature can be added.

(f) Yes, adding a component of a vector to the same vector, is meaningful because both vectors are of same dimensionsm but it is done by using vector law of addition.

Question 5 Read each of the following statements carefully and state with reasons, if it is true or false.

(a) The magnitude of a vector is always a scalar.

(b) Each component of a vector is always a scalar.

(c) The total path length is always equal to the magnitude of the displacement vector of a particle.

(d) The average speed of a particle, defined as total path length divided by the time taken to cover the path, is either greater or equal to the magnitude of average velocity of the particle over the same interval of time.

(e) Three vectors not lying in a plane can never add up to give a null vector.

Sol.

(a) True; because the magnitude of a vector is always a pure number, which is a scalar.

(b) False; because each component of a vector is always a vector, as each component has particular direction.

(c) True; only when a particle is moving along a straight line in same direction, otherwise it is false.

(d) True; because average speed $= \dfrac{\text{Total path length}}{\text{Total time taken}}$

and average velocity $= \dfrac{\text{Total displacement}}{\text{Total time taken}}$

But, the total path length is always greater or equal to the magnitude of the displacement in same interval of time. Therefore, average speed is either greater or equal to the magnitude of average velocity of the particle over the same interval of time.

(e) True; because three vectors not lying in a plane can never represent three sides of a triangle taken in the same order.

Question 6 Establish the following vector inequalities geometrically or otherwise

(a) $|\mathbf{a} + \mathbf{b}| \le |\mathbf{a}| + |\mathbf{b}|$ (b) $|\mathbf{a} + \mathbf{b}| \ge |\mathbf{a}| - |\mathbf{b}|$

(c) $|\mathbf{a} - \mathbf{b}| \le |\mathbf{a}| + |\mathbf{b}|$ (d) $|\mathbf{a} - \mathbf{b}| \ge ||\mathbf{a}| - |\mathbf{b}||$

When does the equality sign above apply?

◎ ***Thinking Process*** From the properties of a triangle, one side of a triangle is always less than the sum of the lengths of its two other sides.

Sol. Let two vectors **a** and **b** be represented by the sides **OP** and **PQ** of the triangle *OPQ* taken in the same order and their resultant is represented by **OQ**.

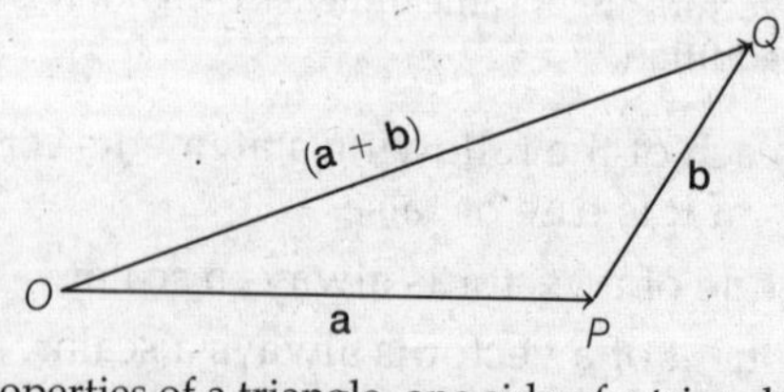

(a) From the properties of a triangle, one side of a triangle is always less than the sum of the lengths of its two other sides.

∴ In ΔOPQ,

$$OQ < OP + PQ$$

or $$|\mathbf{a} + \mathbf{b}| < |\mathbf{a}| + |\mathbf{b}| \qquad \text{...(i)}$$

If the two given vectors **a** and **b** are acting in same direction along the same straight line, then magnitude of the resultant vector,

$$|\mathbf{a} + \mathbf{b}| = \sqrt{a^2 + b^2 + 2ab\cos\theta}$$

$$= \sqrt{a^2 + b^2 + 2ab\cos\theta} \qquad (\because \theta = 0^\circ)$$

$$= \sqrt{(a + b)^2} = (a + b)$$

$$|\mathbf{a} + \mathbf{b}| = |\mathbf{a}| + |\mathbf{b}| \qquad \text{...(ii)}$$

From Eqs. (i) and (ii), we get

$$|\mathbf{a} + \mathbf{b}| \leq |\mathbf{a}| + |\mathbf{b}|$$

The equality sign applies, if **a** and **b** are acting in same direction, along the same straight line.

(b) From the properties of a triangle one side of a triangle is more than the difference of two other sides.

Therefore in ΔOPQ,

$$OQ > |OP - PQ|$$

The modulus of $(OP - PQ)$ has been taken because in LHS, OQ is positive but in RHS, $(OP - PQ)$ can be negative, if $PQ > OP$.

$$\therefore \qquad |\mathbf{a} + \mathbf{b}| > |\mathbf{a}| - |\mathbf{b}| \qquad \text{...(iii)}$$

If the two given vectors **a** and **b** are acting in opposite directions along the same straight line, then

$$|\mathbf{a} + \mathbf{b}| = |\mathbf{a}| - |\mathbf{b}| \qquad \text{...(iv)}$$

From Eqs. (iii) and (iv), we get

$$|\mathbf{a} + \mathbf{b}| \geq |\mathbf{a}| - |\mathbf{b}|$$

The equality sign applies, if **a** and **b** are acting in opposite directions along the same straight line.

(c) If **PR** represents $-\mathbf{b}$ then, the resultant of **a** and $-\mathbf{b}$ is represented by **OR**. From the properties of a triangle, one side of a triangle is less than the sum of the lengths of the other two sides of the triangle. Therefore, in triangle OPR,

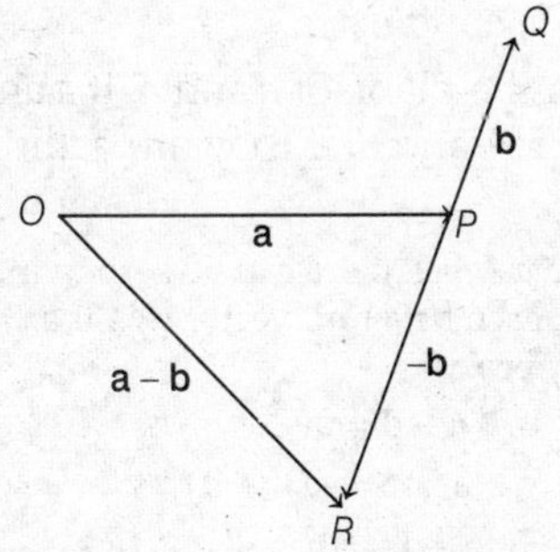

$\therefore$ $$OR < OP + PR$$

$$|\mathbf{a} - \mathbf{b}| < |\mathbf{a}| + |-\mathbf{b}|$$

But $|-\mathbf{b}| = |\mathbf{b}|$, as modulus of a vector is always positive.

or $$|\mathbf{a} - \mathbf{b}| < |\mathbf{a}| + |\mathbf{b}| \quad \text{...(v)}$$

If vector **a** and **b** are acting in opposite directions along a straight line, then

$$|\mathbf{a} - \mathbf{b}| = |\mathbf{a}| + |\mathbf{b}| \quad \text{...(vi)}$$

From Eqs. (v) and (vi), we get

$$|\mathbf{a} - \mathbf{b}| \le |\mathbf{a}| + |\mathbf{b}|$$

(d) From the properties of a triangle, one side of a triangle is more than the difference of its two other sides.

$\therefore$ In triangle *OPR*,

$$OR > |OP - PR|$$

The modulus of $(OP - PR)$ has been taken because in LHS, *OR* is positive but in RHS, $(OP - PR)$ can be negative, if $PR > OP$.

$\therefore$ $$|\mathbf{a} - \mathbf{b}| > |\mathbf{a}| - |-\mathbf{b}|$$

$$|\mathbf{a} - \mathbf{b}| > |\mathbf{a}| - |\mathbf{b}| \quad \text{...(vii)}$$

If the two given vectors **a** and **b** are acting in same direction along the same straight line, then

$$|\mathbf{a} - \mathbf{b}| = |\mathbf{a}| - |\mathbf{b}| \quad \text{...(viii)}$$

From Eqs. (vii) and (viii), we get

$$|\mathbf{a} - \mathbf{b}| \ge |\mathbf{a}| - |\mathbf{b}|$$

The equality sign applies, if **a** and **b** are acting in same direction along the same straight line.

Question 7 Given $a + b + c + d = 0$, which of the following statements are correct?

(a) a, b, c and d must each be a null vector.

(b) The magnitude of $(a + c)$ equals the magnitude of $(b + d)$.

(c) The magnitude of a can never be greater than the sum of the magnitudes of b, c and d.

(d) $b + c$ must lie in the plane of a and d, if a and d are not collinear and in the line of a and d, if they are collinear?

Sol.

(a) Incorrect, because $\mathbf{a} + \mathbf{b} + \mathbf{c} + \mathbf{d}$ can be zero in many ways other than **a**, **b**, **c** and **d** must each be a null vector *e.g.*, If $\mathbf{a} = -\mathbf{b}$ and $\mathbf{c} = -\mathbf{d}$ then their resultant be zero.

(b) Correct, since $\mathbf{a} + \mathbf{b} + \mathbf{c} + \mathbf{d} = 0$

$\therefore$ $$\mathbf{a} + \mathbf{c} = -(\mathbf{b} + \mathbf{d})$$

or $$|\mathbf{a} + \mathbf{c}| = |\mathbf{b} + \mathbf{d}|$$

(c) Correct, since $\mathbf{a} + \mathbf{b} + \mathbf{c} + \mathbf{d} = 0$

$$\therefore \quad \mathbf{a} = -(\mathbf{b} + \mathbf{c} + \mathbf{d})$$

$$\text{or} \quad |\mathbf{a}| = |\mathbf{b} + \mathbf{c} + \mathbf{d}|$$

Therefore, the magnitude of **a** is equal to the magnitude of (**b** + **c** + **d**). As magnitude of (**b** + **c** + **d**) can be equal or less than the sum of magnitudes of **b**, **c** and **d** but can never be greater.

Therefore, **a** also can never be greater than the sum of the magnitude of **b**, **c** and **d**.

(d) Correct, since $\mathbf{a} + \mathbf{b} + \mathbf{c} + \mathbf{d} = 0$

$$\text{or} \quad \mathbf{a} + (\mathbf{b} + \mathbf{c}) + \mathbf{d} = 0$$

The resultant of three vectors **a**, (**b** + **c**) and **d** can be zero only when they lie in a plane and can be represented by the three sides of triangle taken in one order.

If **a** and **d** are collinear, then (**b** + **c**) must be in the line of **a** and **d**, only then the vector sum of all the vectors will be zero.

Question 8 Three girls skating on a circular ice ground of radius 200 m start from a point *P* on the edge of the ground and reach a point *Q* diametrically opposite to *P* following different paths as shown. What is the magnitude of the displacement vector for each? For which girl is this equal to the actual length of path skated?

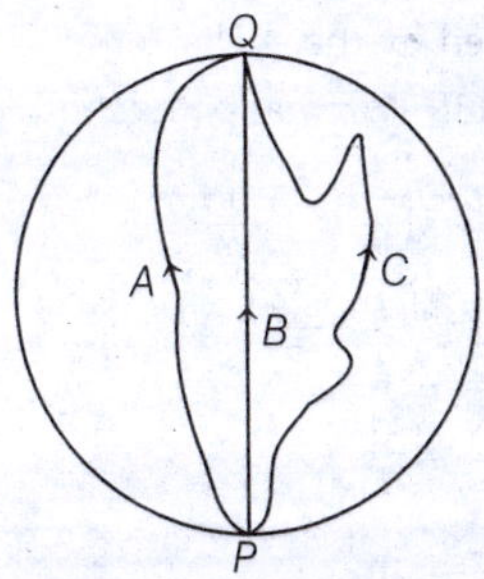

◎ *Thinking Process* Displacement is the shortest distance between initial and final positions. Distance is the length of actual path covered by body.

Sol. Given, radius of the circular track = 200 m

Displacement for each girl is equal to the diameter of the circular track.

$\therefore$ Displacement = Diameter of the circular track

$$= 2 \times 200$$

$$= 400 \text{ m}$$

For girl *B*, the displacement is equal to the actual length of path skated.

Question 9 A cyclist starts from the centre *O* of a circular park of radius 1 km, reaches the edge *P* of the park, then cycles along the circumference and returns to the centre along *QO* as shown. If the round trip takes 10 min, what is the (a) net displacement, (b) average velocity and (c) average speed of the cyclist?

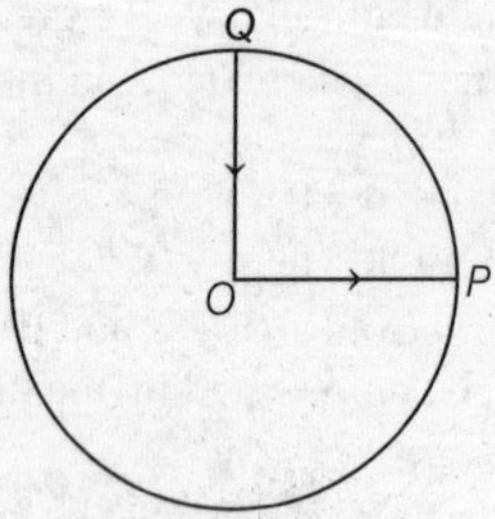

Sol. Given, radius of circular park = 1 km

(a) As cyclist return to its initial state, therefore the net displacement of the cyclist is zero.

(b) $$\text{Average velocity} = \frac{\text{Total displacement}}{\text{Total time taken}}$$

$$= \frac{0}{\text{Total time taken}} = 0$$

(c) Total distance travelled by the cyclist

$$= OP + \text{Actual path length of } PQ + QO$$

$$= r + \left(\frac{1}{4} \times 2\pi r\right) + r$$

$$= 1 + \left(\frac{1}{2} \times \frac{22}{7} \times 1\right) + 1$$

$$= 2 + \frac{11}{7}$$

$$= \frac{25}{7} \text{ km}$$

$$\text{Total time taken} = 10 \text{ min} = \frac{10}{60} \text{ h} = \frac{1}{6} \text{ h}$$

$$\therefore \text{ Average speed of the cyclist} = \frac{\text{Total distance travelled}}{\text{Total time taken}}$$

$$= \frac{25/7}{1/6} = \frac{150}{7} = 21.43 \text{ km/h}$$

Mistake Alert Don't take the same formula of average velocity and average speed.

Question 10 On an open ground, a motorist follows a track that turns to his left by an angle of 60° after every 500 m. Starting from a given turn, specify the displacement of the motorist at the third, sixth and eighth turn. Compare the magnitude of the displacement with the total path length covered by the motorist in each case.

Thinking Process As motorist is taking turn to his left at an angle 60° after every 500 m therefore, he is moving on a regular hexagon.

Sol. The distance after which motorist take a turn = 500 m

As motorist takes a turn at an angle of 60° each time, therefore motorist is moving on a regular hexagonal path. Let the motorist starts from point *A* and reaches at point *D* at the end of third turn and at initial point *A* at the end of sixth turn and at point C at the end of eight turn.

Displacement of the motorist at the third turn = *AD*

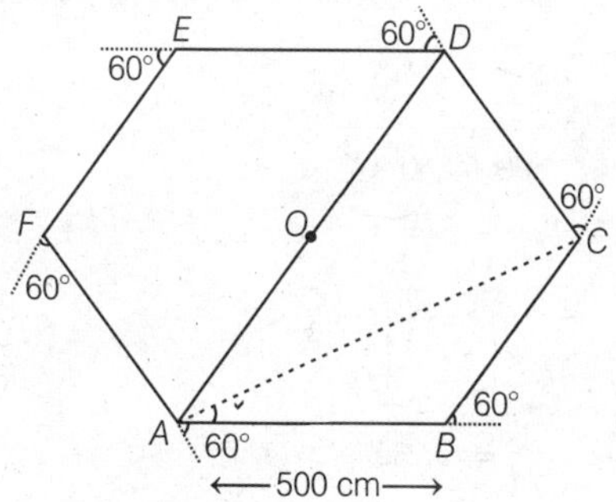

$= AO + OD$

$= 500 + 500 = 1000$ m

Displacement is 1000 m at than angle of 60° from the initial direction of motion.

Total path length $= AB + BC + CD$

$= 500 + 500 + 500$

$= 1500$ m

Total path length is 500 m more than displacement.

At the sixth turn motorist is at the starting point *A*.

$\therefore$ Displacement of the motorist at the sixth turn = 0

Total path length $= AB + BC + CD + DE + EF + FA$

$= 500 + 500 + 500 + 500 + 500 + 500$

$= 3000$ m

Total path length is 3000 m more than displacement.

At the eight turn, the motorist is point C.

$\therefore$ Displacement of the motorist = AC

Using triangle law of vector addition,

$$AC = \sqrt{AB^2 + BC^2 + 2AB \cdot BC\cos 60^\circ}$$
$$= \sqrt{(500)^2 + (500)^2 + 2 \times 500 \times 500 \times \frac{1}{2}}$$
$$= \sqrt{3 \times (500)^2}$$
$$= 500\sqrt{3} \text{ m}$$
$$= 500 \times 1.732 \text{ m} = 866 \text{ m}$$

If it is inclined at an angle β from the direction of **AB**, then

$$\tan\beta = \frac{500\sin 60^\circ}{500 + 500\cos 60^\circ}$$
$$= \frac{500 \times \frac{\sqrt{3}}{2}}{500 + 500 \times \frac{1}{2}}$$
$$= \frac{500 \times \frac{\sqrt{3}}{2}}{500\left(1 + \frac{1}{2}\right)} = \frac{\frac{\sqrt{3}}{2}}{\frac{3}{2}}$$
$$= \frac{1}{\sqrt{3}} = \tan 30^\circ$$

or $\beta = 30^\circ$

$\therefore$ Displacement of the motorist at the end of eighth turn is 866 m making an angle 30° with the initial direction of motion.

Total path length = 8 × 500 = 4000 m

Total path length is 2134 m more than displacement.

Question 11 A passenger arriving in a new town wishes to go from the station to a hotel located 10 km away on a straight road from the station. A dishonest cabman takes him along a circuitous path 23 km long and reaches the hotel in 28 min. What is (a) the average speed of the taxi and (b) the magnitude of average velocity? Are the two equal?

Note Distance and displacement are equal in magnitude if body is moving in straight line. In terms of magnitude, distance can either greater or equal to displacement.

Sol. Given, shortest distance between the station and the hotel = 10 km

$\therefore$ Displacement of the taxi = 10 km

Distance travelled by the taxi = 23 km

Time taken by the taxi = 28 min

$$= \frac{28}{60} = \frac{7}{15} \text{ h}$$

(a) Average speed of the taxi $= \dfrac{\text{Total distance travelled}}{\text{Total time taken}}$

$$= \frac{23}{(7/15)} = \frac{345}{7} \text{ km/h}$$

$$= 49.3 \text{ km/h}$$

(b) Magnitude of average velocity

$$= \frac{\text{Magnitude of the total displacement}}{\text{Total time taken}}$$

$$= \frac{10}{(7/15)} = \frac{150}{7} \text{ km/h}$$

$$= 21.43 \text{ km/h}$$

No, the average speed of the taxi is not equal to the magnitude of the average velocity of the taxi.

Question 12 The ceiling of a long hall is 25 m high. What is the maximum horizontal distance that a ball thrown with a speed of 40 m/s can go without hitting the ceiling of the hall?

◎ **Thinking Process** Maximum height attained by a projectile is given by,

$$H = \frac{u^2 \sin^2 \theta}{2g}$$

and horizontal range is given by

$$R = \frac{u^2 \sin 2\theta}{g}$$

Sol. Given, initial velocity (u) = 40 m/s

Height of the hall (H) = 25 m

Let the angle of projection of the ball be θ, when maximum height attained by it be 25 m.

Maximum height attained by the ball

$$H = \frac{u^2 \sin^2 \theta}{2g}$$

$$25 = \frac{(40)^2 \sin^2 \theta}{2 \times 9.8}$$

$$\text{or} \qquad \sin^2\theta = \frac{25 \times 2 \times 9.8}{1600} = 0.3063$$

$$\text{or} \qquad \sin\theta = 0.5534 = \sin 33.6^\circ$$

$$\text{or} \qquad \theta = 33.6^\circ$$

$$\therefore \text{ Horizontal range } (R) = \frac{u^2 \sin 2\theta}{g}$$

$$= \frac{(40)^2 \sin(2 \times 33.6^\circ)}{9.8}$$

$$= \frac{1600 \times \sin 67.2^\circ}{9.8}$$

$$= \frac{1600 \times 0.9219}{9.8} = 150.5 \text{ m}$$

Question 13 A cricketer can throw a ball to a maximum horizontal distance of 100 m. How much high above the ground can the cricketer throw the same ball?

◎ ***Thinking Process*** Horizontal range is maximum when angle of projection is 45° and height is maximum when angle of projection is 90°.

Sol. Horizontal range of a projectile is given by

$$R = \frac{u^2 \sin 2\theta}{g}$$

If $\theta = 45^\circ$, then R is maximum and is equal to

$$R_{max} = \frac{u^2}{g}$$

$$\text{Given,} \qquad R_{max} = 100 \text{ m}$$

$$\therefore \qquad 100 = \frac{u^2}{g} \qquad \text{...(i)}$$

When cricketer throws the ball vertically upward, then ball goes upto height H. Using equation of motion,

$$v^2 = u^2 + 2as$$

$$(0)^2 = u^2 + 2(-g)H$$

$$\text{or} \qquad H = \frac{u^2}{2g} = \frac{1}{2}\left(\frac{u^2}{g}\right)$$

$$= \frac{1}{2} \times 100 \qquad \text{[Using Eq. (i)]}$$

$$= 50 \text{ m}$$

Quick Solution

$$R = \frac{u^2 \sin 2\theta}{g}$$

For maximum range $\theta = 45°$

$$R_{max} = \frac{u^2}{g} = 100 \text{ m} \quad \ldots(i)$$

Now, $$H = \frac{u^2 \sin^2 \theta}{2g}$$

For maximum height $\theta = 90°$

$$H_{max} = \frac{u^2}{2g} = \frac{R_{max}}{2}$$

$$= \frac{100}{2} = 50 \text{ m}$$

Question 14 A stone tied to the end of a string 80 cm long is whirled in a horizontal circle with a constant speed. If the stone makes 14 revolutions in 25 s, what is the magnitude and direction of acceleration of the stone?

Sol. Radius of the horizontal circle = Length of the strain

$$= 80 \text{ cm} = 0.80 \text{ m}$$

Frequency of revolution $(n) = \frac{14}{25} \text{ s}^{-1}$

Angular speed of the revolution of the stone

$$\omega = 2\pi n$$

$$= 2 \times \frac{22}{7} \times \frac{14}{25}$$

$$= \frac{88}{25} \text{ rad/s}$$

Centripetal acceleration of the stone $(a) = r\omega^2$

$$= 0.80 \times \left(\frac{88}{25}\right)^2$$

$$= 0.80 \times \frac{88}{25} \times \frac{88}{25} = 9.91 \text{ m/s}^2$$

The direction of the acceleration is towards the centre of the horizontal circle, along its radius.

Mistake Alert Student generally does not change the unit according to mentioned value or unit in the question.

Question 15 An aircraft executes a horizontal loop of radius 1 km with a speed of 900 km/h. Compare its centripetal acceleration with the acceleration due to gravity.

Sol. Radius of horizontal loop $(r) = 1\,\text{km} = 1000\text{ m}$

Speed of aircraft $(v) = 900\text{ km/h}$

$$= 900 \times \frac{5}{18}\text{ m/s} \qquad \left(\because 1\text{ km/h} = \frac{5}{10}\text{ m/s}\right)$$

$$= 250\text{ m/s}$$

Centrepetal acceleration of the aircraft

$$a = \frac{v^2}{r}$$

$$= \frac{(250)^2}{1000} = \frac{62500}{1000} = 62.5\text{ m/s}^2$$

Acceleration due to gravity $(g) = 9.8\text{ m/s}^2$

$$\therefore \quad \frac{\text{Centrepetal acceleration }(a)}{\text{Acceleration due to gravity }(g)} = \frac{62.5}{9.8} = 6.38$$

Question 16 Read each of the following statements carefully and state with reasons, if it is true or false.

(a) The net acceleration of a particle in the circular motion is always along the radius of the circle towards the centre.

(b) The velocity vector of a particle at a point is always along the tangent to the path of the particle at that point.

(c) The acceleration vector of a particle in uniform circular motion averaged over one cycle is a null vector.

Sol.

(a) *False,* because in uniform circular motion, the centripetal acceleration is along the radius of the circle towards the centre, but in non-uniform circular motion, the direction of the resultant acceleration is not along the radius of the circle.

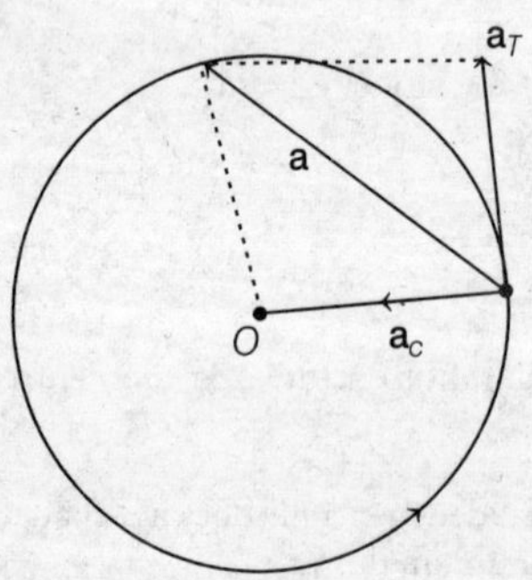

(b) *True,* the velocity vector of a particle is always along the tangent to the path of the particle either it is in rectilinear, circular or curvilinear motion.

(c) *True,* the direction of acceleration vector in uniform circular motion is directed towards the centre of the circular path, which is continuously changing with time. Therefore, the resultant of all these vectors over one cycle will be a null vector.

Question 17 The position of a particle is given by

$$\mathbf{r} = 3.0\,t\,\hat{\mathbf{i}} - 2.0\,t^2\hat{\mathbf{j}} + 4.0\,\hat{\mathbf{k}}\text{ m}$$

where, t is in second and the coefficients have the proper units for r to be in metres.

(a) Find the **v** and **a** of the particle?

(b) What is the magnitude and direction of velocity of the particle at $t = 2$ s?

Sol. Position vector of the particle

$$\mathbf{r} = 3.0t\,\hat{\mathbf{i}} - 2.0t^2\,\hat{\mathbf{j}} + 4.0\,\hat{\mathbf{k}}\text{m}$$

(a) Velocity of the particle,

$$\mathbf{v} = \frac{d\mathbf{r}}{dt} = \frac{d}{dt}(3.0t\hat{\mathbf{i}} - 2.0t^2\hat{\mathbf{j}} + 4.0\hat{\mathbf{k}})$$

$$= (3.0\,\hat{\mathbf{i}} - 4.0t\hat{\mathbf{j}})\text{ m/s}$$

Acceleration of the particle

$$\mathbf{a} = \frac{d\mathbf{v}}{dt} = \frac{d}{dt}(3.0\,\hat{\mathbf{i}} - 4.0t\hat{\mathbf{j}})$$

$$= 0\cdot\hat{\mathbf{i}} - 4.0\hat{\mathbf{j}} = (-4.0\,\hat{\mathbf{j}})\text{ m/s}^2$$

(b) Velocity of the particle at $t = 2$ s

$$\mathbf{v} = (3.0\hat{\mathbf{i}} - 4.0 \times 2\hat{\mathbf{j}})\text{ m/s}$$

$$= (3.0\,\hat{\mathbf{i}} - 8.0\,\hat{\mathbf{j}})\text{ m/s}$$

or $$v = \sqrt{(3.0)^2 + (8.0)^2} = \sqrt{9 + 64} = \sqrt{73}$$

$$= 8.54\text{ m/s}$$

If velocity **v**, makes an angle θ with X-axis, then

$$\tan\theta = \frac{v_y}{v_x} = -\frac{8.0}{3.0} = -2.667 = -\tan 69.5^\circ$$

$$\theta = 69.5^\circ\text{, below the X-axis}$$

$\therefore$ Velocity of the particle at $t = 2$ s is 8.45 m/s making an angle 69.5° below the X-axis.

Question 18 A particle starts from the origin at $t = 0$ s with a velocity of $10.0\hat{\mathbf{j}}$ m/s and moves in the X-Y plane with the constant acceleration of $(8.0\,\hat{\mathbf{i}} + 2.0\,\hat{\mathbf{j}})\text{ m/s}^2$.

(a) At what time is the x-coordinate of the particle 16 m? What is the y-coordinate of the particle at that time?

(b) What is the speed of the particle at that time?

Sol. Given, at $t = 0$, $\mathbf{u} = 10.0\hat{\mathbf{j}}$ m/s

Acceleration $(\mathbf{a}) = \dfrac{d\mathbf{v}}{dt} = (8.0\hat{\mathbf{i}} + 2.0\hat{\mathbf{j}})$ m/s^2

or $\quad d\mathbf{v} = (8.0\hat{\mathbf{i}} + 2.0\hat{\mathbf{j}})dt$

Integrating both sides within limits of motion

$$\int_{\mathbf{u}}^{\mathbf{v}} d\mathbf{v} = \int_0^t (8.0\hat{\mathbf{i}} + 2.0\hat{\mathbf{j}})\, dt$$

$$\mathbf{v} - \mathbf{u} = (8.0\hat{\mathbf{i}} + 2.0\hat{\mathbf{j}})t$$

or $\quad \mathbf{v} = \mathbf{u} + 8.0t\hat{\mathbf{i}} + 2.0t\hat{\mathbf{j}}$

But $\quad \mathbf{v} = \dfrac{d\mathbf{r}}{dt}$

or $\quad d\mathbf{r} = \mathbf{v}dt$

$$= (\mathbf{u} + 8.0t\hat{\mathbf{i}} + 2.0t\hat{\mathbf{j}})\, dt$$

Integrating both sides within proper limits,

$$\int_0^{\mathbf{r}} d\mathbf{r} = \int_0^t (\mathbf{u} + 8.0t\hat{\mathbf{i}} + 2.0t\hat{\mathbf{j}})\, dt$$

$$\mathbf{r} - 0 = \mathbf{u}t + 8.0 \times \frac{t^2}{2}\hat{\mathbf{i}} + 2.0 \times \frac{t^2}{2}\hat{\mathbf{j}}$$

or $\quad \mathbf{r} = 10.0t\,\hat{\mathbf{j}} + 4.0t^2\,\hat{\mathbf{i}} + t^2\,\hat{\mathbf{j}}$

or $\quad x\hat{\mathbf{k}} + y\hat{\mathbf{j}} = 4.0t^2\hat{\mathbf{i}} + (10.0t + t^2)\hat{\mathbf{j}}$

$\therefore \quad x = 4.0t^2$ and $y = 10.0t + t^2$

(a) When $x = 16$ m, then

$$16 = 4.0t^2$$

or $\quad t^2 = 4 \Rightarrow t = 2$ s (since time cannot be negative)

$\therefore \quad y = 10.0 \times 2 + (2)^2$

$$= 24 \text{ m}$$

(b) Velocity of the particle (speed of particle is same as velocity of particle at $t = 2$ s).

$$\mathbf{v} = \mathbf{u} + 8.0t\,\hat{\mathbf{i}} + 2.0t\,\hat{\mathbf{j}}$$

$$= 10.0\,\hat{\mathbf{j}} + 8.0t\,\hat{\mathbf{i}} + 2.0t\,\hat{\mathbf{j}}$$

At $t = 2$ s,

$$\mathbf{v} = 10\,\hat{\mathbf{j}} + 8 \times 2\,\hat{\mathbf{i}} + 2 \times 2\,\hat{\mathbf{j}} = 16\,\hat{\mathbf{i}} + 14\,\hat{\mathbf{j}}$$

$\therefore \quad v = \sqrt{(16)^2 + (14)^2} = 21.26$ m/s

Quick Solution

$u_x = 0,\ u_y = 10\text{ m/s}\ a_x = 8\text{ m/s}^2\ a_y = 2\text{ m/s}^2$

(a) $S_i = 16\text{ m}$

$\therefore \quad S_x = u_x t + \frac{1}{2} a_x t^2$

$16 = \frac{1}{4} \times 8\, t^2$

$\Rightarrow \quad t = 2\text{sec}$

Now, at $t = 2$ sec

$$S_y = u_y t + \frac{1}{2} a_y t^2$$

$$= (10 \times 2) + \frac{1}{2} \times 2 \times 4 = 24$$

(b) at $t = 2$ sec

$$v_x = u_x + a_x t$$

$$= 0 + (8 \times 2) = 16\text{ m/s}$$

$$v_y = u_y + a_y t$$

$$= 10 + (2 \times 2) = 14\text{ m/s}$$

$\therefore \quad v = v_x \hat{\mathbf{i}} + v_y \hat{\mathbf{j}}$

$$= (16\hat{\mathbf{i}} + 14\hat{\mathbf{j}})\text{ m/s}$$

$$v = \sqrt{v_x^2 + v_y^2}$$

$$= \sqrt{(16)^2 + (14)^2} = 21.26\text{ m/s}$$

Question 19 $\hat{\mathbf{i}}$ and $\hat{\mathbf{j}}$ are unit vectors along X and Y axes respectively. What is the magnitude and direction of vectors $\hat{\mathbf{i}} + \hat{\mathbf{j}}$ and $\hat{\mathbf{i}} - \hat{\mathbf{j}}$? What are the components of a vector $A = 2\hat{\mathbf{i}} + 3\hat{\mathbf{j}}$ along the direction $\hat{\mathbf{i}} + \hat{\mathbf{j}}$ and $\hat{\mathbf{i}} - \hat{\mathbf{j}}$? (You may use graphical method).

◎ ***Thinking Process*** The modulus of a vector $\mathbf{A} = A_x \hat{\mathbf{i}} + A_y \hat{\mathbf{j}}$ is given by

$$A = |\mathbf{A}| = \sqrt{A_x^2 + A_y^2}$$

If vector is inclined at an angle θ, from X-axis, then

$$\tan\theta = \frac{A_y}{A_x}$$

Sol. Magnitude of $(\hat{\mathbf{i}} + \hat{\mathbf{j}}) = \sqrt{(1)^2 + (1)^2} = \sqrt{2}$

If vector $(\hat{\mathbf{i}} + \hat{\mathbf{j}})$ makes an angle θ, with the X-axis, then

$$\tan\theta = \frac{A_y}{A_x} = \frac{1}{1} = 1$$

$$= \tan 45^\circ$$

or $$\theta = 45^\circ$$

Magnitude of $(\hat{\mathbf{i}} - \hat{\mathbf{j}}) = \sqrt{(1)^2 + (-1)^2} = \sqrt{2}$

If vector $(\hat{\mathbf{i}} - \hat{\mathbf{j}})$ makes an angle θ, with X-axis, then

$$\tan\theta = \frac{A_y}{A_x} = \frac{(-1)}{1} = -1$$

$$= -\tan 45^\circ$$

or $$\theta = -45^\circ$$

Hence, vector $(\hat{\mathbf{i}} - \hat{\mathbf{j}})$ makes an angle of 45° from X-axis in negative direction.

To determine the component of $\mathbf{A} = 2\hat{\mathbf{i}} + 3\hat{\mathbf{j}}$ in the direction of $(\hat{\mathbf{i}} + \hat{\mathbf{j}})$.

Let $$\mathbf{B} = (\hat{\mathbf{i}} + \hat{\mathbf{j}})$$

$$\mathbf{A}\cdot\mathbf{B} = AB\cos\theta = (A\cos\theta)\cdot B$$

or $$A\cos\theta = \frac{\mathbf{A}\cdot\mathbf{B}}{B}$$

$\therefore$ Magnitude of the component of $\mathbf{A}$ in the direction of $\mathbf{B} = A\cos\theta$

$$= \frac{\mathbf{A}\cdot\mathbf{B}}{B} = \frac{(2\hat{\mathbf{i}} + 3\hat{\mathbf{j}})\cdot(\hat{\mathbf{i}} + \hat{\mathbf{j}})}{\sqrt{(1)^2 + (1)^2}}$$

$$= \frac{2\hat{\mathbf{i}}\cdot\hat{\mathbf{i}} + 3\hat{\mathbf{j}}\cdot\hat{\mathbf{j}}}{\sqrt{2}}$$

$$= \frac{2+3}{\sqrt{2}} = \frac{5}{\sqrt{2}}$$

Unit vector along $(\hat{\mathbf{i}} + \hat{\mathbf{j}})$,

$$\hat{\mathbf{n}} = \frac{(\hat{\mathbf{i}} + \hat{\mathbf{j}})}{|\hat{\mathbf{i}} + \hat{\mathbf{j}}|} = \frac{(\hat{\mathbf{i}} + \hat{\mathbf{j}})}{\sqrt{2}}$$

Component of $\mathbf{A}$ along $(\hat{\mathbf{i}} + \hat{\mathbf{j}})$

$$= \text{Magnitude of the component of } \mathbf{A} \text{ along } (\hat{\mathbf{i}} + \hat{\mathbf{j}})\cdot\hat{\mathbf{n}}$$

$$= \frac{5}{\sqrt{2}}\cdot\frac{(\hat{\mathbf{i}} + \hat{\mathbf{j}})}{\sqrt{2}} = \frac{5}{2}(\hat{\mathbf{i}} + \hat{\mathbf{j}})$$

Magnitude of the component of $\mathbf{A}$ in the direction of $(\hat{\mathbf{i}} - \hat{\mathbf{j}})$

$$= \frac{(2\hat{\mathbf{i}} + 3\hat{\mathbf{j}})\cdot(\hat{\mathbf{i}} - \hat{\mathbf{j}})}{|\hat{\mathbf{i}} - \hat{\mathbf{j}}|}$$

$$= \frac{2\hat{\mathbf{i}}\cdot\hat{\mathbf{i}} - 3\hat{\mathbf{j}}\cdot\hat{\mathbf{j}}}{\sqrt{(1)^2 + (-1)^2}} = \frac{2-3}{\sqrt{2}} = -\frac{1}{\sqrt{2}}$$

Unit vector along $(\hat{\mathbf{i}} - \hat{\mathbf{j}})$

$$\hat{\mathbf{n}} = \frac{(\hat{\mathbf{i}} - \hat{\mathbf{j}})}{|\hat{\mathbf{i}} - \hat{\mathbf{j}}|} = \frac{(\hat{\mathbf{i}} - \hat{\mathbf{j}})}{\sqrt{2}}$$

$\therefore$ Component of **A** along $(\hat{\mathbf{i}} - \hat{\mathbf{j}})$

= Magnitude of the component of **A** along $(\hat{\mathbf{i}} - \hat{\mathbf{j}}) \cdot \hat{\mathbf{n}}$

$$= -\frac{1}{\sqrt{2}} \cdot \frac{(\hat{\mathbf{i}} - \hat{\mathbf{j}})}{\sqrt{2}} = -\frac{1}{2}(\hat{\mathbf{i}} - \hat{\mathbf{j}})$$

Question 20 For any arbitrary motion in space which of the following relations are true?

(a) $\mathbf{v}_{av} = \frac{1}{2}[\mathbf{v}(t_1) + \mathbf{v}(t_2)]$

(b) $\mathbf{v}_{av} = [\mathbf{r}(t_2) - \mathbf{r}(t_1)/(t_2 - t_1)]$

(c) $\mathbf{v}(t) = \mathbf{v}(0) + a\,t$

(d) $\mathbf{r}(t) = \mathbf{r}(0) + \mathbf{v}(0)t + \frac{1}{2}\mathbf{a}t^2$

(e) $\mathbf{a}_{av} = [\mathbf{v}(t_2) - \mathbf{v}(t_1)]/(t_2 - t_1)$

(The average stands for average of the quantity over the time interval t_1 to t_2.)

Sol. Relations (b) and (e) are true for any arbitrary motion in space while relations (a), (c) and (d) are false because they hold good for uniformly accelerated motion.

Question 21 Read each of the following statements carefully and state, with reasons and examples, if it is true or false?

A scalar quantity is one that

(a) is conserved in a process.
(b) can never take negative values.
(c) must be dimensionless.
(d) does not vary from one point to another in space.
(e) has the same values for observers with different orientations of axes.

Sol.

(a) False, because several scalar quantities do not remain conserve in a process. For example, energy being a scalar quantity is not conserved in an inelastic collision.

(b) False, because few scalar quantities can take negative values. For example, temperature being ~~a scalar~~ scalar quantity can take negative values such as –10°C, –33°C etc.

(c) False, because several scalar quantities have dimensions. For example, mass, density, speed and pressure etc. all have dimensions.

(d) False, because few scalar quantities vary from one point to another point in space. For example, density, temperature, charge density etc. vary from one point to another point in space.

(e) True, as orientation of axes does not change the value of a scalar quantity. For example, mass, density etc. are independent of the orientation of axes.

Question 22 An aircraft is flying at a height of 3400 m above the ground. If the angle subtended at a ground observation point by the aircraft positions 10 s apart is 30°, what is the speed of the aircraft?

Sol. Let O is observation point on the ground and aircraft is flying along line PQ at height $OA = 3400$ m. B and C are positions of aircraft 10 seconds apart and A lying at mid-point of BC. Then,

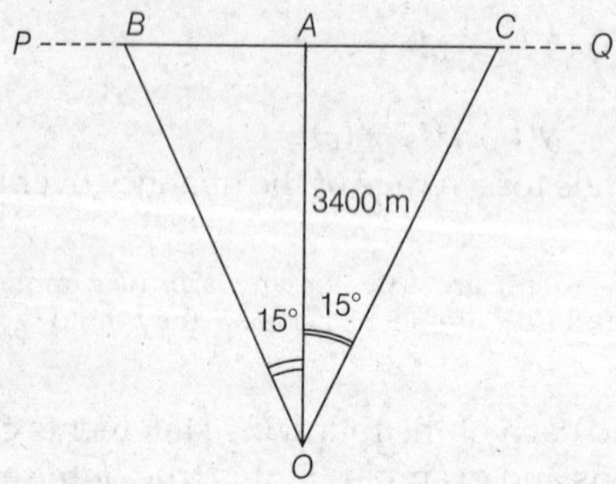

From figure, $\tan 15° = \dfrac{AB}{OA}$

$$3400 \times 0.2679 = AB$$

$$910.86 \text{ m} = AB$$

So, $$BC = 2AB = 1821.72$$

Speed of aircraft is

$$v = \frac{1821.72}{10} = 182.17 \text{ m/s}$$

DIKSHA APP Questions

Multiple Choice Questions

Q.1 A projectile can have the same range for two angles of projection. If T_1 and T_2 be the times of flight in the two cases, then the product of the two times of flight is directly proportional to

(a) R^2
(b) R
(c) $\frac{1}{R}$
(d) $\frac{1}{R^2}$

Sol. (b) We know that projectile has the same range for two complementary angles θ and $90° - \theta$

So, the times of flight for these motion will be $T_1 = \frac{2\,u\sin\theta}{g}$

and $T_2 = \frac{2u\cos\theta}{g}$

Then, $T_1T_2 = \frac{2u^2\;2\sin\theta\cos\theta}{g} = 2R$ $\left(\because R = \frac{u^2\sin 2\theta}{g}\right)$

Thus, it is proportional to R.

Q.2 The x and y coordinates of a particle at any time t is given by $x = 5t - 2t^2$ and $y = 10t$, where x and y are in metre and t in seconds. The acceleration of particle at $t = 3$ s is

(a) zero
(b) 4 m/s^2
(c) 6 m/s^2
(d) 2 m/s^2

Sol. (b)The coordinates of particle are given as $x = 5t - 2t^2$

$$y = 10t$$

So, $v_x = \frac{dx}{dt} = \frac{d}{dt}(5t - 2t^2) = 5 - 4t$

$$v_y = \frac{dy}{dt} = \frac{d}{dt}(10t) = 10$$

Now, $a_x = \frac{dv_x}{dt} = \frac{d}{dt}(5 - 4t) = -4 \Rightarrow a_y = \frac{dv_y}{dt} = \frac{d}{dt}(10) = 0$

Using the pythagoras theorem

$$a = \sqrt{a_x^2 + a_y^2} = \sqrt{(-4)^2 + 0^2} = \sqrt{16} = 4\text{ m/s}^2$$

☐ Long Answer Type

Q.1 What is the angle of projection for a projectile motion whose range R is n times the maximum height H?

Sol. $R = \dfrac{u^2 \sin 2\theta}{g} \Rightarrow H = \dfrac{u^2 \sin^2 \theta}{2g}$

Now, $R = nH$

$$\frac{u^2 \sin 2\theta}{g} = n\left(\frac{u^2 \sin^2 \theta}{2g}\right)$$

$$\sin 2\theta = \frac{n}{2} \sin^2 \theta$$

$$2\sin\theta \cos\theta = \frac{n}{2} \sin^2 \theta$$

$$\frac{2\cos\theta}{\sin\theta} = \frac{n}{2} \Rightarrow 2\cot\theta = \frac{n}{2}$$

Taking the reciprocal gives $\tan\theta = \dfrac{4}{n}$

$$\theta = \tan^{-1}\left(\frac{4}{n}\right)$$

Thus, the angle of projection is $\theta = \tan^{-1}\left(\dfrac{4}{n}\right)$

Q.2 The sum of the magnitude of two forces acting at a point is 18 N and the magnitude of their resultant is 12 N. If the resultant makes an angle of 90° with force of smaller magnitude, what are the magnitudes of two forces ?

Sol. Let P be the smaller force and Q be the greater force, then according to the problems.

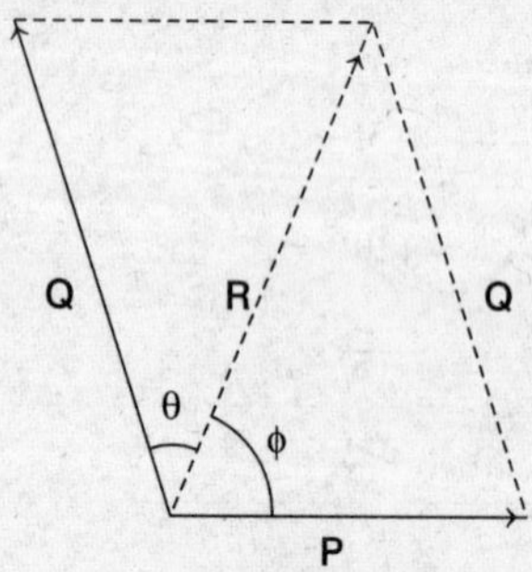

$$P + Q = 18 \quad \text{...(i)}$$

$$P^2 + R^2 = Q^2$$

$$\Rightarrow \quad R^2 = Q^2 - P^2$$

$$\Rightarrow \quad 12^2 = (Q - P)(Q + P)$$

$$\Rightarrow \quad 144 = (Q - P)\,18$$

$$\Rightarrow \quad (Q - P) = 8 \qquad \ldots\text{(ii)}$$

From (i) and (ii), we get

$$Q + P = 18$$

$$Q - P = 8$$

$$\Rightarrow \quad 2Q = 26 \quad \Rightarrow \quad Q = 13$$

Substitute in (i) we get

$$P = 5$$

Q.3 (a) Five vectors are represented by the sides of a closed pentagon taken in the same order. Find their resultant.
(b) At what angle of force $(A + B)$ and $(A - B)$ act so that their resultant is $\sqrt{3A^2 + B^2}$

Sol. (a) If 5 vectors are represented by the side of a closed pentagon taken in same order in both direction and magnitude, then the resultant is a null vector.

AB + BC + CD + DE + EA = 0

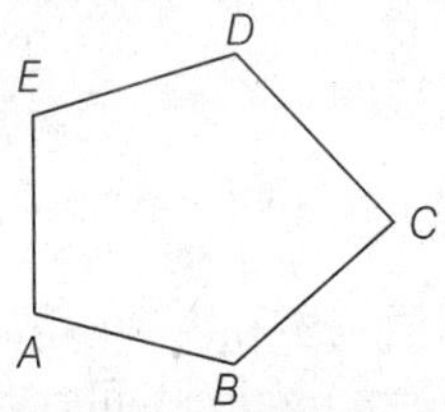

Resultant of these vectors is a null vector.

(b) Use the relation, $R = \sqrt{P^2 + Q^2 + 2PQ\cos\theta}$

$$P = A + B, Q = A - B \text{ and } R = \sqrt{3A^2 + B^2}$$

$$\therefore \quad 3A^2 + B^2 = 2A^2 + 2B^2 + 2(A^2 - B^2)\cos\theta$$

$$A^2 - B^2 = 2(A^2 - B^2)\cos\theta$$

Dividing both sides by $A^2 - B^2$ (assuming $A^2 \neq B^2$)

$$\therefore \quad 1 = 2\cos\theta$$

Thus, $\cos\theta = \frac{1}{2}$

Therefore, $\theta = 60°$ or $\theta = \frac{\pi}{3}$ radians.

Laws of Motion

CHAPTER 04

Important Points

01 Force is an external cause that changes or tries to change the state of rest or state of motion of any object.

02 Inertia is the property of an object by virtue of which it cannot change its state of rest or state of motion or direction of motion on its own. Mass is the measure of inertia.

03 Inertia is of three types

(i) Inertia of rest (ii) Inertia of motion

(iii) Inertia of direction

04 There are three Newton's laws of motion, which are the basis of mechanics.

- **Newton's First Law of Motion** A body at rest will continue to be at rest or in uniform motion will continue in uniform motion, until an external force is applied to it.
- This law is also called law of inertia.
- **Newton's Second Law of Motion** The rate of change of linear momentum of a body is directly proportional to the external force applied on the body.

$$F \propto \frac{dp}{dt} \quad \text{or} \quad F = ma$$

- This law gives a measure of force.
- **Newton's Third Law of Motion** For every action there is an equal and opposite reaction, and both act on two different bodies.

05 **Law of Conservation of Linear Momentum** If net external force acting on a body is zero then its linear momentum remains conserved.

06 **Impulsive Force** A force that acts on a body for a very short interval of time and produces a large change in its linear momentum is called an impulsive force.

07 **Impulse** Impulse of a force is equal to the product of average force and the time interval for which it acts, *i.e.*,

$$\text{Impulse} = \mathbf{F}_{\mathbf{av}} \times t$$

08 Impulse of a force is equal to the change in linear momentum.

09 When an elevator (or lift) is moving upward with an acceleration a, then its apparent weight in lift is given by

$$w = m(g + a)$$

10 When a lift is moving downward with an acceleration a, then its apparent weight in lift is given by

$$w = m(g - a)$$

11 When a lift is moving upward or downward with a constant speed, then its apparent weight in lift is equal to the real weight

$$w = mg$$

12 When a lift accidently falling under gravity, then apparent weight in the lift becomes $w = m(g - g) = 0$

13 When one body moves or tries to move over the surface of the another body then a force comes into play which opposes the relative motion of the objects in contact. This force is called **friction**.

14 Friction is of two types

(i) Static friction (ii) Kinetic friction

15 Static friction is a self adjusting force.

16 Limiting friction is the maximum value of static friction.

17 When limiting friction acts on a body, it is at the verge of starting its motion.

18 Laws of Limiting Friction

(i) Limiting friction is directly proportional to the normal reaction (R),

i.e., $$f_s \propto R$$

(ii) Its direction is in the opposite direction of the intended direction of motion.

(iii) It does not depend upon the actual area of contact.

(iv) It depends upon the nature of the material and nature of the surfaces in contact.

19 Coefficient of Friction

$$\mu = \frac{f_s}{R}$$

20 Angle of Friction The angle between the resultant of limiting friction (f_s) and normal reaction (R) with the direction of R is called angle of friction (θ).

21 Coefficient of friction, $\mu = \tan\theta$

22 Angle of Repose The minimum angle of inclination of a plane with the horizontal, such that a body placed on the plane just start to slide down.

23 Centripetal Force When an object moves on a circular path a force acts on it, whose direction is towards the centre of the path, this force is called centripetal force.

24 Centripetal force acting on a particle of mass m on a circular path of radius r is given by

$$F = \frac{mv^2}{r}$$

Exercises

Question 1 Give the magnitude and direction of the net force acting on

(a) a drop of rain falling down with a constant speed.
(b) a cork of mass 10 g floating on water.
(c) a kite skillfully held stationary in the sky.
(d) a car moving with a constant velocity of 30 km/h on a rough road.
(e) a high-speed electron in space far from all material objects and free of electric and magnetic fields.

◎ ***Thinking Process*** Force $F = ma$, therefore force acting on a particle in unaccelerated ($a = 0$) motion is zero.

Sol.

(a) As drop of rain is falling downward with a constant speed, therefore its acceleration is zero.

According to Newton's second law of motion, net force acting on drop $F = ma = 0$.

(b) In floating condition, the weight of the body is balanced by the upthrust. Therefore, net force acting on a cork floating on water, F = 0.

(c) As the kite is held stationary in the sky, its acceleration is zero. Therefore the net force acting on the kite $F = ma = 0$.

(d) As the car is moving with a constant velocity, its acceleration is zero, *i.e.*, $a = 0$. Therefore, the net force acting on the car $F = ma = 0$.

(e) As the electron is in a space where there are no electric field, magnetic field and gravitational and field acting on it, hence net force acting on electron is zero.

Question 2 A pebble of mass 0.05 kg is thrown vertically upwards. Give the direction and magnitude of the net force on the pebble

(a) during its upward motion.
(b) during its downward motion.
(c) at the highest point where it is momentarily at rest.

Do your answers change if the pebble was thrown at an angle of 45° with the horizontal direction? Ignore air resistance.

Sol. When an object is thrown vertically upward or falls vertically downward under gravity, an acceleration $g = 10\ m/s^2$ acts downward due to earth's gravitational pull.

Mass of pebble (m) = 0.05 kg

(a) **During upward motion**

Net force acting on pebble $(F) = mg$

$= 0.05 \times 10\text{ N}$

$= 0.50\text{ N}$ (Vertically downward)

(b) **During downward motion**

Net force acting on pebble $(F) = mg$

$= 0.05 \times 10\text{ N}$

$= 0.50\text{ N}$ (Vertically downward)

(c) **At the highest point**

Net force acting on pebble $(F) = mg$

$= 0.05 \times 10\text{ N}$

$= 0.50\text{ N}$ (Vertically downward)

If pebble was thrown at an angle of 45° with the horizontal direction then acceleration acting on it and therefore force acting on it will remain unchanged, *i.e.,* 0.50 N (vertically downward). In case (c), at the highest point the vertical component of velocity will be zero but horizontal component of velocity will not be zero.

Note Direction of acceleration due to gravity is always vertically downward towards earth.

Question 3 Give the magnitude and direction of the net force acting on a stone of mass 0.1 kg.

(a) Just after it is dropped from the window of a stationary train,

(b) Just after it is dropped from the window of a train running at a constant velocity of 36 km/h,

(c) Just after it is dropped from the window of a train accelerating with 1 m/s^2,

(d) Lying on the floor of a train which is accelerating with 1 m/s^2, the stone being at rest relative to the train. Neglect air resistance throughout.

◎ *Thinking Process* When any object is thrown from a train, the influence of train on the object become zero at the same moment, *i.e.,* there is no effect of acceleration of train on the object.

Sol. Mass of stone $(m) = 0.1\text{ kg}$

(a) When stone is dropped from the window of a stationary train, it falls freely under gravity.

$\therefore$ Net force acting on stone $(F) = mg = 0.1 \times 10$

$= 1.0\text{ N}$ (Vertically downward)

(b) Just after the stone is dropped from the window of a train running at a constant velocity *i.e.,* acceleration of the train is zero. So, no force acts on the stone and it falls freely under gravity. The force acts on it is due to its weight only.

i.e., acceleration of the train is zero, so no force acts on the stone due to this motion. Net force acting on stone $F = mg = 0.1 \times 10 = 1.0$ N (vertically downward).

(c) As soon as the stone is dropped from accelerating train, influence of train becomes zero, so net force on stone is $F = mg = 0.1 \times 10 = 1.0$ N (vertically downward).

(d) As the stone is on the floor of accelerating train then acceleration of the stone is same as that of train. So force on stone is $F = ma = 0.1 \times 1 = 0.1$ N (along horizontal direction in motion of train).

Weight of stone is balanced by its normal reaction.

Question 4 One end of a string of length l is connected to a particle of mass m and the other to a small peg on smooth horizontal table. If the particle moves in a circle with speed v, the net force on the particle (directed towards the centre) is

(a) T (b) $T - \frac{mv^2}{l}$ (c) $T + \frac{mv^2}{l}$ (d) zero

T is the tension in string. [Choose the correct alternative]

◎ **Thinking Process** When a particle tied with a string moves in a circle, the required centripetal force is provided by the tension in the string.

Sol. (a) When a particle moves in a circle, the centripetal force acting on it is balanced by the tension in the string.

∴ Net force on the particle directed towards centre

$$= \text{centripetal force} = \text{tension in the string} = T = \frac{mv^2}{l}$$

∴ Correct alternative is T.

Question 5 A constant retarding force of 50 N is applied to a body of mass 20 kg moving initially with a speed of 15 m/s. How long does the body take to stop?

Sol. Retarding force $F = -50$ N

Mass of the body $m = 20$ kg

Initial speed $u = 15$ m/s

Final speed $v = 0$

Time $t = ?$

Force $F = ma$

or $$a = \frac{F}{m} = -\frac{50}{20} = -2.5 \text{ m/s}^2 \quad \text{(Retardation)}$$

Using equation of motion $v = u + at$

∴ $$0 = 15 + (-2.5)t$$

or $$t = \frac{15}{2.5} = 6 \text{ s}$$

Question 6 A constant force acting on a body of mass 3.0 kg changes its speed from 2.0 m/s to 3.5 m/s in 25 s. The direction of motion of the body remains unchanged. What is the magnitude and direction of the force?

Sol. Mass of the body $m = 3.0$ kg

Initial speed $u = 2.0$ m/s

Final speed $v = 3.5$ m/s

Time $t = 25$ s

Force $F = ?$

Using the first equation of motion, $v = u + at$

$\therefore \quad 3.5 = 2.0 + a \times 25$

or $\quad a = \frac{3.5 - 2.0}{25}$ m/s^2

Acceleration $a = \frac{1.5}{25}$ m/s^2

$\therefore$ Force acting on the body $F = ma$

$$= 3.0 \times \frac{1.5}{25} = \frac{4.5}{25} \text{ N} = 0.18 \text{ N}$$

As direction of motion of the body remains unchanged, therefore the direction of force acting on the body is along the direction of motion.

Mistake Alert Student can make mistake by incorrectly determining the direction of force.

Question 7 A body of mass 5 kg is acted upon by two perpendicular forces 8 N and 6 N. Give the magnitude and direction of the acceleration of the body.

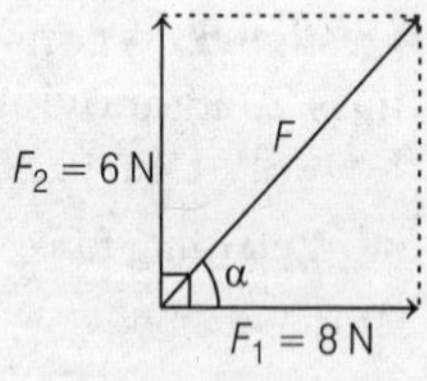

Sol. Mass of the body $m = 5$ kg

Force acting on body $F_1 = 8$ N

and $\quad F_2 = 6$ N

Angle between two forces $\theta = 90°$

Resultant force acting on the body

$$F = \sqrt{F_1^2 + F_2^2 + 2F_1F_2\cos\theta}$$

$$= \sqrt{(8)^2 + (6)^2 + 2 \times 8 \times 6 \times \cos 90°}$$

$$= \sqrt{64 + 36} \quad (\because \cos 90° = 0)$$

$$= 10 \text{ N}$$

If resultant force F makes an angle α with force F_1, then

$$\tan\alpha = \frac{F_2}{F_1} = \frac{6}{8} = 0.75 = \tan 36°53'$$

$\therefore \quad \alpha = 36°53'$

Using relation $\quad F = ma$

Acceleration $a = \frac{F}{m} = \frac{10}{5} = 2\ \text{m/s}^2$

$\therefore$ An acceleration of 2 m/s^2 is acting on body at an angle of 36°53′ from the direction of force $F_1 = 8$ N.

Question 8 The driver of a three wheeler moving with a speed of 36 km/h sees a child standing in the middle of the road and brings his vehicle to rest in 4.0 s just in time to save the child. What is the average retarding force on the vehicle? The mass of the three wheeler is 400 kg and the mass of the driver is 65 kg.

Note Convert the value of physical quantity in SI system preferably.

Sol. Initial speed of the three wheeler $u = 36$ km/h

$$= 36 \times \frac{5}{18}\ \text{m/s} = 10\ \text{m/s} \qquad \left(\because 1\ \text{km/h} = \frac{5}{18}\ \text{m/s}\right)$$

Final speed of the three wheeler $v = 0$

Time $t = 4.0$ s

Mass of the three wheeler $m_1 = 400$ kg

Mass of the driver $m_2 = 65$ kg

Total mass $m = m_1 + m_2 = 400 + 65 = 465$ kg

Using equation of the motion, $v = u + at$

$$0 = 10 + a \times 4.0$$

or $$a = -\frac{10}{4.0}\ \text{m/s}^2 = -2.5\ \text{m/s}^2$$

(Negative sign of acceleration shows that it is retardation)

$\therefore$ Average retarding force acting on the vehicle

$$F = ma$$
$$= 465 \times (-2.5)\ \text{N} = -1162.5\ \text{N}$$

Question 9 A rocket with a lift-off mass 20000 kg is blasted upwards with an initial acceleration of 5.0 m/s^2. Calculate the initial thrust (force) of the blast.

Sol. Initial mass of the rocket $m = 20000$ kg

Initial acceleration $a = 5.0\ \text{m/s}^2$ in upwards direction

Let, initial thrust of the blast be T.

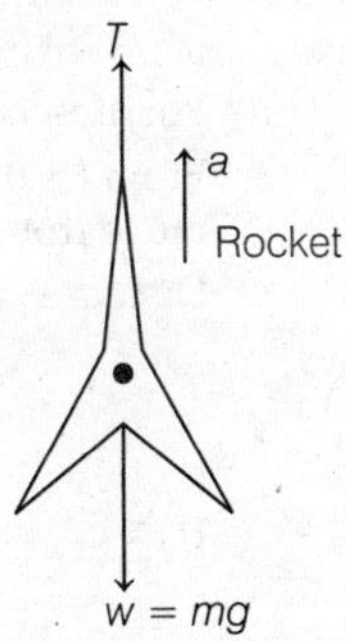

$\therefore$ $$T - mg = ma$$

or $$T = mg + ma$$
$$= m(g + a)$$
$$= 20000 \times (9.8 + 5.0)$$
$$= 2 \times 10^4 \times 14.8\ \text{N}$$
$$= 29.6 \times 10^4\ \text{N} = 2.96 \times 10^5\ \text{N}$$

Question 10 A body of mass 0.40 kg moving initially with a constant speed of 10 m/s to the north is subjected to a constant force of 8.0 N directed towards the south for 30 s. Take the instant the force is applied to be $t = 0$, the position of the particle at that time to be $x = 0$ and predict its position at $t = -5$ s, 25 s, 100 s.

Sol. Mass of the body $m = 0.40$ kg

Initial speed of the body $u = 10$ m/s (Towards north)

Force $F = 8.0$ N (Towards south)

$= -8.0$ N (Negative sign show that it is retarding force)

Time $t = 30$ s

At time $t = 0$, position of the particle $x = 0$

(i) **Position of the body at $t = -5$ s**

From $t = -5$ s to $t = 0$ the motion of the body is unaccelerated motion (towards north).

$\therefore$ Distance covered by the body $(x)_{-5} = u \times t$

$$(x)_{-5} = 10 \times (-5) = -50 \text{ m}$$

(ii) **Position of the body at $t = 25$ s**

From $t = 0$ to $t = 25$ s, body is in accelerated motion.

Acceleration, $a = \dfrac{F}{m}$

(acceleration produced in the particle towards south for $0 \leq t \leq 30$)

$$= -\frac{8.0}{0.40} = -20 \text{ m/s}^2$$

Using equation of motion $s = ut + \dfrac{1}{2}at^2$

$$x_{25} = 10 \times 25 + \frac{1}{2}(-20) \times (25)^2$$

$$= 250 - 6250$$

$$= -6000 \text{ m}$$

$$= -6 \text{ km}$$

(iii) **Position of the body at $t = 100$ s**

From $t = 0$ to $t = 30$ s, body is in accelerated motion after, then it will move from $t = 30$ s to $t = 100$ s with constant speed.

Distance travelled in 30 s.

$$x_{30} = 10 \times 30 + \frac{1}{2}(-20) \times (30)^2$$

$$= 300 - 9000 = -8700 \text{ m}$$

Velocity of the particle at $t = 30$ s.

$$v = u + at = 10 + (-20) \times 30$$

$$= 10 - 600 = -590 \text{ m/s}$$

Distance travelled in time interval from $t = 30$ s to $t = 100$ s

$$x_{70} = vt$$
$$= (-590) \times 70$$
$$= -41300 \text{ m}$$

∴ Position at $t = 100$ s

$$x_{100} = x_{30} + x_{70}$$
$$= -8700 + (-41300) \text{ m}$$
$$= -50000 \text{ m}$$
$$= -50 \text{ km}$$

Question 11 A truck starts from rest and accelerates uniformly with 2 m/s^2. At $t = 10$ s, a stone is dropped by a person standing on the top of the truck (6 m high from the ground). What are the (a) velocity and (b) acceleration of the stone at $t = 11$ s? (Neglect air resistance).

Sol. Initial speed of truck $u = 0$

Acceleration $a = 2 \text{ m/s}^2$

Time $t = 10$ s

Velocity attained by the truck in 10 s

$$v = u + at$$
$$= 0 + 2 \times 10$$
$$= 20 \text{ m/s}$$

(a) Horizontal velocity of the stone which remains unchanged

$$v_x = 20 \text{ m/s}$$

When stone is dropped from the top of the truck initial vertical velocity $u_y = 0$.

Velocity attained in vertical direction by the stone in time interval from $t = 10$ s to $t = 11$ s, *i.e.*, in 1 s.

$$v_y = u_y + gt$$
$$= 0 + 9.8 \times 1$$
$$v_y = 9.8 \text{ m/s}$$

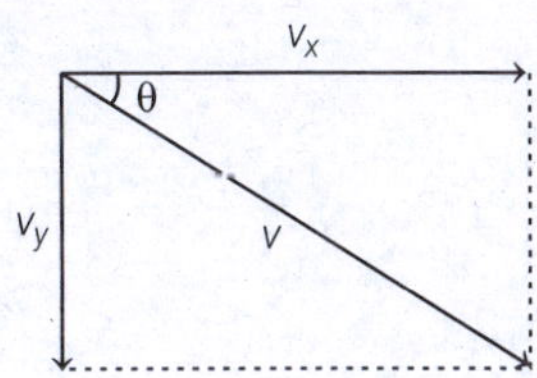

∴ Resultant velocity of the stone

$$v = \sqrt{v_x^2 + v_y^2}$$
$$= \sqrt{(20)^2 + (9.8)^2}$$
$$= 22.3 \text{ m/s}$$

If resultant velocity (v) subtends an angle θ with the horizontal, then

$$\tan\theta = \frac{v_y}{v_x} = \frac{9.8}{20} = 0.49$$

$$= \tan 26^\circ 12'$$

or $$\theta = 26^\circ 12'$$

(b) Just after the stone is dropped from the truck the horizontal force or acceleration acting on stone due to the truck becomes zero ($a_x = 0$) and it falls freely under gravity.

∴ Acceleration of the stone $a_y = g = 9.8\text{ m/s}^2$

Mistake Alert Student can forget to consider the horizontal velocity.

Question 12 A bob of mass 0.1 kg hung from the ceiling of a room by a string 2 m long is set into oscillation. The speed of the bob at its mean position is 1 m/s. What is the trajectory of the bob if the string is cut when the bob is

(a) at one of its extreme positions?

(b) at its mean position?

Thinking Process In simple harmonic motion (SHM), the velocity of the body is zero at extreme position while maximum at mean position.

Sol.

(a) In SHM, the instantaneous velocity of the bob at each extreme position is zero. If string is cut at one of its extreme position, the bob start to fall freely under gravity and therefore, its trajectory will be a vertical straight line path.

(b) In SHM, the instantaneous velocity of the bob at mean position is maximum and its direction is along the tangent to the arc, *i.e.*, in horizontal direction. If string is cut at mean position then the bob will behave as a horizontal projectile whose trajectory will be parabolic path.

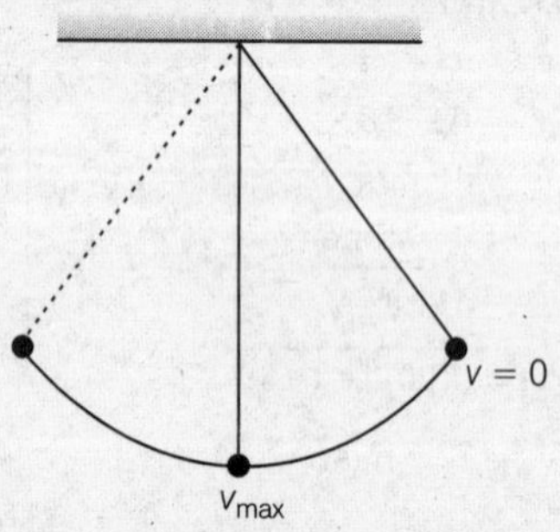

Question 13 A man of mass 70 kg stands on a weighing scale in a lift which is moving

(a) upwards with uniform speed of 10 m/s?

(b) downwards with a uniform acceleration of 5 m/s^2?

(c) upwards with uniform acceleration of 5 m/s^2. What would be the readings on the scale in each case?

(d) What would be the reading if the lift mechanism failed and it hurtled down freely under gravity?

◎ *Thinking Process* When a man is standing on a weighing scale, it will read the normal reaction R as apparent weight.

Sol. Given, mass of man $(m) = 70$ kg

In each case the weighing scale will read the reaction R *i.e.*, the apparent weight.

(a) As lift is moving upward with a uniform speed, therefore its acceleration $a = 0$

$\therefore$ Normal reaction $w = R = mg$

$$= 70 \times 10\,\text{N} = 700\,\text{N}$$

w acts vertically downwards and R acts vertically upwards.

$\therefore$ Reading on weighing scale $= \dfrac{700}{10} = 70$ kg

(b) Acceleration of the lift $a = 5\,\text{m/s}^2(\downarrow)$

$\therefore$ Normal reaction $R = m(g - a)$

$$= 70(10 - 5)\,\text{N}$$

$$= 70 \times 5\,\text{N} = 350\,\text{N}$$

$\therefore$ Reading on weighing scale $= \dfrac{350\text{ N}}{10\text{ m/s}^2} = 35$ kg

(c) Acceleration of the lift $a = 5\,\text{m/s}^2(\uparrow)$

$\therefore$ Normal reaction $R = m(g + a)$

$$= 70(10 + 5) = 1050\,\text{N}$$

$\therefore$ Reading on weighing scale $= \dfrac{1050\text{ N}}{10\text{ m/s}^2} = 105$ kg

(d) Acceleration of the lift when it is falling freely under gravity

$$a = g\,(\downarrow)$$

$\therefore$ Normal reaction $R = m(g - a) = m(g - g) = 0$

$\therefore$ Reading on weighing scale $= 0$

This is the state of weightlessness.

Question 14 Figure below shows the position-time graph of a particle of mass 4 kg. What is the (a) force on the particle for $t<0, t>4$ s, $0<t<4$ s? (b) impulse at $t=0$ and $t=4$ s? (Consider one dimensional motion only).

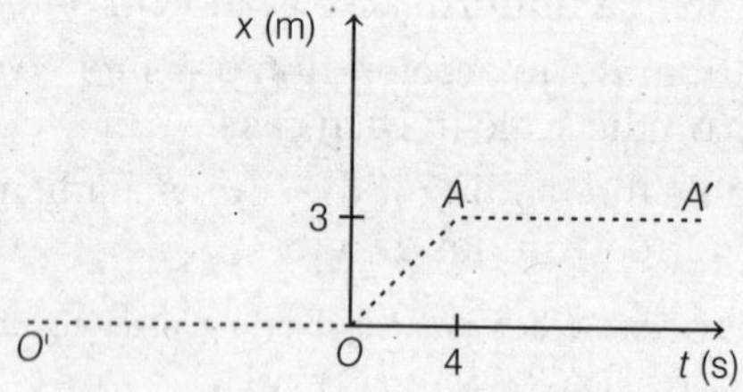

◎ *Thinking Process* Velocity = slope of position-time graph and impulse = change in momentum = $mv - mu$.

Sol.

(a) (i) For $t<0$, the position-time graph is OO'; for which displacement of the particle is zero, therefore particle is at rest at the origin. Hence, acceleration and force acting on particle will also be zero.

(ii) For $t>4$ s, the position-time graph AA' is parallel to time axis. Therefore, for $t>4$ s particle remains at a fixed distance of 3 m from the origin. It means particle is at rest. Therefore, acceleration and force acting on particle will be zero.

(iii) For $0<t<4$ s, the position-time graph OA is a straight line inclined at an angle from time axis, which is representing uniform motion of the particle, *i.e.*, the particle is moving with a constant speed. Therefore, acceleration and force acting on the particle will be zero.

(b) **Impulse at $t=0$**

(i) Impulse = change in momentum

$= mv - mu = m(v-u)$

Before $t=0$, particle is at rest, hence $u=0$

After $t=0$, particle is moving with a constant velocity.

Velocity of the particle = slope of position-time graph

$$= \frac{3 \text{ m}}{4 \text{ s}} = 0.75 \text{ m/s}$$

$\therefore$ Impulse = change in momentum = $4(0.75-0) = 3$ kg-m/s

(ii) **Impulse at $t=4$ s**

Before $t=4$ s, particle is moving with a constant

Speed $u = 0.75$ m/s

After $t=4$ s, particle is again at rest

$\therefore \quad v = 0$

$\therefore$ Impulse = change in momentum = $m(v-u)$

$= 4(0-0.75) = -3$ kg-m/s

Question 15 Two bodies of masses 10 kg and 20 kg respectively kept on a smooth, horizontal surface are tied to the ends of a light string. A horizontal force $F = 600$ N is applied to (a) A, (b) B along the direction of string. What is the tension in the string in each case?

Sol. Mass of body $A(m_1) = 10$ kg

Mass of body $B(m_2) = 20$ kg

Force applied $(F) = 600$ N

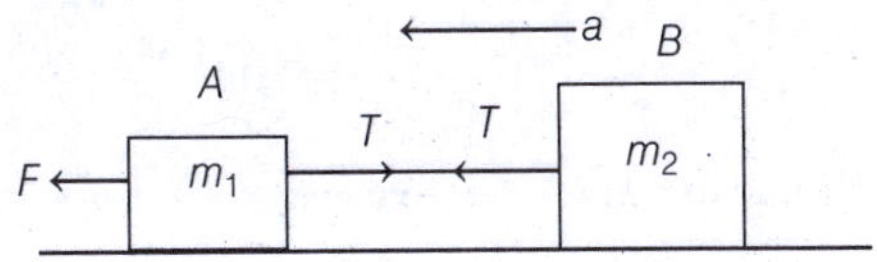

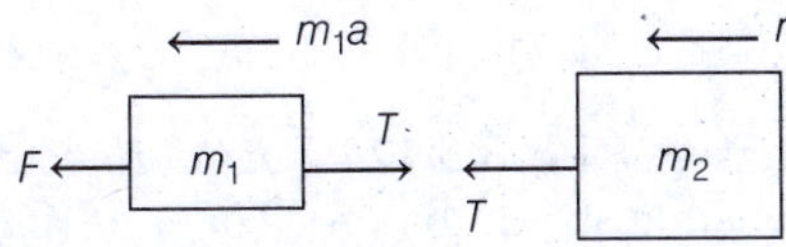

(a) **When force is applied on** A, then

For body A,

$$F - T = m_1a \quad \text{...(i)}$$

For body B,

$$T = m_2a \quad \text{...(ii)}$$

Adding Eqs. (i) and (ii), we get

$$F = (m_1 + m_2)a$$

or

$$a = \frac{F}{m_1 + m_2}$$

$$= \frac{600}{(10 + 20)} = 20 \text{ m/s}^2$$

Substituting value of a in Eq. (ii), we get

$$T = m_2a = 20 \times 20 \text{ N} = 400 \text{ N}$$

(b) **When force is applied on** B, then

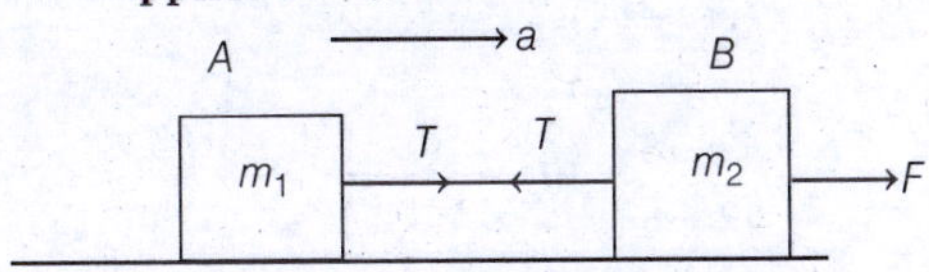

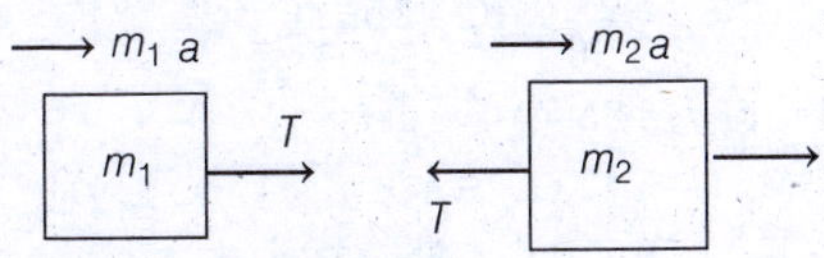

For body A,

$$T = m_1 a \quad \text{...(iii)}$$

For body B,

$$F - T = m_2 a \quad \text{...(iv)}$$

Adding Eqs. (iii) and (iv), we get

$$F = (m_1 + m_2)a$$

or

$$a = \frac{F}{m_1 + m_2}$$

$$= \frac{600}{10 + 20} = 20\,\text{m/s}^2$$

Substituting value of a in Eq. (iii), we get

$$T = m_1 a = 10 \times 20$$

$$= 200\,\text{N}$$

Question 16 Two masses 8 kg and 12 kg are connected at the two ends of a light inextensible string that goes over a frictionless pulley. Find the acceleration of the masses and the tension in the string when the masses are released.

Sol. Masses connected at the two ends of a light inextensible string are

$$m_1 = 8\,\text{kg}, m_2 = 12\,\text{kg}$$

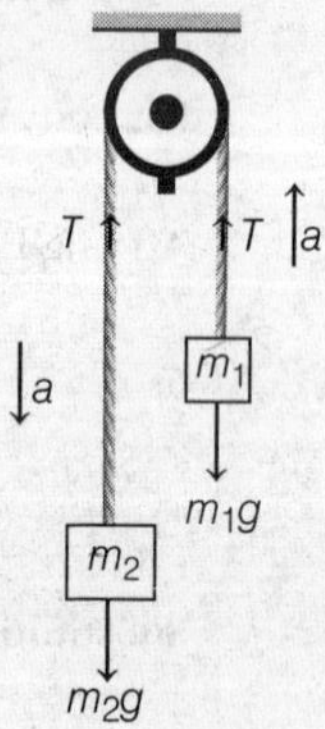

Let T be the tension in the string and masses moves with an acceleration a when masses are released.

For mass m_1

$$T - m_1 g = m_1 a \quad \text{... (i)}$$

For mass m_2

$$m_2 g - T = m_2 a \quad \text{...(ii)}$$

Adding Eqs. (i) and (ii), we get

$$m_2 g - m_1 g = (m_1 + m_2)a$$

$$\therefore \quad a = \frac{(m_2 - m_1)}{(m_1 + m_2)} g \quad \text{...(iii)}$$

$$= \frac{12 - 8}{12 + 8} \times 10$$

$$= \frac{4}{20} \times 10 = 2\,\text{m/s}^2$$

Substituting value of a in Eq. (i), we get

$$T = m_1 g + m_1 a$$

$$= m_1(g + a)$$

$$= 8(10 + 2) = 96\,\text{N}$$

Quick Solution

$$\text{Acceleration, } a = \frac{\text{Net force}}{\text{Total mass}}$$

$$a = \frac{m_2 g - m_1 g}{m_1 + m_2}$$

$$= \frac{120 - 80}{12 + 8}$$

$$= \frac{40}{20} = 2\,\text{m/s}^2$$

and tension,

$$T - m_1 a = m_1 g$$

$$T = m_1(a + b)$$

$$= 8\,[2 + 10]$$

$$= 96\,\text{N}$$

Question 17 A nucleus is at rest in the laboratory frame of reference. Show that if it disintegrates into two smaller nuclei the products must be emitted in opposite directions.

Sol. Nucleus is at rest initially, therefore its initial linear momentum is zero, *i.e.*, $p_i = 0$

Let the given nucleus be disintegrates into two smaller nuclei of masses m_1 and m_2 which move with velocity $\mathbf{v}_1$ and $\mathbf{v}_2$ respectively.

Net momentum of the nuclei after disintegration

$$p_f = m_1 \mathbf{v}_1 + m_2 \mathbf{v}_2$$

According to law of conservation of linear momentum,

$$p_i = p_f$$

or $$0 = m_1 \mathbf{v}_1 + m_2 \mathbf{v}_2$$

or $$\mathbf{v}_2 = -\frac{m_1}{m_2}\mathbf{v}_1$$

Negative sign shows that $\mathbf{v}_1$ and $\mathbf{v}_2$ are emitted opposite in directions.

Mistake Alert Student can incorrectly assume that the two nuclei will move in the same direction.

Question 18 Two billiard balls each of mass 0.05 kg moving in opposite directions with speed 6 m/s collide and rebound with the same speed. What is the impulse imparted to each ball due to the other?

Sol. Mass of each ball $m = 0.05$ kg

Speed of each ball $v = 6$ m/s

Momentum of each ball before collision

$$p_i = mv$$

$$= 0.05 \times 6 = 0.30\,\text{kg-m/s}$$

After collision each ball rebound, therefore momentum of each ball after collision

$$p_f = m(-v)$$
$$= 0.05 \times (-6) = -0.30 \text{ kg-m/s}$$

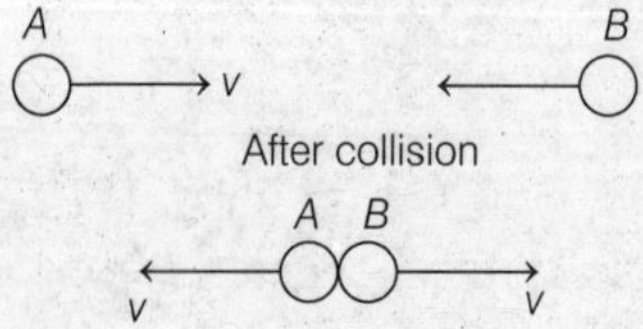

Impulse imparted to each ball = Change in its momentum

$$= p_f - p_i$$
$$= -0.30 - (0.30) = -0.60 \text{ kg-m/s}$$

So, the impulse on each ball is 0.60 kg m/s in terms of magnitude but they are in opposite direction.

Question 19 A shell of mass 0.020 kg is fired by a gun of mass 100 kg. If the muzzle speed of the shell is 80 m/s, what is the recoil speed of the gun?

Sol. Mass of shell $m_1 = 0.020$ kg

Speed of shell $v_1 = 80$ m/s

Mass of the gun $m_2 = 100$ kg

Recoil speed of the gun $v_2 = ?$

Initially gun and shell both are at rest.

$\therefore$ Initial momentum of the gun and shell $p_i = 0$

Final momentum of the gun and shell $p_f = m_1v_1 + m_2v_2$

According to law of conservation of linear momentum,

$$p_i = p_f$$
$$0 = m_1v_1 + m_2v_2$$

or $$v_2 = -\frac{m_1}{m_2}v_1 = -\frac{0.020}{100} \times 80 = -0.016 \text{ m/s}$$

Therefore, the gun recoil with a speed of 0.016 m/s.

Question 20 A batsman deflects a ball by an angle of 45° without changing its initial speed which is equal to 54 km/h. What is the impulse imparted to the ball? (Mass of the ball is 0.15 kg).

Sol. Mass of the ball $m = 0.15$ kg

Velocity of the ball $v = 54$ km/h

$$= 54 \times \frac{5}{18} \text{ m/s} \qquad \left(\because 1 \text{ km/h} = \frac{5}{18} \text{ m/s}\right)$$
$$= 15 \text{ m/s}$$

Let the ball be incident along path *PO*. Batsman deflects the ball by an angle of 45° along path *OQ*.

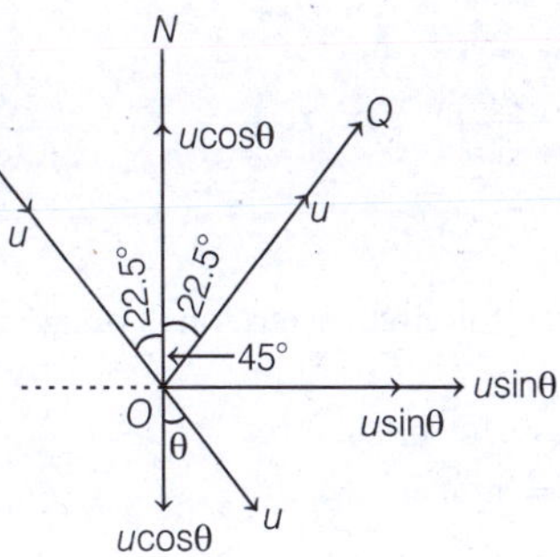

$$\angle PON = \angle NOQ$$
$$= \frac{45^\circ}{2} = 22.5^\circ$$

On resolving the initial velocity of the ball along *PO* and final velocity of the ball along *OQ*, into rectangular components.

The horizontal component of velocity $u\sin\theta$ remains unchanged while vertical component of velocity is just reversed.

$\therefore$ Impulse imparted to the ball = change in linear momentum of the ball

$$= mu\cos\theta - (-mu\cos\theta) = 2mu\cos\theta$$
$$= 2 \times 0.15 \times 15 \times \cos 22.5^\circ$$
$$= 4.5 \times 0.9239 \text{ kg-m/s}$$
$$= 4.16 \text{ kg-m/s}$$

Note If the direction of motion of the particle before collision and just after the collision is not same, then we should resolve linear momentum into rectangular components.

Question 21 A stone of mass 0.25 kg tied to the end of a string is whirled round in a circle of radius 1.5 m with speed 40 rev/min in a horizontal plane. What is the tension in the string? What is the maximum speed with which the stone can be whirled around if the string can withstand a maximum tension of 200 N?

◎ ***Thinking Process*** When a stone tied to one end of a string is whirled in a circle, then required centripetal force is provided by the tension in the string.

Sol. Mass of a stone $m = 0.25$ kg

Radius of the string $r = 1.5$ m

$$\text{Frequency } \nu = 40 \text{ rev/min} = \frac{40}{60} \text{ rev/s} = \frac{2}{3} \text{ rev/s}$$

Centripetal force required for circular motion is obtained from the tension in the string.

$\therefore$ Tension in the string = centripetal force

$$T = mr\omega^2$$

$$= mr(2\pi\nu)^2 \qquad [\because \omega = 2\pi v]$$

$$= mr4\pi^2\nu^2$$

$$= 0.25 \times 1.5 \times 4 \times \left(\frac{22}{7}\right)^2 \times \left(\frac{2}{3}\right)^2$$

$$= 6.6 \text{ N}$$

Maximum tension which can be withstand by the string

$$T_{max} = 200 \text{ N}$$

$$\therefore \quad T_{max} = \frac{mv_{max}^2}{r}$$

$$\text{or} \quad v_{max}^2 = \frac{T_{max} \times r}{m} = \frac{200 \times 1.5}{0.25} = 1200$$

$$\therefore \quad v_{max} = \sqrt{1200} = 34.6 \text{ m/s}$$

Question 22 If in Q. 21, the speed of the stone is increased beyond the maximum permissible value, and the string breaks suddenly, which of the following correctly describes the trajectory of the stone after the string breaks

(a) the stone moves radially outwards,

(b) the stone flies off tangentially from the instant the string breaks,

(c) the stone flies off at an angle with the tangent whose magnitude depends on the speed of the particle?

Sol. When a stone tied to one end of a string is whirled round in a circle then velocity of the stone at any point is along the tangent at that point. If the string breaks suddenly then stone flies off tangentially, along the direction of its velocity.

Question 23 Explain why

(a) a horse cannot pull a cart and run in empty space?

(b) passengers are thrown forward from their seats when a speeding bus stops suddenly?

(c) it is easier to pull a lawn mower than to push it?

(d) a cricketer moves his hands backwards while holding a catch?

Sol.

(a) When a horse tries to pull a cart, it pushes the ground in backward direction at an angle to the horizontal. According to Newton's Third Law of Motion, the ground applies an equal and opposite reaction force on the horses feet. The vertical component of this reaction force balances the weight of the horse and the horizontal component is responsible for motion of the cart. In empty space, as there is no reaction force, therefore a horse cannot pull a cart.

(b) When bus is moving, the passengers sitting in it are also in motion and moving with the speed of the bus. When bus stops suddenly then lower part of the body of passengers which is in contact with the bus slower down with the bus but upper part of the bodies of the passengers continue to remain in motion in initial direction due to its inertia of motion and hence are thrown forward.

(c) While pulling a lawn mower, a force F is applied in upward direction, making an angle θ from the horizontal [Fig. (a)]. Its vertical component in upward and decreasing the effective weight of the mower and making it easier to move.

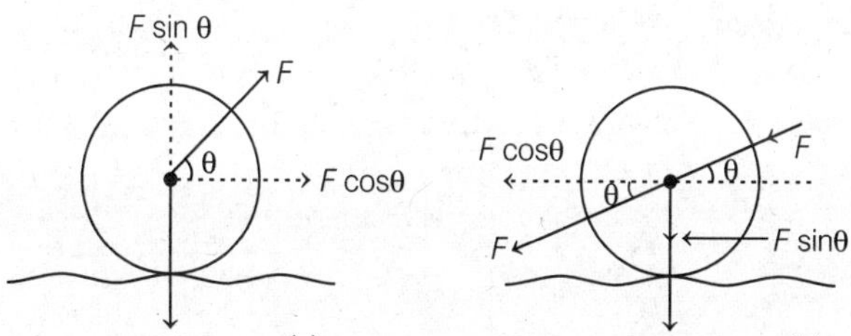

(a) (b)

While pushing a lawn mower, a force F is applied in downward direction, making an angle θ from the horizontal [Fig. (b)]. It vertical component is in downward and increasing the effective weight of the mower. Therefore, it is easier to pull a lawn mower than to push it.

(d) In holding a catch the impulse imparted to the hands $= F \times \Delta t$ = change in momentum of the ball

when a cricketer lowers his hands to take a catch, he increases the time taken to stop the ball. As time t increases the force F applied on the hands of the cricketer by the ball decreases and his hands are hurt lesser.

DIKSHA APP Questions

☐ Multiple Choice Questions

Q.1 Two masses m_1 and m_2 are connected as shown in figure. The system is in equilibrium. Calculate the tensions T_1 and T_2. ($g = 10\ m/s^2$)

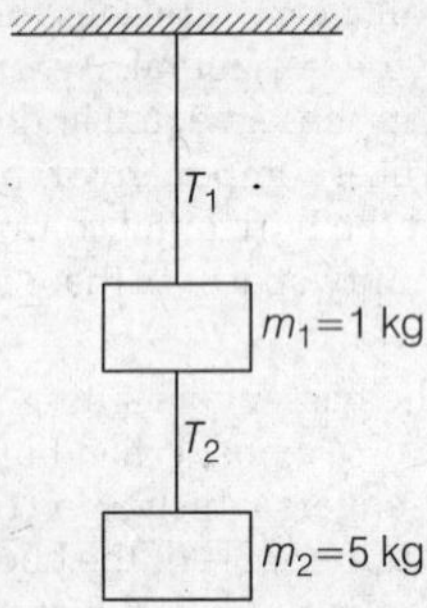

(a) $T_1 = 50\ N, T_2 = 60\ N$ (b) $T = 60\ N, T_2 = 50\ N$
(c) $T_1 = 110\ N, T_2 = 0\ N$ (d) $T_1 = 30\ N, T_2 = 25\ N$

Sol. (b) As the system is in equilibrium so, acceleration $a = 0$.

Free body diagram for $m_2 = 5\ kg$ is

$$m_2 g - T_2 = m_2 a$$

$$5 \times 10 - T_2 = m_2 \times 0 \Rightarrow T_2 = 50\ N$$

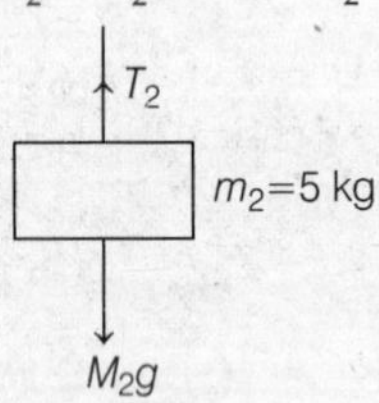

Now, free body diagram for $m_1 = 1\ kg$ is

$$m_1 g + T_2 - T_1 = m_1 a$$

$$1 \times 10 + 50 - T_1 = m_1 \times 0 \Rightarrow T_1 = 60\ N$$

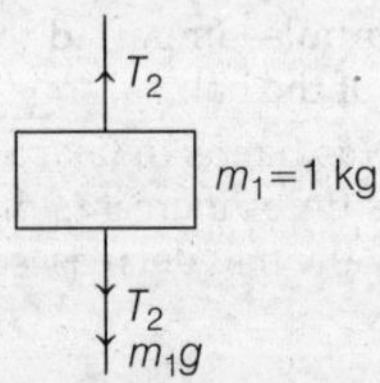

Q.2 A block of mass 13 kg is resting on a horizontal surface as shown in figure.

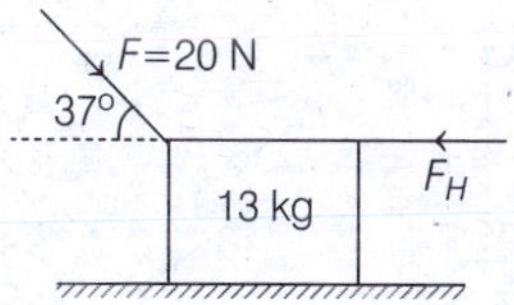

(i) What is the horizontal force required to keep the block in equilibrium?

(ii) What is the normal reaction?

$\left(g = 10\text{ m/s}^2, \cos 37° = \frac{4}{5}, \sin 37° = \frac{3}{5}\right)$

(a) (i) 16 N (ii) 142 N (b) (i) 130 N (ii) $20\sqrt{2}$ N

(c) (i) 12 N (ii) $10\sqrt{2}$ N (d) (i) 20 N (ii) 130 N

Sol. (a) Resolve force 'F' into two rectangular components as shown in figure

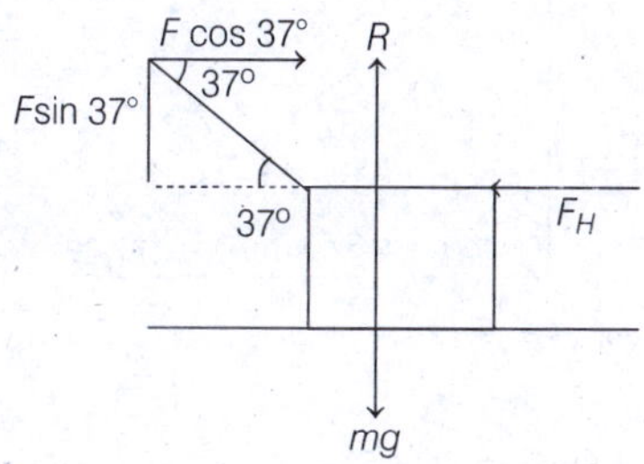

Now, for equilibrium in horizontal direction

$$F\cos 37° - F_H = 0$$

$$20 \times \frac{4}{5} = F_H$$

$$F_H = 16\text{ N}$$

For equilibrium in vertical direction

$$R - (mg + F\sin 37°) = 0$$

$$R = mg + F\sin 37°$$

$$= (13 \times 10) + \left(20 \times \frac{3}{5}\right)$$

$$= 130 + 12$$

$$R = 142\text{ N}$$

Q.3 In the given figure M and m are in equilibrium an an inclined plane. M is

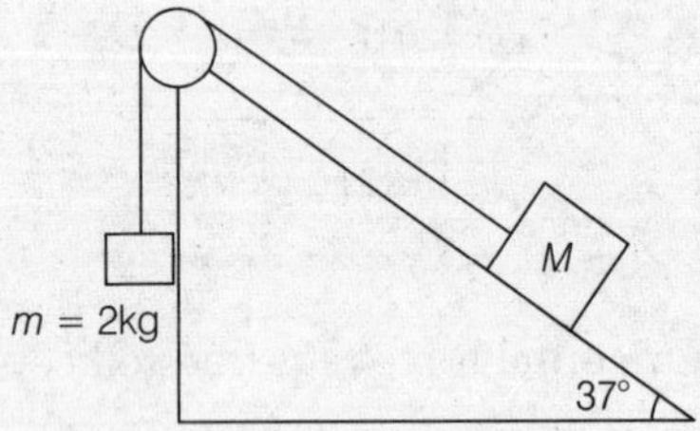

(a) 2 kg (b) 10 kg

(c) 5 kg (d) $\frac{10}{3}$ kg

Sol. (d) From figure

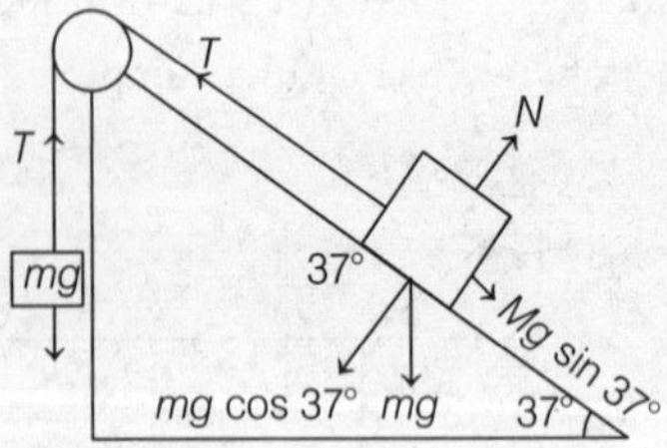

$$Mg\sin 37° = T \quad \text{...(i)}$$

and $$T = mg \quad \text{...(ii)}$$

$\therefore$ $$Mg\sin 37° = mg$$

$$M \times \frac{3}{5} = 2$$

$\Rightarrow$ $$M = \frac{10}{3}\text{ kg}$$

Q.4 The velocity of a body of mass 2 kg as function of t is given by $v = 2t\hat{\mathbf{i}} + t^2\hat{\mathbf{j}}$. Find the momentum and force acting on it at time $t = 2$ second

(a) $8(\hat{\mathbf{i}} + \hat{\mathbf{j}})$ kg m/s, $(4\hat{\mathbf{i}} + 8\hat{\mathbf{j}})$ N (b) 11.31 kg/ms, 8.94 N.

(c) $8(\hat{\mathbf{i}} + \hat{\mathbf{j}})$ kg m/s, $8\hat{\mathbf{j}}$ N (d) $8\hat{\mathbf{i}}$ kg m/s, $(4\hat{\mathbf{i}} + 8\hat{\mathbf{j}})$ N.

Sol. (a) Momentum $\mathbf{P} = m\mathbf{v} = 2(2t\hat{\mathbf{i}} + t^2\hat{\mathbf{j}})$

$$\mathbf{P} = 4t\hat{\mathbf{i}} + 2t^2\hat{\mathbf{j}}$$

at $$t = 2 \text{ seconds}$$

$$\mathbf{P} = 8\hat{\mathbf{i}} + 8\hat{\mathbf{j}} = 8(\hat{\mathbf{i}} + \hat{\mathbf{j}})\ \text{kg m/s.}$$

Now, force is given by $\mathbf{F} = \dfrac{d\mathbf{P}}{dt}$

$$\mathbf{F} = \frac{d}{dt}(4t\hat{\mathbf{i}} + 2t^2\hat{\mathbf{j}}) = (4\hat{\mathbf{i}} + 4t\hat{\mathbf{j}})\ \text{N}$$

at $t = 2$ seconds

$$\mathbf{F} = (4\hat{\mathbf{i}} + 8\hat{\mathbf{j}})\ \text{N}$$

Q.5 Three blocks are resting on a frictionless table, while a force 20 N is applied on the system as shown in figure. Calculate the magnitudes of the acceleration and the normal reaction by block *A* on *B*, and block *C* on *B*.

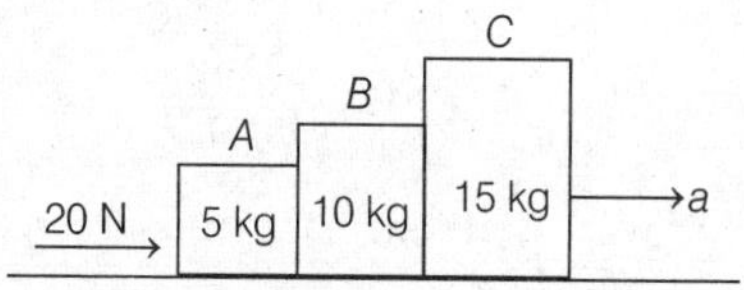

(a) $a = 4\ \text{m/s}^2$, $N_1 = 5\ \text{N}$, $N_2 = 10\ \text{N}$

(b) $a = \dfrac{2}{3}\ \text{m/s}^2$, $N_1 = \dfrac{50}{3}\ \text{N}$, $N_2 = 10\ \text{N}$

(c) $a = 2\ \text{m/s}^2$, $N_1 = 10\ \text{N}$, $N_2 = 5\ \text{N}$

(d) $a = \dfrac{2}{3}\ \text{m/s}^2$, $N_1 = 5\ \text{N}$, $N_2 = \dfrac{50}{3}\ \text{N}$

Sol. (b) Free bodies diagram for *A*, *B* and *C* are as

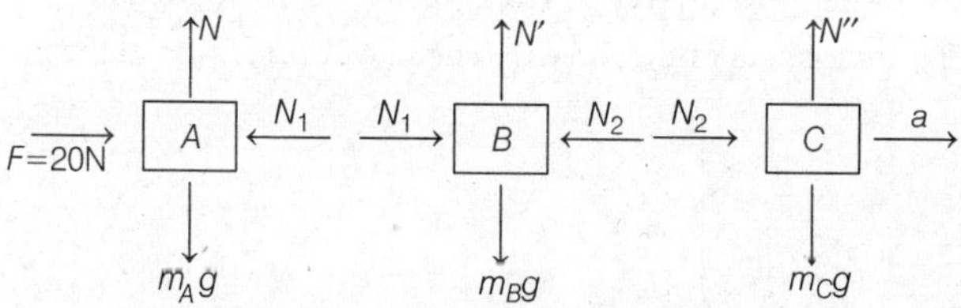

For body *A* $20 - N_1 = 5a$ ...(i)

$[m_A = 5\ \text{kg}, m_B = 10\ \text{kg}, m_C = 15\ \text{kg}]$

For body *B* $N_1 - N_2 = 10a$ ...(ii)

For body *C* $N_2 = 15a$ ...(iii)

Adding equations (i), (ii) and (iii) we get

$$20 - N_1 + N_1 - N_2 + N_2 = 5a + 10a + 15a$$

$$20 = 30a$$

$$\frac{2}{3}\ \text{m/s}^2 = a \quad \text{...(iv)}$$

In equation (i) $20 - n_1 = 5 \times \frac{2}{3}$

$$20 - \frac{10}{3} = N_1$$

$$\frac{50}{3}\text{ N} = N_1 \quad \text{...(v)}$$

In equation (iii) $N_2 = 15 \times \frac{2}{3} = 10\text{ N}$ ...(vi)

Q.6 A bullet of mass m with a velocity v is just able to penetrate a block of width d. If the block offers a uniform resistance R, then v will be given by

(a) $\sqrt{\frac{2Rd}{m}}$ (b) $\sqrt{\frac{2Rdg}{mg + R}}$

(c) $\sqrt{\frac{Rd}{2m}}$ (d) $\sqrt{\frac{Rdg}{mg + R}}$

Sol. (a) KE = Amount of work done against frictional force

$$\frac{1}{2}mv^2 = Rd$$

$$v = \sqrt{\frac{2Rd}{m}}$$

Q.7 An object of mass 5 kg is placed on an inclined plane with angle of inclination as 53°. What is the force that is trying to pull it down the incline ? ($\mu_s = 0.2, \mu_k = 0.1$)

(a) 40 N (b) 8 N (c) 6 N (d) 30 N

Sol. (a) The component of the force that tends to bring it down the incline

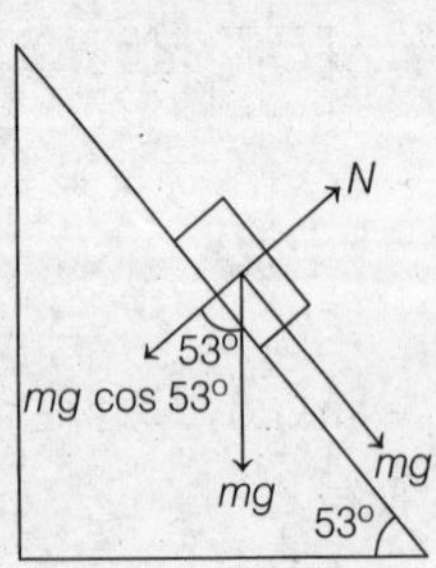

$$F = mg\sin 53°$$

$$= 5 \times 10 \times \frac{4}{5} = 40\text{ N}.$$

Q.8 How much force along the plane is required to move the body of mass 5 kg up to an inclined plane with an acceleration of 1 m/s^2? ($\mu_s = 0.2, \mu_k = 0.1$)

(a) 40 N (b) 44 N

(c) 48 N (d) 45 N

Sol. (c) When body moves with acceleration then coefficient of kinetic friction is used.

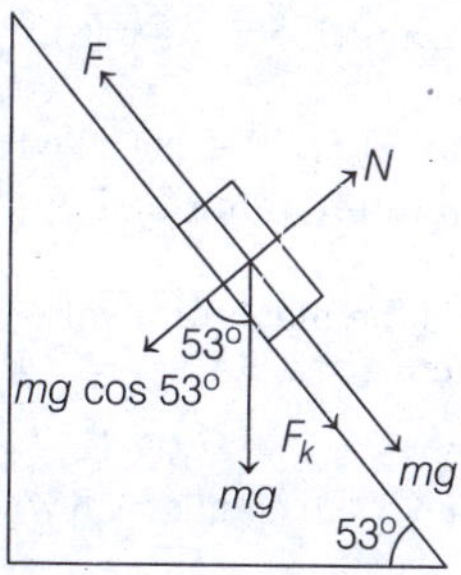

From figure

$$F - F_k - mg\sin 53° = ma.$$

$$F - \left(0.1 \times 5 \times 10 \times \frac{3}{5}\right) - \left(5 \times 10 \times \frac{4}{5}\right) = 5 \times 1 \qquad (\because F_k = \mu_k mg\cos 53°)$$

$$F - 3 - 40 = 5$$

$$F = 5 + 3 + 40 = 48 \text{ N}$$

Q.9 A force F is applied on the body B as shown in figure. The mass of B is m and mass of A is $\frac{m}{2}$. If the coefficient of friction between the floor and body B is 0.1 and between bodies B and A is 0.2. Which of the following statements is true?

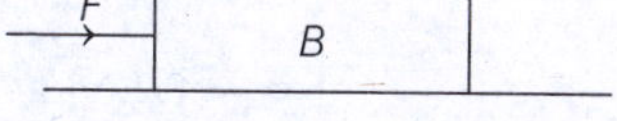

1. The body A will slip with respect to body B if $F = 0.5\, mg$.
2. The two bodies will move together if the value of $F = 0.5\, mg$.
3. The bodies will be at rest if the value of $F = 0.1\, mg$.
4. The two bodies will move together if the value of $F = 0.25\, mg$.

5. The maximum value of F for which the two bodies will move together is 0.45 mg.
   (a) All statements except 3 are false.
   (b) All statements except 3 are true.
   (c) Statements 1, 3, 4 are true and 2 or 5 are false.
   (d) Statements 1, 2, 5 are true and 3 or 4 are false.

Sol. (b) I. *True,* because for the two bodies to start moving together the minimum value of $F = 0.15\,mg$.

II. *True,* because the limiting friction be yord which A will slip over B is 0.45 mg.

III. *False,* because for values of $F > 0.45\,mg$, A will slipover B.

IV. *True,* because the minimum value of F for which two blocks short moving is $F = 0.15\,mg$.

V. *True,* because 0.45 mg is the maximum value of F for which there is no relative motion between A and B.

Explanation

F_{SB} = Limiting frictional force acting on B when A does not move with respect to B.

$$F_{SB} = \mu_{SB} N_B$$
$$= 0.1\left[m + \frac{m}{2}\right]g = 0.1 \times \frac{3}{2}\,mg = 0.15\,mg$$

So, minimum force for system to move is 0.15 mg.

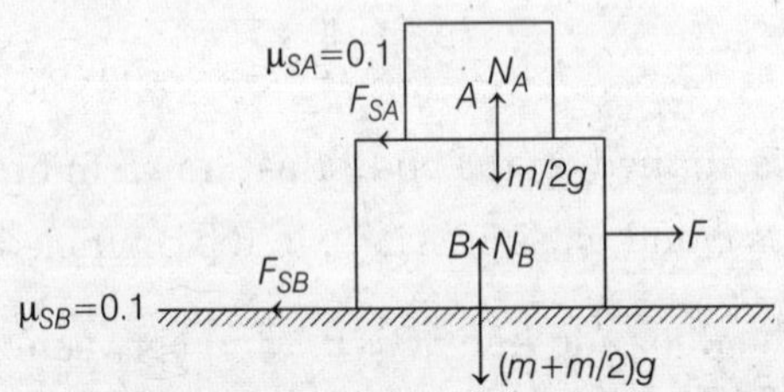

For A to remain at rest with respect to B. A should move with same acceleration as that of B. so

$$\frac{m}{2} a_A = F_{SA} = 0.1\,mg$$

$$a_A = 0.2g\ \text{m/s}^2$$

If A moves with acceleration greater than 0.2 g m/s^2, then A will slip over B. The net force acting on B is

$$F = F - F_{SA} - F_{SB}$$
$$ma_B = F - 0.15\,mg - 0.1\,mg$$

If A is at rest with respect to B then $a_A - a_B$.

$\therefore$ $$m \times 0.2\,g = f - 0.25\,mg = 0.45\,mg = F$$

It is the maximum value of F, so that there is no relative motion between A and B

Q.10 Three forces F_1, F_2 and F_3 acting at a point P on a body. The body moves with uniform speed. Which of the following statements is /are correct?

(i) The forces are coplaner.

(ii) The torque acting on the body about any point due to these three forces is zero.

(a) Both one and two are true.
(b) One is true and two is false.
(c) One is false and two is true.
(d) Both one and two are false.

Sol. (a) The body moves with uniform speed complying no net force or torque acts on it.

(i) For force to balance, they must lie in the same plane (coplanar)

(ii) Zero not torque ensures no rotational acceleration, so that torque about any point is zero.

Thus, both statements are true.

Work, Energy and Power

CHAPTER 05

Important Points

01 **Scalar or Dot Product** Scalar or dot product of two vectors is equal to the product of their magnitudes and the cosine of the angle between them. It is denoted by a dot (•).

$$\mathbf{A} \cdot \mathbf{B} = AB\cos\theta$$

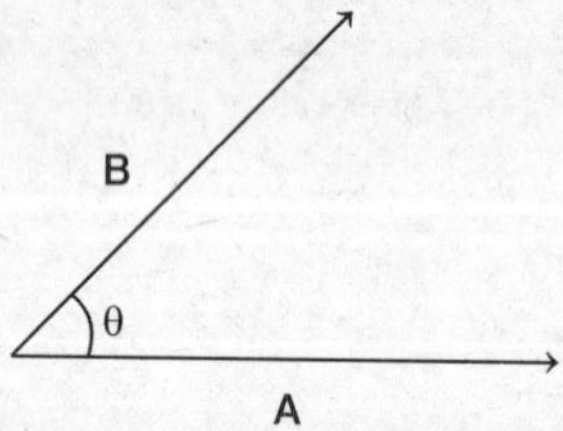

02 Work done by a constant force **F** in displacing a body through distance **s** is given by

$$W = \mathbf{F} \cdot \mathbf{s} = Fs\cos\theta$$

03 Work done by variable force **F** is given by

$$W = \int \mathbf{F} \cdot d\mathbf{s}$$

= Area under the force-displacement graph

04 Work is a scalar quantity and its SI unit is joule and CGS unit is erg.

$$1\text{ J} = 10^7 \text{ erg}$$

05 If **angle** between the force and displacement is

(a) $\theta < 90^\circ$, *i.e.*, acute angle then work done is positive.

(b) $\theta > 90^\circ$, *i.e.*, obtuse angle then work done is negative.

(c) $\theta = 90^\circ$, *i.e.*, right angle then work done is zero.

06 Energy The energy of a body is defined as its ability of doing work.

07 Kinetic Energy The energy possessed by a body due to its motion is called its kinetic energy.

08 If a body of mass m is moving with velocity v, then its kinetic energy $K = \frac{1}{2}mv^2 = \frac{p^2}{2m}$ [p is momentum of body]

09 Potential Energy The energy possessed by a body due to its position or configuration is called its potential energy.

10 Gravitational Potential Energy The energy possessed by an object due to its position above the earth's surface is called gravitational potential energy.

11 If an object of mass m is at height h from the earth's surface then its gravitational potential energy is given by

$$U = mgh$$

where, g is acceleration due to gravity.

12 Elastic Potential Energy The energy possessed by an object due to its stretched or compressed position, is called its elastic potential energy.

13 If a spring is stretched or compressed through a distance x, then its elastic potential energy is given by

$$U = \frac{1}{2}kx^2$$

where, k is the force constant of the spring.

14 Work-energy Theorem It states that the work done by a force on a body is equal to the change in its kinetic energy.

15 Law of Conservation of Energy Energy can neither be created nor be destroyed but can be transformed from one form to another.

16 Power Power is the rate at which work is done. It is given by

$$P = \frac{W}{t}$$

$$\left[\text{Instantaneous power } P = \frac{\mathbf{F}\cdot\mathbf{S}}{t} = \mathbf{F}\cdot\mathbf{V}\right]$$

Its SI unit is watt (W).

17 The FPS unit of power generally used in engineering is horse-power (HP).

1 Horse Power (HP) = 746 W.

18 **Mass Energy Equivalence** If Δm mass is lossed then produced energy is given by

$$E = \Delta mc^2$$

where, c is the speed of light in vacuum.

19 **Elastic Collision** If both linear momentum and kinetic energy of the system remains conserved in a collision then, it is called elastic collision.

20 **Inelastic Collision** A collision is said to be inelastic, if linear momentum remains conserved but kinetic energy is not conserved.

Exercises

Question 1 The sign of work done by a force on a body is important to understand. State carefully, if the following quantities are positive or negative :

(a) work done by a man in lifting a bucket out of a well by means of a rope tied to the bucket.

(b) work done by gravitational force in the above case.

(c) work done by friction on a body sliding down an inclind plane.

(d) work done by an applied force on a body moving on a rough horizontal plane with uniform velocity.

(e) work done by the resistive force of air on a vibrating pendulum in bringing it to rest.

◎ ***Thinking Process*** Work done by an agent is given by $W = \mathbf{F} \cdot \mathbf{s} = Fs \cos\theta$ where, F is the applied force, s is displacement and θ is the smaller angle between **F** and **s**.

(i) If $\theta < 90°$, *i.e.*, acute angle then workdone is positive.

(ii) If $\theta = 90°$, *i.e.*, right angle then work done is zero.

(iii) If $\theta > 90°$, *i.e.*, obtuse angle then work done is negative.

Sol.

(a) In lifting a bucket out of a well by means of a rope tied to the bucket a force equal to the weight of the bucket has to be applied vertically upwards and bucket also moves vertically upwards *i.e.*, angle between the applied force and displacement is 0.

$\therefore$ Work done by the man, $W = Fs\cos 0^\circ = Fs$ i.e. positive

(b) Gravitational force acts vertically downward and bucket moves vertically upwards i.e. angle between the gravitational force and the displacement is 180°.

$\therefore$ Work done by the gravitational force,

$$W = \mathbf{F}\cdot\mathbf{s} = Fs\cos 180^\circ = -Fs \qquad (\because \cos 180^\circ = -1)$$

$\therefore$ Work done by the gravitational force is negative.

(c) Friction opposes the relative motion, therefore friction on a body sliding down an inclind plane is in opposite direction of motion.

$\therefore$ Work done by friction, $W = \mathbf{F}\cdot\mathbf{s} = Fs\cos 180^\circ$

$= -Fs$ *i.e.*, negative

(d) As the body moves along the direction of applied force *i.e.*, $\theta = 0^\circ$.

$\therefore$ Work done by the applied force,

$W = \mathbf{F}\cdot\mathbf{s} = Fs\cos 0^\circ = Fs$ *i.e.*, positive

(e) The resistive force opposes the motion, therefore angle between the resistive force and displacement is 180°. Therefore, workdone by the resistive force,

$$W = \mathbf{F}\cdot\mathbf{s} = Fs\cos 180^\circ = -Fs \text{ i.e., negative} \qquad (\because \cos 180^\circ = -1)$$

Question 2. A body of mass 2 kg initially at rest moves under the action of an applied horizontal force of 7 N on a table with coefficient of kinetic friction = 0.1. Compute the

(a) work done by the applied force in 10 s.

(b) work done by friction in 10 s.

(c) work done by the net force on the body in 10 s.

(d) change in kinetic energy of the body in 10 s and interpret your results.

Sol. Mass of the body $(m) = 2$ kg

Applied force $(F) = 7$ N

Coefficient of kinetic friction $(\mu_k) = 0.1$

Force of kinetic friction $(f) = \mu_k R$

$= \mu_k mg \qquad (\because R = mg)$

$= 0.1 \times 2 \times 9.8$

$= 1.96$ N

$\therefore$ Net force acting on the body $(F') = F - f$

$$= 7 - 1.96$$
$$= 5.04 \text{ N}$$

($\because$ Force of kinetic friction is acting in the direction opposite to applied force)

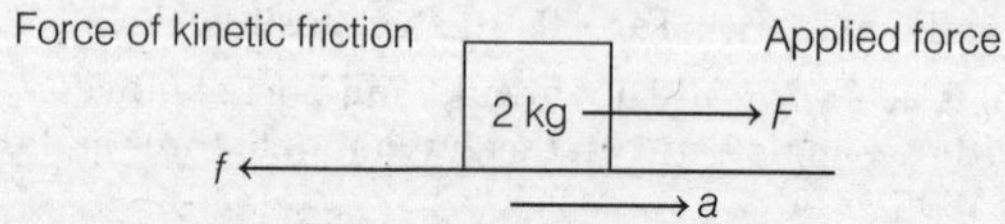

Acceleration of the body $(a) = \dfrac{F'}{m}$ (From Newton's IInd law)

$$= \frac{5.04}{2}$$
$$= 2.52 \text{ m/s}^2$$

Displacement of the body in 10 s,

Using equation of motion $s = ut + \dfrac{1}{2}at^2$

$$= 0 \times 10 + \frac{1}{2} \times 2.52 \times (10)^2$$
$$= 1.26 \times 100 = 126 \text{ m}$$

(a) Work done by the applied force in 10 s,

$$W_1 = \text{Applied force} \times \text{Displacement}$$
$$= F \times s$$
$$= 7 \times 126$$
$$= 882 \text{ J}$$

(b) Work done by the friction force in 10 s,

$$W_2 = \text{Force of kinetic friction} \times \text{Displacement}$$
$$= -f \times s$$
$$= -1.96 \times 126 = -246.9 \text{ J}$$

(c) Work done by the net force in 10 s,

$$W_3 = \text{Net force} \times \text{Displacement}$$
$$= F' \times s$$
$$= 5.04 \times 126 = 635.04 \text{ J}$$

(d) According to work energy theorem,

$$\text{Change in kinetic energy} = \text{Work done} = 635.04 \text{ J}$$

Mistake Alert While calculating acceleration, students generally consider only downwards gravitational force but frictional force also acts opposite to the applied force.

So, acceleration produced is, $a = \dfrac{\text{Net force}}{\text{Mass of body}}$

Question 3 Given below are examples of some potential energy functions in one-dimension. The total energy of the particle is indicated by a cross on the co-ordinate axis. In each case, specify the regions, if any, in which the particle cannot be found for the given energy. Also, indicate the minimum total energy the particle must have in each case. Think of simple physical contexts for which these potential energy shapes are relevant.

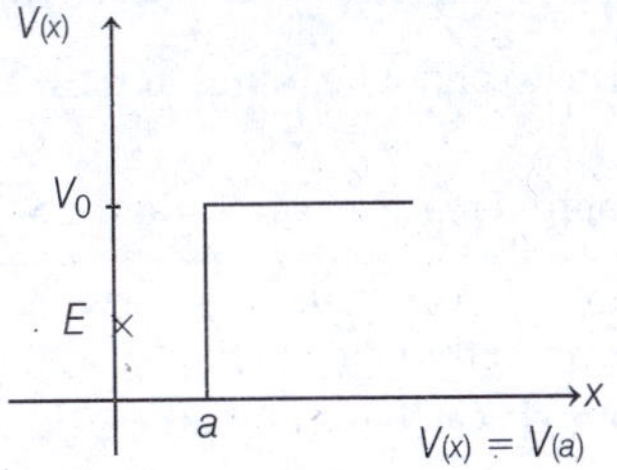

(a)

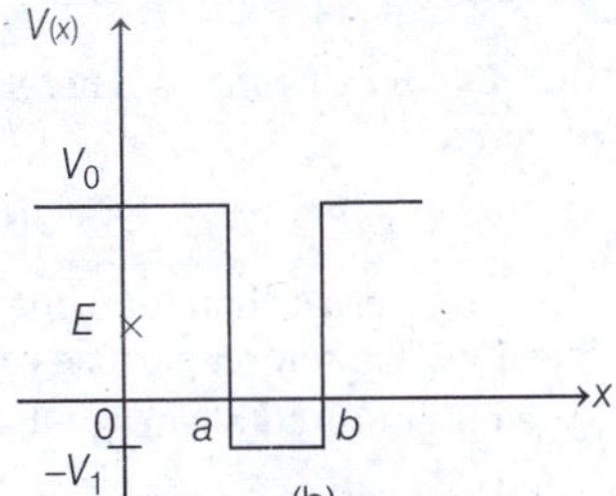

(b)

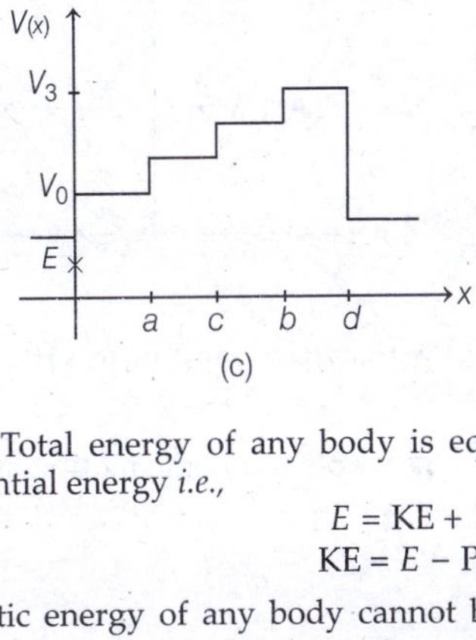

(c)

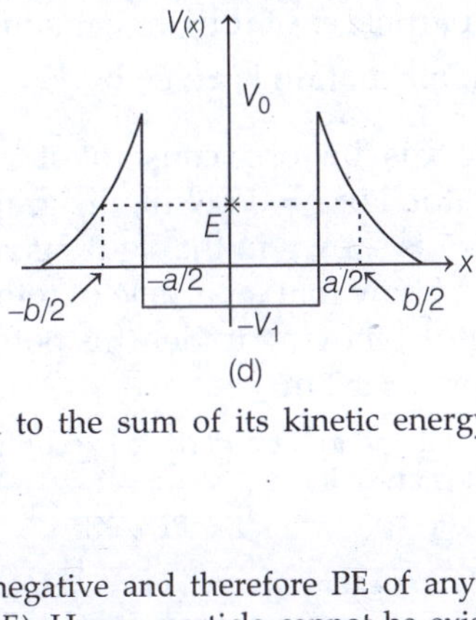

(d)

Sol. Total energy of any body is equal to the sum of its kinetic energy and potential energy *i.e.,*

$$E = \text{KE} + \text{PE}$$

$$\therefore \qquad \text{KE} = E - \text{PE}$$

Kinetic energy of any body cannot be negative and therefore PE of any body cannot be greater than its total energy (E). Hence, particle cannot be exist in a region, where its KE is negative or PE is greater than its total energy (E). Total energy of a particle will be minimum if its kinetic energy is zero.

(a) In region between $x = 0$ and $x = a$, PE (V_0) is zero (on X-axis $y = 0$), so KE is positive. Therefore, the particle can found in this region. The minimum total energy that the particle can have in this case is zero (taking kinetic energy as zero). In the region $x > a$, PE (V_0) is greater than total energy E. So, KE will be negative in this region. Therefore, the particle cannot be found in region $x > a$.

(b) In region $x < a$ and $x > b$ we see that PE is greater than the total energy E, so the KE will be negative ($\because$ KE = E – PE). Therefore, particle cannot found in this region.

In region between $x > a$ and $x < b$, PE is negative, so KE will be positive ($\because$ KE = E − PE). Therefore, particle can be found in this region.

The minimum total energy that particle can have in this case is $-V_1$ (taking kinetic energy zero).

(c) In all regions $x > 0$, PE is greater than the total energy E, so KE will be negative. Therefore, particle cannot be found in all regions, $x > 0$.

The minimum total energy that the particle can have in this case is V_1.

(d) In regions, $-\frac{b}{2} < x < -\frac{a}{2}$ and $\frac{a}{2} < x < \frac{b}{2}$, PE is greater than total energy E, so KE will be negative. Therefore, particle cannot be found in these regions.

In region, $\frac{a}{2} > x > -\frac{a}{2}$, PE is negative and in regions, $x < -\frac{b}{2}$ and $x > \frac{b}{2}$. The PE is lesser than total energy E. So, KE in all these regions will be positive. Therefore, particle can be found in these regions.

The minimum total energy that the particle can have in this case is $-V_1$.

Question 4 The potential energy function for a particle executing linear simple harmonic motion is given by $V(x) = \frac{1}{2}kx^2$ where, k is the force constant of the oscillator. For $k = 0.5$ N/m, the graph $V(x)$ *versus* x is shown in the figure given below. Show that a particle of total energy 1 J moving under this potential must turn back when it reaches $x = \pm 2$ m.

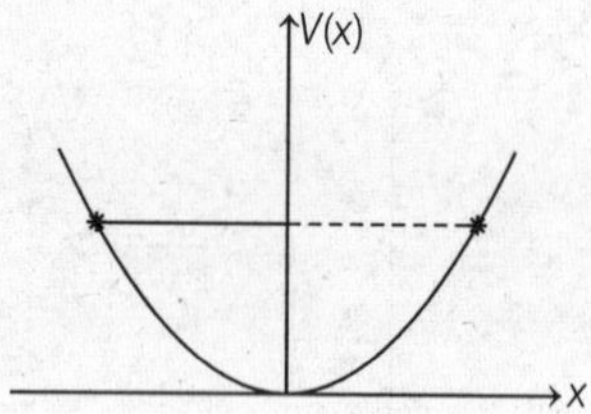

Sol. Total energy of a particle executing linear simple harmonic motion at any instant is given by

$$E = \text{PE} + \text{KE} \quad \ldots\text{(i)}$$

Given, potential energy $V(x) = \frac{1}{2}kx^2$

Total energy $E = 1$ J and $k = 0.5$ N/m

When particle is at extreme position (the position from which the particle starts to come back to its mean position) then speed of the particle is zero and hence, its

$$\text{KE} = \frac{1}{2}mv^2 = 0 \quad (\because v = 0)$$

Substituting values in Eq. (i), we get

$$1 = \frac{1}{2}kx^2 + 0 \Rightarrow 1 = \frac{1}{2} \times 0.5 \times x^2$$

$$x^2 = \frac{2}{0.5} = 4 \text{ or } x = \pm 2\,\text{m}$$

Mistake Alert Student can forget to include both kinetic energy and potential energy in the total energy equation.

Question 5 Answer the following

(a) The casing of a rocket in flight burns up due to friction. At whose expense is the heat energy required for burning obtained? The rocket or the atmosphere?

(b) Comets move around the sun in highly elliptical orbits. The gravitational force on the comet due to the sun is not normal to the comet's velocity in general. Yet the work done by the gravitational force over every complete orbit of the comet is zero. Why?

(c) An artificial satellite orbiting the earth in very thin atmosphere loses its energy gradually due to dissipation against atmospheric resistance, however small. Then, why does its speed increase progressively as it comes closer and closer to the earth?

(d) In figure given below Fig. (i) the man walks 2 m carrying a mass of 15 kg on his hands. In Fig. (ii), he walks the same distance pulling the rope behind him. The rope goes over a pulley and a mass of 15 kg hangs at its other end. In which case is the work done greater?

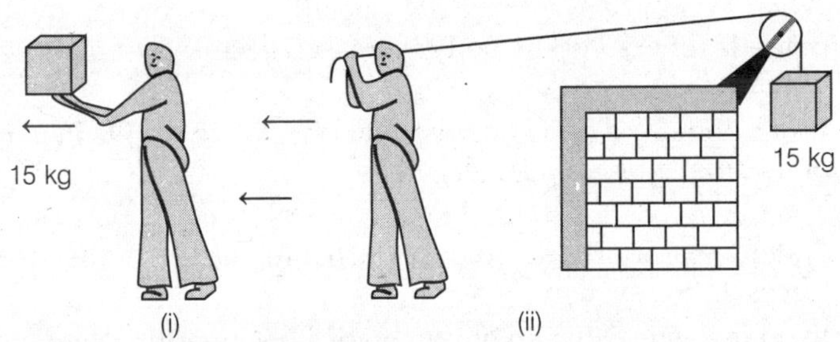

Sol.

(a) The heat energy required for burning of the casing of a rocket in flight is obtained from the rocket itself and not from the atmosphere. When the casing burns up, its mass decreases and therefore, total energy of the rocket decreases.

(b) The gravitational force is a conservative force and work done by a conservative force over a closed path (irrespective of the nature of path) is always zero. Hence, work done by the gravitational force over every complete orbit of the comet is zero.

(c) When an artificial satellite comes closer to the earth, its gravitational potential energy decreases (as its height from the earth surface decreases). Since, according to law of conservation of energy, the sum of kinetic and potential energies remain constant.

Therefore to keep the total energy constant, kinetic energy increases and hence velocity of the satellite increases (KE = $\frac{1}{2}mv^2$, when KE increases velocity will also increase). However, total energy of the satellite continuously decreases at a very small rate due to atmospheric resistance.

(d) In first case, the man applies a force on the mass 15 kg in vertically upward direction, against its weight and walks 2 m in horizontal direction. So, the angle between the applied force and displacement is $Fs \cos 90°$.

$\therefore$ Work done, $W = Fs \cos 90°$

$= 0$ $(\because \cos 90° = 0)$

In second case, the man applies a force in horizontal direction and moves also in horizontal directi . So, angle between the applied force and displacement is 0°.

$\therefore$ Work done, $W = Fs$ c 90°

$= Fs$:. $mg \times s$

$= 15 \times 9.8 \times 2$

$= 294$ J

$\therefore$ Work done is greater in second case.

Question 6 Underline the correct alternative among the following

(a) When a conservative force does positive work on a body, the potential energy of the body increases/decreases/remain unaltered.

(b) Work done by a body against friction always results in a loss of its kinetic/potential energy.

(c) The rate of change of total momentum of a many particle system is proportional to the external force/sum of the internal forces on the system.

(d) In an inelastic collision of two bodies, the quantities which don't change after the collision are the total kinetic energy/total linear moment/total energy of the system of two bodies.

Sol.

(a) Potential energy of the body decreases.
The work done by a conservative force is positive when body displaces in the direction of the applied force and hence, body approaches towards the centre of force, decreasing x. Hence, its potential energy decreases.

(b) Work done by a body against friction always results in a loss of its **kinetic energy.**
Work is done by a body against friction at the expense of its kinetic energy ($\because$ due to friction the speed of an object decreases and hence the kinetic energy). Therefore, its KE decreases.

(c) Internal forces cannot change total momentum of a system of particles. From the law of conservation of momentum we know that if there is no external force on the system then its total momentum remains constant. That means only external force can change the momentum of the system. Therefore, the rate of change of total momentum of a many particle system is proportional to the external force acting on the system.

(d) In an inelastic collision of two bodies, the total linear momentum and total energy of the system by two bodies do not change.

Question 7 State, if each of the following statements are true or false. Give reasons for your answer.

(a) In an elastic collision of two bodies, the momentum and energy of each body is conserved.

(b) Total energy of a system is always conserved, no matter what internal and external forces on the body are persent.

(c) Work done in the motion of a body over a closed-loop is zero for every force in nature.

(d) In an inelastic collision, the final kinetic energy is always less than the initial kinetic energy of the system

Sol.

(a) False, because in an elastic collision of two bodies, total momentum and total energy of the system are conserved and not the momentum and energy of individual body.

(b) False, because the external forces acting on the system can change total energy of the system.

(c) False, because work done in the motion of a body over a closed-loop is zero only for conservative forces such as gravitational force, electrostatic force etc, but it is not zero for non-conservative forces such as frictional forces.

(d) True, because in an inelastic collision, some kinetic energy changes into some other forms of energies such as sound energy, heat energy etc.

Question 8 Answer carefully, with reasons

(a) In an elastic collision of two billiard balls, is the total kinetic energy conserved during the short time of collision of the balls (*i.e.*, when they are in contact)?

(b) Is the total linear momentum conserved during the short time of an elastic collision of two balls?

(c) What are the answers to (a) and (b) for an inelastic collision?

(d) Is the potential energy of two billiard balls depends only on the separation distance between their centres, is the collision elastic or inelastic?

Sol.

(a) No, the total kinetic energy of two billiard balls is not conserved during the short time of collision because a part of kinetic energy is utilized in deforming the balls during that short time of collision and converts into potential energy. In an elastic collision, the kinetic energy before collision and after collision is same.

(b) Yes, the total linear momentum remains conserved during the short time of an elastic collision of two balls.

(c) In an inelastic collision, total kinetic energy do not remain conserved during collision and even after collision but total linear momentum remains conserved during collision as well as after the collision.

(d) The forces involved in collision are conservative, therefore the collision is elastic.

Note We are talking here of potential energy corresponding to the force during collision, not gravitational potential energy.

Question 9 A body is initially at rest. It undergoes one-dimensional motion with constant acceleration. The power delivered to it at time t is proportional to

(a) $t^{1/2}$ (b) t (c) $t^{3/2}$ (d) t^2

Sol. (b) Let a body of mass m which is initially at rest undergoes one-dimensional motion under a constant force F with a constant acceleration a.

Acceleration $$(a) = \frac{F}{m} \quad \text{...(i)}$$

Using equation of motion, $$v = u + at$$

$$\Rightarrow \quad v = 0 + \frac{F}{m} \cdot t \quad (\because u = 0)$$

$$\Rightarrow \quad v = \frac{F}{m} t \quad \text{...(ii)}$$

Power delivered $(P) = Fv$

Substituting the value from Eq. (ii), we get

$$\Rightarrow \quad P = F \times \frac{F}{m} \times t$$

$$\Rightarrow \quad P = \frac{F^2}{m} t$$

Dividing and multiplying by m in RHS,

$$P = \frac{F^2}{m^2} \times mt = a^2 mt \quad \text{[Using Eq. (i)]}$$

As mass m and acceleration a are constant.

$$\therefore \quad P \propto t$$

Question 10 A body is moving unidirectionally under the influence of a source of constant power. Its displacement in time t is proportional to

(a) $t^{1/2}$ (b) t (c) $t^{3/2}$ (d) t^2

Sol. (c) Let a body of mass m be moving uni-directionally under the influence of a source of constant power P. In time t, body is displaced through x and attain a velocity v.

We know that

$$\text{KE} = \text{Work done} = \text{Power} \times \text{Time}$$

But $$\text{KE} = \frac{1}{2}mv^2$$

$\therefore$ $$\text{KE} = \frac{1}{2}mv^2 = P \times t$$

or $$v = \sqrt{\frac{2Pt}{m}} = \sqrt{\frac{2P}{m}}\, t^{1/2} \quad \text{...(i)}$$

The velocity of the body is equal to the time rate of change of displacement x *i.e.*,

$$v = \frac{dx}{dt}$$

or $$dx = vdt$$

Substituting the value of v from Eq. (i), we get

$$dx = \sqrt{\frac{2P}{m}}\, t^{1/2} dt$$

Displacement of the body in time t,

$$\int dx = \int \sqrt{\frac{2P}{m}}\, t^{1/2} dt$$

$$x = \sqrt{\frac{2P}{m}} \left(\frac{t^{\frac{1}{2}+1}}{\frac{1}{2}+1} \right)$$

$$= \sqrt{\frac{2P}{m}} \frac{t^{3/2}}{3/2} = \frac{2}{3}\sqrt{\frac{2P}{m}}\, t^{3/2}$$

Power delivered (P) and mass of the body (m) is constant.

$\therefore$ $$x \propto t^{3/2}$$

Quick Solution

Velocity attained by the body in time t can be obtained using equation of motion,

$$v = u + at$$

$$v = 0 + at \quad (\because u = 0)$$

or $$v = at \quad \text{...(i)}$$

Power delivered, $$P = F \cdot v$$

But $F = ma$

$\therefore$ $P = ma \times at$ [Using Eq. (i)]

$P = ma^2 t$

or $a = \sqrt{\dfrac{P}{mt}}$ ...(ii)

Using equation of motion,

$$s = ut + \frac{1}{2}at^2$$

We get, $x = 0.t + \dfrac{1}{2}\left(\sqrt{\dfrac{P}{mt}}\right) \times t^2$

$$= \frac{1}{2}\sqrt{\frac{P}{m}}\, t^{2-\frac{1}{2}}$$

$$= \frac{1}{2}\sqrt{\frac{P}{m}}\, t^{3/2}$$

As power (P) and mass (m) are constants.

$\therefore$ $x \propto t^{3/2}$

Question 11. A body constrained to move along Z-axis of a coordinate system is subjected to a constant force F given by $F = -\hat{i} + 2\hat{j} + 3\hat{k}$ N where $\hat{i}$, $\hat{j}$ and $\hat{k}$ are the unit vector along the X, Y and Z-axis of the system respectively. What is the work done by this force in moving the body a distance of 4 m along the Z-axis?

◎ *Thinking Process* Work done (W) = $\mathbf{F} \cdot \mathbf{s}$

In scalar (dot) product, $\hat{\mathbf{i}} \cdot \hat{\mathbf{i}} = \hat{\mathbf{j}} \cdot \hat{\mathbf{j}} = \hat{\mathbf{k}} \cdot \hat{\mathbf{k}} = 1$

and $\hat{\mathbf{i}} \cdot \hat{\mathbf{j}} = \hat{\mathbf{j}} \cdot \hat{\mathbf{k}} = \hat{\mathbf{k}} \cdot \hat{\mathbf{i}} = 0$

Sol. Force, $\mathbf{F} = (-\hat{\mathbf{i}} + 2\hat{\mathbf{j}} + 3\hat{\mathbf{k}})$ N

Displacement, $\mathbf{s} = (4\hat{\mathbf{k}})$ m $= (0\hat{\mathbf{i}} + 0\hat{\mathbf{j}} + 4\hat{\mathbf{k}})$ m

$\therefore$ Work done by the force is given by

$$W = \mathbf{F} \cdot \mathbf{s}$$

$$= (-\hat{\mathbf{i}} + 2 + 3\hat{\mathbf{k}}) \cdot (0\hat{\mathbf{i}} + 0\hat{\mathbf{j}} + 4\hat{\mathbf{k}})$$

$$= (-1 \times 0) + (2 \times 0) + (3 \times 4)$$

$= 0 + 12$ [$\because$ $\hat{\mathbf{i}} \cdot \hat{\mathbf{i}} = \hat{\mathbf{j}} \cdot \hat{\mathbf{j}} = \hat{\mathbf{k}} \cdot \hat{\mathbf{k}} = 1$ and $\hat{\mathbf{i}} \cdot \hat{\mathbf{j}} = \hat{\mathbf{j}} \cdot \hat{\mathbf{k}} = \hat{\mathbf{k}} \cdot \hat{\mathbf{i}} = 0$]

$= 12$ J

Question 12 An electron and proton are detected in a cosmic ray experiment, the first with kinetic energy 10 keV and the second with 100 keV. Which is faster, the electron or the proton? Obtain the ratio of their speeds. (Electron mass $= 9.11 \times 10^{-31}$ kg, proton mass $= 1.67 \times 10^{-27}$ kg, 1 eV $= 1.60 \times 10^{-19}$ J)

Sol. Mass of electron, $(m_e) = 9.11 \times 10^{-31}$ kg

Mass of proton, $(m_p) = 1.67 \times 10^{-27}$ kg

We know that 1 eV $= 1.60 \times 10^{-19}$ J

Kinetic energy of electron, $(K_e) = 10\,\text{keV}$ (Given)

$$= 10 \times 10^3 \text{ eV}$$

$$= 10 \times 10^3 \times 1.60 \times 10^{-19} \text{ J} = 1.6 \times 10^{-15} \text{ J}$$

If the electron is moving with speed v_e then kinetic energy of electron

$$K_e = \frac{1}{2} m_e v_e^2$$

but $$K_e = 1.6 \times 10^{-15} \text{ J}$$

$\therefore$ $$\frac{1}{2} m_e v_e^2 = 1.6 \times 10^{-15}$$

On substituting the values $\frac{1}{2} \times 9.11 \times 10^{-31} v_e^2 = 1.6 \times 10^{-15}$ J

or $$v_e = \sqrt{\frac{2 \times 1.6 \times 10^{-15}}{9.11 \times 10^{-31}}} = \sqrt{\frac{3.2}{9.11} \times 10^{16}}$$

or $$v_e = 5.93 \times 10^7 \text{ m/s}$$

Kinetic energy of proton, $(K_p) = 100\,\text{keV}$

$$= 100 \times 10^3 \text{ eV}$$

$$= 100 \times 10^3 \times 1.60 \times 10^{-19} \text{ J}$$

$$= 1.6 \times 10^{-14} \text{ J}$$

If the proton is moving with speed v_p then kinetic energy of proton

$$K_p = \frac{1}{2} m_p v_p^2$$

but $$K_p = 1.6 \times 10^{-14} \text{ J}$$

$\therefore$ $$\frac{1}{2} m_p v_p^2 = 1.6 \times 10^{-14}$$

Substituting the values $\frac{1}{2} \times 1.67 \times 10^{-27} v_1^2 = 1.6 \times 10^{-14}$

or $$v_p = \sqrt{\frac{2 \times 1.6 \times 10^{-14}}{1.67 \times 10^{-27}}} = \sqrt{\frac{3.2}{1.67} \times 10^{13}}$$

or $$v_p = 4.38 \times 10^6 \text{ m/s}$$

We found that $v_e > v_p$

Therefore, the speed of electron is greater than the speed of the proton *i.e.*, the electron moves faster than the proton.

Ratio of their speeds

$$\frac{v_e}{v_p} = \frac{5.93 \times 10^7}{4.38 \times 10^6} = \frac{5930}{438} = 13.5$$

Quick Solution

$$\frac{K \cdot E_e}{K \cdot E_p} = \frac{\frac{1}{2} m_e v_e^2}{\frac{1}{2} m_p v_p^2} = \frac{10 \text{ keV}}{100 \text{ keV}}$$

$$\frac{v_e}{v_p} = \sqrt{\frac{1}{10} \times \frac{m_p}{m_e}} = \sqrt{\frac{1.67 \times 10^{-27}}{10 \times 9.1 \times 10^{-31}}} = 13.5$$

$\therefore \quad v_e > v_p$

Question 13 A rain drop of radius 2 mm falls from a height of 500 m above the ground. It falls with decreasing acceleration (due to viscous resistance of the air) until at half its original height, it attains its maximum (terminal) speed and moves with uniform speed thereafter. What is the work done by the gravitational force on the drop in the first and second half of its journey? What is the work done by the resistive force in the entire journey, if its speed on reaching the ground is 10 m/s?

Sol. Radius of the rain drop $(r) = 2 \text{ mm} = 2 \times 10^{-3}$ m

Density of water $(\rho) = 10^3 \text{ kg/m}^3$

Volume of the rain drop $(V) = \frac{4}{3}\pi r^3$ (as the drop is spherical)

$$= \frac{4}{3} \times 3.14 \times (2 \times 10^{-3})^3$$

$$= \frac{4 \times 3.14 \times 8 \times 10^{-9}}{3} \text{ m}^3$$

$$= 3.35 \times 10^{-8} \text{ m}^3$$

Mass of the rain drop (m) = Volume × Density

$$= 3.35 \times 10^{-8} \times 10^3$$

$$= 3.35 \times 10^{-5} \text{ kg}$$

(The drop will attain the terminal speed when the net force on the drop becomes zero.)

Gravitational force on rain drop = Weight of the rain drop

$$F = mg$$

$$= 3.35 \times 10^{-5} \times 9.8 = 32.83 \times 10^{-5}$$

$$= 3.28 \times 10^{-4} \text{ N}$$

Distance travelled in first half of its journey

$$S = \frac{H}{2} = \frac{500}{2} = 250 \text{ m}$$

$\therefore$ Work done by the gravitational force on the drop in first half of its journey is given by

$$W = F \times s$$
$$= 3.28 \times 10^{-4} \times 250$$
$$= 820.00 \times 10^{-4} \text{ J} = 0.082 \text{ J}$$

Gravitational force acting in second half of journey is same and distance travelled is also same.

$\therefore$ Work done by the gravitational force in second half of journey

= Work done by the gravitational force in first half of journey

= 0.082 J

If the rain drop is initially at rest then, initial velocity $(u) = 0$

Final velocity on reacting the ground $(v) = 10$ m/s (Given)

$\therefore$ Change in KE of the rain drop = Final kinetic energy – Initial kinetic energy

$$\Delta E_k = \frac{1}{2}mv^2 - \frac{1}{2}mu^2$$
$$= \frac{1}{2}mv^2 - 0 \quad \left(\because u = 0, \text{ so } \frac{1}{2}mu^2 = 0\right)$$
$$= \frac{1}{2} \times 3.35 \times 10^{-5} \times (10)^2$$
$$= 1.675 \times 10^{-3} \text{ J}$$
$$= 0.001675 \text{ J}$$

Total work done on the rain drop by the gravitational force

$$W = 0.082 + 0.082 = 0.164 \text{ J}$$

Work done by the resistive force in the entire journey

= Change in KE – Work done by the gravitational force

= 0.001675 – 0.164

= – 0.16225 J = – 0.162 J

It means work done by the resistive force is negative.

Question 14 A molecule in a gas container hits a horizontal wall with speed 200 m/s and angle 30° with the normal and rebounds with the same speed. Is momentum conserved in the collision? Is the collision elastic or inelastic?

◎ ***Thinking Process*** Linear momentum remains conserved in elastic collision as well as in inelastic collision but kinetic energy remains conserved only in an elastic collision.

Sol. Yes, linear momentum is conserved in this collision either it is elastic or inelastic collision because linear momentum remains conserved in both types of collisions.

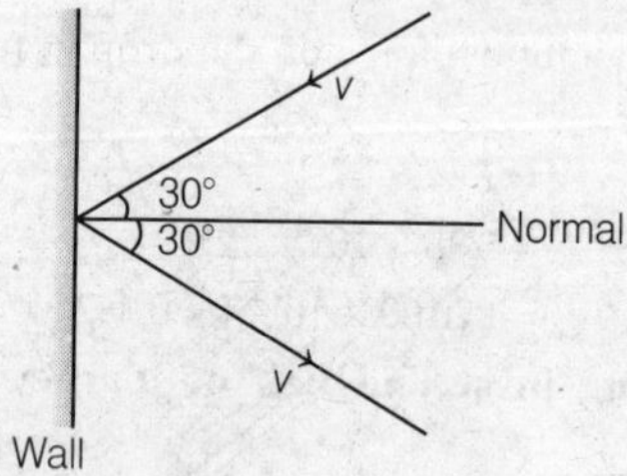

Given that the speed of the molecule of gas is same before and after the collision, therefore its kinetic energy is conserved. Hence, the collision is elastic.

Question 15 A pump on the ground floor of a building can pump up water to fill a tank of value 30 m^3 in 15 min. If the tank is 40 m above the ground and the efficiency of the pump is 30%, how much electric power is consumed by the pump?

Sol. Volume of the tank $(V) = 30\ m^3$

Density of water $(\rho) = 10^3\ kg/m^3$

$\therefore$ Mass of the water to be pumped up to fill the tank

$$m = V \times \rho \qquad \left(\because \text{Density} = \frac{\text{Mass}}{\text{Volume}}\right)$$

$$= 30 \times 10^3$$

$$= 3 \times 10^4\ kg$$

Height of the tank $(h) = 40$ m

Work done by the pump in filling the tank

$$W = mgh$$

$$= 3 \times 10^4 \times 9.8 \times 40$$

$$= 1.176 \times 10^7\ J$$

Time taken to fill the tank = 15 min

$$= 15 \times 60 = 900\ s$$

$$\therefore \quad \text{Power required } (P) = \frac{\text{Work done}}{\text{Time taken}}$$

$$P = \frac{1.176 \times 10^7}{900}$$

$$= 13.07 \times 10^3\ W$$

$$= 13.07\ kW$$

$$\text{Efficiency of the pump } (\eta) = \frac{\text{Output power}}{\text{Input power}} \times 100$$

$$\therefore \qquad \text{Input power} = \frac{\text{Output power}}{\eta} \times 100$$

$$= \frac{13.07}{30} \times 100 = 43.6 \text{ kW}$$

The pump consumed 43.6 kW electric power.

> **Mistake Alert** Student might make mistakes in converting units of time (minutes to seconds) or volume (cubic meters to litre).

Question 16 Two identical ball bearings in contact with each other and resting on a frictionless table are hit head-on by another ball bearing of the same mass moving initially with a speed v. If the collision is elastic, which of the following is a possible result after collision?

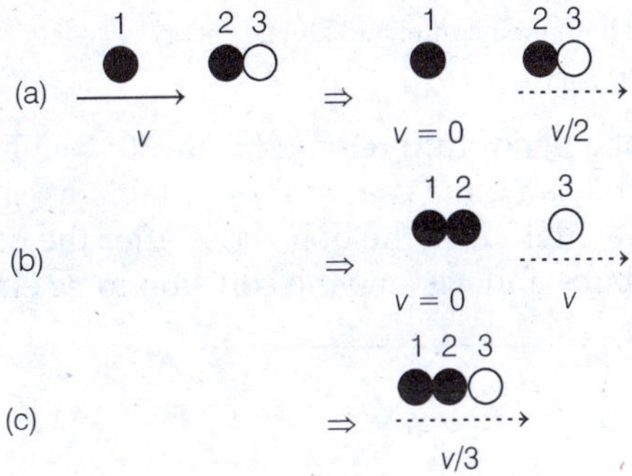

Sol. Let mass of each ball bearings be m.

Before collision

Total KE of the ball bearings

$$= \frac{1}{2}mv^2 + \frac{1}{2}m(0)^2 + \frac{1}{2}m(0)^2$$

$$= \frac{1}{2}mv^2$$

After collision

In first case, kinetic energy of ball bearings

$$= \frac{1}{2}m(0)^2 + \frac{1}{2}m\left(\frac{v}{2}\right)^2 + \frac{1}{2}m\left(\frac{v}{2}\right)^2$$

$$= 0 + \frac{1}{2}\frac{mv^2}{4} + \frac{1}{2}\frac{mv^2}{4}$$

$$= \frac{mv^2}{4}$$

In second case, kinetic energy of ball bearings

$$= \frac{1}{2}m(0)^2 + \frac{1}{2}m(0)^2 + \frac{1}{2}mv^2$$

$$= \frac{1}{2}mv^2$$

In third case, kinetic energy of ball bearings

$$= \frac{1}{2}m\left(\frac{v}{3}\right)^2 + \frac{1}{2}m\left(\frac{v}{3}\right)^2 + \frac{1}{2}m\left(\frac{v}{3}\right)^2$$

$$= 3 \times \frac{1}{2}m\frac{v^2}{9}$$

$$= \frac{mv^2}{6}$$

In an elastic collision, the KE remains conserved. In second case, kinetic energy of ball bearings is conserved.

Therefore, only case second is possible after collision.

> **Note** In elastic collision both momentum and kinetic energy of system remains conserved.

Question 17 The bob A of a pendulum released from 30° to the vertical hits another bob B of the same mass at rest on a table as shown in figure given below. How high does the bob A rise after the collision? Neglect the size of the bobs and assume the collision to be elastic.

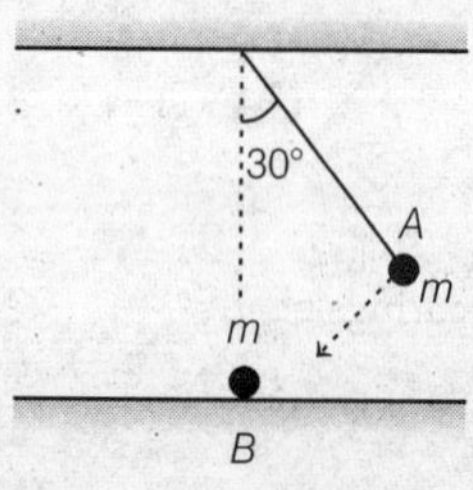

Sol. When a perfectly elastic head-on collision takes place between two bodies of equal masses, their velocities are interchanged. In the given case, bob B is at rest and bob A collides with bob B with some speed. Therefore after collision bob A comes to rest and bob B will start to move with the speed of bob A. Hence, bob A will not rise after the collision.

> ***Mistake Alert*** Students may misunderstand the concept of conservation of linear momentum in elastic collisions.

Question 18 The bob of a pendulum is released from a horizontal position A as shown in the figure. If the length of the pendulum is 1.5 m, what is the speed with which the bob arrives at the lower most point B, given that it dissipated 5% of its initial energy against air resistance?

Sol. Length of the pendulum = 1.5 m

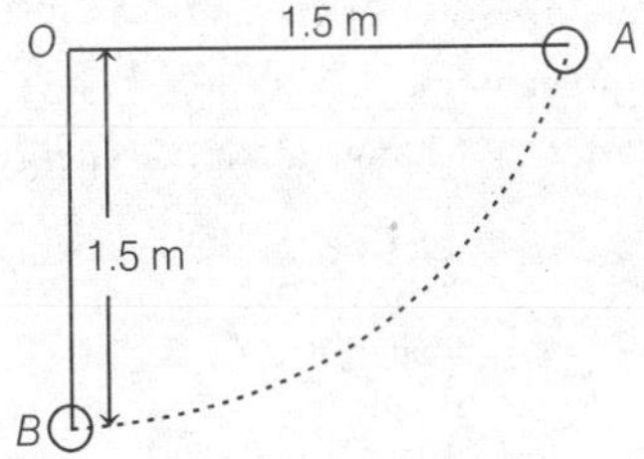

Potential energy of the bob at position $A = mgh$

As bob moves from position A towards position B its potential energy converted into kinetic energy. 5% of its potential energy is dissipated against air resistance.

$\therefore$ KE at position B = 95% of its PE at position A

$$\frac{1}{2}mv^2 = \frac{95}{100} \times mgh$$

or

$$v = \sqrt{\frac{2 \times 95 \times gh}{100}} = \sqrt{\frac{19}{10} \times 9.8 \times 1.5}$$

$$= 5.28 \text{ m/s}$$

Question 19 A trolley of mass 300 kg carrying a sand bag of 25 kg is moving uniformly with a speed of 27 km/h on a frictionless track. After a while, sand starts leaking out of a hole on the floor of trolley at the rate of 0.05 kg/s. What is the speed of the trolley after the entire sand bag is empty?

Sol. The trolley carrying a sand bag is moving uniformly with a constant speed. Therefore, the external force acting on it is zero. The weight of the trolley carrying a sand bag is balanced by the normal reaction of the floor. When sand start leaking out of a hole on the trolley's floor, it does not apply any external force on the trolley and therefore, speed of trolley will not change. Thus, the speed of the trolley after emptying the sand is 27 km/h.

Note In absence of any external force momentum of system remains conserved.

Question 20 A body of mass 0.5 kg travels in a straight line with velocity, $v = ax^{3/2}$, where $a = 5 \text{ m}^{-1/2}\text{/s}$. What is the work done by the net force during its displacement from $x = 0$ to $x = 2$ m?

Sol. Mass of the body $(m) = 0.5$ kg

Velocity of the body $(v) = ax^{3/2}$

where, $a = 5\text{m}^{-1/2}\text{/s}$

Velocity of the body at $x = 0$,

$$v_1 = 5 \times 0 = 0$$

Velocity of the body at $x = 2$ m,

$$v_2 = 5 \times (2)^{3/2} \text{ m/s}$$

According to work-energy theorem,

$$\text{Work done} = \text{Change in kinetic energy}$$
$$= \frac{1}{2}mv_2^2 - \frac{1}{2}mv_1^2$$
$$= \frac{1}{2}m(v_2^2 - v_1^2)$$
$$= \frac{1}{2} \times 0.5[\{5(2)^{3/2}\}^2 - (0)^2]$$
$$= \frac{1}{2} \times 0.5 \times 25 \times 8$$
$$= 50 \text{ J}$$

Question 21 The blades of a windmill sweep out a circle of area A.

(a) If the wind flows at a velocity v perpendicular to the circle, what is the mass of the air passing through it in time t ?

(b) What is the kinetic energy of the air?

(c) Assume that windmill converts 25% of the wind's energy into electrical energy and that $A = 30 \text{ m}^2$, $v = 36$ km/h and the density of air is 1.2 kg/m^3. What is the electrical power produced?

Sol.

(a) Volume of the air passing through the windmill per second $= Av$

Volume of the air passing through the windmill in time $t = Av \times t$

$\therefore$ Mass of the air passing through the windmill in time t,

$$m = Avt \times \rho \qquad (\because \text{Mass} = \text{Volume} \times \text{Density})$$
$$= Av\rho t$$

(b) Kinetic energy of the air $= \frac{1}{2}mv^2$

$$= \frac{1}{2} Av\rho t \times v^2$$
$$= \frac{1}{2} Av^3\rho t$$

(c) Electrical energy produced = 25% of KE of air

$$E = \frac{25}{100} \times \frac{1}{2} Av^3\rho t$$
$$= \frac{1}{8} Av^3\rho t$$

$\therefore$ Electric power produced $= \frac{E}{t} = \frac{1}{8}\frac{Av^3\rho t}{t} = \frac{1}{8}Av^3\rho$

Area of the circle sweep out by the blades of the windmill

$$A = 30\,m^2$$

Velocity of wind (v) = 36 km/h

$$= 36 \times \frac{5}{18}\,m/s = 10\,m/s \qquad \left(\because 1\,km/h = \frac{5}{18}\,m/s\right)$$

Density of air (ρ) = 1.2 kg/m^3

$$\therefore \text{Electric power produced} = \frac{1}{8} \times 30 \times (10)^3 \times 1.2$$

$$= 4500\,W = 4.5\,kW$$

Question 22 A person trying to loose weight (dieter) lifts a 10 kg mass one thousand times to a height of 0.5 m each time. Assume that the potential energy lost each time she lowers the mass is dissipated.

(a) How much work does she do against the gravitational force?

(b) Fat supplies 3.8×10^7 J of energy per kilogram, which is converted to mechanical energy with a 20% efficiency rate. How much fat will the dieter use up?

Sol. Mass m = 10 kg

Height h = 0.5 m

Number of times the mass lifted (n) = 1000

(a) Work done against gravitational force $= n \times mgh$

$$= 1000 \times 10 \times 9.8 \times 0.5$$

$$= 49000\,J$$

(b) Energy supplied by fat per kilogram = 3.8×10^7 J

Mechanical energy supplied by fat per kilogram

$$= 20\% \text{ of total energy supplied by fat}$$

$$= \frac{20}{100} \times 3.8 \times 10^7$$

$$= 0.76 \times 10^7\,J/kg$$

$$\text{Fat used up by the dieter} = \frac{1}{0.76 \times 10^7} \times 49000$$

$$= 6.45 \times 10^{-3}\,kg$$

Question 23 A family uses 8 kW of power.

(a) Direct solar energy is incident on the horizontal surface at an average rate of 200 W per square metre. If 20% of this energy can be converted to useful electrical energy, how large an area is needed to supply 8 kW?

(b) Compare this area to that of the roof of a typical house.

Sol. Power used by a family $(P) = 8\,\text{kW}$

(a) Solar energy incident on horizontal surface per square metre

$$= 200\,\text{W}$$

Electrical energy obtained from solar energy per unit area

$$= 200 \times \frac{20}{100}\,\text{W}$$

$$= 40\,\text{W}$$

$\therefore$ Area needed to supply 8 kW $= \dfrac{8\,\text{kW}}{40\,\text{W}}$

$$= \frac{8000}{40} = 200\,\text{m}^2$$

(b) This area is comparable to the roof of a large house of 250 m^2.

DIKSHA APP Questions

☐ Multiple Choice Questions

Q.1 A body of mass 2 kg is initially at rest and it moves under the action of applied horizontal force of 18 N on a horizontal table. The coefficient of kinetic friction between the body and the table is 0.1. Take $g = 10\,\text{m/s}^2$, the work done by applied force and force of friction on the body in 10 seconds are respectively equal to

(a) 7200 J and –800 J (b) –7200 J and +800 J
(c) 8100 J and –900 J (d) – 8100 J and +900 J

Sol. (a) Force of friction $F_f = \mu N = \mu mg = 0.1 \times 2 \times 10 = 2\,\text{N}$.

Applied force, $F = 18\,\text{N}$

Net force applied, $F_{\text{net}} = 18 - 2 = 16\,\text{N}$.

Acceleration produced, $a = \dfrac{F_{net}}{m} = \dfrac{16}{2} = 8\,\text{m/s}^2$

Distance moved in 10 s is

$$S = ut + \frac{1}{2}at^2$$

$$= 0 + \frac{1}{2} \times 8 \times 10 \times 10 = 400\,\text{m}$$

Work done by applied force $= FS = 18 \times 400 = 7200\,\text{J}$.

Work done by frictional force $= F_f S = -2 \times 400 = -800\,\text{J}$.

Note Work done by frictional force is negative as F_f acts opposite to motion of body.

Q.2 A particle is moved from point $P(1,2,3)$ to point $Q(3,4,5)$ by the application of constant force $\mathbf{F}$ given by $\mathbf{F}=-2\hat{\mathbf{i}}+3\hat{\mathbf{j}}+4\hat{\mathbf{k}})$N. The work done by the force on the particle is

(a) 4 J
(b) 6 J
(c) 8 J
(d) 10 J

Sol. (d) Work done by constant force is $W = \mathbf{F}\cdot\mathbf{S}$

Here $\mathbf{S} = (x_2 - x_1)\hat{\mathbf{i}} + (y_2 - y_1)\hat{\mathbf{j}} + (z_2 - z_1)\hat{\mathbf{k}}$

$$= (3-1)\hat{\mathbf{i}} + (4-2)\hat{\mathbf{j}} + (5-3)\hat{\mathbf{k}} = 2\hat{\mathbf{i}} + 2\hat{\mathbf{j}} + 2\hat{\mathbf{k}}.$$

$$\therefore \quad W = \mathbf{F}\cdot\mathbf{S} = (-2\hat{\mathbf{i}} + 3\hat{\mathbf{j}} + 4\hat{\mathbf{k}})\cdot(2\hat{\mathbf{i}} + 2\hat{\mathbf{j}} + 2\hat{\mathbf{k}})$$

$$= -4 + 6 + 8$$

$$= 10 \text{ J}$$

Q.3 A ball of mass 'm' when pushed down form the point P, with a speed v, just manages to react the top and Q of the smooth hemispherical bowl of radius R as shown in figure. The velocity v is equal to

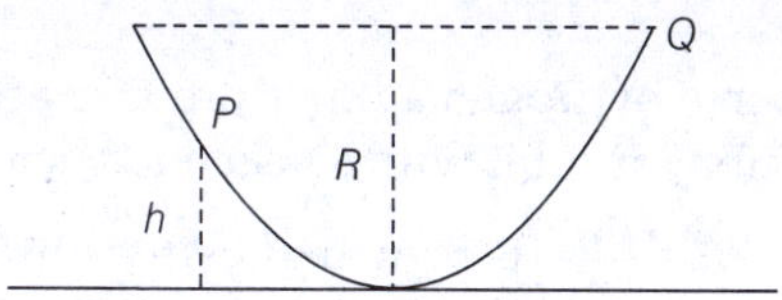

(a) $\sqrt{2gR}$
(b) $\sqrt{2g(R-h)}$
(c) $\sqrt{2g(R+h)}$
(d) $\sqrt{2gh}$

Sol. (b) Using law of conservation of energy

KE at point P + PE at point P = PE point Q

(As at point Q, KE = 0)

$$\frac{1}{2}mv^2 + mgh = mgR$$

$$\frac{v^2}{2} = g(R-h)$$

$$v = \sqrt{2g(R-h)}$$

Q.4 A particle is sliding down an inclined plane having a uniform dynamic friction, from a height h. The variation in kinetic energy with x which is the distance through which the particle moves is given by which one among the following ?

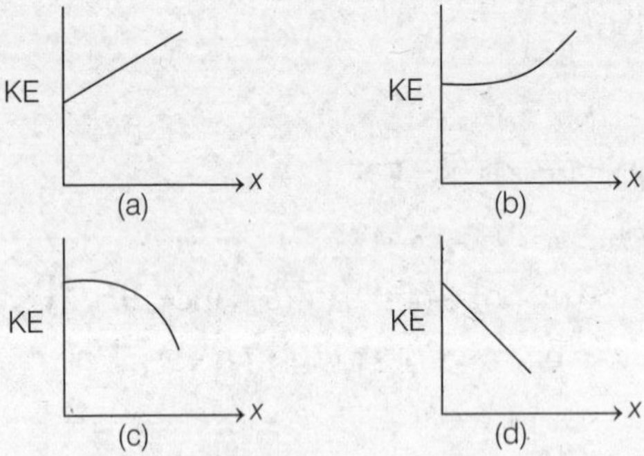

Sol. (d) Let m be the mass of particle and θ is the angle of slope of inclined plane. If F is the dynamic frictional force then KE of particle is given by

$$\text{KE} = \text{Loss in PE} - Fx$$
$$= mgh - Fx$$

So the graph of KE *versus* x is a straight line with a negative slope and intercept with $x = 0$ is $mgh\sin\theta$.

Q.5 The electron, in a hydrogen atom is orbiting around the nuclens in a circular orbit with a speed v. The needed centripetal force $\left(\frac{mv^2}{r}\right)$ is provided by the attractive coulomb force $= \left(\frac{ke^2}{r^2}\right)$ between the electron and the proton of the hydrogen nuclens. If the radius of the electron orbit were to decrease to $\frac{r}{2}$. The kinetic energy of the electron would

(a) increase by an amount of $\left(\frac{ke^2}{r}\right)$

(b) increase by an amount of $\left(\frac{ke^2}{2r}\right)$

(c) decrease by an amount of $\left(\frac{ke^2}{r}\right)$

(d) decrease by an amount of $\left(\frac{ke^2}{2r}\right)$

Sol. (b) In first case centripetal force = coulombian force

$$\frac{mv_1^2}{r} = \frac{ke^2}{r^2}$$

$$\Rightarrow \qquad mv_1^2 = \frac{ke^2}{r}$$

$\therefore$ initial kinetic energy $= \frac{1}{2}\frac{ke^2}{r}$ ...(i)

If the orbit of radius is $\frac{r}{2}$ then

new centripetal force = New coulumbian force

$$\frac{mv_2^2}{\left(\frac{r}{2}\right)} = \frac{ke^2}{\left(\frac{r}{2}\right)^2} \Rightarrow mv_2^2 = \frac{2ke^2}{r}$$

New kinetic energy $\frac{1}{2}mv_2^2 = \frac{ke^2}{r}$ ...(ii)

Increase in kinetic energy $= \frac{ke^2}{r} - \frac{ke^2}{2r} = \frac{ke^2}{2r}$

Q.6 Two springs (1) and (2) have spring constant k_1 and k_2 respectively, with $k_1 < k_2$. The springs are stretched

(i) by applying equal force on them and

(ii) so that their lengths increase by same amount

Let the work done an the two springs in cases (i) and (ii) be (W_{1a} and W_{2a}) and (W_{1b} and W_{2b}) respectively. We would then have

(a) $(W_{1a} > W_{2a})$ and $(W_{1b} = W_{2b})$ (b) $(W_{1a} > W_{2a})$ and $(W_{1b} < W_{2b})$
(c) $(W_{1a} < W_{2a})$ and $(W_{1b} < W_{2b})$ (d) $(W_{1a} > W_{2a})$ and $(W_{1b} < W_{2b})$

Sol. (d) The work done when spring is stracted by amount x is

$$W = \frac{1}{2}kx^2$$

In case (i) $\frac{W_{1a}}{W_{2a}} = \frac{\frac{1}{2}k_1x_1^2}{\frac{1}{2}k_2x_2^2} = \frac{k_1^2x_1^2}{k_2^2x_2^2} \times \frac{k_2}{k_1} = \frac{F^2k_2}{F^2k_1}$ $(\because F = k_1x_1 = k_2x_2)$

$$\frac{W_{1a}}{W_{2b}} = \frac{k_2}{k_1}$$

As $k_1 < k_2$ so $W_{1a} > W_{2a}$.

In case (ii) $\frac{W_{1b}}{W_{2b}} = \frac{\frac{1}{2}k_1x^2}{\frac{1}{2}k_2x^2} = \frac{k_1}{k_2}$

As $\qquad k_1 < k_2$ so $W_{1b} < W_{2b}$.

Q.7 A givén spring when compressed by an amount x_0 can cause an object of mass m kept on it, to 'thrown up' through maximum vertical height h. The spring constant k of this spring equals

(a) $\frac{mgh}{x_0^2}$ (b) $\frac{mgh}{2x_0^2}$ (c) $\frac{2mgh}{3x_0^2}$ (d) $\frac{2mgh}{x_0^2}$

Sol. (d) According to law of conservation of energy.

PE stored in spring = PE gained by object

$$\frac{1}{2}kx_0^2 = mgh \Rightarrow k = \frac{2mgh}{x_0^2}.$$

Q.8 It is known that comets move around the sun in elliptical orbits of very high eccentricity. In general instantaneous gravitational force, on the coment due to the sun is not normal to its instantaneous velocity. The net work done by the gravitational force of the sun, on the comet over one complete orbit of the comet would then be

(a) a non zero positive work; dependent on the eccentricity of the orbit
(b) a non zero negative work; dependent on the eccentricity of the orbit
(c) zero only if the elliptical orbit approaches a circular shape.
(d) zero; irrespective of the eccentricity of the orbit.

Sol. (d) For a complete orbit the final position and speed of comet is same as that of initial position. Hence, here is no change in PE and KE of the comet. It means the net work done on the comet by gravitational force of the sun (over complete orbit) is zero.

Note Gravitational force is conservative force and work done for conservative force over complete closed path is zero.

Q.9 A ball initially at rest (at $t = 0$) from a height H onto a floor. If the coefficient of restitution between the ball and the floor is e the time instant, at which the ball would be just making its second impact on the floor, would be

(a) $\sqrt{\frac{2H}{g}}(1+2e)$

(b) $\sqrt{\frac{2H}{g}}(1-2e)$

(c) $\sqrt{\frac{2H}{g}}(1-e)$

(d) $\sqrt{\frac{2H}{g}}(1+e)$

Sol. (a) Let in time t_1, the ball makes first impact with the floor, So

$$H = ut + \frac{1}{2}gt_1^2$$

$$H = 0 + \frac{1}{2}gt_1^2$$

$$\sqrt{\frac{2H}{g}} = t_1 \qquad \text{...(i)}$$

The ball will rebound to velocity $e\sqrt{2gH}$. Hence in time, t_2 ball reaches new height is given by

$$v' = u' + gt_2$$

$$0 = e\sqrt{2gH} - gt_2$$

$$e\sqrt{\frac{2H}{g}} = t_2 \qquad \text{...(ii)}$$

The ball would again take time t_2 before it impact second time on floor. Hence, the time instant at which it would make second impact on floor is given by

$$T = t_1 + t_2 + t_2$$

$$= \sqrt{\frac{2H}{g}} + e\sqrt{\frac{2H}{g}} + e\sqrt{\frac{2H}{g}} = \sqrt{\frac{2H}{g}}(1 + 2e)$$

Q.10 A ball initially at rest is dropped vertically from a height H onto a floor. If the coefficient of restitution between the ball and the floor equals e. The height to which the ball would rise after the third impact would be

(a) e^3H (b) e^6H (c) e^2H (d) e^4H

Sol. (b) Let v_1 is the velocity with which ball hits the floors, so just before the first impact

$$v_1^2 - u^2 = 2gH$$

$$\Rightarrow \quad v_1 = \sqrt{2gH}. \qquad \text{...(i)}$$

The velocity of rebound is given by $v_2 = e\sqrt{2gH}$.

The new height upto which ball will rise is

$$v'^2 - v_2^2 = -2gh_1$$

$$e^2 \cdot 2gH = 2gh_1$$

$$e^2H = h_1 \qquad \text{...(ii)}$$

Now the ball makes second impact on floor with velocity v_2, and rebounds with velocity ev_2. So the new height h_2 to which ball rises is

$$0 - e^2v_2^2 = -2gh_2 \qquad [v^2 - u^2 = 2gH]$$

$$e^2 \cdot e^2 \cdot 2gH = 2gh_2$$

$$e^4H = h_2 \qquad \text{...(iii)}$$

Containing in same manner, the height h_3 to which ball would rise after third impact is given by

$$e^6H = h_3 \qquad \text{...(iv)}$$

System of Particles and Rotational Motion

CHAPTER 06

Important Points

01 **Centre of Mass** Centre of mass of a body is a point at which the entire mass of the body can be supposed to be concentrated.

02 Centre of mass of two particles of masse-s m_1 and m_2, having position vectors $\mathbf{r}_1$ and $\mathbf{r}_2$ is given by

$$\mathbf{r}_{CM} = \frac{m_1\mathbf{r}_1 + m_2\mathbf{r}_2}{m_1 + m_2}$$

03 For a n-particles system, $\mathbf{r}_{CM} = \dfrac{m_1\mathbf{r}_1 + m_2\mathbf{r}_2 + \ldots + m_n\mathbf{r}_n}{m_1 + m_2 + \ldots + m_n}$

04 The centre of mass of an isolated system is either at rest or it moves with a uniform velocity along a straight line.

05 **Torque** The turning effect of a force about the axis of rotation is called moment of force or torque.

06 Torque is equal to the product of the magnitude of the force and the perpendicular distance of the line of action of the force from the axis of rotation *i.e.*,

$$\tau = \mathbf{r} \times \mathbf{F}$$

07 **Angular Momentum** The moment of linear momentum about the axis of rotation is called angular momentum. It is denoted by **L**.

$$\mathbf{L} = \mathbf{r} \times \mathbf{p} \text{ or } L = mvr$$

Its unit is joule-second.

08 Relation between torque and angular momentum is given by

$$\tau = \frac{d\mathbf{L}}{dt}$$

09 **Law of Conservation of Angular Momentum** If the total external torque acting on a system is zero, then its angular momentum remains conserved *i.e.*, when $\tau_{ext} = 0$

then, $L = \text{constant}$

10 **Moment of Inertia** The moment of inertia of a body is equal to the sum of the products of masses of its various particles and the square of their distances from axis of rotation *i.e.*,

$$I = m_1r_1^2 + m_2r_2^2 + m_3r_3^2 + \ldots + m_nr_n^2$$
$$= \sum_i m_ir_i^2$$

Its SI unit is kg-m^2.

11 **Radius of Gyration** $K = \sqrt{\frac{I}{M}}$

where, I is the moment of inertia and M is the mass of the body.

12 **Theorem of Perpendicular Axis** The moment of inertia of a plane lamina about an axis perpendicular to its plane is equal to the sum of the moments of inertia of the lamina about any two mutually perpendicular axes in its plane and intersecting each other at the point, where the perpendicular axis passes through the lamina *i.e.*,

$$I_Z = I_X + I_Y$$

13 **Theorem of Parallel Axis** The moment of inertia of a rigid body about any axis is equal to the moment of inertia of the body about a parallel axis through its centre of mass plus the product of the mass of the body and the square of the perpendicular distance between the axes.

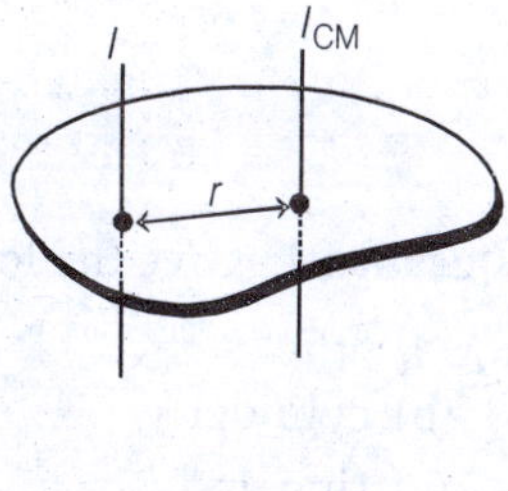

i.e., $I = I_{CM} + MR^2$

14 **Moment of Inertia**

(a) Moment of inertia of a rod about an axis passing through its centre of mass and perpendicular to its length *i.e.*,

$$I = \frac{Ml^2}{12}$$

(b) Moment of inertia of a circular ring about an axis passing through its centre and perpendicular to its plane, $I = MR^2$

(c) Moment of inertia of a circular ring along the diameter

$$I = \frac{1}{2}MR^2$$

(d) Moment of inertia of a right circular solid cylinder about its axis of symmetry, $I = \frac{1}{2}MR^2$

(e) Moment of inertia of a right circular hollow cylinder about its axis of symmetry,

$$I = MR^2$$

(f) Moment of inertia of a solid sphere about any of its diameter,

$$I = \frac{2}{5}MR^2$$

(g) Moment of inertia of a hollow sphere about its any diameter

$$I = \frac{2}{3}MR^2$$

15 **Kinetic Energy of Rotation** $K = \frac{1}{2}I\omega^2$

where I and ω are moment of inertia and angular velocity respectively.

16 Relation between torque and moment of inertia is given by, $\tau = I\alpha$ where, α is the angular acceleration.

Exercises

Question 1 Give the location of the centre of mass of a

(a) sphere,

(b) cylinder,

(c) ring and

(d) cube each of uniform mass density.

Does the centre of mass of a body necessarily lie inside the body?

Sol.

(a) Centre of mass of a sphere lies at its geometrical centre.

(b) Centre of mass of a cylinder lies at its geometrical centre *i.e.*, at the mid-point of its axis of symmetry.

(c) Centre of mass of a ring lies at its geometrical centre.

(d) Centre of mass of a cube lies at its geometrical centre *i.e.*, at the point of intersection of its diagonals.

No, it does not necessary that centre of mass of a body lie inside it, because in some cases such as a ring, a hollow cylinder, a hollow sphere and a hollow cube, centre of mass lies outside.

Question 2 In the HCl molecule, the separation between the nuclei of the two atoms is about 1.27 Å (1 Å $= 10^{-10}$ m). Find the approximate location of the centre of mass of the molecule, given that a chlorine atom is about 35.5 times as massive as a hydrogen atom and nearly all the mass of an atom is concentrated in its nucleus.

◎ ***Thinking Process*** If two masses m_1 and m_2 have position vectors $\mathbf{r}_1$ and $\mathbf{r}_2$ then position vector of centre of mass of the system is given by

$$\mathbf{r}_{CM} = \frac{m_1 \mathbf{r}_1 + m_2 \mathbf{r}_2}{m_1 + m_2}$$

Sol. Given, separation between the nuclei of H and Cl = 1.27Å

$$= 1.27 \times 10^{-10} \text{ m}$$

Let mass of hydrogen atom = m

∴ Mass of chlorine atom = $35.5m$

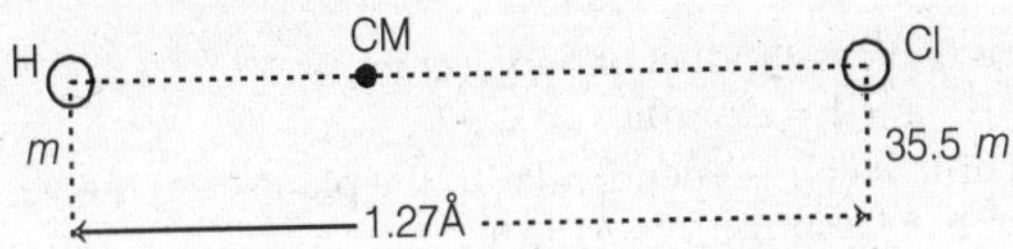

Let hydrogen atom be at origin *i.e.*, position vector of it, $r_1 = 0$

∴ Position vector of chlorine atom, $r_2 = 1.27 \times 10^{-10}$ m

Position vector of centre of mass is given by

$$r_{CM} = \frac{m_1 r_1 + m_2 r_2}{m_1 + m_2} = \frac{m \times 0 + 35.5m \times 1.27 \times 10^{-10}}{m + 35.5m}$$

$$= \frac{35.5 \times 1.27 \times 10^{-10}}{36.5}$$

$$= 1.235 \times 10^{-10} \text{ m} = 1.24 \text{ Å}$$

From hydrogen atom on the line joining H and Cl atoms.

Question 3 A child sits stationary at one end of a long trolley moving uniformly with a speed v on a smooth horizontal floor. If the child gets up and runs about on the trolley in any manner, what is the speed of centre of mass of the (trolley + child) system?

Sol. The speed of centre of mass of the (trolley + child) system will remain unchanged *i.e.* v, because the state of any system can be changed only by external force and the forces involved in running on the trolley are internal forces.

Note In absence of any external force, velocity of centre of mass remains the same.

Question 4 Show tha area of the triangle contained between the vectors $\mathbf{a}$ and $\mathbf{b}$ is one-ı f of the magnitude of $\mathbf{a} \times \mathbf{b}$.

Sol. Let the vectors $\mathbf{a}$ and $\mathbf{b}$ represent the two adjacent sides of the triangle OAB and angle between them be θ. The height of the triangle be h.

$\therefore \quad OA = a, OB = b, AC = h$ and $\angle AOB = \theta$

In ΔOCA, $\quad \sin\theta = \dfrac{AC}{OA}$ or $AC = OA\sin\theta$

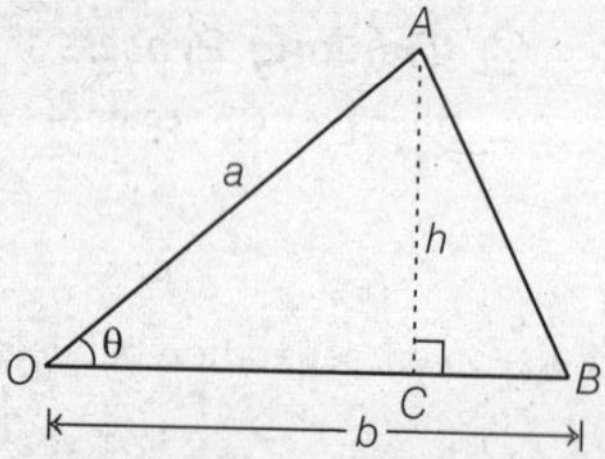

$$h = a\sin\theta$$

$$\text{Area of } \Delta OAB = \frac{1}{2} \times \text{Base} \times \text{Height}$$

$$= \frac{1}{2} \times OB \times AC$$

$$= \frac{1}{2} \times b \times a\sin\theta$$

$$= \frac{1}{2} ab\sin\theta \quad \text{...(i)}$$

By the definition of cross-product of two vectors,

$$\mathbf{a} \times \mathbf{b} = ab\sin\theta\hat{\mathbf{n}}$$

where, $\hat{\mathbf{n}}$ is the unit vector perpendicular to the plane carrying vectors $\mathbf{a}$ and $\mathbf{b}$.

Now, $\quad |\mathbf{a} \times \mathbf{b}| = |ab\sin\theta\, \hat{\mathbf{n}}| \quad = ab\sin\theta$

$|\hat{\mathbf{n}}| = 1)$ ...(ii)

From Eqs. (i) and (ii),

Area of $\Delta CAB = \frac{1}{2}|\mathbf{a} \times \mathbf{b}| = \frac{1}{2}$ |magnitude of $(\mathbf{a} \times \mathbf{b})$|

Question 5 Show that $\mathbf{a} \cdot (\mathbf{b} \times \mathbf{c})$ is equal in magnitude to the volume of the parallelopiped formed on the three vectors $\mathbf{a}$, $\mathbf{b}$ and $\mathbf{c}$.

Sol. Let a parallelopiped be formed of three vectors $\mathbf{OA} = \mathbf{a}, \mathbf{OB} = \mathbf{b}$ and $\mathbf{OC} = \mathbf{c}$.

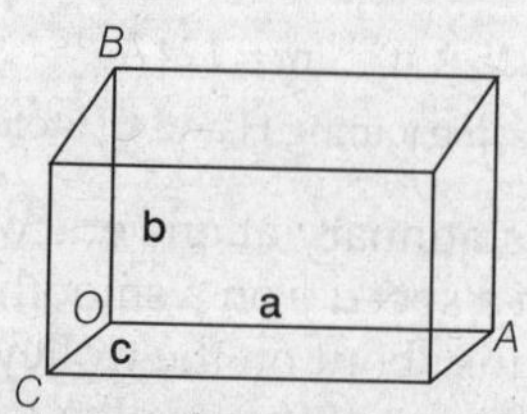

Cross product of vector $\mathbf{b}$ and $\mathbf{c}$ is given by, $(\mathbf{b} \times \mathbf{c}) = bc\sin 90^\circ \cdot \hat{\mathbf{n}} = bc\, \hat{\mathbf{n}}$

where, $\hat{\mathbf{n}}$ is a unit vector along $\mathbf{OA}$, perpendicular to the plane containing $\mathbf{b}$ and $\mathbf{c}$.

$\therefore$ $$\mathbf{a}\cdot(\mathbf{b}\times\mathbf{c}) = \mathbf{a}\cdot(bc\,\hat{\mathbf{n}}) = a(bc)\cos 0^\circ = abc$$

which is equal to the magnitude of the volume of the parallelopiped.

Question 6 (a) Find the components along *X*, *Y* and *Z*-axes of the angular momentum **L** of a particle, whose position vector is **r** with components *x*, *y* and *z* and momentum is **p** with components p_x, p_y and p_z.

(b) Show that if the particle moves only in *X*-*Y* plane, the angular momentum has only a *z*-component.

Sol.

(a) Let a particle be at a point *P*, having position vector **r** and linear momentum **p**.

In Cartesian coordinates, $\mathbf{r} = x\,\hat{\mathbf{i}} + y\,\hat{\mathbf{j}} + z\,\hat{\mathbf{k}}$ and $\mathbf{p} = p_x\,\hat{\mathbf{i}} + p_y\,\hat{\mathbf{j}} + p_z\,\hat{\mathbf{k}}$

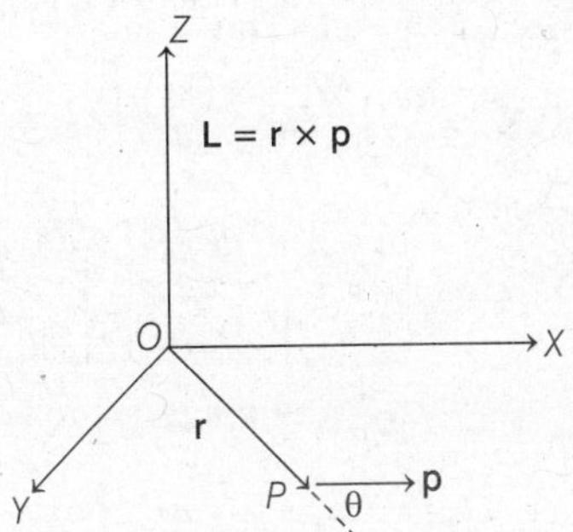

Angular momentum of the particle $\mathbf{L} = \mathbf{r}\times\mathbf{p}$

$$= (x\hat{\mathbf{i}} + y\hat{\mathbf{j}} + z\hat{\mathbf{k}}) \times (p_x\,\hat{\mathbf{i}} + p_y\,\hat{\mathbf{j}} + p_z\,\hat{\mathbf{k}})$$

$$= \begin{vmatrix} \hat{\mathbf{i}} & \hat{\mathbf{j}} & \hat{\mathbf{k}} \\ x & y & z \\ p_x & p_y & p_z \end{vmatrix}$$

If components of **L** along *X*, *Y* and *Z*-axes are L_x, L_y and L_z, then

$$L_x\,\hat{\mathbf{i}} + L_y\,\hat{\mathbf{j}} + L_z\,\hat{\mathbf{k}} = \hat{\mathbf{i}}(yp_z - zp_y) - \hat{\mathbf{j}}(xp_z - zp_x) + \hat{\mathbf{k}}(xp_y - yp_x)$$

Comparing on both sides, we get

$$L_x = yp_z - zp_y,\; L_y = zp_x - xp_z$$
$$L_z = xp_y - yp_x$$

(b) According to the question, particle moves only in X-Y plane.

$\therefore$ The torque experienced by a particle moving in X-Y plane is given by

$$\tau_z = xF_y - yF_x \quad \text{...(i)}$$

where τ_z is the component of torque acting along Z-axis on the particle moving in X-Y plane.

Let m be the mass of the particle having velocity v in X-Y plane and v_x and v_y be its velocity components along X and Y-axes respectively.

From the Newton's second law of motion,

$$F_x = \frac{d}{dt}(p_x) = \frac{d}{dx}(mv_x) = m\frac{dv_x}{dt}$$

and $$F_y = \frac{d}{dt}(p_y) = m\frac{dv_y}{dt}$$

Putting this value in Eq. (i), we get

$$\tau_z = xm\frac{d}{dt}(v_y) - ym\frac{d}{dt}(y_x)$$

$$= m\left[x\frac{dv_y}{dt} - \frac{dv_x}{dt}y\right] \quad \text{...(ii)}$$

Now $$\frac{d}{dt}(xv_y - yv_x) = \frac{d}{dt}(xv_y) - \frac{d}{dt}(yv_x)$$

$$= \left[x\frac{d}{dt}v_y + v_y\frac{d}{dt}x\right] - \left[y\frac{d}{dt}v_x + v_x\frac{d}{dt}y\right]$$

$$= x\frac{d}{dt}v_y + v_xv_y - y\frac{d}{dt}v_x - v_xv_y$$

$$= x\frac{d}{dt}v_y - y\frac{d}{dt}v_x \quad \text{...(iii)}$$

From Eqs. (ii) and (iii), we get

$$\tau_z = m\frac{d}{dt}(xv_y - yv_x)$$

$$= \frac{d}{dt}(xmv_y - ymv_x) \quad \text{...(iv)}$$

$\because$ $$p_y = mv_y \text{ and } p_x = mv_x \quad (\because \text{momentum } p = mv)$$

$\therefore$ $$\tau_z = \frac{d}{dt}(xp_y - yp_x)$$

$$\tau_z = \frac{d}{dt}L_z \quad \text{[From part (a) of Eq. (ii)]}$$

Hence, we conclude that a particle moving in X-Y plane has only one component of **L** *i.e.*, L_z acting along Z-axis.

Question 7 Two particles, each of mass m and speed v, travel in opposite directions along parallel lines separated by a distance d. Show that the vector angular momentum of the two particle system is the same whatever be the point about which the angular momentum is taken.

Sol. Given, mass of each particle = m

Speed of each particle = v

Particles are moving in opposite directions along two parallel lines separated by a distance d.

Let P_1 and P_2 be the positions of the particles at any instant t.

Let $\mathbf{L}_1$, $\mathbf{L}_2$ and $\mathbf{r}_1$, $\mathbf{r}_2$ are the angular momenta and position vectors of the particles at that instant about any arbitrary point O.

Angular momentum of the particles,

$$\mathbf{L}_1 = \mathbf{r}_1 \times m\mathbf{v} \quad \text{and} \quad \mathbf{L}_2 = \mathbf{r}_2 \times m\mathbf{v}$$

If resultant angular momentum of the system is $\mathbf{L}$, then

$$\mathbf{L} = \mathbf{L}_1 + \mathbf{L}_2 = \mathbf{r}_1 \times m\mathbf{v} + (-\mathbf{r}_2 \times m\mathbf{v})$$

Negative sign shows that both particles are moving in opposite directions.

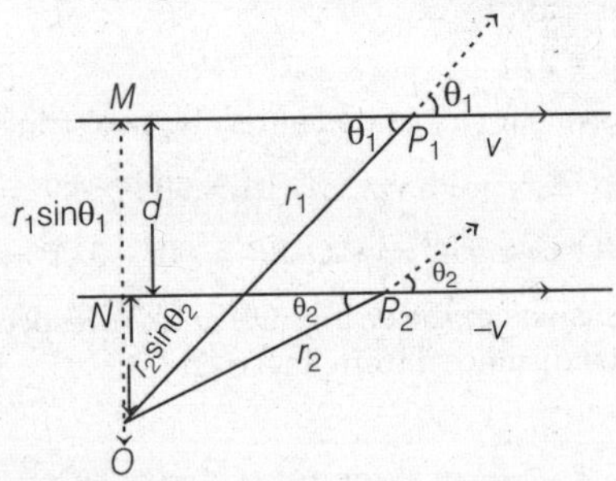

$$\therefore \quad |\mathbf{L}| = mvr_1 \sin\theta_1 - mvr_2 \sin\theta_2$$

$$= mv(r_1 \sin\theta_1 - r_2 \sin\theta_2) \quad \text{...(i)}$$

where, θ_1 and θ_2 are the angles between $\mathbf{r}_1$, $\mathbf{v}$ and $\mathbf{r}_2$, $\mathbf{v}$ respectively.

When particles changes their position with time, their direction of motion ($\mathbf{v}$) remains unchanged and therefore, distances $OM = r_1 \sin\theta_1$ and $ON = r_2 \sin\theta_2$ remains same.

But $\quad OM - ON = MN = d \quad$ (Given)

$$\therefore \quad r_1 \sin\theta_1 - r_2 \sin\theta_2 = d \quad \text{...(ii)}$$

From Eqs. (i) and (ii), we get

$$|\mathbf{L}| = mvd$$

It is constant with time.

The direction of $\mathbf{L}$ is perpendicular to the plane of $\mathbf{r}$ and $\mathbf{v}$ and is inward to the plane of paper, which also remains unchanged with time.

Therefore, the vector angular momentum ($\mathbf{L}$) of the two particle system remains same.

Question 8 A non-uniform bar of weight w is suspended at rest by two strings of negligible weight as shown in the figure. The angles made by the strings with the vertical are 36.9° and 53.1° respectively. The bar is 2 m long. Calculate the distance of the centre of gravity of the bar from its left end.

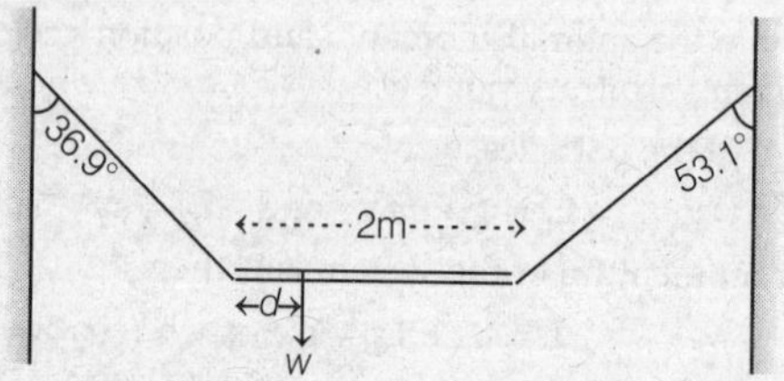

Sol. Weight of the bar = w

Length of the bar = 2 m

Let AB be a non-uniform bar suspended at rest by two strings OA and $O'B$.

Given, $\angle AOA' = 36.9° \Rightarrow \angle OAA' = 90° - 36.9° = 53.1°$

$\angle BO'B' = 53.1° \Rightarrow \angle O'BB' = 90° - 53.1° = 36.9°$

Let T_1 and T_2 be the tensions in the strings OA and OB respectively. The centre of gravity of the rod is at a distance d from its left end A.

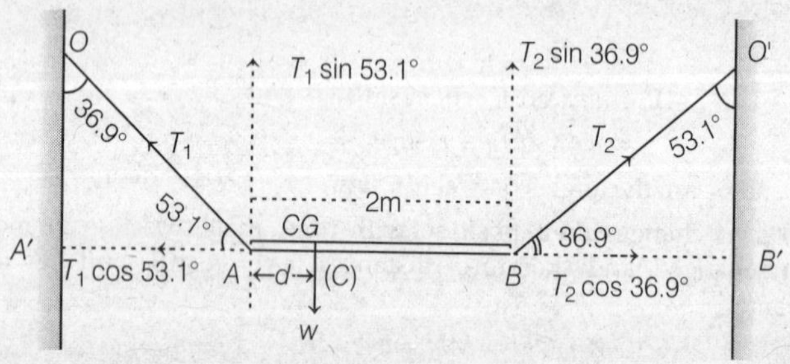

Different forces acting on the system are

(i) Tension in first string T_1 acting along the string in upward direction ($\because$ the bar pulls the string downward so tension in the string will be upward). It can be splitted into two components $T_1 \cos 53.1°$ (horizontal component) and $T_1 \sin 53.1°$ (vertical component).

(ii) Tension in second string T_2 where horizontal and vertical components are $T_2 \cos 3.69°$ and $T_2 \sin 36.9°$ respectively.

(iii) Weight of the bar w acting downward (weight of an object always acts downward).

The system is in equilibrium *i.e.*, the net force on the system is zero. It means different forces balance each other. So, horizontal forces will balance each other and vertical forces will balance each other.

$$T_1 \cos 53.1^\circ = T_2 \cos 36.9^\circ \quad \text{...(i)}$$

($\because$ horizontal forces balance each other)

Similarly vertical forces will balance each other.

Total force in upward direction = Total force in downward direction.

$$\therefore \quad T_1 \sin 53.1^\circ + T_2 \sin 36.9^\circ = w \quad \text{...(ii)}$$

Taking torque about point A, $T_2 \sin 36.9^\circ \times 2 = w \times d$

$$\text{or} \quad T_2 = \frac{wd}{2\sin 36.9^\circ} \quad \text{...(iii)}$$

Using Eqs. (ii) and (iii), we get

$$T_1 \sin 53.1^\circ = w - T_2 \sin 36.9^\circ = w - \frac{wd}{2}$$

$$\text{or} \quad T_1 = \frac{w}{\sin 53.1^\circ}\left(1 - \frac{d}{2}\right) \quad \text{...(iv)}$$

Substituting values of T_1 and T_2 from Eqs. (iii) and (iv) in Eq. (i), we get

$$\frac{w\left(1 - \frac{d}{2}\right)}{\sin 53.1^\circ} \cos 53.1^\circ = \frac{wd}{2\sin 36.9^\circ} \cdot \cos 36.9^\circ$$

$$\frac{\left(1 - \frac{d}{2}\right)}{\tan 53.1^\circ} = \frac{d}{2\tan 36.9^\circ}$$

$$\frac{\left(1 - \frac{d}{2}\right)}{1.3319} = \frac{d}{2 \times 0.7508}$$

$$1 - \frac{d}{2} = \frac{d}{2} \times \frac{1.3319}{0.7508} = \frac{d}{2} \times 1.7740$$

$$1 - 0.5d = 0.8870d \quad \text{or } 1 = 1.3870d$$

$$\text{or} \quad d = \frac{1}{1.3870} = 0.721\,\text{m} = 72.1\,\text{cm}$$

Question 9 A car of weight 1800 kg. The distance between its front and back axles is 1.8 m. Its centre of gravity is 1.05 m behind the front axle. Determine the force exerted by the level ground on each front wheel and each back wheel.

◎ ***Thinking Process*** Moment of forces about centre of gravity is zero.

Sol. Total mass of the car = 1800 kg

Let m and $(900 - m)$ kg be the masses of each front wheel and each back wheel respectively.

Distance of centre of gravity from the front axle = 1.05 m

$\therefore$ Distance of centre of gravity from the back axle = 1.80 − 1.05 = 0.75 m

Taking torque about centre of gravity, $m \times 1.05 = (900 - m) \times 0.75$

or $1.05m + 0.75m = 900 \times 0.75$ or $1.80m = 900 \times 0.75$

or $$m = \frac{900 \times 0.75}{1.80} = 375 \text{ kg}$$

$\therefore$ $(900 - m) = 900 - 375 = 525$ kg

$\therefore$ Weight of each front wheel $(w_1) = m_1 g$

$$w_1 = 375 \times 9.8 = 3675 \text{ N}$$

Force exerted by the level ground on each front wheel

= Force exerted by each front wheel on the level ground (w_1)

= 3675 N

Weight of each back wheel $(w_2) = m_2 g$

$$w_2 = 525 \times 9.8 = 5145 \text{ N}$$

$\therefore$ Force exerted by the level ground on each back wheel

= Force exerted by each back wheel on level ground (w_2)= 5145 N

Quick Solution

Let R_1 and R_2 be the reaction forces exerted by the level ground on each front and back wheels respectively.

According to Newton's third law of motion,

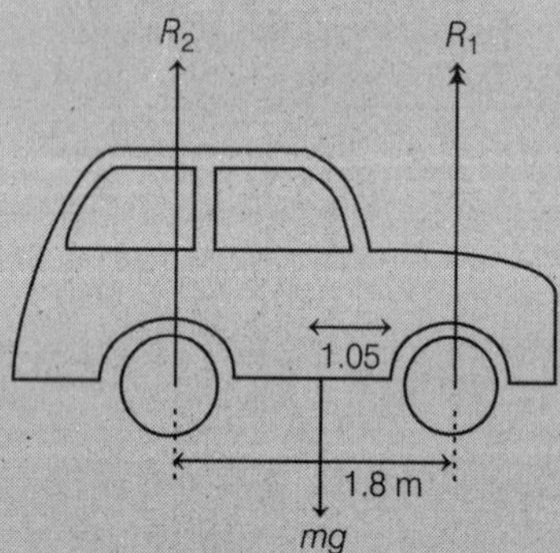

Reaction = Action

$$R_1 + R_2 = mg$$

$$R_1 + R_2 = 1800 \times 9.8 \quad \text{...(i)}$$

Distance of centre of gravity from front axle = 1.05 m

$\therefore$ Distance of centre of gravity from back axle = 1.80 − 1.05 = 0.75 m

Taking moment about centre of gravity, we get

$$R_1 \times 1.05 = R_2 \times 0.75$$

or $$R_1 = \frac{0.75}{1.05} R_2 = \frac{5}{7} R_2 \quad \text{...(ii)}$$

Substituting value of R_1 in Eq. (i), we get

$$\frac{5}{7}R_2 + R_2 = 1800 \times 9.8$$

$\therefore$ $$\frac{12}{7}R_2 = 17640.0$$

or $$R_2 = 17640 \times \frac{7}{12} = 10290\text{ N}$$

$\therefore$ Reaction force on each back wheel $= \frac{R_2}{2} = \frac{10290}{2} = 5145\text{ N}$

From Eq. (ii), we get $R_1 = \frac{5}{7} \times 10290 = 7350\text{ N}$

$\therefore$ Reaction force on each front wheel $= \frac{R_1}{2} = \frac{7350}{2} = 3675\text{ N}$

Question 10 Torques of equal magnitude are applied to a hollow cylinder and a solid sphere, both having the same mass and radius. The cylinder is free to rotate about its standard axis of symmetry and the sphere is free to rotate about an axis passing through its centre. Which of the two will acquire a greater angular speed after a given time?

Sol. Let M and R be the mass and radius of the solid sphere and hollow cylinder.

Moment of inertia of the hollow cylinder about its axis of symmetry,

$$I_1 = MR^2$$

Moment of inertia of the solid sphere about its diameter, $I_2 = \frac{2}{5}MR^2$

Let torque τ of equal magnitude be applied on hollow cylinder and solid sphere. The angular accelerations produced in it are α_1 and α_2 respectively.

$\therefore$ $$\tau = I_1\alpha_1$$

and $$\tau = I_2\alpha_2$$

Therefore, $I_1\alpha_1 = I_2\alpha_2$

or $$\frac{\alpha_1}{\alpha_2} = \frac{I_2}{I_1} = \frac{\frac{2}{5}MR^2}{MR^2} = \frac{2}{5}$$

or $$\alpha_2 = \frac{5}{2}\alpha_1$$

$$= 2.5\alpha_1 \quad \text{...(i)}$$

Let after time t, ω_1 and ω_2 be the angular speeds of the hollow cylinder and solid sphere respectively.

$\therefore$ $$\omega_1 = \omega_0 + \alpha_1 t \quad \text{...(ii)}$$

and $$\omega_2 = \omega_0 + \alpha_2 t$$

$$= \omega_0 + 2.5\alpha_1 t \quad \text{...(iii)}$$

From Eqs. (ii) and (iii), we get

$$\omega_2 > \omega_1$$

Therefore, solid sphere will acquire a greater angular speed after a given time.

Mistake Alert Student sometimes use the wrong axis for calculating the moment of inertia.

Question 11 A solid cylinder of mass 20 kg rotates about its axis with angular speed 100 rad/s. The radius of the cylinder is 0.25 m. What is the kinetic energy associated with the rotation of the cylinder? What is the magnitude of angular momentum of the cylinder about its axis?

Sol. Given, $M = 20\text{ kg}$

$\omega = 100\text{ rad/s}$

$R = 0.25\text{ m}$

Moment of inertia of the solid cylinder about its axis of symmetry,

$$I = \frac{1}{2}MR^2 = \frac{1}{2} \times 20 \times (0.25)^2$$

$$= 10 \times 0.0625 = 0.625\text{ kg-m}^2$$

Kinetic energy associated with the rotation of the cylinder is given by

$$K = \frac{1}{2}I\omega^2 = \frac{1}{2} \times 0.625 \times (100)^2$$

$$= 0.3125 \times 10000 = 3125\text{ J}$$

Angular momentum, $L = I\omega = 0.625 \times 100 = 62.5\text{ J-s}$

Question 12

(a) A child stands at the centre of a turn table with his two arms outstretched. The turn table is set rotating with an angular speed of 40 rev/min. How much is the angular speed of the child if he folds his hands back and thereby reduces his moment of inertia to 2/5 times the initial value? Assume that the turn table rotates without friction.

(b) Show that the child's new kinetic energy of rotation is more than the initial kinetic energy of rotation. How do you account for this increase in kinetic energy?

Thinking Process According to law of conservation of angular momentum, if total external torque acting on a system is zero then, its angular momentum remains conserved *i.e.*, $L = I\omega = \text{constant}$.

Sol.

(a) Given, $\omega_1 = 40\text{ rev/min}$

Let moment of inertia of the child be I.

$\therefore \quad I_1 = I \quad \text{and} \quad I_2 = \frac{2}{5}I$

According to law of conservation of angular momentum

$$I_1\omega_1 = I_2\omega_2$$

$$\therefore \quad \omega_2 = \frac{I_1}{I_2}\omega_1 = \frac{I}{\frac{2}{5}I} \times 40 = \frac{5}{2} \times 40 = 100 \text{ rad/s}$$

(b) $$\frac{\text{Final KE of rotation}}{\text{Initial KE of rotation}} = \frac{\frac{1}{2}I_2\omega_2^2}{\frac{1}{2}I_1\omega_1^2} = \frac{\left(\frac{2}{5}I\right)(100)^2}{I \times (40)^2} = \frac{2}{5} \times \frac{10000}{1600} = \frac{5}{2}$$

$\therefore$ Final KE of rotation $= \frac{5}{2}$(Initial KE of rotation)

Therefore, final KE of rotation of the child is greater than its initial KE of rotation, and it is obtained from the muscular energy of the child when he fold back his hands.

Question 13 A rope of negligible mass is wound round a hollow cylinder of mass 3 kg and radius 40 cm. What is the angular acceleration of the cylinder if the rope is pulled with a force of 30 N? What is the linear acceleration of the rope? Assuming that there is no slipping.

Sol. Given, $M = 3$ kg

$R = 40$ cm $=$ 0 m

$F = 30$ N

Moment of inertia of the hollow cylinder about its axis of symmetry

$$I = MR^2 = 3 \times (0.40)^2 = 0.48 \text{ kg-m}^2$$

Torque acting on the cylinder by the applied force,

$$\tau = F \times R = 30 \times 0.40 = 12 \text{ N-m.}$$

Angular acceleration produced in cylinder,

$$\alpha = \frac{\tau}{I} = \frac{12}{0.48} = 25 \text{ rad/s}^2$$

Linear acceleration, $a = R\alpha = 0.40 \times 25 = 10.0 \text{ m/s}^2$

Question 14 To maintain a rotor at a uniform angular speed of 200 rad/s, an engine needs to transmit a torque of 180 N-m. What is the power required by the engine?

Sol. Given, $\omega = 200$ rad/s

$\tau = 180$ N-m

Power required by the engine $(P) = \tau\omega = 180 \times 200 = 36000 \text{ W} = 36 \text{ kW}$

Note Uniform angular velocity in the absence of friction implies zero torque. In practice, applied torque is needed to counter frictional torque. Assume that the engine is 100% efficient.

Question 15 From a uniform disc of radius R, a circular section of radius $\frac{R}{2}$ is cut out. The centre of the hole is at $\frac{R}{2}$ from the centre of the original disc. Locate the centre of gravity of the resulting flat body.

Sol. Let mass per unit area of the disc be m.

$\therefore$ Mass of the disc (M) = Total area of disc $\times$ Mass per unit area $= \pi R^2 m$

Mass of the portion removed from the disc (M')

$$= \pi\left(\frac{R}{2}\right)^2 m = \frac{\pi R^2}{4} m = \frac{M}{4}$$

The centre of mass of the original disc is O and the centre of mass of the removed part is O_1 and let centre of mass of the remaining part be O_2.

According to the question, figure can be drawn as.

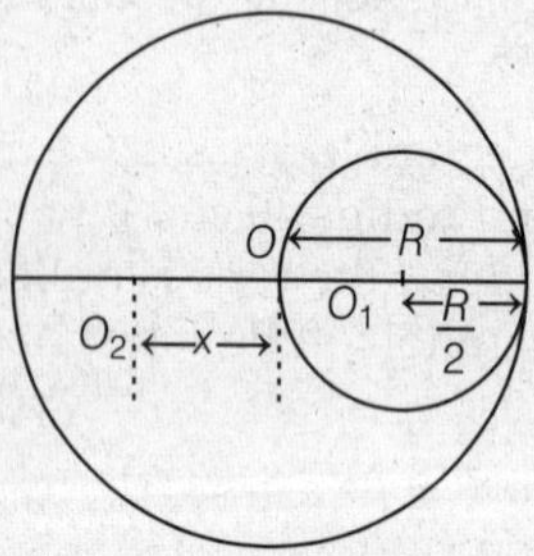

Here, $OO_1 = \frac{R}{2}$

The remaining portion of the disc can be considered as a system of two masses M at O and $-M' = -\frac{M}{4}$ at O_1.

If the distance of the centre of mass of the remaining part from the centre O is at a distance x, then

$$x = \frac{M \times 0 - M' \times \frac{R}{2}}{M - M'} = \frac{-\frac{M}{4} \times \frac{R}{2}}{M - \frac{M}{4}} = -\frac{MR}{8} \times \frac{4}{3M} = -\frac{R}{6}$$

Therefore, centre of mass of the remaining part is at $\frac{R}{6}$ to the left of centre O.

Mistake Alert Student sometimes forget to account the change in distribution of mass.

Question 16 A metre stick is balanced on a knife edge at its centre. When two coins, each of mass 5 g are put one on top of the other at the 12 cm mark, the stick is found to be balanced at 45.0 cm. What is the mass of the metre stick?

Sol. Let total mass of the metre stick be M kg.

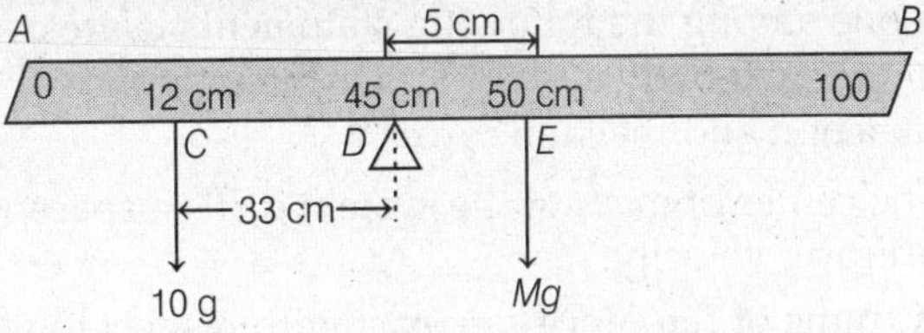

Distance between mid-point E and new centre of gravity (DE),

$$= 50 - 45 = 5 \text{ cm}$$

Distance between 12 cm mark and new centre of gravity (CD),

$$= 45 - 12 = 33 \text{ cm}$$

From principle of moments in equilibrium,

$$Mg \times DE = (2 \times 5g) \times CD$$

$$M \times 5 = 10 \times 33 \text{ or } M = 66 \text{ g}$$

$\therefore$ Mass of the metre stick is 66 g.

Question 17 The oxygen molecule has a mass of 5.30×10^{-26} kg and a moment of inertia of 1.94×10^{-46} kg-m^2 about an axis through its centre perpendicular to the lines joining the two atoms. Suppose the mean speed of such a molecule in a gas is 500 m/s and that is KE of rotation is $\frac{2}{3}$ of its KE translation. Find the average angular velocity of the molecule.

Sol. Mass of oxygen molecule $(M) = 5.30 \times 10^{-26}$ kg

Moment of inertia $I = 1.94 \times 10^{-46}$ kg-m^2

Mean speed of the molecule $(v) = 500$ m/s

Given, KE of rotation $= \frac{2}{3} \times$ KE of translation

$$\frac{1}{2} I\omega^2 = \frac{2}{3} \times \frac{1}{2} Mv^2$$

or

$$\omega = \sqrt{\frac{2Mv^2}{3I}} = \sqrt{\frac{2 \times 5.30 \times 10^{-26} \times (500)^2}{3 \times 1.94 \times 10^{-46}}}$$

$$= 1.35 \times 10^{10} \times 500$$

$$= 6.75 \times 10^{12} \text{ rad/s}$$

DIKSHA APP Questions

☐ Multiple Choice Questions

Q.1 Which one among the following statements is/are correct with respect to a two-body system under the influence of their mutual action and reaction forces ?

(p) The center of mass of the system drift in space with uniform velocity.

(q) A frame of reference can exist with respect to which the center of mass remain's at rest.

(r) The two equations representing the motion of two bodies can be reduced to a single equation in terms of the relative coordinates of the two bodies.

(a) Only (p)
(b) Only (q)
(c) All three (p), (q), and (r)
(d) (p) and (q) but not (r)

Sol. (c) Because the motion of the center of mass remains unaffected in th absence of external unbalanced forces.

Q.2 For a two particle system with masses 1 kg and 2 kg, the velocity of the first particle about the center of mass is 2 m/s along a straight line *AB*. The velocity of the second particle about the centre of mass will be

(a) 1 m/s along *AB*
(b) 1 m/s along *BA*
(c) 2 m/s along *AB*
(d) 2 m/s along *BA*

Sol. (b) Given, $m_1 = 1\,\text{kg}$

$$m_2 = 2\,\text{kg}$$

$$v_1 = 2\,\text{m/s}$$

$$v_2 = ?$$

We know that

$$m_1\mathbf{v}'_1 + m_2\mathbf{v}'_2 = 0$$

$$\therefore \quad \mathbf{v}'_2 = \frac{m_1}{m_2}\mathbf{v}_1 = \frac{-1}{2}\cdot 2\hat{\mathbf{AB}}\,\text{m/s}$$

$$= 1\,\text{m/s along } BA.$$

Q.3 A bomb is thrown and it explodes while moving in its trajectory. The center of mass of the fragments after exlusion will follows a/an

(a) parabolic path
(b) elliptical path
(c) linear path
(d) hyperbolic path

Sol. (a) In absence of any external force the path of center of mass remains same. Here, the original path of bomb is parabolic in nature.

Q.4 If w_1, w_2 and w_3 are the angular speeds of the seconds hand, minute hand and hour hand respectively of a watch, then $w_1 : w_2 : w_3$ is equal to

(a) 360 : 6 : 1 (b) 360 : 12 : 1
(c) 720 : 10 : 1 (d) 720 : 12 : 1

Sol. (d) $w = \frac{2\pi}{T}$ where T is time period so,

$$w_1 = \frac{2\pi}{60} \text{ rad/s}, \; w_2 = \frac{2\pi}{60 \times 60} \text{ rad/s.}$$

$$w_3 = \frac{2\pi}{12 \times 60 \times 60} \text{ rad/s.}$$

$$\therefore \quad w_1 : w_2 : w_3 = \frac{2\pi}{60} : \frac{2\pi}{60 \times 60} : \frac{2\pi}{12 \times 60 \times 60}$$

$$= 1 : \frac{1}{60} : \frac{1}{12 \times 60}$$

$$= 720 : 12 : 1$$

Q.5 A body rotating about an axis has an initial angular velocity w_0 and angular acceleration α. The angle described by it during the tenth second is

(a) $w_0 + 9.5\alpha$ (b) $w_0 + 4\alpha$
(c) $5(w_0 + \alpha)$ (d) $5w_0 + 4\alpha$

Sol. (a) Using equations of rotational motion, $\theta = w_0 t + \frac{1}{2}\alpha t^2$.

$$\theta_n = \theta_{10} - \theta_9 = 10\omega_0 + \frac{1}{2}\alpha(10)^2 - 9\omega_0 - \frac{1}{2}\alpha(9)^2$$

$$= \omega_0 + \frac{\alpha}{2}(100 - 81) = \omega_0 + 9.5\alpha$$

Q.6 A body executing uniformly accelerated circular motion describes 8π radian during the first 2 seconds and 30π radian in the first 6 seconds. What is the number of revolutions undergone by the body in 10 seconds?

(a) 10 (b) 20 (c) 30 (d) 40

Sol. (c) Using equations $w_0 t + \frac{1}{2}\alpha t^2 = \theta$

Now $8\pi = 2w_0 + 2\alpha$ ....(i)

and $30\pi = 6w_0 + 18\alpha$ ...(ii)

An solving we get $\alpha = \frac{\pi}{2}$ rad/ sec and $w_0 = \frac{7\pi}{2}$ rad/sec.

Angle describe in 10 seconds.

$$\theta = w_0 t + \frac{1}{2}\alpha t^2$$

$$= \frac{7\pi}{2} \times 10 + \frac{1}{2} \times \frac{\pi}{2} \times 100 = 60\pi$$

Number of revolutions $= \frac{60\pi}{2\pi} = 30.$

Q.7 Given below are three statements about the moment of a couple

(p) Its value does not depend on the location of the fulcrum.

(q) Its value depends on the location of the fulcrum.

(r) Its value becomes zero if the fulcrum point lies on the line of action of any of the forces constituting the couple which among the following is/are true?

(a) only (p) (b) only (q)

(c) only (r) (d) (q) and (r)

Sol. (a) Let O be the point of fulcrum.

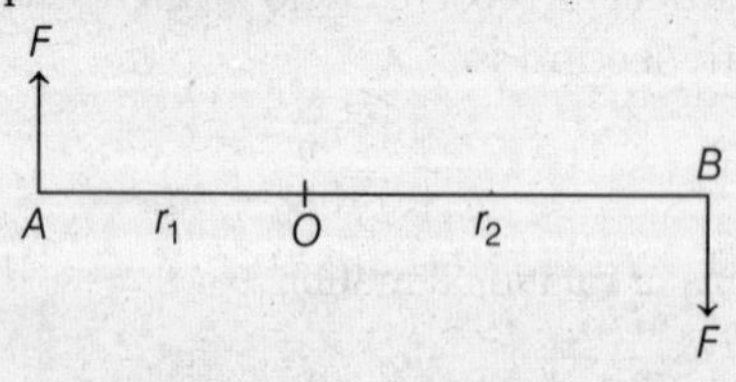

Moment about O is given by

$$r_1 \times (F) + r_2 \times F = (r_1 + r_2) \times F = AB \times F$$

So, it is independent of the choice of origin O.

Q.8 A circular plate of radius R has a mass M. Its moment of inertia about one of its diameter is

(a) MR^2 (b) $\frac{1}{4}MR^2$

(c) $\frac{1}{3}MR^2$ (d) $\frac{1}{2}MR^2$

Sol. (b) Let I_1 and I_2 are the MI about two perpendicular diameters then

$$I_1 + I_2 = \frac{1}{2}MR^2$$

As $$I_1 = I_2 \text{ so } I_1 = \frac{1}{4}MR^2$$

Q.9 Four bodies (a hollow cylinder, a solid cylinder, a hollow sphere, a solid sphere) each of the same radius, are made to roll without slipping down an inclined plane. If the velocities of the bodies on reaching the base are v_1, v_2, v_3 and v_4 respectively then

(a) $v_3 > v_2 > v_4 > v_1$ (b) $v_3 > v_4 > v_2 > v_1$

(c) $v_4 > v_3 > v_2 > v_1$ (d) $v_4 > v_2 > v_3 > v_1$

Sol. (d) Using law of conservation of energy

$$\frac{1}{2}mv^2 + \frac{1}{2}Iw^2 = mgh$$

$$\frac{1}{2}mv^2 + \frac{1}{2}mk^2\frac{v^2}{r^2} = mgh$$

$$\frac{v^2}{2}\left[1 + \frac{k^2}{r^2}\right] = gh$$

$$v^2 = \frac{2gh}{1 + \frac{k^2}{r^2}} \quad \text{...(i)}$$

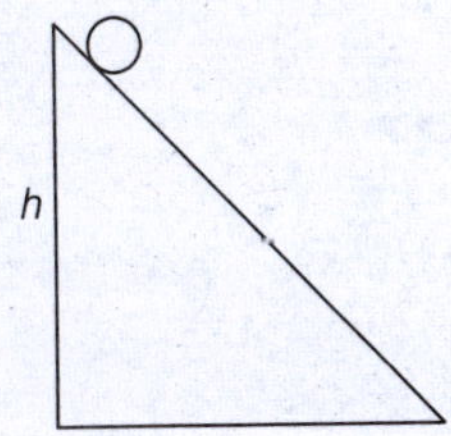

For hollow cylinder, $\frac{1}{1 + \frac{k^2}{r^2}} = \frac{1}{2} = 0.5$

For solid cylinder, $\frac{1}{1 + \frac{k^2}{r^2}} = \frac{2}{3} = 0.67$

For hollow sphere, $\frac{1}{1 + \frac{k^2}{r^2}} = \frac{3}{5} = 0.6$

and for solid sphere, $\frac{1}{1 + \frac{k^2}{r^2}} = \frac{5}{7} = 0.71$

So, $$v_4 > v_2 > v_3 > v_1$$

Q.10 A young girl stands at the center of a turn table with her two arms outstretched. The turn table is set into rotation with an angular speed of 60 rev/min. How much is the angular speed of the girl, if she folds her hands back and there by reduces her moment of inertia to 60% of its initial value ? Assume that the turn-table rotates without friction.

(a) $\frac{2\pi}{5}$ rad/s

(b) $\frac{5\pi}{4}$ rad/s

(c) $\frac{10\pi}{3}$ rad/s

(d) $\frac{12\pi}{3}$ rad/s

Sol. (c) Using law of conservation of angular momentum

$$I_1 w_1 = I_2 w_2$$

$$I \times 60 \times 2\pi = \frac{60I}{100} w_2$$

$$2\pi \times 100 \text{ rev/min} = w_2$$

$$w_2 = 2\pi \times \frac{100}{60} \frac{\text{rev}}{\text{sec}} = \frac{10\pi}{3} \text{ rad/s}$$

Gravitation

CHAPTER 07

Important Points

01 **Gravitation** Every object in the universe attracts every other object with a force, which is called the force of gravitation.

02 **Newton's Law of Gravitation** The gravitational force acting between two point objects is directly proportional to the product of their masses and inversely proportional to the square of the distance between them, *i.e.*,

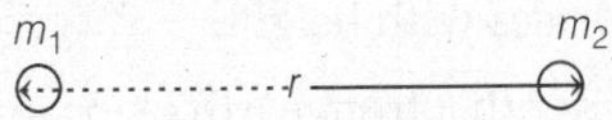

$$F \propto \frac{m_1 m_2}{r^2}$$

or $$F = G\frac{m_1 m_2}{r^2}$$

where, G is the universal gravitational constant.

03 The value of G is 6.67×10^{-11} N-m^2/kg^2 and remains the same throughout the universe.

04 Gravitational force is a central as well as conservative force and it is the weakest fundamental force in nature.

05 **Acceleration due to Gravity** The time rate of change of velocity of a freely falling body under gravity is called acceleration due to gravity (g). It always acts towards the centre of earth.

06 Relation between g and G is given by $g = \frac{GM_e}{R_e^2}$

where, M_e and R_e are the mass and radius of the Earth respectively.

07 If ω is the angular velocity of rotation of earth about its own axis then acceleration due to gravity at any place on earth

$$g' = g - R_e\omega^2 \cos^2 \lambda$$

where, λ is the latitude of that place.

08 At equator $\lambda = 0°$

$\therefore$ $g' = g - R_e\omega^2$

At poles $\lambda = 90°$

$\therefore$ $g' = g$

09 Therefore, acceleration due to gravity is maximum at poles and minimum at the equator on earth.

10 The value of g at height h from earth's surface is given by

$$g' = \frac{g}{\left(1 + \frac{h}{R_e}\right)^2}$$

Therefore, g decreases with height.

11 The value of g at depth h from earth's surface is given by

$$g' = g\left(1 - \frac{h}{R_e}\right)$$

Therefore, g decreases with depth and becomes zero at the earth's centre.

12 **Intensity of Gravitational Field** The gravitational force acting per unit mass at any point in gravitation field is called intensity of gravitational field

It is given by

$$I \text{ or } E_g = \frac{F}{m}$$

Its unit is N/Kg.

13 Intensity of the gravitational field at a distance r from a body of mass M is given by

$$I \text{ or } E_g = \frac{GM}{r^2}$$

14 **Gravitational Potential** At any point, the gravitational potential is equal to the work done per unit mass in bringing a very light body from infinity to that point in the gravitational field.

$$V_g = \frac{W}{m} = -\frac{GM}{r}$$

Its unit is J/kg.

15 Gravitational potential energy between two masses m_1 and m_2 separated by a distance r, is given by

$$U = -\frac{Gm_1m_2}{r}$$

16 A satellite is a celestial object that revolve around a planet due to gravitational attraction.

17 Artificial satellites are of two types

(i) geostationary or parking satellites

(ii) polar satellites

18 Orbital velocity of a satellite is given by

$$v_o = \sqrt{\frac{GM_e}{r}} = R_e\sqrt{\frac{g}{(R_e + h)}}$$

where, M_e = Mass of the earth, R_e = Radius of the earth

h = Height of the satellite from earth surface

19 When a satellite revolve near the earth's surface, then its orbital velocity

$$v_o = \sqrt{gR} \approx 7.92 \text{ km/h(s)}$$

20 Time period of a satellite

$$T = 2\pi\sqrt{\frac{r^3}{GM_e}} = \frac{2\pi}{R}\sqrt{\frac{(R_e + h)^3}{g}} \qquad \left(\because g = \frac{GM_e}{R_e^2}\right)$$

21 When a satellite revolves near the earth's surface, then the time period is given by

$$T = 2\pi\sqrt{\frac{R_e}{g}} \approx 84.6 \text{ min}$$

22 Total energy of a satellite $(E) = -\frac{GM_em}{2r}$

22 Binding energy of a satellite is the minimum energy required to remove a satellite from its orbit around the earth (planet) to infinity.

Binding energy of a satellite $= -\frac{GM_em}{2r}$

24 Escape Velocity The minimum velocity with which a body must be projected vertically upwards from the earth's surface, so that it just escapes the earth's gravitational field and never returns.

25 Escape velocity $(v_e) = \sqrt{\frac{2GM_e}{R}} = \sqrt{2gR_e}$

26 Escape velocity at earth is 11.2 km/s.

27 Kepler's Laws of Planetary Motion

(i) **Law of Orbit** Every planet revolves around the Sun in an elliptical orbit with the sun is at its one of the focus.

(ii) **Law of Area** The areal velocity of any planet around the sun is constant *i.e.*,

$$\frac{d\mathbf{A}}{dt} = \frac{\mathbf{L}}{2m} = \text{constant}$$

(iii) **Law of Period** The square of the time period of revolution of a planet around the sun is directly proportional to the cube of semi-major axis of its elliptical orbit, *i.e*,

$$T^2 \propto a^3$$

where, a = semi-major axis of the elliptical orbit.

Exercises

Question 1 Answer the following

(a) You can shield a charge from electrical forces by putting it inside a hollow conductor. Can you shield a body from gravitational influence of nearby matter by putting it inside a hollow sphere or by some other means?

(b) An astronaut inside a small spaceship orbiting around the earth cannot detect gravity. If the space station orbiting around the earth has a large size can he hope to detect gravity?

(c) If you compare the gravitational force on the earth due to the sun to that due to the moon, you would find that the sun's pull is greater than moon's pull. (You can check this yourself using the data available in the succeeding exercises). However, the tidal effect of the moon's pull is greater than the tidal effect of the sun, why?

Sol.

(a) No, any body cannot be shield from gravitational influence of nearby matter by putting it inside a hollow sphere because gravitational forces does not depend upon the nature of the intervening medium, while electrical forces depends upon the nature of the intervening medium.

(b) Yes, an astronaut can hope to detect gravity if the size of the spaceship is very large because in this condition the magnitude of the gravity of the spaceship will become appreciable and may become measurable.

(c) Tidal effect is not governed by the inverse square law of the gravitational force, but it inversely proportional to the cube of the distance.
Earth-moon distance is very small as compared to the earth-sun distance. Therefore, tidal effect of moon is more effective than the tidal effect of sun.

Question 2 Choose the correct alternatives.

(a) Acceleration due to gravity increases/decreases with increasing altitude.

(b) Acceleration due to gravity increases/decreases with increasing depth (assume the earth to be a sphere of uniform density).

(c) Acceleration due to gravity is independent of the mass of the earth/mass of the body.

(d) The formula $-GMm\left(\frac{1}{r_2}-\frac{1}{r_1}\right)$ is more/less accurate than the formula $mg(r_2 - r_1)$ for the difference of potential energy between two points r_2 and r_1 distance away from the centre of earth.

Sol.

(a) Acceleration due to gravity at altitude h from earth's surface is given by

$$g' = \frac{g}{\left(1+\frac{h}{R_e}\right)^2}$$

where R_e is the radius of the earth.

Therefore, acceleration due to gravity **decreases** with increasing altitude.

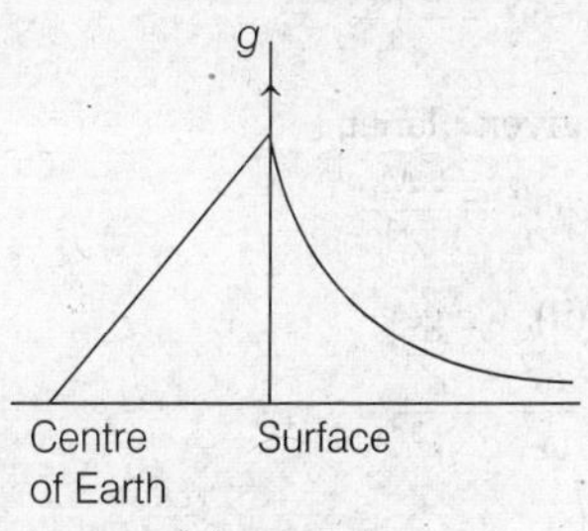

(b) Acceleration due to gravity at depth x from earth's surface is given by

$$g' = g\left(1 - \frac{x}{R_e}\right)$$

Therefore, acceleration due to gravity decreases with increasing depth.

(c) Acceleration due to gravity is independent of the mass of the body. It depends on the mass of the earth. $\left(g = \frac{GM_e}{R_e^2}\right)$

(d) The formula $-GMm\left(\frac{1}{r_2} - \frac{1}{r_1}\right)$ is more accurate than the formula $mg(r_2 - r_1)$ for the difference of potential energy between two points r_2 and r_1 distance away from the centre of earth.

Question 3 Suppose there existed a planet that went around the sun twice as fast as the earth. What would be its orbital size as compared to that of the earth?

◎ ***Thinking Process*** The centripetal force required for the orbital motion of any planet is obtained from the gravitational force between the planet and the sun, so by equating centripetal force and gravitational force we can calculate the orbital radius.

Sol. Let M_s = Mass of the sun

M_e = Mass of the earth

r = Radius of the orbit of the earth around the sun

r' = Radius of the planet around the sun

ω = Angular speed of the earth

ω' = Angular speed of the planet

The centripetal force required for the orbital motion of earth is obtained from the gravitational force between the earth and the sun.

$$\therefore \quad \frac{M_e v^2}{r} = \frac{GM_s M_e}{r^2} \text{ or } v^2 = \frac{GM_s}{r}$$

But linear velocity $v = r\omega$

$$\therefore \quad (r\omega)^2 = \frac{GM_s}{r}$$

$$\text{or} \quad \omega^2 = \frac{GM_s}{r^3} \quad \text{...(i)}$$

Similarly, for the other given planet,

$$\omega'^2 = \frac{GM_s}{r'^3} \quad \text{...(ii)}$$

Dividing Eq. (i) by Eq. (ii), we get

$$\frac{\omega^2}{\omega'^2} = \frac{r'^3}{r^3}$$

or $$r'^3 = \left(\frac{\omega}{\omega'}\right)^2 r^3$$

or $$r' = \left(\frac{\omega}{\omega'}\right)^{2/3} r \qquad \text{...(iii)}$$

But the planet went round the sun twice as fast as the earth, therefore $\omega' = 2\omega$

From Eq. (iii), we get

$$r' = \left(\frac{\omega}{2\omega}\right)^{2/3} r$$

$\therefore$ $$r' = \frac{r}{(2)^{2/3}} = \frac{r}{(4)^{1/3}}$$

$$= \frac{r}{1.587} = 0.63r$$

Therefore, the planet's orbital size is smaller than the orbital size of the Earth by a factor of 0.63.

Quick Solution

According to Kepler's third law of planetary motion

$$\left(\frac{T_e}{T_p}\right)^2 = \left(\frac{R_e}{R_p}\right)^3 \text{ or } R_p = R_e\left(\frac{T_p}{T_e}\right)^{2/3}$$

$$R_p = R_e\left(\frac{1}{2}\right)^{2/3} = 0.63\,\text{Re}$$

Question 4 I_0, one of the satellites of jupiter has an orbital period of 1.769 days and the radius of the orbit is 4.22×10^8 m. Show the mass of jupiter is about one-thousandth that of the sun.

Sol. Given, time period of a satellite of jupiter

$$T = 1.769 \text{ days}$$
$$= (1.769 \times 24 \times 60 \times 60)\text{ s}$$
$$= 1.528 \times 10^5 \text{ s}$$

Radius of orbit $(r) = 4.22 \times 10^8$ m

$G = 6.67 \times 10^{-11}$ N-m^2/kg^2

Mass of the sun $M_s = 2 \times 10^{30}$ kg

Let mass of the jupiter be m_J.

Centripetal force required for the orbital motion of the satellite

= Gravitational force between planet and satellite

$$\frac{mv^2}{r} = \frac{GM_J m}{r^2}$$

or $$v^2 = \frac{GM_J}{r}$$

$$(r\omega)^2 = \frac{GM_J}{r} \qquad (\because v = r\omega)$$

$$\therefore \quad \omega^2 = \frac{GM_J}{r^3}$$

But $\omega = \frac{2\pi}{T}$, where T is the time period.

$$\therefore \quad \left(\frac{2\pi}{T}\right)^2 = \frac{GM_J}{r^3}$$

or

$$M_J = \frac{4\pi^2 r^3}{T^2 G}$$

$$= \frac{4 \times (3.14)^2 \times (4.22 \times 10^8)^3}{(1.528 \times 10^5)^2 \times 6.67 \times 10^{-11}}$$

$$= 1.9 \times 10^{27} \text{ kg}$$

$$\approx 2 \times 10^{27} \text{ kg}$$

Now,

$$\frac{M_J}{M_s} = \frac{2 \times 10^{27}}{2 \times 10^{30}} \approx \frac{1}{1000}$$

or

$$M_J = \frac{1}{1000} M_s$$

Therefore, the mass of jupiter is about one thousandth of the mass of the sun.

> *Mistake Alert* Students sometimes forget to convert days into second.

Question 5 Let us assume that our galaxy consists of 2.5×10^{11} stars each of one solar mass. How long will a star at a distance of 50000 light years from the galactic centre take to complete one revolution? Take the diameter of the milky way to be 10^5 light years.

Sol. Number of stars in our galaxy $(N) = 2.5 \times 10^{11}$

Mass of each star (m) = One solar mass

$$= 2 \times 10^{30} \text{ kg}$$

Total mass of the stars in one galaxy $= N \times m$

$$= 2.5 \times 10^{11} \times 2 \times 10^{30}$$

$$= 5.0 \times 10^{41} \text{ kg}$$

Radius of orbit of a star r = 50000 light years

But 1 light year $= 9.46 \times 10^{15}$ m

$$\therefore \quad r = 50000 \times 9.46 \times 10^{15} \text{ m}$$

Diameter of the milky way $= 10^5$ light years.

The centripetal force required for orbital motion is obtained from the gravitational force.

$\therefore$ Centripetal force = Gravitational force

$$\therefore \quad \frac{mv^2}{r} = \frac{GMm}{r^2}$$

$$\text{or} \quad v^2 = \frac{GM}{r}$$

$$(r\omega)^2 = \frac{GM}{r} \qquad (\because v = r\omega)$$

$$\text{or} \quad \omega^2 = \frac{GM}{r^3}$$

$$\left(\frac{2\pi}{T}\right)^2 = \frac{GM}{r^3} \qquad \left(\because \omega = \frac{2\pi}{T}\right)$$

$$\text{or} \quad T^2 = \frac{4\pi^2 r^3}{GM}$$

$$T = \sqrt{\frac{4 \times (3.14)^2 \times (5 \times 9.46 \times 10^{15})^3}{6.67 \times 10^{-11} \times 5 \times 10^{41}}}$$

$$= \sqrt{12527.5 \times 10^{28}}$$

$$= 111.93 \times 10^{14} \text{ s}$$

$$= \frac{111.93 \times 10^{14}}{365 \times 24 \times 3600} \text{ yr}$$

$$= 3.55 \times 10^8 \text{ yr}$$

Question 6 Choose the correct alternative.

(a) If the zero of potential energy is at infinity, the total energy of an orbiting satellite is negative of the kinetic/potential energy.

(b) The energy required to rocket an orbiting satellite out of earth's gravitational influence is more/less than the energy required to project a stationary object at the same height (as the satellite) out of earth's influence.

Sol.

(a) Potential energy of satellite $U = \frac{-GMm}{r}$

Kinetic energy of satellite $K = \frac{GMm}{2r}$

Total energy $E = U + K$

$$= \frac{-GMm}{r} + \frac{GMm}{2r} = \frac{-GMm}{2r}$$

$$= -K$$

i.e., negative of kinetic energy.

(b) The energy required to rocket an orbiting satellite out of earth's gravitational influence is less than the energy required to project a stationary object, because in case of orbiting satellite the gravitational pull of earth acting on it is balanced by centripetal force so work is required only in rocketing it (no work is required against the gravitational pull).

Question 7 Does the escape velocity of a body from the earth depend on (a) the mass of the body, (b) the location from which it is projected, (c) the direction of projection, (d) the height of the location from where the body is launched?

Sol. Escape velocity is given by $v_e = \sqrt{\frac{2GM}{R}} = \sqrt{2gR}$.

At distance r from earth's surface the escape velocity $v_e = \sqrt{\frac{2GM}{r}}$

where, M and R are the mass and radius of the earth and r is the distance of the point of projection from earth's centre.

(a) No, from the formula it is clear that the escape velocity does not depend on the mass of the body.

(b) Yes, the escape velocity depends on the location from which it is projected, *i.e.*, on the altitude and latitude of the point of projection.

$$\text{Escape velocity } v_e = \sqrt{2gR}$$

and the value of g is different at different latitudes and altitudes.

(c) No, the escape velocity does not depend on the direction of projection.

(d) Yes, the escape velocity depends on the height of location from where the body is launched.

Question 8 A comet orbits the sun in highly elliptical orbit. Does the comet has a constant (a) linear speed, (b) angular speed, (c) angular momentum, (d) kinetic energy, (e) potential energy and (f) total energy throughout its orbit? Neglect any mass loss of the comet when it comes very close to sun.

Sol.

(a) According to law of conservation of linear momentum,
$L = mvr =$ constant, therefore the comet moves faster when it is close to the sun and moves slower when it is farther away from the sun. Therefore, the speed of the comet does not remain constant.

(b) As the linear speed varies, the angular speed also varies. Therefore, angular speed of the comet does not remain constant.

(c) As no external torque is acting on the comet, therefore, according to law of conservation of angular momentum, the angular momentum of the comet remain constant.

(d) Kinetic energy of the comet $= \frac{1}{2}mv^2$

As the linear speed of the comet changes, its kinetic energy also changes. Therefore, its KE does not remains constant.

(e) Potential energy of the comet changes as its kinetic energy changes.

(f) Only angular momentum and total energy of a comet remain constant throughout its orbit.

Mistake Alert Students sometimes use the formulas of potential energy and kinetic energy of satellite interchangeably and also forget to use proper signs with energy.

Question 9 Which of the following symptoms is likely to afflict an astronaut in space?

(a) Swollen feet (b) Swollen face

(c) Headache and (d) Orientational problem

Sol. (b), (c), (d) *i.e.*, swollen face, headache and orientational problems are the symptoms likely to afflict an astronaut in space. In space, the pressure inside the body of astronaut is higher than the outside pressure, so due to high flow of blood, astronaut can have these problems. In space, astronaut is in weight-lessness state so swallen feet may not affect his working.

Question 10 Choose the correct answer among the given ones. The gravitational intensity at the centre of a hemispherical shell of uniform mass density has the direction indicated by the arrow (see in the figure.) (i) *a*, (ii) *b*, (iii) *c*, (iv) zero.

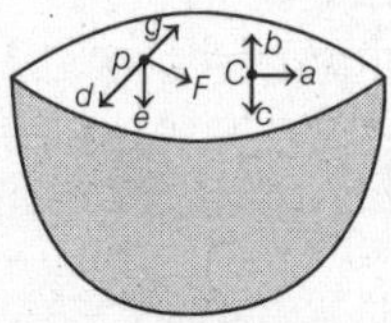

Sol. (iii) The gravitational potential is constant at all points inside a spherical shell.

∴ Gravitational potential gradient inside the spherical shell

$$\frac{dV}{dr} = \frac{d}{dr}(\text{constant}) = 0$$

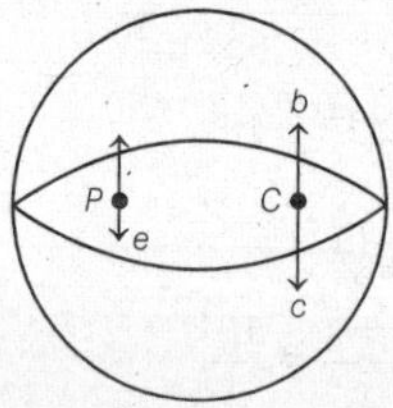

Gravitational intensity is equal to the negative of the gravitational potential gradient. Therefore, gravitational intensity is also zero at all points insides the spherical shell and hence gravitational force acting on any particle at all points inside the spherical shell will be equal.

If upper hemisphere shell is removed then gravitational force acting on particle placed at centre *C* will be downward. Therefore, the gravitational force acting per unit mass, *i.e.*, gravitational intensity will be downward is shown by arrow (c).

Question 11 For the above problem, the direction of the gravitational intensity at an arbitrary point *P* is indicated by the arrow (i) *d*, (ii) *e*, (iii) *f*, (iv) *g*.

Sol. (ii) As point *P* lies on the face of semispherical shell and hence gravitational intensity at point *P* will be downward *i.e.* along *e*.

Question 12 A rocket is fired from the earth towards the sun. At what distance from the earth's centre is the gravitational force on the rocket zero? Mass of the sun $= 2 \times 10^{30}$ kg, mass of earth $= 6.0 \times 10^{24}$ kg. Neglect the effect of the other planets etc. (Orbital radius $= 1.5 \times 10^{11}$ m).

Sol. Mass of the sun $(M_s) = 2 \times 10^{30}$ kg

Mass of the earth $(M_e) = 6.0 \times 10^{24}$ kg

Orbital radius $(r) = 1.5 \times 10^{11}$ m

Let gravitational force acting on the rocket be zero at a distance x from earth's centre. The mass of the rocket be m.

Gravitational force between rocket and the sun (f_s)

= Gravitational force between rocket and the earth (f_e)

$$\frac{GM_s m}{(r-x)^2} = \frac{GM_e m}{x^2}$$

or
$$\frac{M_s}{(r-x)^2} = \frac{M_e}{x^2}$$

or
$$\frac{2 \times 10^{30}}{(r-x)^2} = \frac{6 \times 10^{24}}{x^2}$$

or
$$\frac{(r-x)^2}{x^2} = \frac{2 \times 10^{30}}{6 \times 10^{24}}$$

$$\frac{(r-x)^2}{x^2} = \frac{10^6}{3}$$

Taking square root on both sides,

or
$$\frac{r-x}{x} = \frac{10^3}{\sqrt{3}}$$

$$\frac{r}{x} - 1 = \frac{10^3 \times \sqrt{3}}{3} = \frac{1.732 \times 1000}{3}$$

or
$$\frac{r}{x} = 1 + \frac{1732}{3} \Rightarrow \frac{r}{x} = \frac{1735}{3}$$

or
$$x = \frac{3}{1735} \times r$$

$$= \frac{3 \times 1.5 \times 10^{11}}{1735} = 2.594 \times 10^8 \text{ m}$$

$$x = 2.6 \times 10^8 \text{ m}$$

Question 13 How will you weight the sun *i.e.,* estimate its mass? You will need to know the period of one of its planets and the radius of the planetary orbit. The mean orbital radius of the earth around the sun is 1.5×10^8 km. Estimate the mass of the sun.

Sol. Mean orbital radius of the earth around the sun

$$r = 1.5 \times 10^8 \text{ km} = 1.5 \times 10^{11} \text{ m}$$

Time period of earth around the sun = 1 yr

$$= 365 \text{ days} = 365 \times 24 \times 60 \times 60 \text{ s}$$

As required centripetal force is obtained from the gravitational force, therefore

Centripetal force = Gravitational force

$$\frac{mv^2}{r} = \frac{GM_s m}{r^2}$$

$$v^2 = \frac{GM_s}{r}$$

$$(r\omega)^2 = \frac{GM_s}{r} \qquad (\because v = r\omega)$$

or $$\omega^2 = \frac{GM_s}{r^3}$$

But $$\omega = \frac{2\pi}{T}$$

$\therefore$ $$\left(\frac{2\pi}{T}\right)^2 = \frac{GM_s}{r^3}$$

or $$M_s = \frac{4\pi^2 r^3}{GT^2}$$

$$= \frac{4 \times (3.14)^2 \times (1.5 \times 10^{11})^3}{6.67 \times 10^{-11}(365 \times 24 \times 60 \times 60)^2}$$

$$\approx 2 \times 10^{30} \text{ kg}$$

Question 14 A saturn year is 29.5 times the earth year. How far is the saturn from the sun if the earth is 1.50×10^8 km away from the sun?

◎ **Thinking Process** According to Kepler's law of periods, the square of the time period of a planet is directly proportional to the cube of the average radius of the orbit, *i.e.,* $T^2 \propto r^3$

Sol. Earth year $T_e = 1$ yr

Saturn year $T_s = 29.5$ yr

Radius of earth's orbit $(R_e) = 1.50 \times 10^8$ km

Radius of saturan's orbit $(R_s) = ?$

According to Kepler's planetery law of period,

$$T^2 \propto R^3$$

or $$\frac{T_e^2}{T_s^2} = \frac{R_e^3}{R_s^3}$$

$$\left(\frac{1}{29.5}\right)^2 = \frac{(1.50 \times 10^8)^3}{R_s^3}$$

$$R_s^3 = (29.5)^2 \times (1.50 \times 10^8)^3$$
$$= (2.947 \times 10^{27}\,\text{km})$$
$$R_s = (2.937 \times 10^{27})$$
$$= 1.43 \times 10^9\ \text{km}$$
$$= 1.43 \times 10^{12}\ \text{m}$$

Question 15 The weight of a body on the surface of earth is 63 N. What is the gravitational force on it due to the earth at a height equal to half the radius of earth?

◎ *Thinking Process* To calculate the gravitational force at height, we have to calculate acceleration due to gravity at altitude h which is given by

$$g' = \frac{g}{\left(1 + \frac{h}{R_e}\right)^2}$$

Sol. Given $h = \frac{R_e}{2}$

Acceleration due to gravity at altitude h is given by

$$g' = \frac{g}{\left(1 + \frac{h}{R_e}\right)^2}$$

$$= \frac{g}{\left(1 + \frac{R_e/2}{R_e}\right)^2} = \frac{g}{\left(1 + \frac{1}{2}\right)^2}$$

$$g' = \frac{g}{(3/2)^2} = \frac{4}{9}g \qquad \ldots\text{(i)}$$

Weight of the body at earth's surface

$$w = mg = 63\,\text{N} \qquad \ldots\text{(ii)}$$

Weight of the body at altitude $h = R_e / 2$

$$w' = mg' = \frac{4}{9}mg \qquad \ldots\text{(iii)}$$

Using Eq. (ii), we get

$$w' = \frac{4}{9} \times 63$$

$$w' = 28 \text{ N}$$

Quick Solution

$$\frac{mg'}{mg} = \left[\frac{R_e}{R_e + h}\right]^2$$

$$\frac{mg'}{63} = \left[\frac{R_e}{R_e + \frac{R_e}{2}}\right]^2 = \left(\frac{2}{3}\right)^2$$

$$w' = \frac{4}{9} \times 63 = 28 \text{ N} \qquad (\because W = mg')$$

Question 16 Assuming the earth to be a sphere of uniform mass density, how much would body weight half way down to the centre of earth if it weighed 250 N on the surface?

◎ **Thinking Process** To calculate the weight of the body down the centre of earth we have to calculate. The acceleration due to gravity at depth h from earth's surface which is given by

$$g' = g\left(1 - \frac{h}{R_e}\right)$$

Sol. Weight of the body at earth's surface

$$w = mg = 250 \text{ N} \qquad \text{...(i)}$$

Acceleration due to gravity at depth h from earth's surface

$$g' = g\left(1 - \frac{h}{R_e}\right)$$

Here, $h = R_e / 2$

$\therefore$
$$g' = g\left(1 - \frac{R_e / 2}{R_e}\right) = g\left(1 - \frac{1}{2}\right)$$

$$g' = \frac{g}{2}$$

$\therefore$ Weight of the body at depth h

$$w' = mg' = \frac{mg}{2}$$

Using Eq. (i), we get

$$w' = \frac{250}{2}$$

$$= 125 \text{ N}$$

$\therefore$ Weight of the body will be 125 N.

Question 17 A rocket is fired vertically with a speed of 5 km/s from the earth's surface. How far from the earth does the rocket go before returning to the earth?

Mass of the earth $= 6.0 \times 10^{24}$ kg, mean radius of earth $= 6.4 \times 10^6$ m, $G = 6.67 \times 10^{-11}$ N-m^2/kg^2.

Sol. Let a rocket of mass m be fired vertically with a speed v and it reach at height h from earth's surface.

KE of the rocket $= \frac{1}{2}mv^2$

PE of the rocket at earth's surface

$$(U_0) = -\frac{GM_e m}{R_e}$$

PE of the rocket at height h from earth's surface

$$U_h = -\frac{GM_e m}{(R_e + h)}$$

$\therefore$ Increase in PE $(\Delta U) = U_h - U_0$

$$\Delta U = -\frac{GM_e m}{(R_e + h)} - \left(-\frac{GM_e m}{R_e}\right)$$

$$= GM_e m\left[\frac{1}{R_e} - \frac{1}{(R_e + h)}\right]$$

$$= GM_e m\left[\frac{R_e + h - R_e}{R_e(R_e + h)}\right]$$

$$= GM_e m \times \frac{h}{R_e(R_e + h)}$$

But $\quad GM_e = gR_e^2$

$\therefore$
$$\Delta U = gR_e^2 \times m \times \frac{h}{R_e(R_e + h)}$$

$$= \frac{mgh}{\frac{R_e(R_e + h)}{R_e^2}}$$

$$= \frac{mgh}{\left(1 + \frac{h}{R_e}\right)}$$

According to law of conservation of energy,

KE of the rocket = Increase in PE

$$\frac{1}{2}mv^2 = \frac{mgh}{\left(1 + \frac{h}{R_e}\right)}$$

$$v^2\left(1+\frac{h}{R_e}\right) = 2gh$$

$$v^2 + \frac{v^2h}{R_e} = 2gh$$

or $$v^2R_e + v^2h = 2ghR_e$$

$$v^2R_e = h(2gR_e - v^2)$$

or $$h = \left(\frac{v^2R_e}{2gR_e - v^2}\right)$$

Here, speed of the rocket $v = 5\text{ km/s} = 5 \times 10^3$ m/s

Mass of the earth $M_e = 6.0 \times 10^{24}$ kg

Radius of the earth $R_e = 6.4 \times 10^6$ m,

Acceleration due to gravity $g = 9.8\text{ m/s}^2$

$$\therefore \quad h = \frac{(5 \times 10^3)^2 \times 6.4 \times 10^6}{(2 \times 9.8 \times 6.4 \times 10^6) - (5 \times 10^3)^2}$$

$$= \frac{25 \times 6.4 \times 10^{12}}{9.8 \times 12.8 \times 10^6 - 25 \times 10^6} = 1.6 \times 10^6 \text{ m}$$

$$= 1600 \times 10^3 \text{ m} = 1600 \text{ km}$$

$\therefore$ Distance from the centre of the earth $r = R_e + h$

$$= 6.4 \times 10^6 + 1.6 \times 10^6 = 8.0 \times 10^6 \text{ m}$$

Mistake Alert Student sometime use formula of PE without – *ve* sign *i.e.*, PE of the rocket at earths surface $= \frac{GM_em}{R_e}$.

Question 18 The escape speed of a projectile on earth's surface is 11.2 km/s. A body is projected out with thrice this speed. What is the speed of the body far away from the earth? Ignore the presence of sun and other planets.

Sol. v = speed of projection of body

v_{esc} = escape velocity

v' = speed of projectile when far away from earth.

According to law of conservation of energy

$$\frac{1}{2}mv^2 = \frac{1}{2}mv_{esc}^2 + \frac{1}{2}mv'^2$$

$$(3v_{esc})^2 = v_{esc}^2 + v'^2$$

$$2\sqrt{2}\, v_{esc} = v'$$

or $$v' = 2 \times 1.414 \times 11.6 = 31.68 \text{ km/s}$$

Question 19 A satellite orbits the earth at a height of 400 km above the surface. How much energy must be expended to rocket the satellite out of the earth's gravitational influence? Mass of the satellite $= 200$ kg, mass of the earth $= 6.0 \times 10^{24}$ kg, radius of the earth $= 6.4 \times 10^6$ m,
$G = 6.67 \times 10^{-11}$ N-m^2/kg^2.

Sol. Given, height of the satellite above the earth's surface

$$(h) = 400 \text{ km} = 0.4 \times 10^6 \text{ m}$$

Mass of the satellite $(m) = 200$ kg

Radius of earth $(R_e) = 6.4 \times 10^6$m

Mass of earth $(M_e) = 6.0 \times 10^{24}$ kg

Gravitational constant $(G) = 6.67 \times 10^{-11}$ N-m^2/kg^2

Energy required to send a satellite out of earth's gravitational influence is called its binding energy.

Binding energy of a satellite = (total energy of the orbiting satellite).

$$= \frac{GM_e m}{2(R_e + h)}$$

$$= \frac{6.67 \times 10^{-11} \times 6.0 \times 10^{24} \times 200}{2(6.4 \times 10^6 + 0.4 \times 10^6)}$$

$$= \frac{6.67 \times 12 \times 10^{15}}{2 \times 6.8 \times 10^6}$$

$$= 5.885 \times 10^9 \text{ J}$$

$$= 5.9 \times 10^9 \text{ J}$$

Question 20 Two stars each of 1 solar mass $(= 2 \times 10^{30}$ kg) are approaching each other for a head on collision. When they are at a distance 10^9 km, their speeds are negligible. What is the speed with which they collide? The radius of each star is 10^4 km. Assume the stars to remain undistorted until they collide. (Use the known value of G).

Sol. Mass of each star $(m) = 2 \times 10^{30}$ kg

Initial distance between them $(r_1) = 10^9$ km $= 10^{12}$ m

Radius of each star $(R) = 10^4$ km $= 10^7$ m

Initial speed of each star when they are very far away $(v_1) = 0$

$\therefore$ Initial KE of the star = 0

Initial PE of the star $= -\dfrac{Gmm}{r} = -\dfrac{Gm^2}{r}$

Let stars collide with each other with a speed v'.

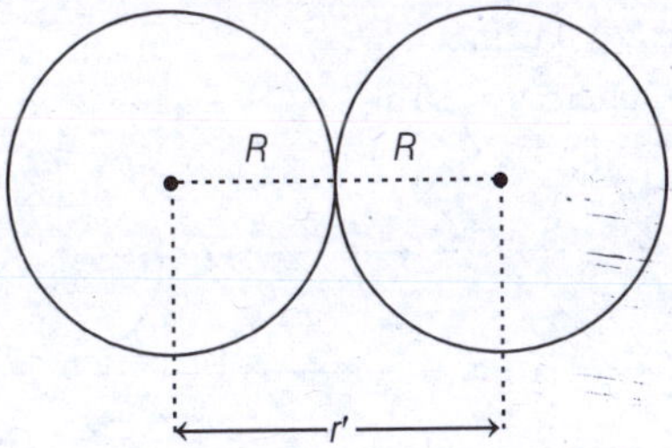

Distance between the stars when they collide with each other

$$r' = 2R$$

$\therefore$ KE of the stars $= \frac{1}{2}mv'^2 + \frac{1}{2}mv'^2$

$= mv'^2$

$\therefore$ PE of the stars $= -\frac{Gmm}{r'} = -\frac{Gm^2}{2R}$

According to law of conservation of energy

Total initial energy of stars = Final energy of stars

$$0 + \left(-\frac{Gm^2}{r}\right) = mv'^2 + \left(-\frac{Gm^2}{2R}\right)$$

or
$$mv'^2 = Gm^2\left[\frac{1}{2R} - \frac{1}{r}\right]$$

$$v'^2 = Gm\left[\frac{1}{2R} - \frac{1}{r}\right]$$

$$= 6.67 \times 10^{-11} \times 2 \times 10^{30}\left[\frac{1}{2 \times 10^7} - \frac{1}{10^{12}}\right]$$

$$= 13.34 \times 10^{19}[5 \times 10^{-8} - 10^{-12}]$$

$$= 13.34 \times 10^{19} \times 4.999 \times 10^{-8}$$

$$= 6.6699 \times 10^{12}$$

or
$$v' = \sqrt{6.6699 \times 10^{12}}$$

$$= 2.583 \times 10^6 \text{ m/s}$$

$$v' = 2.6 \times 10^6 \text{ m/s}$$

Question 21 Two heavy spheres each of mass 100 kg and radius 0.10 m are placed 1.0 m apart on a horizontal table. What is the gravitational force and potential at the mid-point of the line joining the centres of the spheres? Is an object placed at that point in equilibrium? If so, is the equilibrium stable or unstable?

Sol. Given, mass of each sphere $m = 100$ kg

Radius of each sphere $R = 0.10$ m

Distance between the spheres $r = 1.0$ m

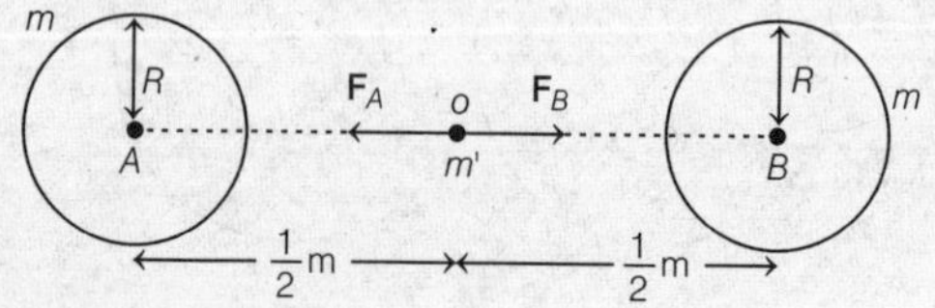

Distance of mid-point from each sphere

$$d = \frac{r}{2} = \frac{1}{2}\text{ m}$$

Let an object of very small mass m' be placed at mid-point O of AB.

Force acting on m' due to sphere A

$$\mathbf{F}_A = \frac{Gmm'}{d^2}, \text{ along } \mathbf{OA}$$

Force acting on m' due to sphere B

$$\mathbf{F}_B = \frac{Gmm'}{d^2}, \text{ along } \mathbf{OB}$$

$\therefore$ Net force on m' at point O

$$\mathbf{F} = \mathbf{F}_A + \mathbf{F}_B$$

$$= \frac{Gmm'}{d^2} + \left(\frac{-Gmm'}{d^2}\right)$$

$$\mathbf{F} = 0$$

$\therefore$ Gravitational force at mid-point O is zero.

Gravitational potential at mid-point O, due to sphere A

$$V_A = -\frac{Gm}{d}$$

Similarly, gravitational potential at mid-point O, due to sphere B

$$V_B = -\frac{Gm}{d}$$

$\therefore$ Resultant gravitational potential at mid-point O

$$V = V_A + V_B$$

$$= \left(-\frac{Gm}{d}\right) + \left(-\frac{Gm}{d}\right)$$

$$= -2 \times \frac{GM}{d} = -\frac{2 \times 6.67 \times 10^{-11} \times 100}{1/2}$$

$$= -26.68 \times 10^{-9}$$

$$= -2.7 \times 10^{-8} \text{ J/kg}$$

As gravitational potential is not zero at the mid-point therefore, the equilibrium is unstable.

DIKSHA APP Questions

Multiple Choice Questions

Q.1 A satellite is in a circular orbit around the earth. Due to some reason it loses some of its energy. What is the new trajectory?

(a) Follows a hyperbolic path and falls to earth.
(b) Follows a parabolic path and falls to earth.
(c) Follows new circular orbit of smaller radius.
(d) Follows an elliptical orbit around earth with earth at one of the two focal points.

Sol. (d) It is according to keplar's first law of planetary motion.

Q.2 Mass M is divided into two parts xM and $(1-x)M$. For a given separation the value of x for which the gravitational attraction between the two pieces becomes maximum is

(a) $\frac{1}{3}$ (b) $\frac{1}{2}$
(c) $\frac{3}{4}$ (d) 1

Sol. (b) For of attraction, $F = \frac{GM_1M_2}{r^2}$

$$F = \frac{GxM(1-x)M}{r^2}$$

For F to be maximum (for same r)

$$\frac{dF}{dx} = 0$$

$$\frac{d}{dx}[x - x^2] = 0$$

$$1 - 2x = 0$$

$$\Rightarrow \quad x = \frac{1}{2}.$$

Q.3 The time period of an artificial satellite orbiting around earth is proportional to the nth power of its orbital radius. What is the value of n?

(a) 0.5 (b) −1 (c) 1.5 (d) −2

Sol. (c) Using Keplar's third law of planetary motion

$$T^2 \propto r^3 \Rightarrow T \propto r^{3/2}$$

$$\Rightarrow \quad T \propto r^{1.5}$$

So, the value of n will be 1.5.

Q.4 Composition of the materials of the two planets are the same. Their radii are r_1 and r_2. The ratio of the acceleration due to planets g_1 / g_2 at the surface of the two planets are

(a) $\frac{r_1}{r_2}$ (b) $\frac{r_2}{r_1}$

(c) $\left(\frac{r_1}{r_1}\right)^2$ (d) $\left(\frac{r_2}{r_1}\right)^2$

Sol. (a) We know that, $g = \frac{GM}{R^2} = \frac{G}{R^2} \times \frac{4}{3}\pi R^3 \rho = \frac{4}{3}\pi G R \rho$

(Assuming planet of uniform density and perfectly spherical)

$$\therefore \quad \frac{g_1}{g_2} = \frac{\frac{4}{3}\pi G \rho r_1}{\frac{4}{3}\pi G \rho r_2} = \frac{r_1}{r_2}$$

Q.5 The escape velocity from the earth surface is v. The escape velocity from the surface of another planet having a radius twice that of earth and the same mean density will be

(a) v (b) $\sqrt{2}v$

(c) $2v$ (d) $2\sqrt{2}v$

Sol. (c) $v_{esc} = \sqrt{\frac{2GM}{R}} = \sqrt{\frac{2G}{R} \times \frac{4}{3}\pi R^3 \rho} = R\sqrt{\frac{8}{3}\pi G \rho}$

$$\therefore \quad v_{esc} \propto R$$

$$\Rightarrow \quad \frac{v_P}{v_e} = \frac{R_P}{R} = 2$$

$$\Rightarrow \quad v_P = 2v$$

Q.6 A satellite of mass m is moving in a circular orbit of radius R, close to the Earth's surface. Then the work required to be done, to move it to a circular orbit of radius $2R$ is (where M is mass of the Earth)

(a) $\frac{2GMm}{R}$ (b) $\frac{GMm}{R}$

(c) $\frac{GMm}{2R}$ (d) $\frac{GMm}{4R}$

Sol. (d) Total energy of satellite in a circular orbit of radius R is

$$E_1 = \frac{1}{2}mv^2 - \frac{GMm}{R}$$

$$= \frac{GMm}{2R} - \frac{GMm}{R} \qquad \left[\frac{mv^2}{R} = \frac{GMm}{R^2}\right]$$

$$= -\frac{GMm}{2R}$$

New energy of satellite in a circular orbit of radius $2R$ is

$$E_2 = -\frac{GMm}{4R}$$

$\therefore$ Work done $W = E_2 - E_1 = \frac{-GMm}{4R} - \left(-\frac{GMm}{2R}\right) = \frac{GMm}{4R}$

Q.7 A satellite is to be projected for the purpose of communication. Which of the following is not true ?

(a) Its time period should be 24 hr.
(b) It should be in polar orbit.
(c) It should move from west to east.
(d) It should be at the same height above the earth's surface as that of other communication satellites.

Sol. (b) For communication purposes satellites are placed in geostationary orbit which moves in the equatorial orbit.

Q.8 An astronaut in a space station orbiting earth experiences weightlessness. Which of the following is not the correct reason?

(a) Earth's gravity at the space station is zero.
(b) Space station is falling towards earth with acceleration g.
(c) In the frame of reference of the space station the centrifugal force neutralizes the gravitational attraction.
(d) g at the space station is the same as $w^2 r$.

Sol. (a) At the space station acceleration due to gravity is

$$g = \frac{GM}{r^2} \neq 0$$

Q.9 An astronaut orbiting the earth in a circular orbit satellite above the surface of the earth gently drops an object out of the satellite. The object will

(a) fall vertically down to the earth
(b) move in an orbit around the earth
(c) will move in an irregular way and fall down to the earth
(d) will escape out of earth's gravity

Sol. (b) As astronaut gently drops the object, the gravitational force between earth and object provides required centripetal force to revolve around earth with same speed as before.

Q.10 The areal velocity versus time graph for a planet around the sun

(a) is a straight line with zero intercept and positive slope.
(b) is a straight line with non-zero intercept and positive slope.
(c) is a straight line with zero intercept and negative slope.
(d) is a straight line with non-zero intercept and negative slope.

Sol. (a) According to Kepler's second law of planetary motion, the areal velocity of a planet revolving around sun remains constant.

Mechanical Properties of Solids

CHAPTER 08

Important Points

01 A force which produces a change in configuration of the object on applying it, is called a **deforming force.**

02 **Elasticity** is that property of the object by virtue of which it regain its original configuration after the removal of the deforming force.

03 No material is perfectly elastic but quartz and phospher-bronze are practically taken as **perfectly elastic**.

04 Those bodies which do not regain its original configuration at all on the removal of deforming force are called **perfectly plastic** bodies.

05 No material is perfectly plastic but putty and paraffin wax are practically taken as perfectly plastic.

06 **Stress** The internal restoring force acting per unit area of a deformed body is called **stress**.

$$\text{Stress} = \frac{\text{Restoring force}}{\text{Area}}$$

07 Its SI unit is newton-metre^{-2} and its dimensions is $[ML^{-1}T^{-2}]$.

08 **Strain** The fractional change in configuration is called strain.

$$\text{Strain} = \frac{\text{Change is configuration}}{\text{Original configuration}}$$

It has no unit and is a dimensionless quantity.

09 According to the change in configuration, the strain is of three types

(i) Longitudinal strain $= \dfrac{\text{Change in length}}{\text{Original length}}$

(ii) Volumetric strain $= \dfrac{\text{Change in volume}}{\text{Original volume}}$

(iii) Shearing strain = Angular displacement of the plane perpendicular to the fixed surface.

10 **Limit of Elasticity** The maximum value of deforming force for which elasticity is present in the body is called its limit of elasticity.

11 **Hooke's Law** Within the limit of elasticity, the stress is directly proportional to the strain *i.e.,*

$$\text{Stress} \propto \text{Strain}$$

or

$$\text{Stress} = E \times \text{Strain}$$

where E is the modulus of elasticity of the material of the body.

12 **Types of Modulus of Elasticity**

(i) Young's modulus of elasticity $(Y) = \dfrac{\text{Normal stress}}{\text{Longitudinal strain}}$

$$= \frac{F/A}{\Delta l / l} = \frac{Fl}{A\Delta l}$$

(ii) Bulk modulus of elasticity $(K) = \dfrac{\text{Normal stress}}{\text{Volumetric strain}}$

$$= \frac{-p}{\Delta V / V} = \frac{-pV}{\Delta V}$$

(iii) Modulus of rigidity $(\eta) = \dfrac{\text{Tangential stress}}{\text{Shearing stress}}$

$$= \frac{F/A}{\theta} = \frac{F}{A\theta}$$

13 Compressibility of a material is the reciprocal of its bulk modulus of elasticity.

$$\text{Compressibility}\ (C) = \frac{1}{\text{Bulk modulus}\ (K)}$$

14 **Breaking Stress** The minimum value of stress required to break a wire, is called breaking stress.

15 Breaking stress is fixed for a material but breaking force varies with area of cross-section of the wire.

$$\text{Lateral strain} = \frac{\text{Change in the lateral dimension}}{\text{Original lateral dimension}}$$

$$\text{Poisson's Ratio} = \frac{\text{Lateral strain}}{\text{Longitudinal strain}}$$

$$\Rightarrow \quad \frac{\Delta d / d}{\Delta L / L} = \frac{\Delta d}{\Delta L} \frac{L}{d}$$

16 **Brittleness** The property of a material by virtue of which it split into small pieces on beating, is called brittleness.

These materials show very small plastic range beyond elastic limit.

Glass, cast iron, salt etc., are brittle materials.

17 **Elastomers** Elastomers are those materials for which strain produced is much larger than the stress applied, with in the limit of elasticity. Elastomers have no plastic range.

Examples Rubber, the elastic tissue of aorta, the large vessel carrying blood from heart etc.

18 Elastic potential energy in a stretched wire is given by

$$U = \text{Average force} \times \text{Increase in length}$$
$$= \frac{1}{2} F \times \Delta l = \frac{1}{2} \times \text{Stress} \times \text{Strain} \times \text{Volume}$$

19 Elastic potential energy of a stretched spring $= \frac{1}{2} \times kx^2$

where k = force constant and x = change in length.

20 A beam clamped at one end and loaded at free end is called a **cantilever**.

21 Depression at the free end of a cantilever is given by,

$$\delta = \frac{Wl^3}{3YI_G}$$

where, W = load, l = length of the cantilever
Y = Young's modulus of elasticity
I_G = geometrical moment of inertia.

22 For beam of rectangular cross-section having breadth b and thickness d,

$$I_G = \frac{bd^3}{12}$$

23 For a beam of circular cross-section area having radius r,

$$I_G = \frac{\pi r^4}{4}$$

24 Depression in a beam supported at two ends and loaded at the middle is given by

$$\delta = \frac{Wl^3}{48YI_G}$$

Exercises

Question 1 A steel wire of length 4.7 m and cross-sectional area $3.0 \times 10^{-5}\ m^2$ stretches by the same amount as a copper wire of length 3.5 m and cross-sectional area $4.0 \times 10^{-5}\ m^2$ under a given load. What is the ratio of the Young's modulus of steel to that of copper?

Sol. Given,

For steel wire

$$\text{Length } (l_1) = 4.7\ \text{m}$$

$$\text{Area of cross-section } (A_1) = 3.0 \times 10^{-5}\ \text{m}^2$$

For copper wire

$$\text{Length } (l_2) = 3.5\ \text{m}$$

$$\text{Area of cross-section } (A_2) = 4.0 \times 10^{-5}\ \text{m}^2$$

Let F be the given load under which steel and copper wires be stretched by the same amount Δl.

Young's modulus $(Y) = \dfrac{F/A}{\Delta l / l} = \dfrac{F \times l}{A \times \Delta l}$

For steel, $Y_s = \dfrac{F \times l_1}{A_1 \times \Delta l}$ ...(i)

For copper, $Y_c = \dfrac{F \times l_2}{A_2 \times \Delta l}$ ...(ii)

Dividing Eq. (i) by Eq. (ii), we get

$$\frac{Y_s}{Y_c} = \frac{F \times l_1}{A_1 \times \Delta l} \times \frac{A_2 \times \Delta l}{F \times l_2} = \frac{l_1}{l_2} \times \frac{A_2}{A_1}$$

$$= \frac{4.7}{3.5} \times \frac{4.0 \times 10^{-5}}{3.0 \times 10^{-5}}$$

$$= \frac{18.8}{10.5} = 1.79 \simeq 1.8$$

Question 2 Figure shows the strain-stress curve for a given material. What are (a) Young's modulus and (b) approximate yield strength for this material?

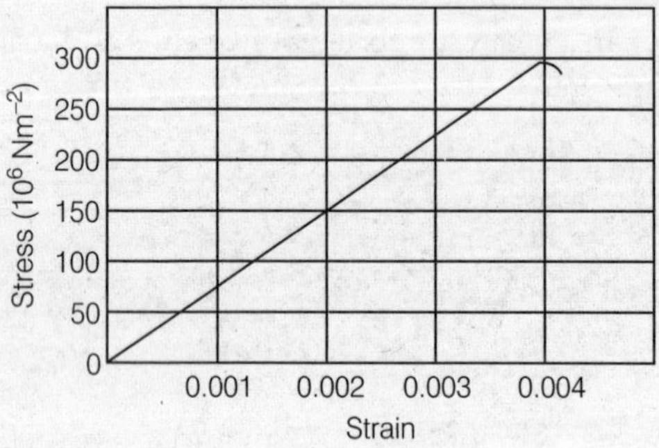

◎ *Thinking Process* The slope of straight line portion of strain-stress curve for a given material represents its Young's modulus.

The maximum stress a material can sustain is called its yield strength.

Sol.

(a) Young's modulus of the given material (Y)

$$= \text{Slope of strain-stress curve}$$

$$Y = \frac{150 \times 10^6}{0.002} = 75 \times 10^9 \text{ N/m}^2 = 7.5 \times 10^{10} \text{ N/m}^2$$

(b) Yield strength of the given material

= Maximum stress the material can sustain

$= 300 \times 10^6 \text{ N/m}^2 = 3 \times 10^8 \text{ N/m}^2$ (approximately)

Question 3 The stress-strain graphs for materials A and B are shown in Fig. (a) and Fig. (b)

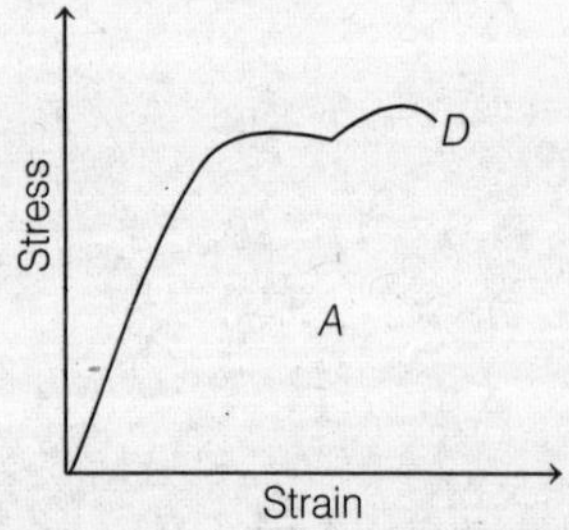

(a)

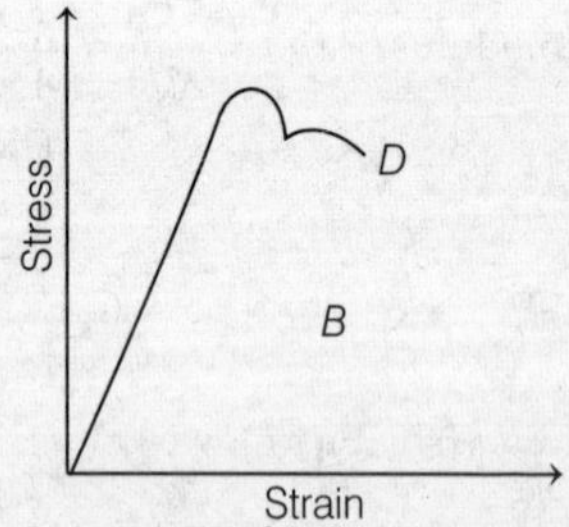

(b)

The graphs are drawn to the same scale.

(a) Which of the materials has greater Young's modulus?

(b) Which of the two is the stronger material?

Sol.

(a) In the two graphs, the slope of graph in Fig. (a) is greater than the slope of graph in Fig. (b), so material *A* has greater Young's modulus.

(b) Material *A* is stronger than material *B*, become it can with stand more load without breaking. For material *A* the break even point (*D*) is higher.

Question 4 Read the following two statements below carefully and state, with reasons, if it is true or false.

(a) The Young's modulus of rubber is greater than that of steel.

(b) The stretching of a coil is determined by its shear modulus.

Sol.

(a) False, because more stress is required to produce same strain in steel wire in comparison to a identical rubber wire. Therefore, Young's modulus of steel is greater than that of rubber.

(b) True, because when a coil is stretched there is neither a change in its length nor a change in its volume and change takes place only in its shape. Therefore, stretching of a coil is determined by its shear modulus.

Question 5 Two wires of diameter 0.25 cm, one made of steel and other made of brass are loaded as shown in figure. The unloaded length of steel wire is 1.5 m and that of brass wire is 1.0 m. Young's modulus of steel is 2.0×10^{11} Pa. Compute the elongations of steel and brass wires. (1 Pa = 1 N/m^2).

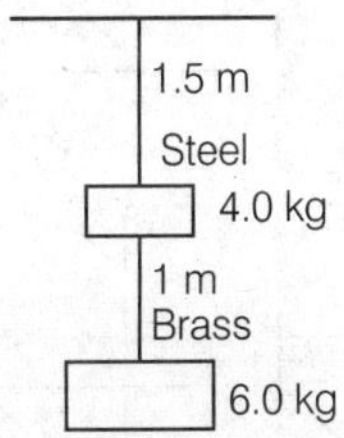

Sol. Given, diameter of wires $(2r) = 0.25$ cm

$$\therefore \quad r = 0.125 \text{ cm} = 1.25 \times 10^{-3} \text{ m}$$

For steel wire,

$$\text{Load } (F_1) = (4 + 6) \text{ kgf} = 10 \times 9.8 \text{ N} = 98 \text{ N}$$

$$\text{Length of steel wire } (l_1) = 1.5 \text{ m}$$

$$\text{Young's modulus } (Y_1) = 2.0 \times 10^{11} \text{ Pa}$$

$$\text{Young's modulus } (Y) = \frac{F_1 \times l_1}{A_1 \times \Delta l_1}$$

$\therefore$ Change in length $(\Delta l_1) = \dfrac{F_1 \times l_1}{A_1 \times Y_1}$

$$= \frac{F_1 \times l_1}{\pi r_1^2 \times Y_1}$$

$$= \frac{98 \times 1.5}{3.14 \times (1.25 \times 10^{-3})^2 \times 2.0 \times 10^{11}}$$

$$= 1.5 \times 10^{-4} \text{ cm}$$

For brass wire,

Load $(F_2) = 6 \text{ kg } f = 6 \times 9.8 \text{ N} = 58.8 \text{ N}$

Length of brass wire $(l_2) = 1.0 \text{ m}$

Young's modulus $(Y_2) = 0.91 \times 10^{11}$ Pa

Change in length $(l_2) = \dfrac{F_2 \times l_2}{\pi r_2^2 \times Y_2}$

$$= \frac{58.8 \times 1.0}{3.14 \times (1.25 \times 10^{-3})^2 \times 0.91 \times 10^{11}}$$

$$= 1.3 \times 10^{-4} \text{ m}$$

Question 6 The edge of an aluminium cube is 10 cm long. One face of the cube is firmly fixed to a vertical wall. A mass of 100 kg is then attached to the opposite face of the cube. The shear modulus of aluminium is 25 GPa. What is the vertical deflection of this face?

Sol.

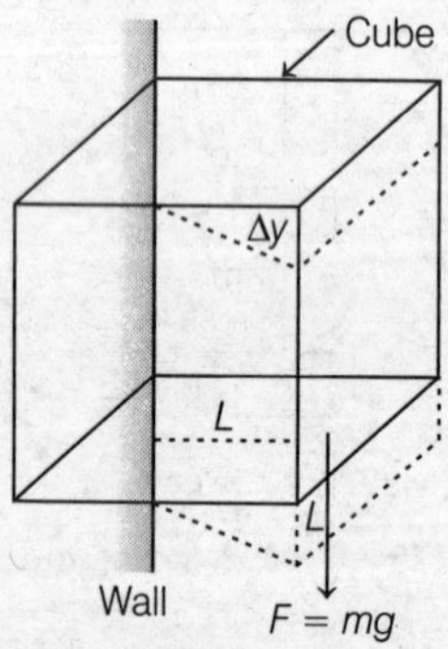

Given, side of a cube $(l) = 10 \text{ cm} = 0.1 \text{ m}$

Area its each face $(A) = l^2 = (0.1)^2 = 0.01 \text{ m}^2$

Load $(m) = 100 \text{ kg}$

Tangential force acting on one face of the cube,

$$F = mg = 100 \times 9.8 = 980 \text{ N}$$

Shear stress acting on this face $= \dfrac{F}{A}$

$$= \frac{980}{0.01}\ \text{N/m}^2$$

$$= 9.8 \times 10^4\ \text{N/m}^2$$

Shear modulus of aluminium $(\eta) = 25$ GPa

$$= 25 \times 10^9\ \text{N/m}^2$$

$$\text{Shear modulus } (\eta) = \frac{\text{Shearing stress}}{\text{Shearing strain}}$$

$$\text{or shearing strain} \left(\frac{\Delta y}{L}\right) = \frac{\text{Shearing stress}}{\text{Shear modulus}}$$

$$\text{or vertical deflection } \Delta y = \frac{\text{Shearing stress}}{\text{Shear modulus}} \times L$$

$$= \frac{9.8 \times 10^4}{25 \times 10^9} \times 0.1$$

$$= 0.0392 \times 10^{-5}\ \text{m}$$

$$= 3.92 \times 10^{-7}\ \text{m}$$

Mistake Alert Student sometime use shear modulus $(\eta) = \dfrac{\text{Shearing strain}}{\text{Shearing stress}}$

Question 7 Four identical hollow cylindrical columns of mild steel support a big structure of mass 50000 kg. The inner and outer radii of each column are 30 cm and 60 cm respectively. Assuming the load distribution to be uniform, calculate the compressional strain of each column. Young's modulus, $Y = 2.0 \times 10^{11}$ Pa.

Sol. Given, total mass supported by cylindrical columns $(m) = 50000$ kg

$\therefore$ Total weight supported by cylindrical columns $= mg = 50000 \times 9.8$

$$= 490000\ \text{N}$$

$\therefore$ Force acting on each cylindrical support

$$F = \frac{mg}{4} = \frac{490000}{4}\ \text{N} = 122500\ \text{N}$$

Inner radius of each column $(r_1) = 30$ cm $= 0.3$ m

Outer radius of each column $(r_2) = 60$ cm $= 0.6$ m

$\therefore$ Area of cross-section of each cylindrical column

$$A = \pi r_2^2 - \pi r_1^2$$

$$= \pi(r_2^2 - r_1^2)$$

$$= 3.14\ [(0.6)^2 - (0.3)^2]$$

$$= 3.14 \times 0.27\ \text{m}^2$$

Young's modulus $(Y) = 2 \times 10^{11}$ Pa

Compressional strain of each column = ?

$$\text{Young's modulus } (Y) = \frac{\text{Compressional stress}}{\text{Compressional strain}}$$

$$\text{or Compressional strain} = \frac{\text{Compressional stress}}{\text{Young's modulus}}$$

$$= \frac{F/A}{Y} = \frac{F}{AY}$$

$$= \frac{122500}{(3.14 \times 0.27) \times 2 \times 10^{11}}$$

$$= 0.722 \times 10^{-6}$$

$$= 7.22 \times 10^{-7}$$

Question 8 A piece of copper having a rectangular cross-section of 15.2 mm × 19.1 mm is pulled in tension with 44500 N force, producing only elastic deformation. Calculate the resulting strain? Y for copper $= 1.1 \times 10^{11}$ N/m^2.

Sol. Given, cross-section area of copper piece (A)

$$= 15.2 \text{ mm} \times 19.1 \text{ mm}$$

$$= (15.2 \times 19.1) \times 10^{-6} \text{ m}^2$$

Force applied (F) = 44500 N

Young's modulus (Y) = 1.1×10^{11} Nm^{-2}

$$\text{Young's modulus } (Y) = \frac{\text{Longitudinal stress}}{\text{Longitudinal strain}}$$

$$\text{or longitudinal strain} = \frac{\text{Longitudinal stress}}{\text{Young's modulus}} = \frac{(F/A)}{Y} = \frac{F}{AY}$$

$$= \frac{44500}{15.2 \times 19.1 \times 10^{-6} \times 1.1 \times 10^{11}}$$

$$= 139.34 \times 10^{-3} = 0.139$$

Mistake Alert Student sometime forget to change millimeter to meter.

Question 9 A steel cable with a radius of 1.5 cm supports a chair lift at a ski area. If the maximum stress is not to exceed 10^8 N/m^2, what is the maximum load the cable can support?

Note Breaking stress is constant for a given material.

Sol. Given, radius of steel cable (r) = 1.5 cm = 1.5×10^{-2} m

Maximum stress = 10^8 N/m^2

Area of cross-section of steel cable (A) = πr^2

$$= 3.14 \times (1.5 \times 10^{-2})^2 \text{ m}^2$$

$$= 3.14 \times 2.25 \times 10^{-4} \text{ m}^2$$

$$\text{Maximum stress} = \frac{\text{Maximum force}}{\text{Area of cross - section}}$$

or $$\text{Maximum force} = \text{Maximum stress} \times \text{Area of cross-section}$$

$$= 10^8 \times (3.14 \times 2.25 \times 10^{-4})\text{ N}$$

$$= 7.065 \times 10^4 \text{ N}$$

$$= 7.1 \times 10^4 \text{ N}$$

Question 10 A rigid bar of mass 15 kg is supported symmetrically by three wires each 2 m long. Those at each end are of copper and the middle one is of iron. Determine the ratios of their diameters if each is to have the same tension.

Sol. Young's modulus of copper $(Y_1) = 110 \times 10^9 \text{ N/m}^2$

Young's modulus of steel $(Y_2) = 190 \times 10^9 \text{ N/m}^2$

Let d_1 and d_2 be the diameters of steel and copper wires.

Since tension in each wire is same, therefore each wire has same extension. As each wire in of same length, hence each wire has same strain.

$$\text{Young's modulus } (Y) = \frac{\text{Strees}}{\text{Strain}} = \frac{F/A}{\text{Strain}}$$

or $$Y = \frac{F}{\left(\frac{\pi d^2}{4}\right)\text{Strain}} = \frac{4F}{\pi d^2 \times \text{Strain}}$$

$\therefore$ $$Y \propto \frac{1}{d^2} \text{ or } d^2 \propto \frac{1}{Y}$$

$\therefore$ $$\frac{d_1^2}{d_2^2} = \frac{Y_2}{Y_1}$$

or $$\frac{d_1}{d_2} = \sqrt{\frac{Y_2}{Y_1}} = \sqrt{\frac{190 \times 10^9}{110 \times 10^9}}$$

$$= \sqrt{\frac{19}{11}} = \sqrt{1.73}$$

$$= 1.31$$

$\therefore$ $$d_1 : d_2 = 1.31 : 1$$

Question 11 A 14.5 kg mass, fastened to one end of a steel wire of unstretched length 1 m is whirled in a vertical circle with an angular frequency of 2 rev/s at the bottom of the circle. The cross-sectional area of the wire is 0.065 cm^2. Calculate the elongation of the wire when the mass is at the lowest point of its path.

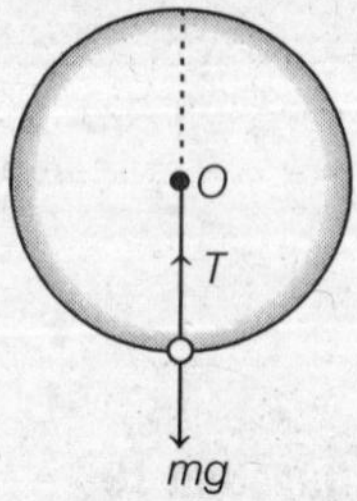

Sol. Given, mass $(m) = 14.5\,\text{kg}$

Length of wire $(l) = 1\,\text{m}$

Angular frequency $(\nu) = 2\,\text{rev/s}$

Angular velocity $(\omega) = 2\pi\nu$

$= 2\pi \times 2\,\text{rad/s}$

$= 4\pi\,\text{rad/s}$

Area of cross-section of wire $(A) = 0.065\,\text{cm}^2$

$= 6.5 \times 10^{-6}\,\text{m}^2$

Young's modulus for steel $(Y) = 2 \times 10^{11}\,\text{N/m}^2$.

At lowest point of the vertical circle, $\left[\frac{mv^2}{l} = \frac{m(lw)^2}{l}\right]$

$$T - mg = ml\omega^2$$

or $$T = mg + ml\omega^2$$

$$= (14.5 \times 9.8) + (14.5 \times 1 \times 4\pi)^2$$

$$= 14.5(9.8 + 16\pi^2)$$

$$= 14.5(9.8 + 16 \times 9.87) \quad (\because \pi^2 = 9.87)$$

$$= 14.5 \times 167.72\,\text{N}$$

$$= 2431.94\,\text{N}$$

Young's modulus $(Y) = \frac{\text{Stress}}{\text{Strain}} = \frac{(T/A)}{\Delta l/l}$

$$= \frac{Tl}{A \cdot \Delta l}$$

$\therefore$ $$\Delta l = \frac{T \cdot l}{A \cdot Y}$$

$$= \frac{2431.94 \times 1}{6.5 \times 10^{-6} \times 2 \times 10^{11}}$$

$$= 1.87 \times 10^{-3}\,\text{m}$$

$$= 1.87\,\text{mm}$$

Question 12 Compute the bulk modulus of water from the following data : initial volume = 100.0 L, pressure increase = 100.0 atm (1 atm = 1.013×10^5 Pa), final volume = 100.5 L. Compare the bulk modulus of water with that of air (at constant temperature). Explain in simple terms why the ratio is so large?

Sol. Given, initial volume $(V_1) = 100.0\,\text{L}$

Final volume $(V_2) = 100.5\,\text{L}$

$\therefore$ Increase in volume $(\Delta V) = V_2 - V_1$

$= 100.5 - 100.0$

$$= 0.5 \text{ L}$$
$$= 0.5 \times 10^{-3} \text{ m}^3 \qquad (\because 1 \text{ L} = 10^{-3} \text{ m}^3)$$

$$\text{Increase in pressure } (\Delta p) = 100.0 \text{ atm}$$
$$= 100.0 \times 1.013 \times 10^5 \text{Pa} \, (\because 1 \text{ atm} = 1.013 \times 10^5 \text{Pa})$$
$$= 1.013 \times 10^7 \text{ Pa}$$

$$\text{Bulk modulus of water } (K_w) = \frac{\Delta p}{(\Delta V / V)} = \frac{\Delta p \cdot V}{\Delta V}$$
$$= \frac{1.013 \times 10^7 \times 100 \times 10^{-3}}{0.5 \times 10^{-3}}$$
$$= \frac{10.13}{5} \times 10^9 \text{ Pa} = 2.026 \times 10^9 \text{ Pa}$$

$$\text{Bulk modulus of air } (K_a) = 1.0 \times 10^5 \text{ Pa}$$
$$\therefore \quad \frac{\text{Bulk modulus of water } (K_w)}{\text{Bulk modulus of air } (K_a)} = \frac{2.026 \times 10^9}{1.0 \times 10^5} = 2.026 \times 10^4$$

This ratio is too large as gases are more compressible than those of liquids. In liquids interatomic forces are more strong than that for gases.

Question 13 What is the density of water at a depth where pressure is 80.0 atm, given that its density at the surface is 1.03×10^3 kg/m^3, compressibility of water is 45.8×10^{-11} Pa^{-1}.

◎ ***Thinking Process*** According to question, given SI unit of compressibility of water and Si unit of pressure should be same.

Sol. Density of water at the surface $(\rho_0) = 1.03 \times 10^3$ kg/m^3

$$\text{Pressure } (p) = 80.0 \text{ atm}$$
$$= 80.0 \times 1.013 \times 10^5 \text{ Pa} \qquad (\because 1 \text{ atm} = 1.013 \times 10^5 \text{ Pa})$$
$$\text{Compressibility of water} \left(\frac{1}{K}\right) = 45.8 \times 10^{-11} \text{ Pa}^{-1}$$

Let V and V' be the volumes of certain mass of water at the surface and at a given depth. The density of water at the given depth be ρ'.

Volume of water at the surface, $V = \dfrac{m}{\rho}$

At the given depth, $\quad V' = \dfrac{m}{\rho'}$

$\therefore$ Change in volume, $\quad \Delta V = V - V'$

$$= m\left(\frac{1}{\rho} - \frac{1}{\rho'}\right)$$

$$\text{Volumetric strain} = \frac{\Delta V}{V} = m\left(\frac{1}{\rho} - \frac{1}{\rho'}\right) \times \frac{\rho}{m}$$

$$= \left(1 - \frac{\rho}{\rho'}\right)$$

$$\text{Compressibility} = \frac{1}{\text{Bulk modulus }(K)}$$

$$= \frac{1}{\dfrac{p}{(\Delta V / V)}} = \frac{\Delta V}{pV}$$

$$45.8 \times 10^{-11} = \left(1 - \frac{\rho}{\rho'}\right) \times \frac{1}{80 \times 1.013 \times 10^5}$$

$$45.8 \times 10^{-11} \times 80 \times 1.013 \times 10^5 = 1 - \frac{1.03 \times 10^3}{\rho'}$$

$$3.712 \times 10^{-3} = 1 - \frac{1.03 \times 10^3}{\rho'}$$

$$\frac{1.03 \times 10^3}{\rho'} = 1 - 3.712 \times 10^{-3}$$

or $$\rho' = \frac{1.03 \times 10^3}{1 - 0.003712} = 1.034 \times 10^3 \text{ kg/m}^3$$

Question 14 Compute the fractional change in volume of a glass slab, when subjected to a hydraulic pressure of 10 atm.

Sol. Pressure (p) = 10 atm = $10 \times 1.013 \times 10^5$ Pa ($\because$ 1 atm = 1.013×10^5 Pa)

$$= 1.013 \times 10^6 \text{ Pa}$$

Bulk modulus for glass (K) = 37×10^9 N/m^2

(Using value from table given in Book)

Fractional change in volume $\left(\dfrac{\Delta V}{V}\right) = ?$

$$\text{Bulk modulus }(K) = \frac{p}{\Delta V / V} = \frac{pV}{\Delta V}$$

$$\therefore \quad \frac{\Delta V}{V} = \frac{p}{K}$$

$$= \frac{1.013 \times 10^6}{37 \times 10^9}$$

$$= \frac{101.3}{37} \times 10^{-5} = 2.74 \times 10^{-5}$$

$\therefore$ Fractional change in volume $\left(\dfrac{\Delta V}{V}\right) = 2.74 \times 10^{-5}$

Question 15 Determine the volume contraction of a solid copper cube, 10 cm on an edge, when subjected to a hydraulic pressure of 7×10^6 Pa.

Sol. Given, each side of cube $(l) = 10\text{ cm} = 0.1\text{ m}$

Hydraulic pressure $(p) = 7 \times 10^6$ Pa

Bulk modulus for copper $(K) = 140 \times 10^9$ Pa

Volume contraction $(\Delta V) = ?$

Volume of the cube $(V) = l^3$

$$= (0.1)^3 = 1 \times 10^{-3}\text{ m}^3$$

$$\text{Bulk modulus for copper } (K) = \frac{p}{\Delta V / V} = \frac{pV}{\Delta V}$$

or

$$\Delta V = \frac{pV}{K}$$

$$\Delta V = \frac{7 \times 10^6 \times 1 \times 10^{-3}}{140 \times 10^9}$$

$$= \frac{1}{20} \times 10^{-6}\text{ m}^3$$

$$= 0.05 \times 10^{-6}\text{ m}^3$$

$$= 5 \times 10^{-8}\text{ m}^3$$

Question 16 How much should the pressure on a litre of water be changed to compress it by 0.10%?

Sol. Change in volume, $\Delta V = V \times \frac{0.10}{100}$

or

$$\frac{\Delta V}{V} = \frac{0.10}{100} = 1 \times 10^{-3}$$

Bulk modulus of water $(K) = 2.2 \times 10^9\text{ N/m}^2$

Pressure on water $(\Delta p) = ?$

$$\text{Bulk modulus of water } (K) = \frac{\Delta p}{\Delta V / V}$$

or

$$\Delta p = K \times \frac{\Delta V}{V}$$

$$= 2.2 \times 10^9 \times 1 \times 10^{-3}$$

$$= 2.2 \times 10^6\text{ N/m}^2$$

Mechanical Properties of Fluids

CHAPTER 09

Important Points

01 Fluids are those substances which can flow. Liquids and gases are fluids.

02 Pressure $= \dfrac{\text{Force}}{\text{Area}}$

It is a scalar quantity and its unit is N/m^2.

03 Liquids apply pressure on bottom and walls of the container in which they are filled.

04 Pressure exerted by a liquid column at depth h is given by

$$p = h\rho g$$

where, ρ = density of the liquid

g = acceleration due to gravity

h = depth of the below surface

05 **Pascal's Law** States that the increase in pressure at one point of the enclosed liquid in equilibrium of rest is transmitted equally to all other points of the liquid in all directions.

06 Hydraulic brakes, hydraulic lift, hydraulic press etc., works on the basis of Pascal's law.

07 **Equation of Continuity**

$$a_1 v_1 = a_2 v_2$$

where a_1, a_2 and v_1, v_2 are area of cross-section and velocity of liquids at two positions in a tube.

08 Flow of Liquid

(i) **Streamline Flow** The flow of liquid in which each of its particle passing through a point follows the same path as followed by the proceeding particle, is called streamlined flow.

(ii) **Laminar Flow** The steady flow of a liquid over a horizontal surface in the form of layers of different velocities, is called laminar flow.

(iii) **Turbulent Flow** The flow of liquid in which each of its particle passing through a point does not follow the same path as followed by the proceeding particle, is called turbulent flow.

09 Bernoulli's Theorem If an ideal liquid is flowing in streamlined flow, then total energy *i.e.*, sum of pressure energy, kinetic energy and potential energy per unit volume of the liquid remains constant at every cross-section of the tube.

Mathematically,

$$p + \frac{1}{2}\rho v^2 + \rho g h = \text{constant}$$

or

$$\frac{p}{\rho g} + \frac{v^2}{2g} + h = \text{constant}$$

where, $\frac{p}{\rho g}$ = pressure head

$\frac{v^2}{2g}$ = velocity head

h = gravitational head

10 For horizontal flow of fluid,

$$p + \frac{1}{2}\rho v^2 = \text{constant}$$

11 Torricelli's Theorem

Velocity of efflux $v = \sqrt{2gh}$

where, h = depth of orifice below the free surface of liquid.

12 **Critical Velocity** The velocity of liquid flow below which its flow is streamlined and above which it becomes turbulent, is called critical velocity.

Critical velocity $v_e = \frac{k\eta}{r\rho}$

where, k = reynolds number

η = coefficient of viscosity of liquid

r = radius of capillary tube

ρ = density of the liquid

13 The height of liquid column in a capillary tube is given by

$$h = \frac{2S\cos\theta}{r\rho g}$$

where, r is the radius of the capillary tube, θ is angle of contact and ρ is the density of the liquid.

Reynolds number (k) is a pure number which tells about the flow of liquid.

If $0 < k < 2000$, then flow of liquid is streamlined.

If $2000 < k < 3000$, the flow of liquid is variable between streamline and turbulent.

If $k > 3000$, then flow of liquid is turbulent.

14 **Magnus Effect** The Magnus effect is the sideways force that make a spinning object curve in air or water.

15 **Viscosity** The property of a fluid by virtue of which an internal frictional force acts between its different layers, which opposes their relative motion is called viscosity.

16 These internal frictional force is called viscous force.

$$\text{Viscous force } (F) = \eta A \frac{dv}{dx}$$

where, A = area of cross-section.

$\frac{dv}{dx}$ = rate of change of velocity with distance called velocity gradient and η is the coefficient of viscosity.

17 **Surface Tension** The property of a liquid by virtue of which it tries to acquire minimum surface area, is called surface tension.

Poiseuille's Formula The rate of flow of liquid through a horizontal pipe for steady flow is given by $V = \frac{\pi}{8} \frac{pr^4}{\eta l}$

where, p = pressure difference across the ends of the pipe
r = radius of the pipe, l = length of time pipe
η = coefficient of viscosity of the liquid.

18 Surface tension is defined as the force acting per unit length at the imaginary line drawn at the surface of the liquid. It is denoted by 'S'.

$$\text{Surface tension } (S) = \frac{F}{l}$$

Its unit is 'N/m'.

19 **Surface Energy** Surface energy of a given liquid surface is equal to the work done against the force of surface tension, in forming the liquid surface of given area at a constant temperature.

Surface energy $(E) = S \times \Delta A$

20 **Angle of Contact** The angle subtended between the tangent drawn at liquid surface and tangent drawn as solid surface inside the liquid, at the point of contact, is called angle of contact.

If angle of contact θ is acute, then liquid surface in capillary tube is concave. If angle of contact θ is obtuse, then liquid surface in capillary tube is convex.

21 Excess of pressure inside a liquid drop $p = \frac{2S}{R}$

Excess of pressure inside a soap bubble $p = \frac{4S}{R}$

Excess of pressure inside an air bubble in a liquid

$$p = \frac{2S}{R}$$

where, S is the surface tension and R is the radius of the drop of bubble.

22 The phenomena of rising or falling of liquid in a capillary tube is called capillarity.

Exercises

Question 1 Explain why?

(a) The blood pressure in humans is greater at the feet than the brain.

(b) Atmospheric pressure at a height of about 6 km decreases to nearly half its value at the sea level though the height of the atmosphere is more than 100 km.

(c) Hydrostatic pressure is a scalar quantity even though pressure is force divided by area.

Sol.

(a) The pressure of liquid column is given by $p = h\rho g$, where h is depth, ρ is density and g is acceleration due to gravity. Therefore, pressure of liquid column increases with depth. The height of blood column in human body is more at feet than at the brain. Therefore, the blood pressure in humans is greater at the feet than the brain.

(b) The density of air is maximum near the surface of the earth and decreases rapidly with height. At a height of 6 km, the density of air decreases to nearly half of its value at the sea level. Beyond 6 km height, the density of air decreases very slowly with height. Hence, the atmospheric pressure at a height of about 6 km decreases to nearly half of its value at the sea level.

(c) When force is applied on a liquid, the pressure is transmitted equally in all directions inside the liquid. Therefore, hydrostatic pressure has no fixed direction and hence, it is a scalar quantity.

Question 2 Explain why?

(a) The angle of contact of mercury with glass is obtuse, while that of water with glass is acute.

(b) Water on a clean glass surface tends to spread out while mercury on the same surface tends to form drops. (Put differently, water wets and glass while mercury does not.)

(c) Surface tension of a liquid is independent of the area of the surface.

(d) Water with detergents dissolved in it should have small angles of contact.

(e) A drop of liquid under no external forces is always spherical in shape

Sol.

(a) When a small quantity of a liquid is poured on a solid, three types of interfaces namely liquid-air, solid-air and solid-liquid are formed.

The surface tension corresponding to these three interfaces are S_{LA}, S_{SA} and S_{SL} respectively. If θ is the angle of contact between solid and liquid then,

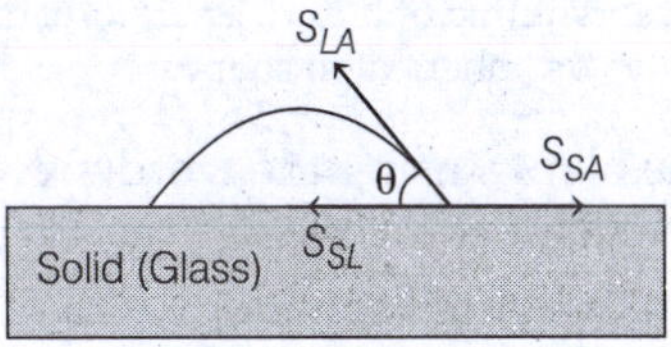

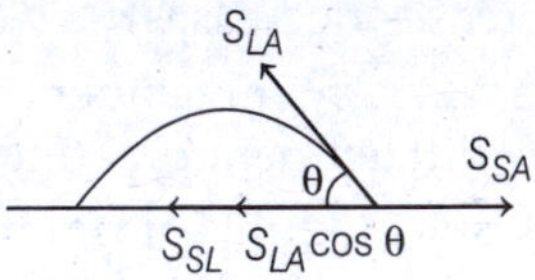

$$S_{SL} + S_{LA}\cos\theta = S_{SA}$$

or
$$S_{LA}\cos\theta = S_{SA} - S_{SL}$$

$$\cos\theta = \frac{S_{SA} - S_{SL}}{S_{LA}} \quad \text{...(i)}$$

For mercury and glass $S_{SA} < S_{SL}$, therefore from Eq. (i) cos θ is negative and therefore θ > 90° *i.e.*, obtuse.

For water and glass $S_{SA} > S_{SL}$, therefore from Eq. (i) cos θ is positive and therefore θ < 90° *i.e.*, acute.

(b) For equilibrium of a liquid drop on a solid surface

$$S_{SL} + S_{LA}\cos\theta = S_{SA}$$

In case of mercury and glass, $S_{SL} > S_{SA}$, therefore for equilibrium cos θ should be negative *i.e.*, θ should be obtuse. In order to achieve this obtuse value of angle of contact, the mercury tends to form a drop. In case of water and glass, $S_{SA} > S_{SL}$, therefore for equilibrium cos θ should be positive *i.e.*, θ should be acute.

In order to achieve this acute value of angle of contact, the water tends to spread.

(c) Surface tension of a liquid is defined as the force acting per unit length on an imaginary line drawn tangentially to the liquid surface at rest. Therefore, surface tension is independent of the area of the liquid surface.

(d) The rise of liquid in a capillary tube is given by

$$h = \frac{2s\cos\theta}{r\rho g}$$

$$\therefore \quad h \propto \cos\theta$$

The cloth has narrow spaces in the form of fine capillaries. If angle of contact θ is small, then the value of cos θ will be large and hence detergent will rise more in fine capillaries in the cloth. Now, the detergent solution will penetrate more in cloth and remove dust from the cloth.

(e) In the absence of external forces, the size of a liquid drop is decided only by the force due to surface tension. Due to surface tension, a liquid drop tends to acquire minimum surface area. As surface area is minimum for a sphere for a given volume of liquid. Therefore, under no external force a liquid drop is always spherical in shape.

Question 3 Fill in the blanks using the word(s) from the list appended with each statement.

(a) Surface tension of liquids generally .... with temperature. (increases/decreases)

(b) Viscosity of gases .... with temperature, whereas viscosity of liquids .... with temperature. (increases/decreases)

(c) For solids with elastic modulus of rigidity, the shearing force is proportional to ...., while for fluids it is proportional to .... (shear strain/rate of shear strain)

(d) For a fluid in a steady flow, the increase in flow speed at a constriction follows from ...., while the decrease of pressure there follows from .... (conservation of mass/Bernoulli's principle).

(e) For the model of a plane in a wind tunnel, turbulence occurs at a .... speed that the critical speed for turbulence for an actual plane. (greater/smaller)

Sol.

(a) decreases.

(b) increases, decreases.

(c) shear strain, rate of shear strain.

(d) conservation of mass, Bernoulli's principle.

(e) greater.

Question 4 Explain why?

(a) To keep a piece of paper horizontal, you should blow over, not under it.

(b) When we try to close a water tap with our fingers, fast jets of water gush through the opening between our fingers.

(c) The size of the needle of a syringe controls flow rate better than the thumb pressure exerted by a doctor while administering an injection.

(d) A fluid flowing out of a small hole in a vessel results in a backward thrust on the vessel.

(e) A spinning cricket ball in air does not follow a parabolic trajectory.

◎ *Thinking Process* According to Bernoulli's theorem, for horizontal flow of fluids,

$$p + \frac{1}{2}\rho v^2 = \text{constant}$$

Therefore, when velocity of a fluid increases, its pressure decreases and *vice-versa.*

Sol.

(a) When we blow over a piece of paper, the velocity of air above the paper increases. So, in accordance with Bernoulli's theorem $\left(p + \frac{1}{2}\rho v^2 = \text{constant}\right)$, the pressure of air decreases above the paper. Due to the pressure difference of air between below and above the paper a lifting force acts on paper and hence, it remain horizontal.

(b) According to equation of continuity for steady flow of liquid the product of area of cross-section of the tube and velocity of liquid remains constant at each point *i.e.,*

$$A_1 v_1 = A_2 v_2$$

When we try to close a water tap with our fingers, the area of cross-section of the outlet of water jet is reduced due to the restriction provided by the fingers and therefore, the velocity of water increases and fast jets of water gush through the openings between our fingers.

(c) According to Bernoulli's theorem,

$$p + \frac{1}{2}\rho v^2 = \text{constant}$$

In this relation pressure (p) occurs with one power while velocity (v) occurs with two powers. Therefore, the influence of velocity is higher than pressure.

The size of the needle controls the velocity of flow and the thumb pressure controls pressure. Therefore, size of the needle of a syringe controls flow rate better than thumb pressure.

(d) A fluid flowing out of a small hole in a vessel have a large velocity and therefore a large momentum. As no external force is acting therefore according to law of conservation of momentum equal momentum in opposite direction and hence, a backward velocity is attained by the vessel. Therefore, a backward thrust $\left(F = \frac{dp}{dt}\right)$ acts on the vessel.

(e) A spinning cricket ball in air does not follow a parabolic trajectory due to Magnus effect.

Let a spinning cricket ball is moving forward with a velocity v and spinning clockwise with velocity u. As ball moves forward, if leaves a lower pressure region behind it. To fill this region, air moves backward with velocity v. The layers of air in contact with the ball spins with ball with velocity u.

Therefore, the resultant velocity of air above the ball is $(v - u)$ and below the ball is $(v + u)$. According to Bernoulli's theorem $p + \frac{1}{2}\rho v^2 = \text{constant}$.

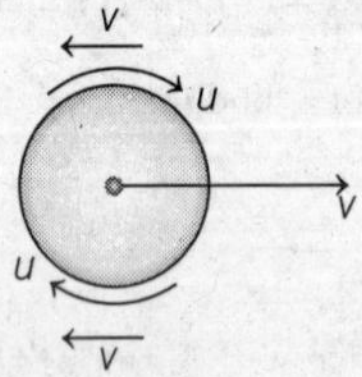

Therefore, pressure below the ball becomes lower than above the ball. Due to this pressure difference a force acts on ball in downward direction. Therefore, the ball follows a curved path in spite of a parabolic trajectory.

Question 5 A 50 kg girl wearing high heel shoes balances on a single heel. The heel is circular with a diameter 1.0 cm. What is the pressure exerted on the horizontal floor?

Sol. Given, mass of girl $(m) = 50$ kg

Diameter of circular heel $(2r) = 1.0$ cm

$\therefore$ Radius $(r) = 0.5$ cm

$= 5 \times 10^{-3}$ m

Area of circular heel $(A) = \pi r^2 = 3.14 \times (5 \times 10^{-3})^2 \text{ m}^2$

$= 78.50 \times 10^{-6} \text{m}^2$

$\therefore$ Pressure exerted on the horizontal floor

$$p = \frac{F}{A} = \frac{mg}{A} = \frac{50 \times 9.8}{78.50 \times 10^{-6}}$$

$$= 6.24 \times 10^6 \text{ Pa}$$

Mistake Alert The most common mistakes is forgetting to convert the diameter or radius from centimeters to meters.

Question 6 Torricelli's barometer used mercury. Pascal duplicated it using French wine of density 984 kg/m^3. Determine the height of the wine column for normal atmospheric pressure.

Thinking Process The pressure exerted by a liquid column, $p = h\rho g$

where, h = height of liquid column

ρ = density of liquid

g = acceleration due to gravity

Sol. Atmospheric pressure (p) = 1.013×10^5 Pa

Density of French wine (ρ) = 984 kg/m^3

Let h be the height of the wine column for normal atmospheric pressure.

For normal atmospheric pressure (p) = $h\rho g$

$$\therefore \quad h = \frac{p}{\rho g} = \frac{1.013 \times 10^5}{984 \times 9.8}$$

$$= 10.5 \text{ m}$$

Question 7 A vertical off-shore structure is built to withstand a maximum stress of 10^9 Pa. Is the structure suitable for putting up on top of an oil well in the ocean? Take the depth of the ocean to be roughly 3 km and ignore ocean currents.

Sol. Given, depth of ocean (h) = 3 km = 3000 m

Density of water (ρ) = 10^3 kg/m^3

Pressure exerted by water column, $p = h\rho g = 3000 \times 10^3 \times 9.8$

$$= 29.4 \times 10^6 = 2.94 \times 10^7 \text{ Pa}$$

Maximum stress which can be withstand by
the vertical off-shore structure = 10^9 Pa

As $\quad 10^9 \text{ Pa} > 2.9 \times 10^7 \text{ Pa}$

Therefore, the vertical structure is suitable for putting up on top of an oil well in the ocean.

Question 8 A hydraulic automobile lift is designed to lift cars with a maximum mass of 3000 kg. The area of cross-section of the piston carrying the load is 425 cm^2. What maximum pressure would the smaller piston have to bear?

Sol. Given, maximum mass that can be lifted (m) = 3000 kg

Area of cross-section (A) = 425 cm^2 = 4.25×10^{-2} m^2 [1 cm^2 = 10^{-4} m^2]

$\therefore$ Maximum pressure on the bigger piston.

$$p = \frac{F}{A} = \frac{mg}{A} = \frac{3000 \times 9.8}{4.25 \times 10^{-2}} = 6.92 \times 10^5 \text{ Pa}$$

According to Pascal's law, the pressure applied on an enclosed liquid is transmitted equally in all directions.

$\therefore$ Maximum pressure on smaller piston

= Maximum pressure on bigger piston

$$p' = p = 6.92 \times 10^5 \text{ Pa}$$

Question 9 A U-tube contains water and methylated spirit separated by mercury. The mercury columns in the two arms are in level with 10.0 cm of water in one arm and 12.5 cm of spirit in the other. What is the specific gravity of spirit?

Sol.

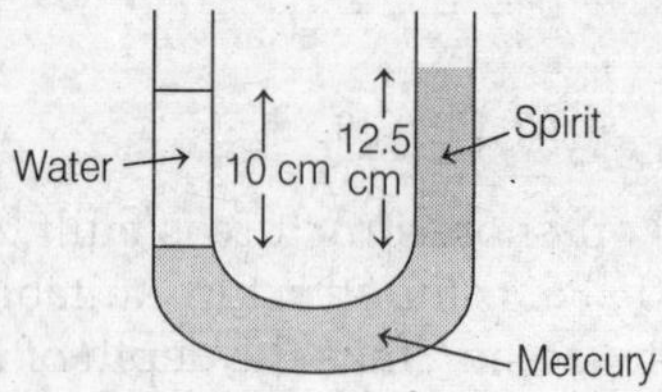

Height of water column $h_1 = 10.0$ cm

Density of water $(\rho_1) = 1\ g/cm^3$

Height of spirit column $(h_2) = 12.5$ cm

Density of spirit $(\rho_2) = ?$

The mercury column in both arms of the U-tube are at same level, therefore pressure in both arms will be same.

$\therefore$ Pressure exerted by water column = Pressure exerted by sprit column

$\therefore$
$$p_1 = p_2$$
$$h_1\rho_1 g = h_2\rho_2 g$$

or
$$\rho_2 = \frac{h_1\rho_1}{h_2} = \frac{10 \times 1}{12.5} = 0.80\ g/cm^3$$

$$\text{Specific gravity of spirit} = \frac{\text{Density of spirit}}{\text{Density of water}} = \frac{0.80}{1} = 0.80$$

Question 10 In the Q. 9 if 15.0 cm of water and spirit each are further poured into the respective arms of the tube, what is the difference in the levels of mercury in the two arms? (Specific gravity of mercury = 13.6)

Sol. When 15.0 cm of water is poured in each arm then,

height of water column $(h_1) = 10 + 15 = 25$ cm

Height of spirit column $(h_2) = 12.5 + 15 = 27.5$ cm

Density of water $(\rho_w) = 1\ g/cm^3$

Density of spirit $(\rho_s) = 0.80\ g/cm^3$

Density of mercury $(\rho_m) = 13.6\ g/cm^3$

Let in equilibrium, the difference in the level of mercury in both arms be h cm.

[Since, specific gravity of spirit is less then water, so mercury will rise in arm containing spirit.]

$\therefore$
$$h\rho_m g = h_1\rho_w g - h_2\rho_s g$$

or
$$h = \frac{h_1\rho_w - h_2\rho_s}{\rho_m} = \frac{25 \times 1 - 27.5 \times 0.80}{13.6}$$
$$= 0.221 \text{ cm}$$

Therefore, mercury will rise in the arm containing spirit by 0.221 cm.

Mistake Alert Student might forget to add the additional height of water and spirit to the initial height.

Question 11 Can Bernoulli's equation be used to describe the flow of water through a rapid in a river? Explain.

Sol. No, Bernoulli's equation cannot be used to describe the flow of water through a rapid in a river because Bernoulli's equation can be utilized only for streamlined flow.

Question 12 Does it matter if one uses gauge instead of absolute pressures in applying Bernoulli's equation? Explain.

Sol. No, it does not matter if one uses gauge instead of absolute pressures in applying Bernoulli's equation unless the atmospheric pressure at the two points where Bernoulli's equation is applied are significantly different.

Question 13 Glycerine flows steadily through a horizontal tube of length 1.5 m and radius 1.0 cm. If the amount of glycerine collected per second at one end is 4.0×10^{-3} kg/s. What is the pressure difference between the two ends of the tube? (Density of glycerine = 1.3×10^3 kg/m^3 and viscosity of glycerine = 0.83 Pa-s). (You may also like to check if the assumption of laminar flow in the tube is correct.)

Thinking Process The velocity above which flow of fluid becomes turbulent is known as critical velocity.
For critical velocity Reynolds number > 3000.

Sol. Given, length of the tube (l) = 1.5 m

Radius of the tube (r) = 1.0 cm = 1×10^{-2} m

Mass of glycerine flowing per second = 4×10^{-3} kg/s

Density of glycerine (ρ) = 1.3×10^3 kg/m^3

Viscosity of glycerine (η) = 0.83 Pa-s

Volume of glycerine flowing per second *i.e.*, rate of flow (V) = $\frac{m}{\rho}$

$$\left[\because \text{Density} = \frac{\text{Mass}}{\text{Volume}}\right]$$

$$= \frac{4 \times 10^{-3}}{1.3 \times 10^3} \text{ m}^3/\text{s}$$

$$= \frac{4}{1.3} \times 10^{-6} \text{ m}^3/\text{s}$$

According to Poiseuille's formula, the rate of flow of liquid through a tube

$$V = \frac{\pi\, pr^4}{8\, \eta \rho}$$

where, p is the pressure difference between the two ends of the tube.

or $$p = \frac{8\eta\rho V}{\pi r^4} = \frac{8 \times 0.83 \times 1.5 \times 4 \times 10^{-6}}{3.14 \times (1 \times 10^{-2})^4 \times 1.3}$$

$$= 975.37 \text{ Pa}$$

$$= 9.75 \times 10^2 \text{ Pa}$$

To check the laminar flow in the tube, the value of Reynolds number should be less than 2000.

Reynolds number $k = \frac{\rho D v_c}{\eta}$

where, v_c is the critical velocity and D is the diameter of the tube.

Critical velocity $v_c = \frac{\text{Volume flowing out per second}}{\text{Area of cross - section}}$

$$= \frac{m/\rho}{A} = \frac{m}{\rho \pi r^2} \qquad (\because A = \pi r^2)$$

$\therefore$ $$\text{Reynolds number } k = \frac{\rho D}{\eta} \times \frac{m}{\rho \pi r^2}$$

$$= \frac{2r \times m}{\eta \pi r^2} \qquad (\because D = 2r)$$

$$= \frac{2m}{\pi r \eta} = \frac{2 \times 4 \times 10^{-3}}{3.14 \times 10^{-2} \times 0.83} = 0.31$$

As $k < 2000$, therefore flow of glycerine is laminar.

Question 14 In a test experiment on a model aeroplane in a wind tunnel, the flow speeds on the upper and lower surfaces of the wing are 70 m/s and 63 m/s respectively. What is the lift on the wing, if its area is 2.5 m^2? Take the density of air to be 1.3 kg/m^3.

Sol Let the lower and upper surface of the wings of the aeroplane be at the same height h and speeds of air on the upper and lower surfaces of the wings be v_1 and v_2

Speed of air on the upper surface of the wing $v_1 = 70$ m/s

speed of air on the lower surface of the wings $v_2 = 63$ m/s

Density of the air $\rho = 1.3$ kg/m^3

Area $A = 2.5$ m^2

According to Bernoulli's theorem,

$$p_1 + \frac{1}{2}\rho v_1^2 + \rho g h = p_2 + \frac{1}{2}\rho v_2^2 + \rho g h$$

or $$p_2 - p_1 = \frac{1}{2}\rho(v_1^2 - v_2^2)$$

$\therefore$ Lifting force acting on the wings,

$$F = (p_2 - p_1) \times A = \frac{1}{2}\rho(v_1^2 - v_2^2) \times A \qquad \left[\because \text{Pressure} = \frac{\text{Force}}{\text{Area}}\right]$$

$$= \frac{1}{2} \times 1.3 \times [(70)^2 - (63)^2] \times 2.5$$

$$= \frac{1}{2} \times 1.3\,[4900 - 3969] \times 2.5$$

$$= \frac{1}{2} \times 1.3 \times 931 \times 2.5 = 1.51 \times 10^3 \text{ N}$$

Mistake Alert Some student might forget to include the pressure terms in bernoullis equation or might incorrectly equate the pressure term.

Question 15 Figs. (a) and (b) refer to the steady flow of a (non-viscous) liquid. Which of the two figures is incorrect? Why?

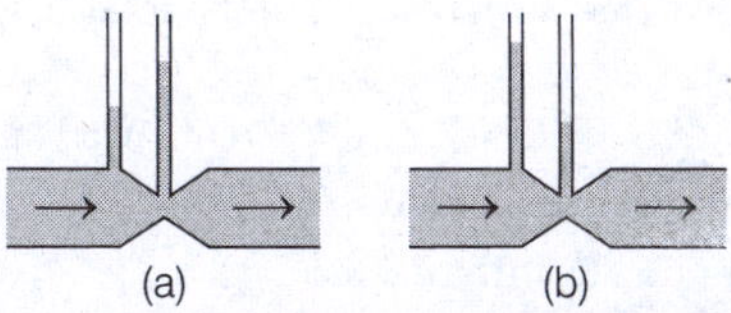

Sol. Fig. (a) is incorrect. From equation of continuity, the speed of liquid is larger at smaller area. According to Bernoulli's theorem due to larger speed the pressure will be lower at smaller area and therefore, height of liquid column will also be at lesser height, while in Fig. (a) height of liquid column at narrow area is higher.

Question 16 The cylindrical tube of a spray pump has a cross-section of 8.0 cm^2 one end of which has 40 fine holes each of diameter 1.0 mm. If the liquid flow inside the tube is 1.5 m/min, what is the speed of ejection of the liquid through the holes?

Sol. Area of cross-section of tube $(A) = 8 \text{ cm}^2 = 8 \times 10^{-4} \text{ m}^2$

Number of holes $(N) = 40$

Diameter of each hole $(2r) = 1.0$ mm

$\therefore$ Radius of each hole $(r) = 0.5$ mm

$= 5 \times 10^{-4}$ m

Velocity of liquid flow in tube $= 1.5 \text{ m/min} = \frac{1.5}{60}$ m/s

$= 2.5 \times 10^{-2}$ m/s

Total area of holes $= N \times \pi r^2$

$= 40 \times 3.14 \times (5 \times 10^{-4})^2 = 3.14 \times 10^{-5} \text{ m}^2$

According to equation of continuity,

$$A_1 v_1 = A_2 v_2$$

or $$v_2 = \frac{A_1 v_1}{A_2} = \frac{8 \times 10^{-4} \times 2.5 \times 10^{-2}}{3.14 \times 10^{-5}}$$

$$= \frac{20}{3.14} \times 10^{-1} = 0.64 \text{ m/s}$$

Question 17 A U-shaped wire is dipped in a soap solution and removed. The thin soap film formed between the wire and a light slider supports a weight of 1.5×10^{-2} N (which includes the small weight of the slider). The length of the slider is 30 cm. What is the surface tension of the film?

Sol. Length of the slider (l) = 30 cm.

As a soap film has two free surfaces, therefore total length of the film to be supported

$$l' = 2l = 2 \times 30 = 60 \text{ cm} = 0.60 \text{ m}$$

Let S be the surface tension of the soap Sol..

Total force on the slider due to surface tension, $F = S \times 2l$

$$F = S \times 0.60 \text{ N} \quad \text{...(i)}$$

Weight (w) supported by the slider (w) = 1.5×10^{-2} N

In equilibrium,

Force on the slider due to surface tension = weight supported by the slider

$\therefore$ $$F = w$$

$$S \times 0.60 = 1.5 \times 10^{-2}$$

or $$S = \frac{1.5 \times 10^{-2}}{0.60} = 2.5 \times 10^{-2} \text{ N/m}$$

Mistake Alert Student can forget to consider the two free surface of the soap film.

Question 18 Fig. (a) shows a thin liquid film supporting a small weight = 4.5×10^{-2}N. What is the weight supported by a film of the same liquid at the same temperature in Figs. (b) and (c)? Explain your answer physically.

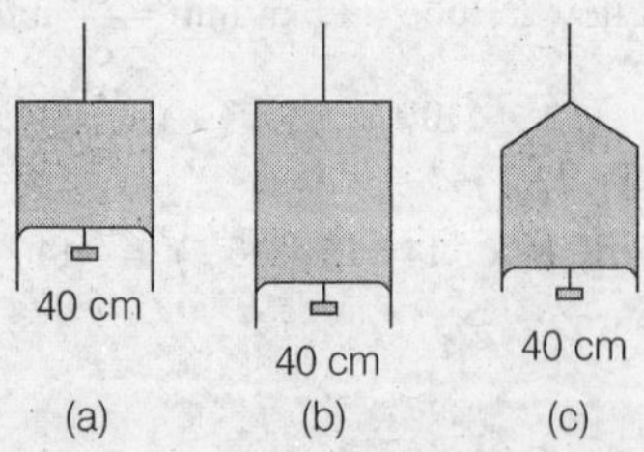

Sol. As liquid is same, temperature is same and the length of the film supporting the weight is also same, therefore in Figs. (b) and (c), the film will support same weight *i.e,* 4.5×10^{-2}N.

Question 19 What is the pressure inside the drop of mercury of radius 3.00 mm at room temperature? Surface tension of mercury at that temperature (20° C) is 4.65×10^{-1} N/m. The atmospheric pressure is 1.01×10^5 Pa. Also give the excess pressure inside the drop.

◎ **Thinking Process** Excess pressure inside a liquid drop is given by

$\Delta p = \dfrac{2S}{R}$ (as liquid drophas one free surface)

where, S = Surface tension of the liquid

R = Radius of the drop.

Sol. Given, radius of drop (R) = 3.00 mm = 3×10^{-3} m

Surface tension of mercury (S) = 4.65×10^{-1} N/m

Atmospheric pressure (p_0) = 1.01×10^5 Pa

Pressure inside the drop = Atmospheric pressure + Excess pressure inside the liquid drop

$$= p_0 + \frac{2S}{R}$$

$$= 1.01 \times 10^5 + \frac{2 \times 4.65 \times 10^{-1}}{3 \times 10^{-3}}$$

$$= 1.01 \times 10^5 + 3.10 \times 10^2$$

$$= 1.01 \times 10^5 + 0.00310 \times 10^5$$

$$= 1.01310 \times 10^5 \text{ Pa}$$

Excess pressure inside the drop (Δp) $= \dfrac{2S}{R} = \dfrac{2 \times 4.65 \times 10^{-1}}{3 \times 10^{-3}}$

$$= 3.10 \times 10^2 = 310 \text{ Pa}$$

Question 20 What is the excess pressure inside a bubble of soap solution of radius 5.00 mm, given that the surface tension of soap solution at the temperature (20° C) is 2.50×10^{-2} N/m? If an air bubble of the same dimension were formed at a depth of 40.0 cm inside a container containing the soap solution (of relative density 1.20), what would be the pressure inside the bubble? (1 atmospheric pressure is 1.01×10^5 Pa.)

◎ **Thinking Process** The excess pressure inside a soap bubble is given by

$\Delta p = \dfrac{4S}{R}$ (as liquid bubble has two free surfaces)

where, S = surface tension of the soap solution.

R = radius of the bubble.

Sol. Given, surface tension of soap solution $(S) = 2.5 \times 10^{-2}$ N/m

Density of soap solution $(\rho) = 1.2 \times 10^3$ kg/m^3

Radius of soap bubble $(r) = 5.00$ mm

$= 5.0 \times 10^{-3}$ m

Atmospheric pressure $(p_0) = 1.01 \times 10^5$ Pa

Excess pressure inside the soap bubble $= \dfrac{4S}{r}$

$$= \frac{4 \times 2.5 \times 10^{-2}}{5.0 \times 10^{-3}} = 20 \text{ Pa}$$

Excess pressure inside the air bubble $= \dfrac{2S}{R} = \dfrac{2 \times 2.5 \times 10^{-2}}{5.0 \times 10^{-3}} = 10$ Pa

$\therefore$ Pressure inside the air bubble = Atmospheric pressure + Pressure due to 40 cm of soap solution column + Excess pressure inside the bubble

$$= (1.01 \times 10^5) + (0.40 \times 1.2 \times 10^3 \times 9.8) + 10$$
$$= (1.01 \times 10^5) + 4.704 \times 10^3 + 10$$
$$= 1.01 \times 10^5 + 0.04704 \times 10^5 + 0.00010 \times 10^5$$
$$= 1.05714 \times 10^5 \text{ Pa}$$
$$= 1.06 \times 10^5 \text{ Pa}$$

DIKSHA APP Questions

☐ Multiple Choice Questions

Q.1 A vessal is filled with a liquid of density d upto a height h. The pressure exerted on the bottom of the vessal will be maximum when the vessal is

(a) on the surface of earth

(b) on top of a hill

(c) deep inside a mine

(d) on the surface of the moon

Sol. (a) Pressure at point is given by $p = h\rho g$.

As g is maximum on the surface of earth.

Q.2 A tank with a square base is divided by a vertical partition in the middle as shown in figure. The bottom of the partition has a small hinged door. The two parts of the tank are filled to the same height with different liquids of densities ρ_1 and ρ_2 $(\rho_1 > \rho_2)$. The door experiences

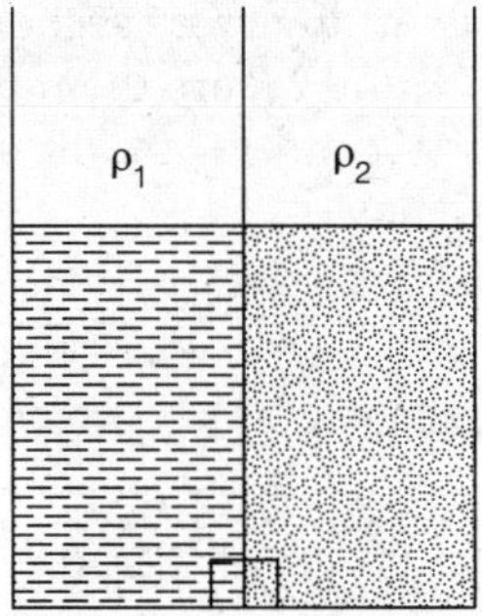

(a) a net force directed towards the right
(b) a net force directed towards the left
(c) no net force
(d) a net force along the vertical.

Sol. (a) As pressure at a point is $P = h\rho g$. Since height of both liquid columns are same and

$$\rho_1 > \rho_2 \text{ so } p_{\text{left}} > p_{\text{right}}$$

Force, $F = p \times A$.

Hence, force from left side is more as compare to right side. Therefore, door experiences a net force towards right.

Q.3 A manometer reads the pressure of a gas in an enclosure as shown in fig. (a). When the pump removes some of the gas, the manometer reads as shown in fig. (b). The change in pressure in the enclosure expressed in terms of the length of the liquid column is

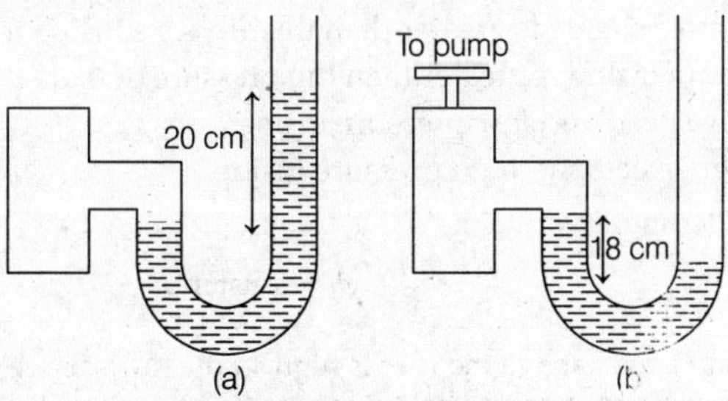

(a) 2 cm (b) 38 cm (c) 40 cm (d) 36 cm

Sol. (b) In figure (a) $P_{Gas} - P_{atm} = 20$ cm of liquid column.

In figure (b) $P_{atm} - P'_{Gas} = 18$ cm of liquid column.

So, change in pressure

$$\Delta P = P_{Gas} - P_{atm} - (P_{atm} - P'_{Gas}) = 20 - (-18)$$
$$= 38 \text{ cm of liquid column.}$$

Q.4 A horizontal tube of varying cross section has a streamlined flow of ideal liquid. R and $2R$ are the radii of the tube at points P and Q respectively. V_P and V_Q are the speeds of flow of the liquid at P and Q. We have

(a) $V_P = 2V_Q$ (b) $2V_P = V_Q$
(c) $V_P = 4V_Q$ (d) $4V_P = V_Q$

Sol. (c) Using equation of continuity

$$A_P V_P = A_Q V_Q$$
$$\pi R^2 V_P = \pi(2R)^2 V_Q$$
$$V_P = 4V_Q$$

Q.5 A horizontal cylindrical tube of radius R open at one end has a plate having N holes each of radius r fixed at the other end. A liquid in streamlined flow enters the open end of the tube with speed v. The speed of liquid emerging out of each hole at the other end is

(a) $\frac{Rv}{Nr}$ (b) $\frac{NRv}{r}$ (c) $\frac{R^2v}{Nr^2}$ (d) $\frac{NR^2v}{r^2}$

Sol. (c) Using equation of continuity

$$a_1v_1 = a_2v_2$$
$$\pi R^2 v = N\pi r^2 v'$$
$$\frac{R^2 v}{Nr^2} = v'$$

Q.6 During storms, the thatched roofs sometime get blown off because.

(a) pressure outside is greater than the pressure inside the room
(b) pressure inside is greater than the pressure outside the room
(c) of low speed and low pressure inside
(d) of high speed and high pressure inside

Sol. (b) Using Bernoulli's principle

$$\frac{P}{\rho} + \frac{v^2}{2} + gh = \text{constant.}$$

Since, wind speed above the roof is high so pressure above roof will be less as compare to pressure below the roof. This pressure difference sometimes lifted up the roof and blow away by storm.

Q.7 The surface of a liquid stored in a glass container is concave. The angle of contact for liquid – glass is θ. We have

(a) $F_{Cohesion} > F_{Adhesion}$ and $\theta > 90°$
(b) $F_{Cohesion} < F_{Adhesion}$ and $\theta < 90°$
(c) $F_{Cohesion} > F_{Adhesion}$ and $\theta < 90°$
(d) $F_{Cohesion} < F_{Adhesion}$ and $\theta > 90°$

Sol. (b) For concave liquid surface adhesive force is greater than cohesive force and angle of contact is acute in nature.

Q.8 Two mercury droplets of radii 0.1 cm and 0.2 cm coalesc into single drop. The surface tension of mercury is 435.5×10^{-3} N/m. The amount of energy released is

(a) -3.7×10^{7} J
(b) 3.2×10^{-6} J
(c) 7.4×10^{-6} J
(d) 3.7×10^{-2} J

Sol. (b) Let r_1, r_2 and R are the radius of first two drops and coalesced drop, then

Initial volume = Final volume

$$\frac{4}{3}\pi r_1^3 + \frac{4}{3}\pi r_2^3 = \frac{4}{3}\pi R^3$$

$$(0.1)^3 + (.2)^3 = R^3$$

$$\Rightarrow \quad R = (0.009)^{1/3} \text{ cm} = 0.21 \text{ cm}.$$

Decrease in Area $= \Delta A = 4\pi r_1^2 + 4\pi r_2^2 - 4\pi R^2$

$= 4\pi\,(0.1)^2 + (0.2) - (0.21)^2]\text{ cm}^2$

$= 4\pi \times 0.067 = 0.074 \text{ cm}^2 = 0.074 \times 10^{-4} \text{ m}^2$

Energy released = Surface tension × decrease in area

$= 435.5 \times 10^{-6} \times 0.074 \times 10^{-4}$

$= 3.2 \times 10^{-6}$ J

Q.9 The work done in increasing the size of a soap film from 10 cm × 6 cm to 10 cm × 11 cm is 2×10^{-4} J. The surface tension of the soap solution is

(a) $2 \times 10^{-2}\text{ Nm}^{-1}$
(b) $2 \times 10^{-6}\text{ Nm}^{-1}$
(c) $2 \times 10^{-4}\text{ Nm}^{-1}$
(d) $4 \times 10^{-2}\text{ Nm}^{-1}$

Sol. (a) We know the soap film has two free surfaces. Work done

$W = 2 \times$ Surface tension × change in area

$[\Delta A = 110\text{ cm}^2 - 60\text{ cm}^2 = 50\text{ cm}^2]$

$2 \times 10^{-4} = 2 \times \text{Surface tension} \times 50 \times 10^{-4}$

$2 \times 10^{-4} = 10^{-2} \times \text{surface tension}$

$2 \times 10^{-2}\text{ Nm}^{-1} = \text{surface tension}$

Q.10 Two capillary tubes A and B with radii in the ratio 1:2 are immersed in a liquid. A mass M of the liquid rises in tube A. The mass of liquid that will rise in tube B is

(a) $4M$

(b) $2M$

(c) M

(d) $\frac{M}{2}$

Sol. (b) The height of liquid column in capillary tube is

$$h = \frac{2T\cos\theta}{r\rho g} \qquad \left(\because h \propto \frac{1}{r}\right)$$

So,
$$\frac{h_1}{h_2} = \frac{r_2}{r_1} = \frac{2}{1}$$

Volume of liquid in capillary tube

$$\frac{V_1}{V_2} = \frac{\pi r_1^2 h_1}{\pi r_2^2 h_2} = \frac{1}{4} \times \frac{2}{1} = \frac{1}{2}$$

$$\therefore \qquad \frac{m_1}{m_2} = \frac{V_1\rho}{V_2\rho} = \frac{1}{2}$$

$$\Rightarrow \qquad m_2 = 2m_1 = 2\,M.$$

Thermal Properties of Matter

CHAPTER 10

Important Points

01 Heat is a form of energy which is transfered between two system.

02 Temperature of a body is the degree of hotness or coldness of the body.

03 Celsius, fahrenheit and kelvin scales are three main scales of temperatures.

$$K = C + 273.15$$

$$\frac{C}{5} = \frac{F - 32}{9}$$

04 Expansion in length, area or in volume due to heating is called thermal expansion.

In linear expansion, $\Delta L = L_0 \alpha \Delta t$

and $L = L_0(1 + \alpha \cdot \Delta t)$

In area expansion,

$$\Delta A = A_0 \cdot \beta \Delta t$$

and $A = A_0(1 + \beta \cdot \Delta t)$

In volume expansion,

$$\Delta V = V_0 \cdot \gamma \Delta t$$

and $V = V_0(1 + \gamma \cdot \Delta t)$

$\Rightarrow$ $\alpha : \beta : \gamma = 1 : 2 : 3$

05 Specific heat of any substance is the amount of heat required to raise the temperature of its unit mass through 1°C.

It is denoted by s and its unit is J/kg-K or cal/g-°C.

06 Heat energy required to change the temperature of a body is given by $Q = ms\Delta t$

07 There are two types of specific heats of a gas

(i) Specific heat at constant volume (C_V)

(ii) Specific heat at constant pressure (C_p)

08 Specific heat at constant pressure is greater than the specific heat at constant volume *i.e.,* $C_p > C_V$.

09 When water is heated from 0°C to 4°C, its volume decreases and when heated furth er (greater than 4°C) its volume increases. This shows the anomalous expansion of water. Thus water has maximum density at 4°C.

10 The density of liquids and gases decrease with increase in temperature as

$$\rho' = \rho_0(1 - \gamma\Delta T)$$

11 When two or more than two substances of different temperatures are mixed then heat energy is transferred from a higher temperature body towards a lower temperature body until the temperature of them becomes equal.

In this process,

Heat given by hot body = Heat taken by cold body.

This is called principle of calorimetry.

12 **Latent Heat** The amount of heat energy absorbed or released by unit mass of a substance during change of state at constant temperature is called latent heat.

13 Heat energy absorbed or released during change of state is given by

$$Q = mL$$

14 There are three methods of transfer of heat

(i) Conduction

(ii) Convection

(iii) Radiation

15 The amount of heat energy conducted in a metallic rod is given by

$$Q = \frac{KA\Delta\theta t}{l}$$

where, K = thermal conductivity of the material

A = cross-section of area

l = length

$\Delta\theta$ = temperature difference between two faces of the rod

and t = time

16 **Wien's Displacement Law** The wavelength corresponding to which energy emitted by a black body is maximum is shifted towards shorter wavelength side with rise in temperature. *i.e.,*

$$\lambda_m \propto \frac{1}{T} \text{ or } \lambda_m T = \text{constant } (b)$$

where, b is called Wien's constant and this law is called Wien's displacement law.

17 **Stefan's Law** The amount of radiant energy emitted per second per unit area of a perfectly black body is directly proportional to the fourth power of its absolute temperature *i.e.,*

$$E \propto T^4 \text{ or } E = \sigma T^4$$

where, $\sigma = 5.67 \times 10^{-8} \dfrac{W}{m^2 K^4}$ is called Stefan's constant.

18 A perfectly black body is that which absorbs the radiation of all wavelengths completely, incident on it.

For a perfectly black body $a_\lambda = 1$

a_λ = absorptive power of black body

19 **Newton's Law of Cooling** The rate of loss of heat of a body is directly proportional to the difference in temperature of the body and its surroundings *i.e.,*

$$-\frac{dT}{dt} \propto (T - T_0)$$

where, T = temperature of the body

T_0 = temperature of the surroundings

Exercises

Question 1 The triple point of neon and carbon dioxide are 24.57 K and 216.55 K respectively. Express these temperature on the celsius and fahrenheit scales.

◎ *Thinking Process* If temperature of a body in celsius, kelvin and fahrenheit scales are C, K and F respectively, then

$$K = C + 273.15$$

$$\frac{C}{5} = \frac{F-32}{9}$$

and $$\frac{K-273.15}{5} = \frac{F-32}{9}$$

Sol. Triple point of neon, $(T_1) = 24.57$ K

Triple point of CO_2, $(T_2) = 216.55$ K

On celsius scale, $°C = K - 273.15$

Triple point of neon, $t_1°C = 24.57 - 273.15$

$$= -248.58°C$$

Triple point of CO_2, $t_2°C = 216.55 - 273.15$

$$= -56.60°C$$

On fahrenheit scale,

$$\frac{K-273.15}{5} = \frac{F-32}{9}$$

or $$F = (K_1 - 273.15) \times \frac{9}{5} + 32$$

Triple point of neon,

$$F_1 = (K_1 - 273.15) \times \frac{9}{5} + 32$$

$$= (24.57 - 273.15) \times \frac{9}{5} + 32$$

$$= -248.58 \times \frac{9}{5} + 32 = -415.44°F$$

Triple point of CO_2, $F_2 = (K_2 - 273.15) \times \frac{9}{5} + 32$

$$= (216.55 - 273.15) \times \frac{9}{5} + 32$$

$$= -56.6 \times \frac{9}{5} + 32$$

$$= -69.88°F$$

Question 2 Two absolute scales A and B have triple points of water defined to be 200 A and 350 B. What is the relation between T_A and T_B ?

Sol. Given, triple point of water on scale $A = 200\ A$

Triple point of water on scale $B = 350\ B$

We know that triple point of water on absolute scale = 273.16 K

$$\therefore \quad 200A = 350B = 273.16\text{ K}$$

$$\therefore \quad 1A = \frac{273.16}{200}\text{ K}$$

$$\text{and} \quad 1B = \frac{273.16}{350}\text{ K}$$

If T_A and T_B are the triple point of water on two scales A and B, then

$$\frac{273.16}{200}T_A = \frac{273.16}{350}T_B$$

$$\therefore \quad \frac{T_A}{T_B} = \frac{200}{350} = \frac{4}{7} \text{ or } T_A = \frac{4}{7}T_B$$

Mistake Alert Student can forget to convert the triple point of water from kelvin to the units of scales A and B.

Question 3 The electrical resistance in ohms of a certain thermometer varies with temperature according to the approximate law,

$$R = R_0[1 + 5 \times 10^{-3}(T - T_0)]$$

The resistance is 101.6 Ω at the triple point of water 273.16 K and 165.5 Ω at the normal melting point of lead (600.5 K). What is the temperature when the resistance is 123.4 Ω?

Sol. Given, $R_0 = 101.6\,\Omega,\ T_0 = 273.16\text{ K}$

$R_1 = 165.5\,\Omega,\ T_1 = 600.5\text{ K}$

$R_2 = 123.4\,\Omega,\ T_2 = ?$

We know that

$$R_1 = R_0[1 + \alpha(T_1 - T_0)]$$

$$165.5 = 101.6\,[1 + \alpha(600.5 - 273.16)]$$

$$165.5 = 101.6[1 + \alpha \times 327.34]$$

$$165.5 = 101.6 + \alpha \times 101.6 \times 327.34$$

$$\text{or} \quad \alpha = \frac{165.5 - 101.6}{101.6 \times 327.34} = \frac{63.9}{101.6 + \times 327.34} \quad \text{...(i)}$$

$$\therefore \quad R_2 = R_0[1 + \alpha(T_2 - T_0)]$$

$$123.4 = 101.6\left[1 + \frac{63.9}{101.6 \times 327.34}(T_2 - 273.16)\right]$$

$$= 101.6 + \frac{63.9}{327.34}(T_2 - 273.16)$$

or $$T_2 = \frac{(123.4 - 101.6) \times 327.34}{63.9} + 273.16$$

$$= 111.67 + 273.16$$

$$= 384.83 \text{ K}$$

Question 4 Answer the following

(a) The triple point of water is a standard fixed point in modern thermometry. Why? What is wrong in taking melting point of ice and the boiling point of water as standard fixed points (as was originally done in celsius scale)?

(b) There were two fixed points in the original celsius scale as mentioned above which were assigned the numbers 0°C and 100°C respectively. On the absolute scale, one of the fixed points is the triple point of water, which on the kelvin absolute scale is assigned the number 273.16 K. What is the other fixed point on this (kelvin) scale?

(c) The absolute temperature (kelvin scale) T is related to the temperature T on the celsius scale by $t_c = T - 273.15$. Why do we have 273.15 in this relation and not 273.16?

(d) What is the temperature of triple point of water on an absolute scale whose unit interval size is equal to that of the fahrenheit scale?

Sol.

(a) The triple point of water is a unique condition of pressure and temperature. Therefore, melting point of ice and boiling point of water are not taken as standard fixed points.

The melting point of ice and boiling point of water are pressure depended conditions and also varies as impurities are dissolved in it

(b) 0° K or absolute zero is the other fixed point on the absolute scale of temperature.

(c) The ice point on kelvin scale is 273.15 K and the corresponding value on celsius scale is 0°C. Therefore, celsius scale is related to kelvin scale as $t_c = T - 273.15$.

Triple point of water is 273.16 K and hence, its corresponding value of celsius scale is 0.01°C.

(d) Triple point of water on kelvin scale = 273.16 K

Total number of divisions on kelvin scale = 100

Total number of divisions on fahrenheit scale = 180

∴ Triple point of water on an absolute scale having 180 divisions

$$T = 273.16 \times \frac{180}{100} = 491.69$$

Question 5 Two ideal gas thermometers A and B use oxygen and hydrogen respectively. The following observations are made

Temperature	Pressure thermometer A	Pressure thermometer B
Triple point of water	1.250×10^5 Pa	0.200×10^5 Pa
Normal melting point of sulphur	1.797×10^5 Pa	0.287×10^5 Pa

(a) What is the absolute temperature of normal melting point of sulphur as read by thermometers A and B?

(b) What do you think is the reason for slightly different answers of thermometers A and B? (The thermometers are not faulty). What further procedure is needed in the experiment to reduce the discrepancy between the two readings?

Sol.

(a) Let the melting point of sulphur be T K.

Given, **For thermometer A,**

Pressure at triple point of water $(p_1) = 1.250 \times 10^5$ Pa

Triple point of water $(T_1) = 273.16$ K

Pressure at normal melting point of sulphur $(p_2) = 1.797 \times 10^5$ Pa

Melting point of sulphur $(T_2) = ?$

Using relation, $\frac{p_1}{T_1} = \frac{p_2}{T_2}$

or
$$T_2 = \frac{p_2}{p_1} \times T_1$$
$$= \frac{1.797 \times 10^5}{1.250 \times 10^5} \times 273.16$$
$$= 392.69 \text{ K}$$

For thermometer B,

Pressure at triple point of water $(p_1) = 0.200 \times 10^5$ Pa

Triple point of water $(T_1) = 273.16$ K

Pressure at normal melting point of sulphur $(p_2) = 0.287 \times 10^5$ Pa

Melting point of sulphur $(T_2) = ?$

Using relation, $\frac{p_1}{T_1} = \frac{p_2}{T_2}$

or
$$T_2 = \frac{p_2}{p_1} \times T_1$$
$$= \frac{0.287 \times 10^5}{0.200 \times 10^5} \times 273.16 = 391.98 \text{ K}$$

(b) The reason of slightly different answers of thermometers A and B is that the gases hydrogen and oxygen are not perfectly ideal.

To reduce the discrepancy, reading should be taken at lower and lower pressures because at lower pressure gases behaviour is closer to ideal gas.

Question 6 A steel tape 1 m long is correctly calibrated for a temperature of 27.0°C. The length of a steel rod measured by this tape is found to be 63.0 cm on a hot day, when the temperature is 45.0°C. What is the actual length of the steel rod on that day? What is the length of the same steel rod on a day when temperature is 27.0°C? Coefficient of linear expansion of steel $= 1.20 \times 10^{-5}$/K.

Sol. Given, length of steel tape at 27.0°C $(L_0) = 1\,\text{m} = 100$ cm

Increase in temperature $(\Delta T) = 45° - 27° = 18°$

Coefficient of linear expansion of steel $(\alpha) = 1.20 \times 10^{-5}$/K

Length of steel tape at 45.0°C $(L) = L_0(1 + \alpha\Delta T)$

$$= 100[1 + 1.20 \times 10^{-5} \times 18]$$

$$= 100[1.000216] = 100.0216 \text{ cm}$$

Length of 1 cm mark of steel tape at 45°C $= \dfrac{100.0216}{100}$ cm

∴ Length of 63 cm rod measured by this tape at 45°C

$$= \frac{100.0216}{100} \times 63 = 63.0136 \text{ cm}$$

When temperature is 27°C then, the size of 1 cm mark on the steel tap will be exactly 1 cm.

∴ Length of the same steel rod at 27°C = 63 cm.

Mistake Alert Student can forget to consider the expansion of the steel itself.

Question 7 A large steel wheel is to be fitted on a shaft of the same material. At 27°C, the outer diameter of the shaft is 8.70 cm and the diameter of the central hole in the wheel is 8.69 cm. The shaft is cooled using dry ice. At what temperature of the shaft does the wheel slip on the shaft? Assume the coefficient of linear expansion of the steel to be constant over the required temperature range.

$$\alpha_{\text{steel}} = 1.20 \times 10^{-5}/\text{K}$$

Sol. Given, coefficient of linear expansion of steel

$(\alpha) = 1.20 \times 10^{-5}$/K

Outer diameter $(l_1) = 8.70$ cm

Inner diameter $(l_2) = 8.69$ cm

$T_1 = 27 + 273 = 300$ K

$T_2 = ?$

Change in length due to cooling

$$l_2 = l_1[1 + \alpha(T_2 - T_1)]$$

$$8.69 = 8.70[1 + 1.20 \times 10^{-5}(T_2 - 300)]$$

or $$8.69 = 8.70 + 8.70 \times 1.20 \times 10^{-5}(T_2 - 300)$$

$$8.69 - 8.70 = 8.70 \times 1.20 \times 10^{-5}(T_2 - 300)$$

or $$(T_2 - 300) = \frac{-0.01}{8.70 \times 1.20 \times 10^{-5}}$$

$$T_2 - 300 = -95.78 \text{ K}$$

or $$T_2 = (300 - 95.78) \text{ K}$$

$$= 204.22 \text{ K}$$

or $$T_2 = (204.22 - 273)°\text{C}$$

$$= -68.78°\text{C} \approx -69°\text{C}$$

Question 8 A hole is drilled in a copper sheet. The diameter of the hole is 4.24 cm at 27.0°C. What is the change in the diameter of the hole when the sheet is heated to 227°C? Coefficient of linear expansion of copper is 1.70×10^{-5} K^{-1}.

Sol. Given, diameter of the hole $(d_1) = 4.24$ cm

Initial temperature $T_1 = 27 + 273 = 300$ K

Final temperature $T_2 = 227 + 273 = 500$ K

Coefficient of linear expansion $(\alpha) = 1.70 \times 10^{-5}$ K^{-1}

Coefficient of superficial expansion $(\beta) = 2\alpha = 3.40 \times 10^{-5}$ K^{-1}

Initial area of hole at 27°C $(A_1) = \pi r^2 = \frac{\pi d_1^2}{4} = \frac{\pi}{4}(4.24)^2 = 4.494\pi$ cm^2

Area of hole at 227°C $(A_2) = A_1(1 + \beta \cdot \Delta t)$

$$= 4.494\pi[1 + 3.40 \times 10^{-5} \times (227 - 27)]$$

$$= 4.494\pi\,[1 + 3.40 \times 10^{-5} \times 200]$$

$$= 4.494\pi \times 1.0068 = 4.524\pi$$

If diameter of hole becomes d_2 at 227°C, then $A_2 = \frac{\pi d_2^2}{4}$

$$4.524\pi = \frac{\pi d_2^2}{4}$$

or $$d_2^2 = 4.525 \times 4$$

or $$d_2 = 4.2542 \text{ cm}$$

$\therefore$ Change in diameter $(\Delta d) = d_2 - d_1 = 4.2544 - 4.24$ cm

$$= 0.0142 = 1.42 \times 10^{-2} \text{ cm}$$

Note $\alpha = \frac{\beta}{2} = \frac{\gamma}{3}$

Question 9 A brass wire 1.8 m long at 27°C is held taut with little tension between two rigid supports. If the wire is cooled to a temperature of –39°C, what is the tension developed in the wire, if its diameter is 2.0 mm? Coefficient of linear expansion of brass $= 2.0 \times 10^{-5}$/K. Young's modulus of brass $= 0.91 \times 10^{11}$ Pa.

◎ ***Thinking Process*** When a wire or rod held taut between two rigid supports is cooled then, a stress is produced in it, called thermal stress.

Thermal stress $\left(\frac{F}{A}\right) = Y \alpha \Delta t$

Sol. Given, length of wire $(l_1) = 1.8$ m

Initial temperature $t_1 = 27°$ C

Final temperature $t_2 = -39°$ C

Diameter of wire $(d) = 2.0$ mm $= 2.0 \times 10^{-3}$ m

Coefficient of linear expansion $(\alpha) = 2.0 \times 10^{-5}$/K

Young's modulus $(Y) = 0.91 \times 10^{11}$ Pa

$\therefore$ Tension developed in wire $(F) = YA\alpha\Delta t$

$$= Y\left(\frac{\pi d^2}{4}\right)\alpha\Delta t$$

$$= \frac{0.91 \times 10^{11} \times 3.14 \times (2 \times 10^{-3})^2 \times 2.0 \times 10^{-5} \times (-39 - 27)}{4}$$

$$= 0.91 \times 3.14 \times (-66) \times 2$$

$$= -377 \text{ N}$$

$$= -3.77 \times 10^2 \text{ N}$$

Negative sign shows that force is acting inwards due to contraction of the wire.

Question 10 A brass rod of length 50 cm and diameter 3.0 mm is joined to a steel rod of the same length and diameter. What is the change in length of the combined rod at 250°C, if the original lengths are at 40°C? Is there a thermal stress developed at the junction? The ends of the rod are free to expand. (Coefficient of linear expansion of brass $= 2.0 \times 10^{-5}$/K and of steel $= 1.2 \times 10^{-5}$/K)

Sol. Given, initial temperature $(T_1) = (40 + 273)$ K $= 313$ K

Final temperature $(T_2) = (250 + 273)$ K $= 523$ K

$\therefore$ Increase in temperature $(\Delta T) = 523 - 313 = 210$ K

For brass rod,

Initial length $(l_1) = 50$ cm

Coefficient of linear expansion $\alpha = 2.0 \times 10^{-5}$/K

$$\text{Final length } (l_2) = l_1[1 + \alpha \Delta T]$$
$$= 50[1 + 2.0 \times 10^{-5} \times 210]$$
$$= 50 \times 1.00420$$
$$= 50.21 \text{ cm}$$

$\therefore$ $$\text{Increase in length } (\Delta l) = l_2 - l_1 = 50.21 - 50$$
$$= 0.21 \text{ cm}$$

For steel rod,

Initial length $(l_1') = 50$ cm

Coefficient of linear expansion $\alpha' = 1.2 \times 10^{-5}$/K

$\therefore$ $$\text{Final length } (l_2') = l_1'(1 + \alpha' \Delta T)$$
$$= 50[1 + 1.2 \times 10^{-5} \times 210]$$
$$= 50 \times 1.00252$$
$$= 50.126 \text{ cm}$$

$\therefore$ Increase in length $(\Delta l') = l_2' - l_1'$
$$= 50.126 - 50.0 = 0.126 \text{ cm}$$

$\therefore$ Total increase in length $= \Delta l + \Delta l'$
$$= (0.21 + 0.126) \text{ cm} = 0.336 \text{ cm}$$

No thermal stress will develop at the junction because the ends of the rod are free to expand.

Mistake Alert Student can incorrectly calculate the change in length of each rod.

Question 11 The coefficient of volume expansion of glycerine is 49×10^{-5}/K. What is the fractional change in its density for a 30°C rise in temperature?

Sol. Given, coefficient of volume expansion $(\gamma) = 49 \times 10^{-5}$/K

Rise in temperature $(\Delta t) = 30°C$

Let initial volume of glycerine be V_0.

$\therefore$ Volume of glycerine when temperature is increased by 30°C

$$V = V_0[1 + \gamma \Delta t]$$
$$= V_0[1 + 49 \times 10^{-5} \times 30]$$
$$= V_0[1 + 0.01470]$$
$$= 1.0147 V_0$$

$\therefore$ $$\frac{V_0}{V} = \frac{1}{1.0147} \quad \text{...(i)}$$

If mass of glycerine is m, then

initial density of glycerine $(\rho_0) = \dfrac{m}{V_0}$

and final density of glycerine $(\rho) = \dfrac{m}{V}$

$$\therefore \quad \frac{\rho}{\rho_0} = \frac{m/V}{m/V_0} = \frac{V_0}{V} = \frac{1}{1.0147} \qquad \text{...(ii)}$$

Fractional change in density $= \dfrac{\Delta\rho}{\rho_0}$

$$= \frac{\rho - \rho_0}{\rho_0} = \frac{\rho}{\rho_0} - 1$$

Substituting value from Eq. (ii), we get

Fractional change in density $= \dfrac{1}{1.0147} - 1$

$$= -0.0145 = -1.45 \times 10^{-2}$$

Negative sign shows that the density of glycerine decreases with rise in temperature.

Question 12 10 kW drilling machine is used to drill a bore in a small aluminium block of mass 8.0 kg. How much is the rise in temperature of the block in 2.5 min, assuming 50% of the power is used up in heating the machine itself or lost to the surroundings. Specific heat of aluminium is 0.91 J/g-K.

Sol. Given, power of drilling machine $(P) = 10\text{ kW} = 10 \times 10^3\text{ W}$

Mass $(m) = 8.0$ kg

Time $(t) = 2.5$ min

$= 2.5 \times 60\text{ s} = 150\text{ s}$

Specific heat $(s) = 0.91\text{ J/g-K} = 0.9 \times 10^3\text{ J/kg-K}$

Energy utilized by machine $(E) = P \times t$

$= 10 \times 10^3 \times 150 = 1.5 \times 10^6\text{ J}$

Energy utilized in increasing temperature $(\Delta E) = 1.5 \times 10^6 \times \dfrac{50}{100}\text{ J}$

$$\Delta E = 7.5 \times 10^5\text{ J}$$

If temperature of the block is increases by $\Delta\theta$, then

$$\Delta E = ms\Delta t$$

or
$$\Delta t = \frac{\Delta E}{ms} = \frac{7.5 \times 10^5}{8 \times 0.91 \times 10^3} = 103^\circ\text{C}$$

Mistake Alert Student can assume that all the energy from the machine is used to heat the block, instead of considering the 50% loss.

Question 13 A copper block of mass 2.5 kg is heated in furnace to a temperature of 500°C and then placed on a large ice block. What is the maximum amount of ice that can melt? (Specific heat of copper = 0.39 J/g-K; heat of fusion of water = 335 J/g)

◎ ***Thinking Process*** Heat energy given or taken by any object change of temperature

$$Q = ms\Delta t$$

where, m = mass of the object

s = specific heat of the substance of the object

Δt = change in temperature

Heat energy given or taken in change of state at constant temperature

$Q = mL$, where, L = latent heat of the change of state

Sol. Given, mass of copper block (m) = 2.5 kg

Change in temperature (Δt) = 500°C

Specific heat (s) = 0.39 J/g-K= 0.39×10^3 J/kg-K

= 390 J/kg-K

Latent heat of fusion of water (L) = 335 J/g

$= 335 \times 10^3$ J/kg

Heat energy absorbed by copper block

$$Q_1 = ms\Delta t$$

$$= 2.5 \times 390 \times 500 \text{ J}$$

Let m' kg of ice be melted.

Heat energy required to melt ice, $Q_2 = m'L$

But heat energy absorbed by copper block

= Heat energy utilized by ice in melting

$$Q_1 = Q_2$$

$$ms\Delta t = m'L$$

or

$$m' = \frac{ms\Delta t}{L}$$

$$= \frac{2.5 \times 390 \times 500}{335 \times 10^3}$$

$$= 1.455 \text{ kg}$$

$$\approx 1.5 \text{ kg}$$

Question 14 In an experiment on the specific heat of a metal, a 0.20 kg block of the metal at 150°C is dropped in a copper calorimeter (of water equivalent 0.025 kg) containing 150 cm^3 of water at 27°C. The final temperature is 40°C. Compute the specific heat of the metal. If heat losses to the surroundings are not negligible, is your answer greater or smaller than the actual value for specific heat of the metal?

Sol. Given, mass of metal block $(m_1) = 0.20$ kg

Temperature of metal block $(t_1) = 150°C$

Temperature of calorimeter $(t_2) = 27°C$

Final temperature of the mixture $(t) = 40°C$

Volume of water in calorimeter $= 150\ cm^3$

Mass of water in calorimeter $= V \times \rho$

$$m_2 = (150 \times 10^{-6} m^3) \times (1 \times 10^3 kg/m^3)$$

$$m_2 = 150 \times 10^{-3} kg$$

Water equivalent of calorimeter $W = 0.025\ kg = 25 \times 10^{-3}$ kg

Let s be the specific heat of the metal block.

Heat energy given by metal block

$$Q_1 = m_1 s (t_1 - t_2)$$
$$= 0.20 \times s \times (150 - 40)$$
$$= 0.20 \times s \times 110$$
$$= 22\ s$$

Heat energy taken by calorimeter W and water $Q_2 = (m_2 + w)\ s\ \Delta t$

$$Q_2 = (150 \times 10^{-3} + 25 \times 10^{-3}) \times s_2 \times (40 - 27)$$
$$= 175 \times 10^{-3} \times 4.2 \times 10^3 \times 13$$
$$= 175 \times 4.2 \times 13$$

According to principle of calorimetry

Heat given = Heat taken

$$Q_1 = Q_2$$
$$22s = 175 \times 4.2 \times 13$$
$$s = \frac{175 \times 4.2 \times 13}{22}$$
$$s = 434\ J/kg\text{-}K$$

If heat losses to the surroundings are not negligible than the value of specific heat s of metal will be less than the actual value.

Note Water equivalent of material is the mass of water which shows same rise or fall of temperature as that of material for the same amount of heat absorbed or lost.

Question 15 Given below are observations on molar specific heats at room temperatures of some common gases.

Gas	Molar specific heat (C_V) [cal/mol-K]
Hydrogen	4.87
Nitrogen	4.97
Oxygen	5.02
Nitric oxide	4.99
Carbon monoxide	5.01
Chlorine	6.17

The measured molar specific heats of these gases are markedly different from those for monoatomic gases (typically molar specific heat of a monoatomic gas is 2.92 cal/mol-K). Explain this difference. What can you infer from the somewhat larger (than the rest) value for chlorine?

Sol. All the gases given in the list are diatomic gases. Diatomic gases have 5 degrees of freedom. While monoatomic gases have 3 degrees of freedom. Therefore, molar specific heat of diatomic gas

$$= 5 \times \frac{R}{2} = 5 \times \frac{1.98}{2}$$

$$= 4.95 \text{ cal/mol-K.}$$

It agrees with the molar specific heats of the given gases except chlorine.

Monoatomic gases has only translational motion while diatomic gas molecules has translational, vibrational and rotational motion. Therefore, to increase the temperature of diatomic gas through 1°C, heat energy is supplied to increase its translational, vibrational and rotational energies and hence, molar specific heat of diatomic gases are higher than the molar specific heat of monoatomic gases. The molar specific heat of chlorine is higher due to translational motion along with rotational and vibrational motion while other gases molecule have only translational and rotational motion at room temperature.

Question 16 A child running at a temperature of 101°F is given an antipyrin (*i.e.*, medicine that lowers fever) which causes an increase in the rate of evaporation of sweat from his body. If the fever is brought down to 98°F in 20 min, what is the average rate of extra evaporation caused by the drug. Assume the evaporation mechanism to be the only way by which heat is lost. The mass of child is 30 kg. The specific heat of the human body is approximately the same as that of water and latent heat of evaporation of water at that temperature is about 580 cal/g.

Sol. Given, mass of the child $(m) = 30$ kg

Time taken $(t) = 20$ min

Fall in temperature $= (101 - 98)°F$

$$\Delta T = 3°F = 3 \times \frac{5}{9}°C = \frac{5}{3}°C$$

Specific heat of human body $(s) = 4.2 \times 10^3$ J/kg-°C

Latenl heat of evaporation $(L) = 580$ cal/g $= 580 \times 10^3$ cal/kg

$$= (580 \times 10^3 \times 4.2) \text{ J/kg}$$

Heat given by body during fall in temperature

$$Q_1 = ms\Delta T$$

Let m' be the mass of sweat evaporates from the human body.

Heat taken in evaporation

$$Q_2 = m'L$$

But $\quad Q_1 = Q_2$

$\therefore \quad ms\Delta T = m'L$

or $$m' = \frac{ms\Delta T}{L} = \frac{30 \times 4.2 \times 10^3 \times 5/3}{580 \times 4.2 \times 10^3}$$

$$= \frac{10}{116} = 0.0862 \text{ kg}$$

$\therefore$ Rate of evaporation of sweat $= \dfrac{0.0862}{20}$

$$= 0.00431 \text{ kg/min}$$

$$= 4.31 \text{ g/min}$$

Question 17 A 'thermocole' icebox is a cheap and efficient method for storing small quantities of cooked food in summer in particular. A cubical icebox of side 30 cm has a thickness of 5.0 cm. If 4.0 kg of ice is put in the box, estimate the amount of ice remaining after 6 h. The outside temperature is 45°C and coefficient of thermal conductivity of thermacole is 0.01 J/s-m-K.
[Heat of fusion of water $= 335 \times 10^3$ J/kg]

Sol. Given, each side of cubical icebox $(a) = 30$ cm

Area of 6 faces of box $= 6 \times (30 \times 30)$ cm^2

$$A = 5400 \times 10^{-4} \text{ m}^2 \qquad [1 \text{ cm}^2 = 10^{-4} \text{ m}^2]$$

Thickness of the box $(d) = 5.0$ cm $= 5.0 \times 10^{-2}$ m

Mass of ice $(m) = 4.0$ kg

Time $(t) = 6$ h $= 6 \times 60 \times 60$ s

Difference in temperature $(\Delta\theta) = \theta_1 - \theta_2$

$$= 45° - 0 = 45°C$$

Latent heat of fusion of water $(L) = 335 \times 10^3$ J/kg

Coefficient of thermal conductivity $(K) = 0.01$ J/s-m-K

Let the mass of the ice melted be m' kg.

Heat supplied by the surrounding = Heat taken by ice in melting

$$Q = \frac{KA\Delta\theta t}{d} = m' \cdot L$$

or
$$m' = \frac{KA\Delta\theta t}{Ld}$$

$$= \frac{0.01 \times 5400 \times 10^{-4} \times 45° \times 6 \times 60 \times 60}{335 \times 10^3 \times 5 \times 10^{-2}}$$

$$= 0.313 \text{ kg}$$

$\therefore$ Mass remained in the box unmelted $= m - m'$

$$= 4 - 0.313 = 3.687 \text{ kg}$$

Question 18 A brass boiler has a base area 0.15 m^2 and thickness 1.0 cm. It boils water at the rate of 6.0 kg/min when placed on a gas stove. Estimate the temperature of the part of the flame in contact with the boiler. Thermal conductivity of brass = 109 J/s-m-K. (Heat of vapourization of water $= 2256 \times 10^3$ J/kg)

Sol. Base area of boiler $(A) = 0.15 \text{ m}^2$

Thickness $(d) = 1.0 \text{ cm} = 1 \times 10^{-2}$ m

Rate of water boils $= 6.0 \text{ kg/min} = \frac{6.0}{60} \text{ kg/s} = 0.1 \text{ kg/s}$

Thermal conductivity of brass $(K) = 109$ J/s-m-K

Latent heat of vapourization of water $(L) = 2256 \times 10^3$ J/kg

Let θ_1 be the temperature of the part of the boiler in contact with the stove.

Rate of heat energy supplied = Rate of heat energy utilized in vaporization

$$\frac{KA\Delta\theta}{d} = mL$$

$$\frac{KA(\theta_1 - \theta_2)}{d} = mL$$

$$\frac{109 \times 0.15(\theta_1 - 100)}{1 \times 10^{-2}} = 0.1 \times 2256 \times 10^3$$

$$1635\,(\theta_1 - 100) = 2256 \times 10^2$$

$$\theta_1 = \frac{225600}{1635} + 100 = 137.98 + 100$$

$$= 237.98°\text{C} \approx 238°\text{ C}$$

Mistake Alert Student can misunderstand the heat transfer equation *i.e.* forget to account latent heat of vaporization.

Question 19 Explain why?

(a) A body with large reflectivity is a poor emitter.

(b) A brass tumbler feels much colder than wooden tray on a chilly day.

(c) An optical pyrometer (for measuring high temperatures) calibrated for an ideal black body radiations gives too low a value for the temperature of a red hot iron piece in the open, but gives a correct value for the temperature when the same piece is in the furnace.

(d) The earth without its atmosphere would be inhospitably cold.

(e) Heating systems based on circulation of steam are more efficient in warming a building than those based on circulation of hot water.

Sol.

(a) We know that $a + r + t = 1$

where a, r and t are absorptance, reflectance and transmittance respectively of the surface of the body. t is also called emittance (e). Also according to Kirchhoff's law $e \propto a$ that is good absorbers are good emitters and hence poor reflectors and *vice-versa i.e.,* if r is large (*i.e.,* large reflectively) a is smaller and hence e is smaller *i.e.,* poor emitter.

(b) The thermal conductivity of brass is high *i.e.,* brass is a good conductor of heat. So, when a brass tumbler is touched, heat quickly flows from human body to the tumbler. Consequently, the tumbler appears colder. On the other hand, wood is a bad conductor of heat. So heat does not flow from the human body to the wooden tray, thus it appears relatively hotter.

(c) Let T be the temperature of the hot iron in the furnace. Thus, according to Stefan's law, heat radiated per second per unit area (E) is given by $E = \sigma T^4$. When the body is placed in open at temperature T_0, then the heat radiated/sec/area (E') is given by $E' = \alpha(T^4 - T_0^4)$.

Clearly $E' < E$, so the optical pyrometer gives too low a value for the temperature of a red hot iron piece in open.

(d) Gases are generally insulators. The earth's atmosphere acts like an insulating blanket around it and does not allows heat to escape out but reflects it back to the earth. Had this atmosphere been absent, the earth would naturally be colder as all its heat would have escaped out.

(e) This is because steam has much higher heat capacity (540 cal/g) than the heat capacity of water (80 cal/g) at the same temperature. Thus, evidently steam will heat building better than water.

Question 20 A body cools from 80°C to 50°C in 5 min. Calculate the time it takes to cool from 60°C to 30°C. The temperature of the surroundings is 20°C.

Sol. Given, initial temperature $T_1 = 80°C$

Final temperature $T_2 = 50°C$

Temperature of the surroundings $T_0 = 20°C$

$$t_1 = 5 \text{ min}$$

According to Newton's law of cooling.

Rate of cooling, $$\frac{dT}{dt} = k\left[\frac{T_1 + T_2}{2} - T_0\right]$$

$$\frac{(80 - 50)}{5} = k\left[\frac{80 + 50}{2} - 20\right]$$

$$\frac{30}{5} = k(65 - 20)$$

$$6 = k \times 45$$

or $$k = \frac{6}{45} = \frac{2}{15} \quad \text{...(i)}$$

In second condition,

Initial temperature $T_1' = 60°C$

Final temperature $T_2' = 30°C$

$$t' = ?$$

Now, $$\frac{(60 - 30)}{t'} = \frac{2}{15}\left[\frac{60 + 30}{2} - 20\right]$$

$$\frac{30}{t'} = \frac{2}{15}(45 - 20)$$

or $$t' = \frac{30 \times 15}{2 \times 25} = 9 \text{ min}$$

DIKSHA APP Questions

Multiple Choice Questions

Q.1 The temperature at which celsius scale and fahrenheit scale show the same numerical reading is

(a) −30 (b) −40
(c) 30 (d) 40

Sol. (b) The conversion formula between different scales of temperature is

$$\frac{F-32}{180} = \frac{C}{100}$$

$$\frac{x-32}{180} = \frac{x}{100}$$

$$100x - 3200 = 180x$$

$$\Rightarrow \quad -3200 = 80x$$

$$\Rightarrow \quad -40 = x.$$

Q.2 The triple point of neon is −415.44°F. The corresponding temperatures on kelvin and celsius scale are (nearly)

(a) 24.57 K and −248.58°C (b) 60.12 K and −213.08°C
(c) 92.12 K and −245.08°C (d) 42.35 K and −230.8°C

Sol. (a) Using conversion formula between different scale of temperature we have

$$\frac{F-32}{180} = \frac{K-273.15}{100} = \frac{C}{100}$$

$$= \frac{-415.44-32}{180} = \frac{C}{100}$$

$$-\frac{447.44}{180} \times 100 = C$$

$$-248.58°\text{ C} = C$$

In kelvin scale $K = 273.15 - 248.58 = 24.57$ K.

Q.3 Three rods A, B and C have the same length, area of cross -section and temperature. The coefficients of linear expansion of the materials of rod are α_a, α_b and α_c respectively $(\alpha_c > \alpha_a > \alpha_b)$

The temperature of the three rods is increased by T °C, the change in length L_a, L_b and L_c of the three rods will respectively be

(a) $L_a > L_b < L_c$ (b) $L_a > L_c > L_b$
(c) $L_b > L_a > L_c$ (d) $L_b < L_a < L_c$

Sol. (d) We know that change is length $\Delta L = \alpha L \Delta\theta$

For same length, change in temperature larger the value of α larger will be change in length.

Q.4 The temperature of an aluminium sphere of volume V is increased by 100 K. If the coefficient of volume expansion of aluminium is $7 \times 10^{-5}\ K^{-1}$, the change in volume of sphere will be

(a) 0.00007 V (b) 0.0007 V

(c) 0.00 7 V (d) 0.07 V

Sol. (c) Using formula $\Delta V = rV\Delta\theta$

$$= 7 \times 10^{-5} \times V \times 100$$
$$= 7 \times 10^{-3}\ V$$
$$= 0.007\ V.$$

Q.5 The coefficients of linear expansion of four metal A, B, C and D are $2.5 \times 10^{-5}\ K^{-1}$, $1.8 \times 10^{-5}\ K^{-1}$, $1.7 \times 10^{-5}\ K^{-1}$ and $1.2 \times 10^{-5} K^{-1}$ respectively. The bimetallic strip made from which of the two metals would show maximum bending for the same rise in temperature ?

(a) A and B

(b) B and C

(c) C and D

(d) D and A

Sol. (d) The extent of bending of a bimetallic strip (same length, temperature and area of comes cross-section depends upon the difference between coefficients of linear expansion of constituent metals).

Therefore, option (d) is correct.

Q.6 Specific heat of gas at constant pressure is more than its specific heat at constant volume because

(a) a part of the heat supplied is used to keep the volume of the gas constant

(b) a part of the heat supplied is used in expansion of gas

(c) Boyle's law does not hold as the temperature is not constant

(d) The volume of the gas decreases when the pressure is kept constant

Sol. (b) On heating gas at constant pressure, a part of energy supplied is used for the expansion of gas.

Q.7 One litre of an oil at 30°C in a poly-pack floats in water with $\frac{1}{9}$th of its volume above the water surface. The temperature is decreased by 20°C. Neglecting any change in volume of the packing material. Which of the following statements is correct ?

(a) The density of oil decreases.

(b) The packet still floats with $\frac{1}{9}$th of its volume above the water surface.

(c) The packet floats with more than $\frac{1}{9}$th of its volume above the water surface.

(d) The packet floats with less than $\frac{1}{9}$th of its volume above the water surface.

Sol. (d) On decreasing the temperature, the volume of oil decreases and its density increases. Therefore, the fraction of the volume of oil packet above the water surface decreases.

Q.8 2 kg of water at 70°C is mixed with 8 kg of water at 30°C. Assuming no loss of heat to the surroundings, the final temperature of the mixture will be

(a) 63.6°C (b) 40°C (c) 38°C (d) 36°C

Sol. (c) Heat lost by hot water = Heat gained by cold water

$$m_1 s(70 - T) = m_2 s(T - 30)$$
$$2(70 - T) = - 8(T - 30)$$
$$140 - 2T = 8T - 240$$
$$380 = 10T$$
$$38° \text{ C} = T$$

Q.9 Two liquids A and B have specific heat S_1 and S_2 respectively. 40 gm of A at 10°C is mixed with 25 gm of B at 60°C. The equilibrium temperature of mixture is 30°C. The ratio of thermal capacities of A and B is

(a) 8 : 5 (b) 15 : 16

(c) 2 : 3 (d) 3 : 2

Sol. (d) If C_1 and C_2 be the thermal capacities of liquid A and B. According to principle of calorimetry

$$C_1(30 - 10) = C_2(60 - 30)$$
$$\frac{C_1}{C_2} = \frac{30}{20} = \frac{3}{2}$$

Q.10 C_p and C_v are the molar specific heats of a gas. Given $y(>0)$ is the difference and $z(>1)$ is the ratio of the two specific heats of the gas. Which of the following is correct?

(a) $C_v = \frac{y}{z-1}, C_p = \frac{yz}{z-1}$

(b) $C_p = \frac{y}{z-1}, C_v = \frac{y}{z+1}$

(c) $C_v = \frac{yz}{z-1}, C_p = \frac{y}{z+1}$

(d) $C_p = \frac{yz}{z-1}, C_v = \frac{yz}{z-1}$

Sol. (a) As $C_p > C_v$ and y is a positive number.

$$\therefore \quad C_p - C_v = y \quad \text{...(i)}$$

$$\frac{C_p}{C_v} = z \quad \text{...(ii)}$$

From equation (i) and (ii), we get

$$\Rightarrow \quad zC_v - C_v = y$$

$$C_v(z-1) = y$$

$$\Rightarrow \quad C_v = \frac{y}{(z-1)}$$

$$\Rightarrow \quad C_p = \frac{yz}{(z-1)}$$

Thermodynamics

CHAPTER 11

Important Points

01 When two bodies are placed in contact and there is no exchange of heat between them, then they are called in thermal equilibrium.

02 **Zeroth Law of Thermodynamics** When thermodynamics systems A and B are separately in thermal equilibrium with a third thermodynamic system C, then the systems A and B are in thermal equilibrium with each other also.

03 The equation of state of an ideal gas is represented as

$$pV = nRT$$

where, p is pressure, V is volume, T is absolute temperature, R is gas constant and n is number of moles.

04 **Isothermal Process** A change in pressure and volume of a thermodynamic system taking place at constant temperature is called an isothermal process.

05 It takes place at a very slow rate and follows Boyle's law according to which pV = constant

06 **Adiabatic Process** A change in pressure and volume of a thermodynamic system for which there in no exchange of heat between the system and its surroundings, is called an adiabatic process.

07 Adiabatic process takes place at a very fast speed.

08 For an adiabatic process,

$$pV^{\gamma} = \text{constant}$$

or $$TV^{\gamma - 1} = \text{constant}$$

$$T^{\gamma} p^{1 - \gamma} = \text{constant}$$

09 Slope of an adiabatic curve = γ × Slope of isothermal curve.

10 Work done in an isothermal expansion is given by

$$W = 2.3026\, RT \log_{10}\left(\frac{V_2}{V_1}\right) = 2.3026\, RT \log_{10}\left(\frac{p_1}{p_2}\right)$$

11 Work done in an adiabatic expansion is given by

$$W = \frac{\mu R}{(1 - \gamma)}(T_2 - T_1)$$

12 Work done by a thermodynamic system is given by

$$W = p.\Delta V = p(V_2 - V_1)$$

= Area under p-V curve and X-axis.

13 **Isobaric Process** A process taking place in a thermodynamic system for which pressure remains constant is called an isobaric process.

14 **Isochoric Process** A process taking place in a thermodynamic system for which volume remains constant is called an isochoric process.

15 **Internal Energy** The total energy possessed by a system due to molecular motion and molecular configuration is called internal energy of the system. It is denoted by U.

16 **First Law of Thermodynamics** The energy supplied (ΔQ) to a system is partially utilized in increasing the internal energy of the system (ΔU) and remaining part is utilized in doing work (ΔW)

i.e., $$\Delta Q = \Delta U + \Delta W$$

17 First law of thermodynamics follows law of conservation of energy.

18 Mayers's formula, $C_p - C_V = R$

where C_p and C_V are molar specific heats of a gas at constant pressure and at constant volume respectively.

19 Second Law of Thermodynamics

Clausius Statement It is impossible for a machine, unaided by an external agency to transfer heat from the body at lower temperature to the body at higher temperature.

Kelvin Statement It is impossible to derive a continuous supply of work by cooling a body to a temperature lower than that of the coldest of its surroundings.

20 Heat Engine A heat engine is a device which converts heat energy into mechanical energy.

21 Efficiency of a heat engine is the ratio of useful work done (W) by the engine per cycle to the heat energy absorbed from the source (Q_1) per cycle.

$$\eta = \frac{W}{Q_1} = 1 - \frac{Q_2}{Q_1}$$

where, Q_2 is the heat energy rejected to the sink.

22 If temperatures of the source and sink are T_1 and T_2 respectively, then

$$\eta = 1 - \frac{T_2}{T_1}$$

23 Carnot Engine It is an ideal heat engine. Its working is based on Carnot's cycle, which consists following four steps :

(i) Isothermal expansion
(ii) Adiabatic expansion
(iii) Isothermal compression
(iv) Adiabatic compression

24 A refrigerator (or a heat pump) is a device which absorbs heat (Q_2) from a sink at lower temperature (T_2) and rejected heat (Q_1) to source at higher temperature (T_1).

25 Coefficient of performance of a refrigeration

$$(\beta) = \frac{Q_2}{W} = \frac{Q_2}{Q_1 - Q_2} = \frac{1-\eta}{\eta}$$

where, η is the efficiency.

Exercises

Question 1 A geyser heats water flowing at the rate of 3.0 L/min from 27°C to 77°C. If the geyser operates on a gas burner, what is the rate of consumption of fuel, if its heat of consumption is 4.0×10^4 J/g?

Sol. Rate of flow of water (V) = 3 L/min

$$= 3 \times 10^{-3} \text{m}^3/\text{min} \qquad [\because 1\text{L} = 10^{-3} \text{m}^3]$$

Density of water $(\rho) = 10^3$ kg/m^3

$\therefore$ Mass of water flowing per minute $= 3 \times 10^{-3} \times 10^3$ kg/min

[$\because$ Mass = Volume × Density]

$= 3$ kg/min

Increases in temperature $(\Delta\theta) = 77°\text{C} - 27°\text{C} = 50°\text{C}$

Specific heat of water $(s) = 4.2$ J/g-°C

$= 4.2 \times 10^3$ J/kg-°C

Heat energy taken by water

$$Q = ms\Delta\theta$$
$$= 3 \times 4.2 \times 10^3 \times 50$$
$$= 63 \times 10^4 \text{ J/min} \qquad \text{...(i)}$$

Heat of combustion of fuel $= 4 \times 10^4$ J/g $= 4 \times 10^7$ J/kg

Let m kg of fuel is utilized per minute.

$\therefore$ Heat produced $= m \times 4 \times 10^7$ J/min ...(ii)

But heat energy taken by water = Heat produced by fuel

$$63 \times 10^4 = m \times 4 \times 10^7$$

or

$$m = \frac{63 \times 10^4}{4 \times 10^7} \text{ kg/min}$$

$$= 15.75 \times 10^{-3} \text{ kg/min} = 15.75 \text{ g/min}$$

Mistake Alert Student can forget to convert the flow rate from L/min to m^3/min.

Question 2 What amount of heat must be supplied to 2.0×10^{-2} kg of nitrogen (at room temperature) to raise its temperature by 45°C at constant pressure? (Molecular mass of $N_2 = 28$, $R = 8.3$ J/mol-K).

Thinking Process Heat energy given or taken at constant pressure is given by $Q = nC_p\Delta t$.

Sol. Given, mass of nitrogen $(m) = 2.0 \times 10^{-2}$ kg

Increase in temperature $(\Delta t) = 45°\text{C}$

Molecular mass of $N_2(M) = 28\text{ g} = 28 \times 10^{-3}\text{kg}$

$$R = 8.3\text{ J/mol-K}$$

Number of moles $(n) = \frac{m}{M} = \frac{2 \times 10^{-2}}{28 \times 10^{-3}} = \frac{5}{7}$

Molar specific heat at constant pressure $C_p = \frac{7}{2}R$

$\therefore$ Heat supplied $Q = nC_p\,\Delta t$

$$= \frac{5}{7} \times \frac{7}{2} \times 8.3 \times 45 = 933.75\text{ J}$$

Question 3 Explain why?

(a) Two bodies at different temperatures T_1 and T_2, if brought in thermal contact don't necessarily settle to the mean temperature $(T_1 + T_2)/2$.

(b) The coolant in a chemical or a nuclear plant (*i.e.*, liquid used to prevent the different parts of a plant from getting too hot) should have high specific heat.

(c) Air pressure in a car tyre increases during driving.

(d) The climate of a harbour town is more temperature than that of a town in a desert at the same latitude.

Sol.

(a) When two bodies of different temperatures T_1 and T_2 are brought in thermal contact then heat flows from the body at higher temperature to the body at lower temperature till temperatures become equal. Final temperature of bodies can be the mean temperature *i.e.*, $(T_1 + T_2)/2$ only when heat capacities of the two bodies are equal.

(b) The coolant in a chemical or a nuclear plant is utilized to absorb the heat energy produced in the plant to prevent the different parts of a plant from getting too hot.

The heat energy absorbed by the coolant is directly proportional to its specific heat. Therefore, to absorb more heat energy the specific heat of the coolant should be high.

(c) During driving the temperature of the tyre as well as the air inside it increases due to the friction between the tyres and the road. As volume remains constant therefore according to Charle's law $(p \propto T)$.

Air pressure increases in tyres during driving.

(d) In a harbour town, the relative humidity is more than in a desert town. Therefore, the climate of a harbour town is more temperature than that of a town in a desert at the same latitude.

Question 4 A cylinder with a movable piston contains 3 moles of hydrogen at standard temperature and pressure. The walls of the cylinder are made of heat insulator, and the piston is insulated by having a pile of sand on it. By what factor does the pressure of the gas increase, if the gas is compressed to half its original volume?

◎ ***Thinking Process*** Here the walls of the cylinder are made of heat insulater, so there will be no exchange of heat between system and surrounding *i.e.*, the process taking place will be adiabatic.
For an adiabatic process,

$$pV^{\gamma} = \text{constant}$$

or

$$p_1V_1^{\gamma} = p_2V_2^{\gamma}$$

Sol. Let initial volume of the gas in the cylinder be V.

$$\therefore \quad V_1 = V$$

and

$$V_2 = V/2$$

$$\frac{p_2}{p_1} = ?$$

As hydrogen is a diatomic gas.

$$\therefore \quad \gamma = \frac{7}{5} = 1.4$$

For an adiabatic change,

$$p_1V_1^{\gamma} = p_2V_2^{\gamma}$$

$$\therefore \quad \frac{p_2}{p_1} = \left(\frac{V_1}{V_2}\right)^{\gamma}$$

$$= \left(\frac{V}{V/2}\right)^{1.4} = (2)^{1.4} = 2.64$$

Question 5 In changing the state of a gas adiabatically from an equilibrium state A to another equilibrium state B, an amount of work equal to 22.3 J is done on the system. If the gas is taken from state A to B *via* a process in which the net heat absorbed by the system is 9.35 cal, how much is the net work done by the system in the latter case? (Take 1 cal = 4.19 J).

◎ ***Thinking Process*** According to first law of thermodynamics, if ΔQ heat energy is given (or taken) to a thermodynamic system which is partially utilized in doing work (ΔW) and remaining part increases (or decreases) the internal energy of the system.

$$\Delta Q = \Delta W + \Delta U$$

Sol. Given, work done $(W) = -22.3$ J

Work done is taken negative as work is done on the system.

In an adiabatic change $\Delta Q = 0$

Using first law of thermodynamics

$$\Delta U = \Delta Q - W$$
$$= 0 - (-22.3)$$
$$= 22.3 \text{ J}$$

For another process between state A and state B,

$$\text{Absorbed } (\Delta Q) = +9.35 \text{ cal}$$
$$\text{heat} = +(9.35 \times 4.19) \text{ J}$$
$$= +39.18 \text{ J}$$

Change in internal energy between two states *via* different paths are equal.

$$\therefore \quad \Delta U = 22.3$$

$\therefore$ From first law of ther odynamics

$$\Delta U = \Delta Q - W$$

or
$$W = \Delta Q - \Delta U$$
$$= 39.18 - 22.3$$
$$= 16.88 \text{ J}$$
$$\approx 16.9$$

Note • If work is don: on the system then work done is taken negative and if work is don by the system then the work done is taken positive.

• Heat energy taken by a system is taken positive and heat energy given by a system is taken negative.

• In first law of thermodynamics, all three quantities ΔQ, ΔU and W should be taken in same units.

Question 6 Two cylinders A and B of equal capacity are connected to each other *via* a stopcock. A contains a gas at standard temperature and pressure. B is completely evacuated. The entire system is thermally insulated. The stopcock is suddenly opened.

Answer the following

(a) What is finally pressure of the gas in A and B?

(b) What is the change in internal energy of the gas?

(c) What is the change in temperature of the gas?

(d) Do the intermediate states of the system (before settling to the final equilibrium state) lie on its p-V-T surface?

◎ Thinking Process

- For an isothermal process, temperature remains constant and it follows Boyle's law, according to which $p_1V_1 = p_2V_2$
- These process takes place at a slow rate.
- For an isothermal process, change in internal energy is zero *i.e.*, $\Delta U = 0$.

Sol.

(a) Let capacity of each cylinder be V and atmospheric pressure be p.

$\therefore$ $$p_1 = p$$

Initial volume of gas = Volume of the cylinder A

$\therefore$ $$V_1 = V$$

When stopcock is opened, then volume available for gas becomes $2V$.

$\therefore$ $$V_2 = 2V$$

Final pressure $(p_2) = ?$

As system is thermally insulated therefore, there is no change in temperature during the process and hence, it is an isothermal process.

For an isothermal process (according to Boyle's law),

$$p_1V_1 = p_2V_2$$

or $$p_2 = p_1\frac{V_1}{V_2} = p \times \frac{V}{2V}$$

$$= \frac{p}{2} = \frac{1}{2} \text{ atm} = 0.5 \text{ atm}$$

(b) Change in internal energy $\Delta U = 0$, (being isothermal process) as no work is done on or by the gas.

(c) Change in temperature of the gas is zero as gas does no work in expansion.

(d) No, because free expansion of gas is rapid and cannot be controlled. The intermediate states are non-equilibrium states and do not satisfy the gas equation. Therefore, the intermediate states of the gas does not lie on the p-V-T surface.

Question 7 An electric heater supplies heat to a system at a rate of 100 W. If the system performs work at a rate of 75 J/s. At what rate is the internal energy increasing?

Sol. Heat energy supplied per second by the heater

$$\Delta Q = 100 \text{ W} = 100 \text{ J/s}$$

Work done by the system $(\Delta W) = +75$ J/s

Rate of change in internal energy $(\Delta U) = ?$

According to first law of thermodynamics

$$\Delta U = \Delta Q - \Delta W$$

$$= 100 - 75 = 25 \text{ J/s}$$

$$= 25 \text{ W}$$

Mistake Alert Student can misunderstand the first law of thermodynamics, might use the incorrect equation.

Question 8 A thermodynamic system is taken from an original state D to an intermediate state E by linear process shown in figure here. Then, its volume is reduced to the original value from E to D *via* F by an isobaric process. Calculate the total work done by the gas from D to E to F.

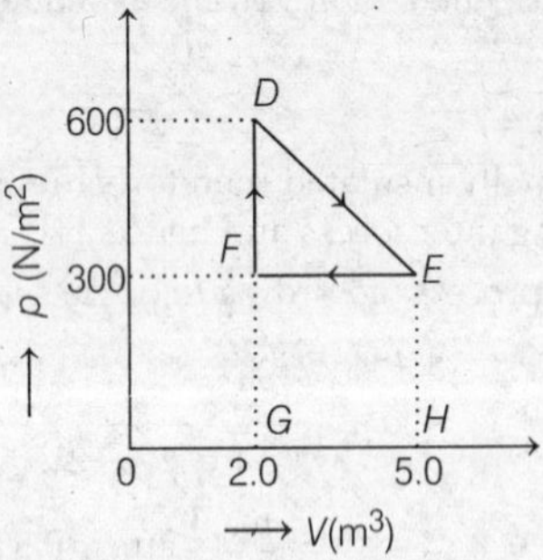

Thinking Process Work done by a thermodynamic system
= Area under p-V curve and V-axis

Work done is positive, if volume increases and negative, if volume decreases.

Sol. Work done in process DE = + Area of $DEHGD$

$$= +[\text{Area of } \Delta DEF + \text{Area of rectangle } EHGF]$$

$$= +\left[\frac{1}{2} \times (600 - 300) \times (5 - 2) + 300 \times (5 - 2)\right]$$

$$= 450 + 900 = 1350 \text{ J}$$

Work done in process EF = $-$[Area of rectangle $EHGF$]

$$= -[300 \times (5 - 2)]$$

$$= -900 \text{ J}$$

$\therefore$ Total work done by the gas from D to E to F

$$W = 1350 - 900$$

$$= 450 \text{ J}$$

DIKSHA APP Questions

Multiple Choice Questions

Q.1 The internal energy, of any general system,

(a) can change only when the temperature of the system (ideal or practical) changes

(b) can change only when potential energy of the system (ideal/practical) changes

(c) can change either when the temperature or potential energy of the system (ideal/practical) changes

(d) never changes irrespective of the changes it may undergo.

Sol. (c) For ideal gas potential energy of system is taken as zero and its kinetic energy is a function of temperature only. Hence for ideal gas internal energy changes with the change in temperature only. For practical (real) gases internal energy is the sum of potential and kinetic energy so, internal energy of practical gas can change only by changing potential energy also for *e.g.*, change of state of solid into liquid or vice versa.

Q.2 Heat is added to a system but its temperature does not change. This could be so because the system must have undergone an

(a) Isothermal change (b) Isobaric change

(c) Isochoric change (d) Adiabatic change

Sol. (a) In isothermal change temperature of system remains constant and hence the internal energy. The heat supplied to the system is used in doing work against surroundings.

Q.3 Two identical containers A and B each of volume V contain respectively (i) monotomic (ii) a diatomic gas at constant temperature. The gas in container A is compressed to a volume $(V/4)$ isothermally while that in container B is compressed to a volume $(v/8)$ adiabatically. the ratio of the final pressure in container B that in container A would be

(a) $(2^{11/5})$ (b) 16 (c) 8 (d) $(2^{16/5})$

Sol. (a) For container A in isothermal condition

$$P_1V = P_{2A}\cdot\frac{V}{4} \Rightarrow P_{2A} = \frac{4PV}{V} = 4P \qquad ...(i)$$

For container B *i.e.*, in adiabatic condition

$$PV^\gamma = P_{2B}\left(\frac{V}{8}\right)^\gamma$$

$$P(8)^\gamma = P_{2B} \qquad ...(ii)$$

$$\therefore \quad \frac{P_{2B}}{p_{2A}} = \frac{(8)^\gamma}{4} = 2^{11/5} \qquad ...(iii)$$

[γ for diatomic gas is $\frac{7}{5}$]

Q.4 Imagine a heat engine following a cycle, represented by the $P-V$ diagram as shown in figure. This cycle is made up of (i) an isothermal from state X to state Y (ii) an adiabatic from state Y to state Z and (iii) an adiabatic from state Z to state X. Such cycle is not permissible because

(a) It shows an isothermal (XY) intersecting with adiabatic (YZ)

(b) It represents a cycle in which mechanical energy gets completely converted into heat which in not in accord with the second law of thermodynamics.

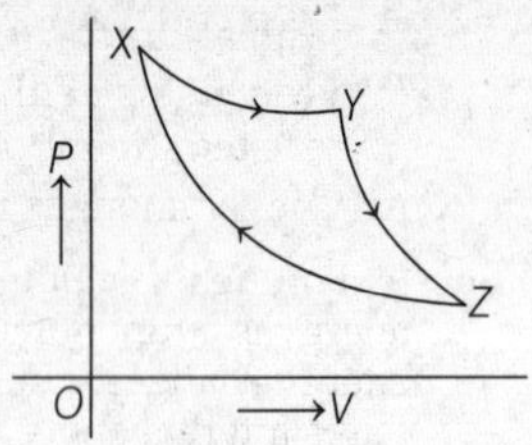

(c) It represents a cycle in which heat gets completely converted into mechanical energy which is not in accord with second law of thermodynamics.

(d) It represents a cycle in which the internal energy (U) of system in all three states have different values *i.e.*, $U_X \neq U_Y \neq U_Z$.

Sol. (c) Option (a) is wrong as isotherm can intersect with adiabatic curve. Option (b) is incorrect because complete conversion of mechanical energy into heat is possible.
Option (c) is correct. As in portion XY temperature is constant so, $dU = 0$ and $dQ = dW$.

In portion YZ and ZX being adiabatic $dQ = 0$ and according to this cycle $dQ = dW$ *i.e.*, heat is completely converted into work which is against the second law of thermodynamics.

Option (d) is incorrect because $U_X = U_Y$ being an isothermal curve in which temperature remains same *i.e.*, internal energy is same.

Q.5 The $P-V$ diagram, for a process of an ideal gas is as shown in figure.

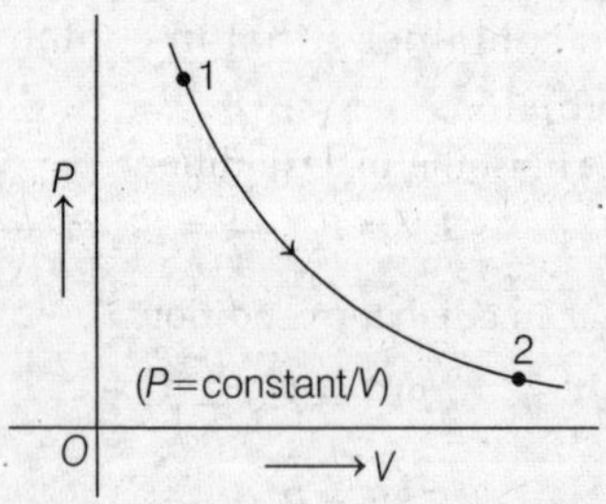

The $(T - P)$ diagram for this gas would have the form

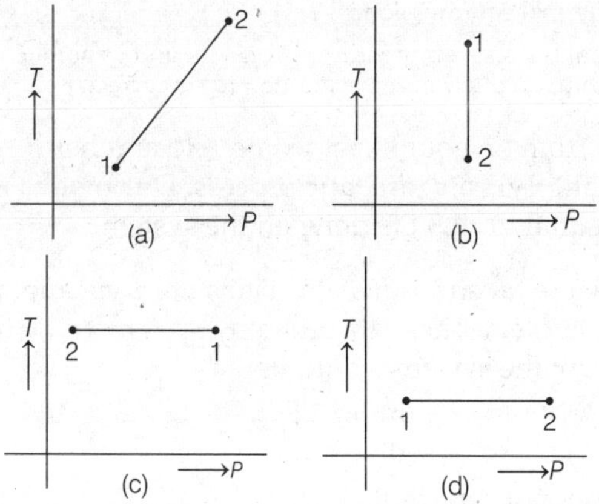

Sol. (c) The given $(P - V)$ diagram represents that gas is obeying Boyle's law and undergoing isothermal expansion.
Hence in $T - P$ diagram temperature will remain constant. In given $(P - V)$ graph pressure at point 1 is more so option (c) is correct.

Q.6 The $P - V$ diagram for an ideal gas is shown in figure.

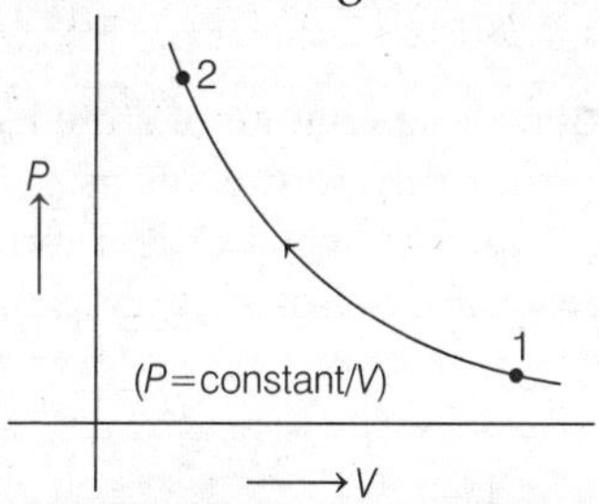

The $T - V$ diagram for this gas would have the form

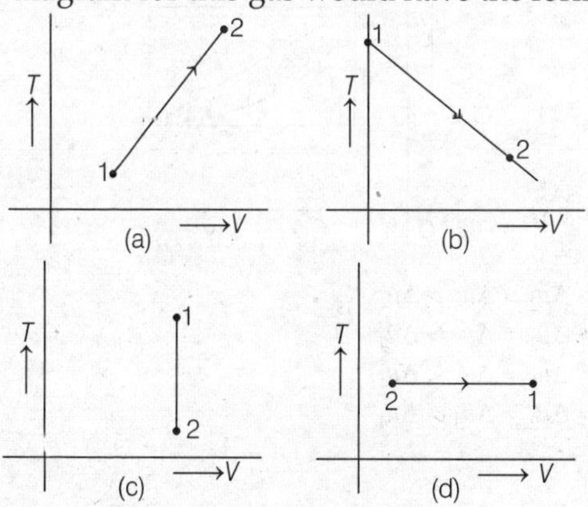

Sol. (d) The given $P-V$ diagram shows gas is obeying Boyle's law and undergoing isothermal compression.

Since in isothermal process temperature is constant and at point 2 volume of gas is less as compared to point 1 so, option (d) is correct.

Q.7 A system goes from on equilibrium state A to another equilibrium state B via an adiabatic process. During this process work equal to 22.3 J is done on the system.

If this system were taken from state A to state B via another process in which the net heat absorbed by system 39.2 J, the net work done by the system would be

(a) 16.9 J (b) 62.3 J
(c) 22.3 J (d) 39.2 J

Sol. (a) During adiabatic process $dQ = 0$

so in first case $dQ = dU + dW$

$$0 = dU + dW \text{ or } du = -(-22.3)$$

$$du = 29.3 \text{ J}$$

In second case, $d\theta = 39.2$ J, the net work done by the system case $dQ = 39.2$ J.

$\therefore$ $$dW = dQ - dU = 39.2 - 22.3 = 16.9 \text{ J}.$$

Q.8 An ideal gas undergoes a change of state from a state A to another state B in four different ways as per the $P-V$ diagram shown in figure. If the changes in the internal energy of the gas, in the four cases are denoted by Δu_1, Δu_2, Δu_3 and Δu_4, we would have

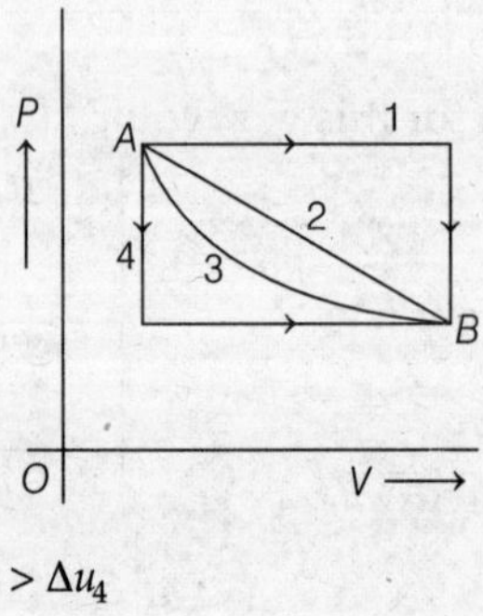

(a) $\Delta u_1 > \Delta u_2 > \Delta u_3 > \Delta u_4$
(b) $\Delta u_1 > \Delta u_2 = \Delta u_3 > \Delta u_4$
(c) $\Delta u_1 < \Delta u_2 = \Delta u_3 < \Delta u_4$
(d) $\Delta u_1 = \Delta u_2 = \Delta u_3 = \Delta u_4$

Sol. (d) The internal energy of gas in given state is the chracteristic of that state (depending upon P, V, and T) and does not depend on the way that state has been arrived. So, values of u_A and u_B is same in all four process.

$\therefore \Delta u = u_B - u_A$ is same in all four processes.

Q.9 A carnot engine is working between a heat source of a temperature $T_1 = 500$ K and a heat sink maintained at temperature $T_2 = 300$ K. The mechanical work produce by engine per cycle is 1 kJ. The heat H_1 taken by the engine from the source and heat H_2 given by the engine to the sink are then equal, respectively to

(a) 5.5. kJ and 4.0 kJ (b) 3.5 kJ and 2.5 kJ

(c) 2.5 kJ and 1.5 kJ (d) 2.0 kJ and 1.0 kJ

Sol. (c) For cannot cycle $\dfrac{H_1}{H_2} = \dfrac{T_1}{T_2} = \dfrac{500}{300} = \dfrac{5}{3}$ ...(i)

$$H_1 - H_2 = W$$

$$H_1 - \frac{3}{5}H_1 = 1\text{kJ}$$

$$H_1 = 2.5\text{kJ}$$

and $$H_2 = 1.5 \text{ kJ}$$

Q.10 A heat engine operating between a sink at a temperature of 27°C and a source at a temperature of 327°C produces 1.4 kJ of mechanical work per cycle per calorie (1 calorie = 4.2 J of heat absorbed from the source. The ratio of efficiency of engine to that of ideal heat engine operating between the same source and sink temperature is

(a) $\dfrac{1}{3}$ (b) $\dfrac{2}{3}$

(c) $\dfrac{1}{2}$ (d) $\dfrac{3}{4}$

Sol. (b) Efficiency of heat engine $= \dfrac{\text{Work done}}{\text{Heat absorbed}}$

$$\eta_1 = \frac{1.4 \times 10^3}{4.2 \times 10^3} = \frac{1}{3} \quad \text{...(i)}$$

For ideal heat engine

$$\eta_2 = 1 - \frac{T_2}{T_1} = 1 - \frac{300}{600} = \frac{1}{2} \quad \text{...(ii)}$$

$$\therefore \quad \frac{\eta_1}{\eta_2} = \frac{\frac{1}{3}}{\frac{1}{2}} = \frac{2}{3}$$

Kinetic Theory

CHAPTER 12

Important Points

01 The ideal gas equation connecting pressure p, volume (V) and absolute temperature (T) is given by

$$pV = nRT = k_B NT$$

where, n is the number of moles and N is the number of molecules.

R an d k_B are universal constants.

$$R = 8.314 \text{ J/mol K}$$

$$K = \frac{R}{N_A}$$

$$= 1.38 \times 10^{-23} \text{ J/K}$$

02 Kinetic theory of an ideal gas given by the relation

$$\text{KE} = \frac{1}{3} nm \overline{v^2}$$

where, n is number density of molecules and $\overline{v^2}$ is the mean of squared speed.

03 Combined with the ideal gas equation, it yields a kinetic interpretation of temperature.

$$\frac{1}{2} m\overline{v^2} = \frac{3}{2} k_B T$$

$$v_{\text{rms}} = (\overline{v^2})^{1/2} = \sqrt{\frac{3k_B T}{m}}$$

04 Average kinetic energy of one mole is given by

$$E = \frac{3}{2} k_B NT$$

This leads to a relation $pV = \frac{2}{3} E$

05 The mean free path λ is the average distance covered by a molecule between two successive collisions.

$$\lambda = \frac{1}{\sqrt{2}\pi n d^2}$$

where, n is the number density and d is the diameter of the molecule.

06 The Avogadro number is the number of molecules in 1 mole of a substance. It's value is 6.022×10^{23} and it is denoted by N.

07 **Degree of Freedom** The number of independent ways in which a molecules can move or store energy.

08 Using the law of equipartition of energy, the molar specific heats of gases can be predicted as for monatomic gases,

$$C_V = \frac{3}{2} R, C_p = \frac{5}{2} R, \gamma = \frac{5}{3} \left[\gamma = \frac{C_p}{C_V}\right]$$

For diatomic gases,

$$C_V = \frac{5}{2} R, C_p = \frac{7}{2} R, \gamma = \frac{7}{5}$$

For polyatomic gases, $C_V = 3R, C_p = 4R, \gamma = \frac{4}{3}$

09 According to Boyle's law, the product of the pressure and the volume of a given mass of gas at constant temperature is constant

i.e., $$PV = \text{constant}$$

10 According to Charles' law, the volume of a given mass of gas at constant pressure is directly proportional to the absolute temperature of the gas *i.e.,* $V \propto T$.

11 According to Dalton's Law of Partial Pressure, the total pressure of a mixture of non- reacting gas is equal to the sum of the partial pressure of each individual gas.

$$P_{\text{total}} = P_1 + P_2 + P_3 \ldots.$$

(Partial pressure)

12 According to law of diffusion, when two gases at the same temperature, pressure diffuse into each other, their rates of diffusion are inversely proportional to the square roots of their densities.

i.e., $$\frac{v_{1\,\text{rms}}}{v_{2\,\text{rms}}} = \sqrt{\frac{\rho_2}{\rho_1}}$$

and $$\frac{R_1}{R_2} = \sqrt{\frac{\rho_2}{\rho_1}} = \sqrt{\frac{M_1}{M_2}}$$

where, R_1 and R_2 be the rates of diffusion of the two gases.

13 The intermolecular force is minimum for the real gases and zero for ideal gases.

14 Real gases don't obey the ideal gas equation $pV = nRT$ at all temperature and pressure.

15 The volume and pressure of ideal gas become zero at the absolute zero temperature.

16 The number of molecules with higher speeds increase with the rise in temperature.

17 Potential energy for the molecules of an ideal gas is zero and they have kinetic energy only.

18 The law of equipartition of energy says that in thermal equilibrium, the total energy is equally distributed among all the degrees of freedom and each degree of freedom contributes $\frac{1}{2}KT$ of energy per molecule.

Exercises

Question 1. Estimate the fraction of molecular volume to the actual volume occupied by oxygen gas at STP. Take the diameter of an oxygen molecule to be 3 Å.

◎ *Thinking Process* 1 mole of an ideal gas occupies 22.4 L at STP. O_2 molecules are treated as made up of two spherical oxygen atoms.

Sol. Diameter of O_2 molecule = 3 Å

$\therefore$ Radius of O_2 $= 1.5$ Å $= 1.5 \times 10^{-8}$ cm

Volume of each molecule $V = \frac{4}{3}\pi r^3$ (each molecule)

Number of molecules in one mole of a gas $= N_A$ = Avagadro's number

$= 6.023 \times 10^{23}$ molecules/mol

$\therefore$ Volume of total molecules at STP $V = \frac{4}{3}\pi r^3 N_A$

$$V = \frac{4}{3} \times 3.14(1.5 \times 10^{-8})^3 \times 6.023 \times 10^{23}$$

$$= 8.51 \text{ cm}^3$$

We know that the volume of one mole of a gas at STP = 22.4 L

$= 22.4 \times 10^3 \text{ cm}^3 = 22400 \text{ cm}^3$

Molecular volume $= \dfrac{8.51}{22400}$

Actual volume occupied by gas

$$= 3.8 \times 10^{-4} \approx 4.0 \times 10^{-4}$$

Note *1 mole of an ideal gas contains exactly 6.023×10^{23} numbers of atoms/molecules only at STP and not any other condition.*

Question 2 Molar volume is the volume occupied by 1 mole of any (ideal) gas at standard temperature and pressure. (STP : 1 atm pressure, 0°C). Show that it is 22.4 L.

Sol. Given, pressure $p = 1 \text{ atm} = 1.013 \times 10^5 \text{ Nm}^{-2}$

Gas constant $R = 8.314 \text{ J mol}^{-1} \text{ K}^{-1}$

Number of mole $n = 1$

Temperature $T = 0°\text{C} = 273.15$ K

Using ideal gas equation $pV = nRT$

or
$$V = \frac{nRT}{p} = \frac{1 \times 8.314 \times 273.15}{1.013 \times 10^5}$$
$$= 0.0224 \text{ m}^3$$
$$= 22.4 \times 10^{-3} \text{ m}^3 \qquad (\text{As } 1 \text{ L} = 10^{-3} \text{ m}^3)$$
$$= 22.4 \text{ L}$$

Mistake Alert Student sometime forget to convert the given data in SI unit before calculation.

Question 3 Figure shows plot of pV/T *versus* p for 1.00×10^{-3} kg of oxygen gas at two different temperatures.

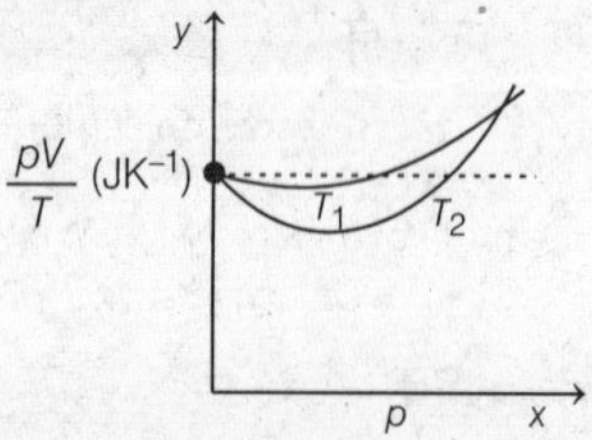

(a) What does the dotted plot signify?
(b) Which is true : $T_1 > T_2$ or $T_1 < T_2$?
(c) What is the value of pV/T where the curves meet on the y-axis?
(d) If we obtained similar plots for 1.00×10^{-3} kg of hydrogen, would we get the same value of pV/T at the point where the curves meet on the y-axis? If not, what mass of hydrogen yields the same value of pV/T (for low pressure high temperature region of the plot)? (Molecular mass of $H_2 = 2.02$ u, $O_2 = 32.0$ u, $R = 8.31 \text{ J mol}^{-1}\text{K}^{-1}$.)

Thinking Process The parts of the question are based on ideal gas equation and the fact that a real gas approaches the ideal gas behaviour at higher temperatures.

Sol. Ideal gas equation
$$pV = nRT$$
or
$$\frac{pV}{T} = nR = \text{constant for a given mass of a gas.}$$

(a) The dotted plot is parallel to x-axis, signifying that nR is independent of p hence representing ideal gas behaviour.
(b) As the graph drawn at temperature T_1 is closer to ideal behaviour than the graph drawn at temperature T_2, hence $T_1 > T_2$. (Higher the temperature, ideal is the behaviour.)

(c) Using $pV = nRT$

$$\frac{pV}{T} = nR$$

Given amount of the gas $= 1.00 \times 10^{-3}$ kg $= 1$ g

Molecular mass of O_2 = 32 amu

Molar mass of O_2 = 32 g

$\therefore$ Number of moles $n = \frac{1}{32}$

$$\therefore \quad nR = \frac{1}{32} \times 8.314$$

$$= 0.26\ \text{JK}^{-1}, \text{ is the required value.}$$

(d) 1.00×10^{-3} kg of H_2 does not represent the same number of moles as that of O_2 as the molar mass of $H_2 = 2.02$ g.

For the same value of $\frac{pV}{T}$. The number of moles must be equal. Hence, number of moles of H_2 required is $\frac{1}{32}$ (= number of moles of O_2.)

$\therefore$ Mass of H_2 required = Number of moles $\times$ Molar mass

$$= \frac{1}{32} \times 2.02 \times 10^{-3}$$

$$= 6.3 \times 10^{-5} \text{ kg}$$

Note Molecular mass is in amu whereas molar mass is in gram. Before going for calculations convert molecular mass to molar mass just by changing amu $(= u)$ to g. 1 mole of a gas or substance is its molecular mass or atomic mass expressed in gram.

Question 4 An oxygen cylinder of volume 30 L has an initial gauge pressure of 15 atm and a temperature of 27°C. After some oxygen is withdrawn from the cylinder, the gauge pressure drops to 11 atm and its temperature drops to 17°C. Estimate the mass of oxygen taken out of the cylinder ($R = 8.31$ J mol^{-1}K^{-1}, molecular mass of $O_2 = 32$ u).

◎ ***Thinking Process*** Whenever masses are taken out of the closed system, no more it is a closed system, hence ideal gas equation should be applied to calculate the change in mass. First number of moles removed should be calculated and then by multiplying with molecular mass of the gas the same can be converted into mass of the gas removed.

Sol. $p_1 = 15 \text{ atm} = 15 \times 1.01 \times 10^5$ Pa

$V_1 = 30 \text{ L} = 30 \times 10^{-3}\ \text{m}^3$

$T_1 = 273.15 + 27 = 300.15$ K

Using ideal gas equation

$$pV = nRT$$

or $$n = \frac{pV}{RT}$$

$$n = \frac{15 \times 1.01 \times 10^5 \times 30 \times 10^{-3}}{8.3 \times 300}$$

$$= 18.253$$

Final $$p_2 = 11 \text{ atm}$$

$$= 11 \times 1.013 \times 10^5 \text{ Pa.}$$

$$V_2 = 30 \text{ L} = 30 \times 10^{-3} \text{m}^3$$

$$T_2 = 273.15 + 17 = 290.15 \text{ K}$$

$$\text{Number of moles} = \frac{p_2 V_2}{RT_2} = \frac{11 \times 1.013 \times 10^5 \times 30 \times 10^{-3}}{8.314 \times 290.15}$$

$$= 13.857$$

Hence, moles removed = 18.253 − 13.847 = 4.395

Mass removed = 4.406 × 32 = 140.65 gm = 141 gm

Mistake Alert Student can use gauge pressure in stead of absolute pressure while calculating initial and final mole.

Question 5 An air bubble of volume 1.0 cm^3 rises from the bottom of a lake 40 m deep at a temperature of 12°C. To what volume does it grow when it reaches the surface, which is at a temperature of 35°C?

Thinking Process Here mass of air trapped inside the bubble remains constant. Other parameters, pressure, volume and temperature varies. Clearly, it is an application of ideal gas equation.

Sol. At the bottom, volume of the bubble

$$V_1 = 1.0 \text{ cm}^3 = 1.0 \times 10^{-6} \text{ m}^3$$

$$\text{Temperature } T_1 = 12°\text{C} = (273.15 + 12) \text{K} = 285.15 \text{ K}$$

At the surface,

$$\text{Temperature, } T_2 = 35°\text{C} = (273.15 + 35) \text{K} = 308.15 \text{ K}$$

$$\text{Pressure, } p_2 = 1 \text{ atm} = 1.013 \times 10^5 \text{ Pa}$$

and pressure at depth $d = 40$ m from below the surface

$$p_1 = 1 \text{ atm} + h\rho g$$

$$= 1.013 \times 10^5 + 40 \times 10^3 \times 9.8$$

$$= 493.3 \times 10^3 \text{ Pa}$$

Using $$\frac{p_1 V_1}{T_1} = \frac{p_2 V_2}{T_2}$$

We have, $$V_2 = \left(\frac{p_1V_1}{T_1}\right)\left(\frac{T_2}{p_2}\right) = \frac{(493.3 \times 10^3) \times (1.0 \times 10^{-6}) \times 308.15}{285 \times 1.013 \times 10^5}$$

$$= 5.265 \times 10^{-6}\,\text{m}^3 = 5.265\,\text{cm}^3$$

Therefore, the volume of the air bubble at the surface of the lake is 5.263 cm^3.

Note While calculating the pressure at depth d don't forget to add 1 atm to the '$d\rho g$' component of hydrostatic pressure. Take care of using units coherently, preferably SI unit, to get error free values.

Question 6 Estimate the total number of air molecules (inclusive of oxygen, nitrogen, water vapour and other constituents) in a room of capacity 25.0 m^3 at a temperature of 27°C and 1 atm pressure.

◎ ***Thinking Process*** Whenever, number of molecules/atoms are to be calculated $pV = nk_BT$ is used

where n = number of molecules/atoms;

k_B = Boltzmann's constant = 1.38×10^{-23} $\text{m}^2\,\text{kg s}^{-2}\,\text{K}^{-1}$.

Sol. Volume of the room = $V = 25.0\,\text{m}^3$

Temperature $T = 27°\text{C} = (273.15 + 27)\,\text{K} = 300.15\,\text{K}$

Pressure $p = 1\,\text{atm} = 1.013 \times 10^5$ Pa

Using the relation $pV = nk_BT$

$$n = \frac{pV}{k_BT} = \frac{1.013 \times 10^5 \times 25}{1.38 \times 10^{-23} \times 300.15}$$

$$= 6.11 \times 10^{26} \text{ molecules}$$

Note Number of molecules should not be confused with number of moles. The equation used above is another form of ideal gas equation.

Question 7 Estimate the average thermal energy of a helium atom at (a) room temperature (27°C), (b) the temperature on the surface of the sum (6000 K), (c) the temperature of 10 million kelvin (the typical core temperature in the case of a star).

◎ ***Thinking Process*** Thermal energy represents that part of internal energy which is translational kinetic in nature. This equal $\frac{3}{2}k_bT$; which only depends on absolute temperature of the gas.

Sol.

(a) Given, $T = 27°\text{C} = (273.15 + 27)\,\text{K} = 300.15\,\text{K}$

Average thermal energy

$$E = \frac{3}{2}k_BT$$

(where k_B = Boltzmann's constant = 1.38×10^{-23} $\text{m}^2\,\text{kg s}^{-2}\,\text{K}^{-1}$)

$$\therefore \quad E = \frac{3}{2} \times 1.38 \times 10^{-23} \times 300.15$$
$$= 6.21 \times 10^{-21} \text{ J}$$

(b) At the temperature

$$T = 6000 \text{ K} \qquad \text{(Surface of the sun)}$$

Average thermal energy $E = \frac{3}{2} k_B T$

$$= \frac{3}{2} \times 1.38 \times 10^{-23} \times 6000 = 1.241 \times 10^{-19} \text{ J}$$

(c) At temperature, $T = 10^7$ K

Average thermal energy $E = \frac{3}{2} k_B T$

$$= \frac{3}{2} \times 1.38 \times 10^{-23} \times 10^7 = 2.07 \times 10^{-16} \text{ J}$$

Note In the given question the gas taken is 'He' which is monoatomic and has only 3 degrees of freedom. Hence, thermal energy is same as that of internal energy. But if gases are diatomic (N_2, O_2 etc.) or polyatomic (NH_3, SO_3 etc.). The thermal energy and internal energy differ, depending on number of degrees of freedom.

Question 8 Three vessels of equal capacity have gases at the same temperature and pressure. The first vessel contains neon (monatomic), the second contains chlorine (diatomic), and the third contains uranium hexafluoride (polyatomic). Do the vessels contain equal number of respective molecules? Is the root mean square speed of molecules the same in the three cases? If not, in which case is v_{rms} the largest?

◎ ***Thinking Process*** Avogadro's hypothesis is an important proposition based on which a variety of questions are framed. It states that equal volume of all gases under similar condition of temperature and pressure contain same number of molecules/atoms. Root mean square speed is directly proportional to absolute temperature of the gas and inversely proportional to its molar mass.

Sol. Yes, according to Avogadro's law equal amount of gases have equal number of molecules/atoms at the same temperature and pressure.
No, root mean square speed of molecules of three given gases is not same. As root mean square speed is given by

$$v_{rms} = \sqrt{\frac{3RT}{M}} \Rightarrow v_{rms} \propto \sqrt{\frac{1}{M}}$$

For constant temperature of samples, atomic mass is least for neon hence v_{rms} is largest for Ne.

Note The average kinetic energy (per molecule) of any (ideal) gas (be it monoatomic like argon, diatomic like chlorine or polyatomic) is always equal to $\frac{3}{2} k_B T$. It depends only on temperature and is independent of the nature of the gas.

Question 9 At what temperature is the root mean square speed of an atom in an argon gas cylinder equal to the rms speed of a helium gas atom at –20°C? (Atomic mass of Ar = 39.9 u, of H = 4.0 u).

◎ *Thinking Process* Comparing the two root mean square speeds will be the easiest approach using the direct relation between v_{rms} and absolute temperature T.

Sol. Root mean square speed of organ atom

$$(v_{rms})_{Ar} = \sqrt{\frac{3RT_{Ar}}{M_{Ar}}} \quad \text{...(i)}$$

Root mean square speed of helium atom

$$(v_{rms})_{He} = \sqrt{\frac{3RT_{He}}{M_{He}}} \quad \text{...(ii)}$$

Dividing Eq. (i) by Eq. (ii)

$$\frac{(v_{rms})_{Ar}}{(v_{rms})_{He}} = \sqrt{\frac{3RT_{Ar}}{M_{Ar}} \times \frac{M_{He}}{3RT_{He}}}$$

Given $(v_{rms})_{Ar} = (v_{rms})_{He}$

$$\Rightarrow \quad 1 = \sqrt{\left(\frac{T_{Ar}}{T_{He}}\right) \cdot \left(\frac{M_{He}}{M_{Ar}}\right)}$$

$$\Rightarrow \quad \frac{M_{He}}{M_{Ar}} = \frac{T_{He}}{T_{Ar}}$$

$$\therefore \quad T_{Ar} = T_{He}\left(\frac{M_{Ar}}{M_{He}}\right)$$

$$= 253.15\left(\frac{39.9}{4}\right) = 2525.171\,\text{K}$$

$$= 2.52 \times 10^3\ \text{K}$$

Mistake Alert Student may use wrong formula for the mean free path can load to incorrect results.

Question 10 Estimate the mean free path and collision frequency of a nitrogen molecule in a cylinder containing nitrogen at 2.0 atm and temperature 17°C. Take the radius of a nitrogen molecule to be roughly 1.0 Å. Compare the collision time with the time the molecule moves freely between two successive collisions (Molecular mass of $N_2 = 28.0$ u).

Sol. Given, pressure $p = 2\text{ atm} = 2 \times 1.013 \times 10^5\ \text{N/m}^2$

$$\text{Temperature}\,(T) = 17 + 273.15\,\text{K} = 290.15\,\text{K}$$

$$\text{Molecular weight}\,(M) = 28\text{g}$$

Root mean square speed $v_{rms} = \sqrt{\frac{3RT}{M}}$

$$v_{rms} = \sqrt{\frac{3 \times 8.314 \times 290.15}{28 \times 10^{-3}}} \quad \text{(putting the values given)}$$

$$= 508.39 \text{ m/s}$$

For mean free path (l) on using

$$l = \frac{1}{\sqrt{2}\pi n d^2} \quad \ldots(i)$$

Here n = number density of gas molecules,
= number of gas molecules per unit volume.

Using $pV = n'kT$, where n' = number of molecules.

$$\therefore \quad \frac{n'}{V} = \frac{p}{kT} = n$$

Putting the value of n in Eq. (i)

$$l = \frac{kT}{\sqrt{2}\pi d^2 \times p}$$

Putting the values $l = \dfrac{1.38 \times 10^{-23} \times 290.15}{\sqrt{2} \times 3.14 \times (2 \times 10^{-10})^2 \times 2 \times 1.013 \times 10^5}$

$$= \frac{1.38 \times 29 \times 10^{-7}}{1.414 \times 3.14 \times 4 \times 2.06} = 1.11 \times 10^{-7} \text{ m}$$

Hence, mean free path, $l = 1.1 \times 10^{-7}$ m

Collision frequency = number of collisions per second

$$= \frac{v_{rms}}{l} = \frac{508.26}{1.11 \times 10^{-7}} = 4.6 \times 10^9 \text{ s}^{-1}$$

Time taken for the collision $= \dfrac{d}{v_{rms}}$

where, d = diameter of a molecule

$$= \frac{2 \times 1 \times 10^{-10}}{508.26} = 3.93 \times 10^{-13} \text{ s}$$

Time taken between successive collisions

$$= \frac{l}{v_{rms}} = \frac{1.11 \times 10^{-7}}{508.26} = 2 \times 10^{-10} \text{ s}$$

Thus the time taken between successive collisions is 500 times the time taken for a collision. Thus a molecule in a gas moves essentially free for most of the time.

Note In the relation $l = \dfrac{1}{\sqrt{2}\pi n d^2}$, note that n is not number of molecules but it is number density of molecules i.e., number of molecules per unit volume. Also note that in the equation $pV = n'k_BT$, n' is the total number of molecules present in the entire volume of the closed container. For a closed container the former may vary but the latter is a constant.

Oscillations

CHAPTER 13

Important Points

01 The motion which repeat themselves are called periodic motion.

02 All oscillatory motion are per iodic motions but all periodic motions may not be oscillatory.

03 The period T is the time required for one complete oscillation or cycle. It is related to the frequency ν by,

$$T = \frac{I}{\nu}$$

04 Simple Harmonic oscillation (SHM) is a special type of oscillatory motion where restoring force is directly proportional to displacement and directed towards mean position.

$$F = -Kx \Rightarrow a^2 = -w^2 x$$

05 Simple Harmonic Motion (SHM) is not any periodic motion, but one which displacement is sinusoidal function of time. General equation of SHM

$$n(t) = A\cos(wt + \phi)$$

A→ amplitude, Wt → angular frequency

$x(t)$ → displacement x as a function of time t, ϕ → phase constant

It is periodic, but not S.H.M because it is not to and for motion about a fixed pairs

06 The angular frequency ω is related to the period and frequency of the motion is given by

$$\omega = \frac{2\pi}{T} = 2\pi\nu$$

07 Velocity of particle executing simple harmonic motion is given by

$$v = r\omega \cos \omega t = \omega\sqrt{r^2 - y^2}$$

08 Acceleration of a particle executing simple harmonic motion is given by $$a = -\omega^2 y$$

09 Acceleration amplitude (*i.e.*, maximum acceleration) is given by

$$a_0 = \omega^2 r$$

10 Velocity of a particle executing SHM is zero at the extreme position and maximum at the mean position.

11 Acceleration is maximum at the extreme position and zero at the mean position.

12 A particle of mass m oscillating under the influence of a Hooke's law restoring force is given by $F = -kx$ exhibits simple harmonic motion with

$$\omega = \sqrt{\frac{k}{m}} \qquad \text{(Angular frequency)}$$

$$T = 2\pi\sqrt{\frac{m}{k}} \qquad \text{(Period)}$$

Such a system is also called a linear oscillator.

13 Time period of mass m suspended by two springs connected in parallel is given by

$$T = 2\pi\sqrt{\frac{m}{k_1 + k_2}}$$

14 Time period of a mass m suspended by two springs connected in series is given by

$$T = 2\pi\sqrt{\left(\frac{1}{k_1} + \frac{1}{k_2}\right)m} = 2\pi\sqrt{\frac{m(k_1 + k_2)}{k_1 k_2}}$$

15 The time period of simple pendulum for massless string is given by

$$T = 2\pi\sqrt{\frac{l}{g}}$$

16 A liquid in a U-tube set in oscillations executes SHM with a period $T = 2\pi\sqrt{\frac{h}{g}}$, where h is the rise or depression of liquid from the mean position in one limb.

17 Time period of simple pendulum in infinite length is 84.6 min.

18 Graph between l^2 and T^2 is a straight line in case of simple pendulum.

19 Time period of pendulum decreases, if it accelerates upward with an acceleration a.

$$T = 2\pi\sqrt{\frac{l}{g+a}}$$

20 Time period of a simple pendulum increases if it accelerates downward with an acceleration a.

$$T = 2\pi\sqrt{\frac{l}{g-a}}$$

21 Time period of simple pendulum increases when it is immersed in a liquid of density σ.

22 The total energy of a particle in SHM is given by $E = 2\pi^2 m\nu^2 a^2$ where a is the amplitude and ν is the frequency of particle.

23 Simple pendulum cannot oscillate in weightlessness but the spring can do so.

24 The work done by simple pendulum in one complete oscillation is zero.

25 The mechanical energy in a real oscillating system decreases during oscillation because external force, such as drag, inhibit the oscillations and convert mechanical energy to thermal energy. The real oscillator and its motion are then said to be damped. The damping force is given by $F_d = -bv$, where v is the velocity of the oscillator and b is a damping constant, then the displacement of the oscillator is given by

$$x(t) = Ae^{-bt/2m}\cos(\omega' t + \phi)$$

where ω', the angular frequency of the damped oscillator, is given by

$$\omega' = \sqrt{\frac{k}{m} - \frac{b^2}{um^2}}$$

26 The mechanical energy E of the damped oscillator is given by

$$E(t) = \frac{I}{2}kA^2 e^{-bt/m}$$

27 The oscillation whose amplitude does not change with time are called undamped oscillations. Such oscillations exist only in vaccum.

Exercises

Question 1 Which of the following examples represent periodic motion?

(a) A swimmer completing one (return) trip from one bank of a river to the other and back.

(b) A freely suspended bar magnet displaced from its *N-S* direction and released.

(c) A hydrogen molecule rotating about its centre of mass.

(d) An arrow released from a bow.

◎ ***Thinking Process*** If the motion is repeated after certain interval of time then, it is periodic. Circular motion is a periodic.

Sol.

(a) There is no repetition of the motion as the swimmer just completes one trip; hence not periodic.

(b) The motion is repeated after a certain interval of time, hence periodic. In fact the bar magnet oscillates about its mean position with a definite period of time.

(c) Rotatory motion is periodic as repeating after fixed time-interval.

(d) There is no repetition, hence not periodic.

Note Periodic motion may be completed in two or more parts with similar or dissimilar time interval. But it must repeat the entire set of events after certain fixed interval of time called time period.

Question 2 Which of the following examples represent (nearly) simple harmonic motion and which represent periodic but not simple harmonic motion?

(a) The rotation of earth about its axis.

(b) Motion of an oscillating mercury column in a U-tube.

(c) Motion of a ball bearing inside a smooth curved bowl, when released from a point slightly above the lower most point.

(d) General vibrations of a polyatomic molecule about its equilibrium position.

◎ ***Thinking Process*** Every SHM is periodic but every periodic motion is not SHM. Only that periodic motion governed by the force law where, $F = -kx$ is simple harmonic.

Sol.

(a) Earth's rotation is periodic as it repeats every 24 hours, but there's no linear restoring force or to-and-fro motion through equilibrium. So, it is not SHM.

(b) This is a periodic motion and as it follows $F = -kx$ (about mean position, to and fro motion) hence it is SHM.

(c) The ball rolls back and forth around the bottom. For small movement, gravity acts like a spring pulling it back, so it behaves like SHM.

(d) A polyatomic molecule has a number of natural frequencies. So, in general, its vibration is a superposition of SHMs of a number of different frequencies. Thus, superposition is periodic but not SHM.

Note A combination of two SHMs with arbitrary amplitudes and phases is not necessarily periodic. It is periodic only if frequency of one motion is an integral multiple of the other's frequency. However, a periodic motion can always be expressed as a sum of infinite number of harmonic motions with appropriate amplitudes.

Question 3 Figures depict four *x*-*t* plots for linear motion of a particle. Which of the plots represent periodic motion? What is the period of motion (in case of periodic motion)?

(a)

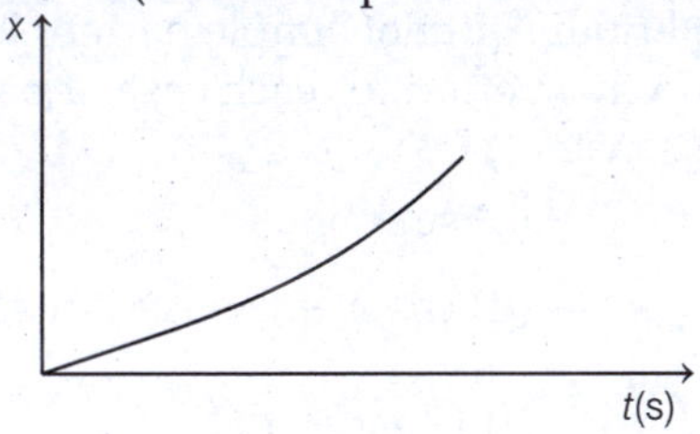

(b)

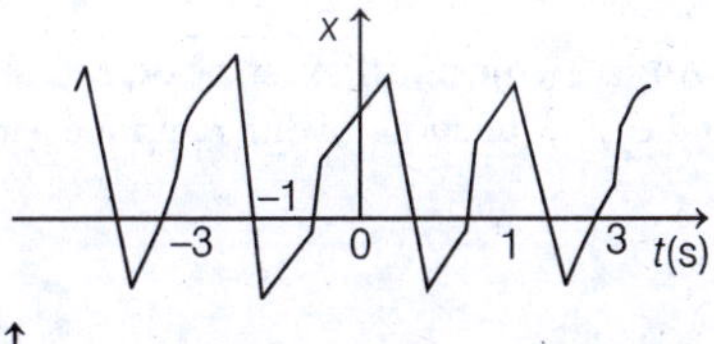

(c)

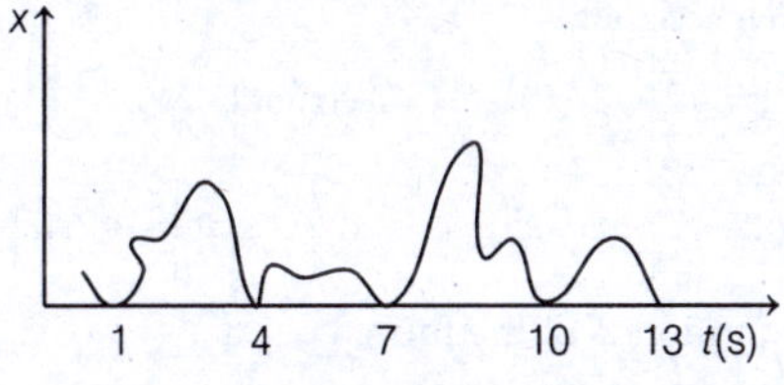

(d)

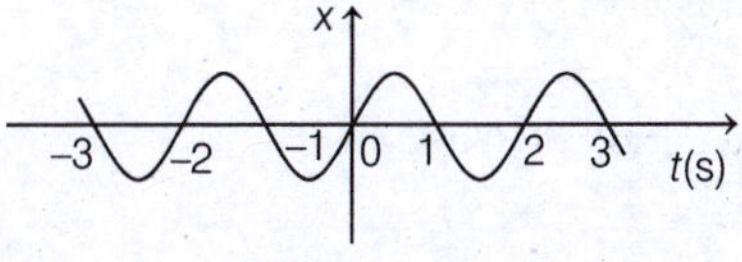

Thinking Process As the graphs are plot between displacements *versus* time, we shall check for repetition to ascertain, whether periodic or not. Also, the minimum time span after which the plot repeats itself will be time period of the motion.

Sol.

(a) No repetition of motion. It's a unidirectional, linear but non-uniform motion of the particle.

(b) Motion repeats after every 2 s. Hence, periodic with time period 2 s.

(c) Repetition of one position or a few positions (but not all) is not enough for motion to be periodic, the entire motion during one period must be repeated successively.

Hence the given x-t plot is not periodic, though there is repetition of a single position ($x = 0$ at every 3s) but other positions are not repeated.

(d) Clearly, the motion repeats itself after every 2 s. Hence, periodic having a time-period of 2 s.

Note The graph may be regular or irregular, but if they repeat successively after a fixed time interval, they are periodic in either case.

Question 4 Which of the following functions of time represent (i) simple harmonic, (ii) periodic but not simple harmonic and (iii) non-periodic motion? Give period for each case of periodic motion (ω is any positive constant).

(a) $\sin \omega t - \cos \omega t$ (b) $\sin^3 \omega t$

(c) $3 \cos\left(\frac{\pi}{4} - 2\omega t\right)$ (d) $\cos \omega t + \cos 3\omega t + \cos 5\omega t$

(e) $\exp(-\omega^2 t^2)$ (f) $1 + \omega t + \omega^2 t^2$

Thinking Process Any periodic function can be expressed as a superposition of sine and cosine functions of different time periods with suitable coefficients.

Sol.

(a) Assuming $(x)t = \sin \omega t - \cos \omega t$

$$= \sqrt{2}\left[\frac{1}{\sqrt{2}}\sin \omega t - \frac{1}{\sqrt{2}}\cos \omega t\right]$$

$$= \sqrt{2}\left[\cos\frac{\pi}{4}\sin \omega t - \sin\frac{\pi}{4}\cos \omega t\right] = \sqrt{2}\sin\left(\omega t - \frac{\pi}{4}\right)$$

Clearly, the above equation is of the form

$$x = A\sin(\omega t \pm \phi)$$

represents SHM.

Again, if $t = \frac{2\pi}{\omega}$ is the period of SHM, then

$$x\left(t+\frac{2\pi}{\omega}\right)=\sqrt{2}\sin\left[\omega\left(t+\frac{2\pi}{\omega}\right)-\frac{\pi}{4}\right]$$

$$=\sqrt{2}\sin\left(\omega t+2\pi-\frac{\pi}{4}\right)=\sqrt{2}\sin\left(\omega t-\frac{\pi}{4}\right)=x(t)$$

Hence, the period $T=\dfrac{2\pi}{\omega}$

and phase angle $=-\dfrac{\pi}{4}$ or $\left(2\pi-\dfrac{\pi}{4}\right)$

(b) Let $x(t)=\sin^3\omega t$

or $x(t)=\dfrac{1}{4}(3\sin\omega t-\sin 3\omega t)$

Using $\sin 3\theta=3\sin\theta-4\sin^3\theta$

The above equation represent two SHMs in combination. The combination is periodic but not SHM.

Period of $\dfrac{3}{4}\sin\omega t=\dfrac{2\pi}{\omega}=T$

Period of $\dfrac{1}{4}\sin 3\omega t=\dfrac{2\pi}{3\omega}=T'=\dfrac{T}{3}$

Thus, period of the combination = Minimum time after which the combined function repeats

$=$ LCM of T and $\dfrac{T}{3}=T$

(c) $x(t)=3\cos\left(\dfrac{\pi}{4}-2\omega t\right)=3\cos\left(2\omega t-\dfrac{\pi}{4}\right)$

As $\cos(-\theta)=\cos\theta$

The above equation is of the form $x(t)=A\cos(\omega t\pm\phi)$

Hence, SHM with period

$$T=\frac{2\pi}{2\omega}=\frac{\pi}{\omega}$$

(d) $x(t)=\cos\omega t+\cos 3\omega t+\cos 5\omega t$

$\cos\omega t$ represents SHM with period $=\dfrac{2\pi}{\omega}=T$ (say)

$\cos 3\omega t$ represents SHM with period $=\dfrac{2\pi}{3\omega}=\dfrac{T}{3}$

$\cos 5\omega t$ represents SHM with period $=\dfrac{2\pi}{5\omega}=\dfrac{T}{5}$

The minimum time after which the combined function repeats its value is T. Hence, the given function represents periodic function but not SHM, with period T.

(e) $x(t)=\exp(-\omega^2t^2)$

The given function is an exponential function. It decreases monotonically

$$x(t)\to 0 \text{ as } t\to\infty$$

There is no repetition of the values. Hence, represents a non-periodic function.

(f) $x(t) = 1 + \omega t + \omega^2 t^2$

Here, as $t \to \infty$

$x(t) \to \infty$

No repetition of values. Hence, it represents non-periodic function.

Note Either a function must be represented in standard form of SHM or alternatively, it can be checked for acceleration $\propto$ –displacement, by double differentiating the $x(t)$ function with respect to t. It is only then SHM nature of the function is confirmed. Superposition of two SHM may or not be a SHM. It must be checked satisfying the above condition for confirming its SHM nature.

Question 5 A particle is in linear simple harmonic motion between two points A and B, 10 cm apart. Take the direction from A to B as the positive direction and give the signs of velocity, acceleration and force on the particle when it is

(a) at the end A.

(b) at the end B.

(c) at the mid-point of AB going towards A.

(d) at 2 cm away from B going towards A.

(e) at 3 cm away from A going towards B.

(f) at 4 cm away from B going towards A.

Thinking Process At either extreme positions in SHM, the velocity is 0 but not the acceleration and force. Acceleration is always directs towards the mean position (point about which SHM is taking place). Further, acceleration decides the direction of force.

Sol. Visualize the situation using the diagram below.

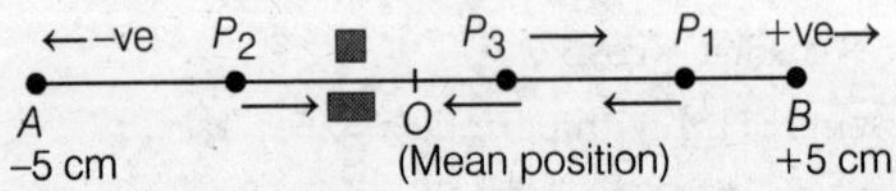

Now,

	Velocity	acceleration	Force
(a) A	0	+	+
(b) B	0	–	–
(c) O	–	0	0.
(d) P_1	–	–	–
(e) P_2	+	+	+
(f) P_3	–	–	–

Note Don't confuse with velocity to that of acceleration both may or may not have same sign. In SHM acceleration and force must be the same. Further at mean position particle has 0 acceleration but maximum velocity. At extreme positions particle has zero velocity but maximum acceleration.

Question 6 Which of the following relationships between the acceleration a and the displacement x of a particle involve simple harmonic motion?

(a) $a = 0.7x$

(b) $a = -200x^2$

(c) $a = -10x$

(d) $a = 100x^3$

Thinking Process All SHM follow the condition acceleration $\propto$ –displacement or acceleration = – constant × displacement. $[a \alpha - x]$

Sol.

(a) No negative sign on RHS hence, not SHM.

(b) Displacement on RHS is squared, hence not SHM.

(c) $a = -10x$ follows the condition of SHM acceleration $\propto$–displacement hence, SHM.

(d) No negative sign on RHS and displacement appears as cubed. Hence, not SHM.

Note All SHM are oscillatory, but not all oscillatory motions are SHM. SHM must follow acceleration α- displacement, meaning they are always in opposite directions.

Question 7 The motion of a particle executing simple harmonic motion is described by the displacement function,

$$x(t) = A\cos(\omega t + \phi)$$

If the initial $(t = 0)$ position of the particle is 1 cm and its initial velocity is ωcm/s, what are its amplitude and initial phase angle? The angular frequency of the particle is $\pi \text{ s}^{-1}$. If instead of the cosine function, we choose the sine function to describe the SHM : $x = B\sin(\omega t + \alpha)$, what are the amplitude and initial phase of the particle with the above initial conditions?

Thinking Process The standard form of SHM should be used to determine the constants of the motion using the given condition.

Sol. Given $x(t) - A\cos(\omega t + \phi)$

At $t = 0$; position $x(t) = 1\,\text{cm}$,

Angular frequency $\omega = \pi \text{s}^{-1}$

$$1 = A\cos(\omega t + \phi)$$

$$1 = A\cos\phi \quad \text{...(i)}$$

Now, $$v(t) = \frac{dx}{dt}(t) = \frac{d}{dt}A\cos(\omega t + \phi)$$

$$= -A\omega\sin(\omega t + \phi)$$

Again at $t = 0$, $v = \omega$ cm/s

$\Rightarrow$ $$\omega = -A\omega\sin\phi$$

$\Rightarrow$ $$-1 = A\sin\phi \quad \text{...(ii)}$$

Squaring and adding Eqs. (i) and (ii),

$$A^2\cos^2\phi + A^2\sin^2\phi = (1)^2 + (-1)^2$$

$$A^2 = 2 \Rightarrow A = \pm\sqrt{2}\text{ cm}$$

Hence, the amplitude = $\sqrt{2}$ cm

Dividing Eq. (ii) by Eq. (i), we have

$$\frac{A\sin\phi}{A\cos\phi} = \frac{-1}{1} \text{ or } \tan\phi = -1$$

$\Rightarrow$ $$\phi = -\frac{\pi}{4} \text{ or } \frac{7\pi}{4}$$

Now, if instead of cosine we choose the sine function, then

$$x(t) = B\sin(\omega t + \alpha)$$

At $t = 0$, $x = 1$ cm

$\Rightarrow$ $$1 = B\sin(0 + \alpha)$$

or $$B\sin\alpha = 1 \quad \text{...(iii)}$$

Velocity $$v(t) = \frac{dx(t)}{dt} = \frac{d}{dt}[B\sin(\omega t + \alpha)]$$

$$= +B\omega\cos(\omega t + \alpha)$$

Again at $t = 0$, $v(t) = \omega$ cm/s

$$\omega = +B\omega\cos(0 + \alpha)$$

$$B\cos\alpha = +1 \quad \text{...(iv)}$$

Squaring and adding Eqs. (iii) and (iv),

$$B^2\sin^2\alpha + B^2\cos^2\alpha = (1)^2 + (+1)^2$$

$\Rightarrow$ $$B^2\sin^2\alpha + B^2\cos^2\alpha = 2$$

$$B^2(\sin^2\alpha + \cos^2\alpha) = 2$$

$$B^2 \cdot 1 = 2 \Rightarrow B = \pm\sqrt{2}\text{ cm}$$

Hence, amplitude of motion = $\sqrt{2}$ cm

Dividing Eq. (iii) by Eq. (iv), we get

$$\frac{B\sin\alpha}{B\cos\alpha} = \frac{1}{1} \text{ or } \tan\alpha = 1$$

$\therefore$ $$\alpha = \frac{\pi}{4}$$

Note By changing sine to cosine or vice-versa only the initial phase of the SHM is changed. Remaining parameters of motion such as amplitude, frequency etc., remains unaffected.

Question 8 A spring balance has a scale that reads from 0 to 50 kg. The length of the scale is 20 cm. A body suspended from this balance, when displaced and released, oscillates with a period of 0.6 s. What is the weight of the body?

◎ *Thinking Process* This is direct application of oscillation of a loaded spring. The parameters required are to be determined from the given conditions of the situation.

Sol. As the length of the scale is 20 cm and it can read upto 50 kg. The maximum extension of 20 cm will correspond to maximum weight of $50 \text{ kg} \times 9.8 \text{ m/s}^2$.

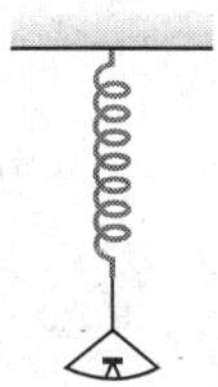

Using, $F = -kx$

$|F| = F = kx$

Here, $x = 20 \times 10^{-2}$ m

$$k = \frac{50 \times 9.8}{20 \times 10^{-2}}$$

$$= 2450 \text{ N/m}$$

We have for loaded oscillation

$$T = 2\pi\sqrt{\frac{m}{k}}$$

or $$T^2 = 4\pi^2 \frac{m}{k}$$

$$m = \frac{T^2 k}{4\pi^2} = \frac{(0.60)^2 \times 2450}{4 \times (3.14)^2} = 22.36 \text{ kg}$$

$\therefore$ Weight $= mg = 22.36 \times 9.8 = 219.13$ N

Note Mass and weight should be distinguished while solving such questions. Though a spring balance reads weight, in questions it might be given, mass. Convert into weight by multiplying 9.8 m/s^2 or more precisely the value of g at the location.

Question 9 A spring having with a spring constant 1200 N/m is mounted on a horizontal table as shown in figure. A mass of 3 kg is attached to the free end of the spring. Then the mass is pulled sideways to a distance of 2.0 cm and released.

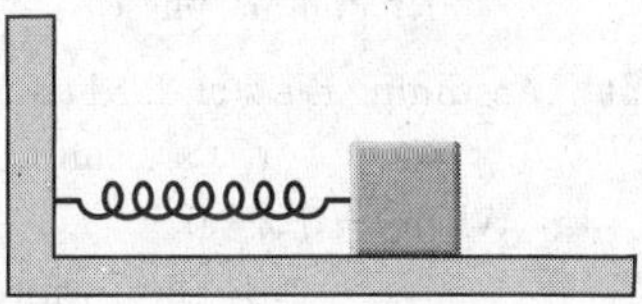

Determine (a) the frequency of oscillations, (b) maximum acceleration of the mass, and (c) the maximum speed of the mass.

◎ *Thinking Process* This is direct application of oscillation of attached mass on horizontal surface.

Sol. (a) Here, spring constant $k = 1200$ N/m, mass $m = 3.0$ kg

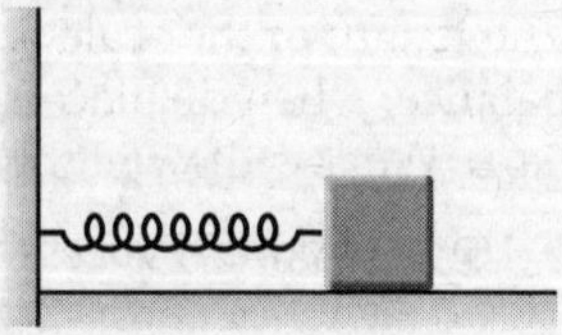

Amplitude $A = 2.0\text{ cm} = 2.0 \times 10^{-2}$ m

Now, frequency of oscillation

$$\nu = \frac{1}{2\pi}\sqrt{\frac{k}{m}} = \frac{1}{2 \times 3.14}\sqrt{\frac{1200}{3.0}}$$

$$= \frac{1}{2 \times 3.14} \times 20 = 3.2/\text{s}$$

(b) Angular frequency $\omega = 2\pi\nu = \sqrt{\frac{k}{m}} = \sqrt{\frac{1200}{3.0}} = 20$ rad/s

Maximum acceleration of the mass

$$|a_{max}| = |-\omega^2 A| = |-(20)^2 \times 2.0 \times 10^{-2}| = 8.0\text{ m/s}^2$$

(c) Maximum speed $= \omega A$

$$= 20 \times 2.0 \times 10^{-2} = 0.4\text{ m/s}$$

Note The pulling of mass side ways from the mean position of the block is considered as the amplitude of motion. There should be no friction between horizontal table and the block.

Question 10 In Q. 9, let us take the position of mass when the spring is unstretched as $x = 0$ and the direction from left to right as the positive direction of X-axis. Given x as a function of time t for the oscillating mass, if at the moment we start the stopwatch ($t = 0$), the mass is

(a) at the mean position,

(b) at the maximum stretched position and

(c) at the maximum compressed position.

In what way do these functions for SHM differ from each other, in frequency, in amplitude or the initial phase?

◎ ***Thinking Process*** Standard equation for SHM should be used with different initial phases.

Sol. Assuming the standard equation

$$x(t) = A\sin(\omega t + \phi)$$

(a) When $t = 0$, $x = 0$ (Mean position)

$$0 = A\sin(\omega \times 0 + \phi)$$

$$A\sin\phi = 0 \quad \text{(As } A \neq 0\text{)}$$

or $\sin\phi = 0$

$\therefore$ $\phi = 0$

$\therefore$ Required function is

$$x(t) = A\sin(\omega t + 0) \text{ or } x(t) = A\sin\omega t$$

$$\omega = \sqrt{\frac{k}{m}} = \sqrt{\frac{1200}{3.0}} = 20 \text{ rad/s}$$

$\therefore \quad x(t) = A\sin 20t \quad \text{or} \quad x(t) = 2\sin 20t$

(b) When $t = 0$, $x = + A$ (Maximum stretched position)

$$x(t) = A\sin(\omega t + \phi) \text{ at } t = 0 \text{ and } x = + A = A\sin(\omega \times 0 + \phi)$$

or $\quad 1 = \sin\phi \Rightarrow \phi = \frac{\pi}{2}$

$\therefore \quad x(t) = A\sin\left(\omega t + \frac{\pi}{2}\right)$

$$= A\cos\omega t = A\cos 20t = 2\cos 20t$$

(c) When the spring is at maximum compressed position.

At $t = 0$, $\quad x(t) = - A$

$\Rightarrow \quad -A = A\sin(\omega \times 0 + \phi)$

or $\quad -1 = \sin\phi \quad \text{or} \quad \phi = \frac{3\pi}{2}$

$\therefore \quad x(t) = A\sin\left(\omega t + \frac{3\pi}{2}\right) = - A\cos\omega t = - 2\cos 20t$

So, the equations only differ in initial phase and remains same in other factors.

Note Sine, cosine and positive, negative changes in SHM does not change the motion and its characteristics features such as frequency, amplitude etc. These changes only change the initial phase of the motion that is initial position of the particle.

Question 11 Figures correspond to two circular motions. The radius of the circle, the period of revolution, the initial position and the sense of revolution (*i.e.*, clockwise or anti-clockwise) are indicated on each figure.

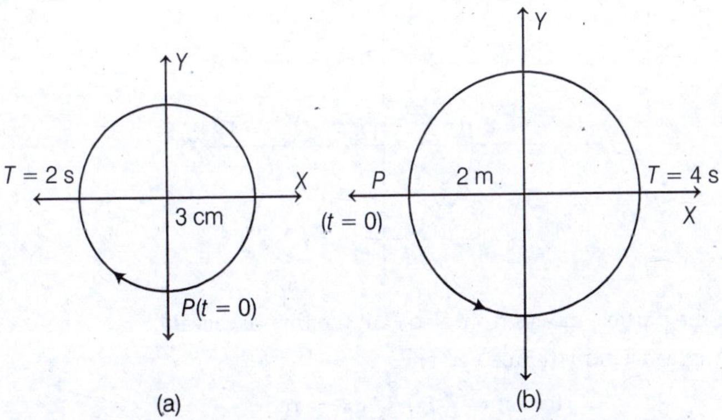

Obtain the corresponding simple harmonic motions of the X-projection of the radius vector of the revolving particle P, in each case.

Thinking Process The projection on the required axis gives the displacement. Initial phase is found from the position of the particle at $t = 0$. The displacement is considered a function of time and equated to the graphical displacement to get the required equation.

Sol. If the particle moves from P to P' in time-interval t, then angle moved by position vector (= radius vector)

$$\theta = \omega t = \frac{2\pi}{T} t = \frac{2\pi}{2} t = \pi t \text{ rad}$$

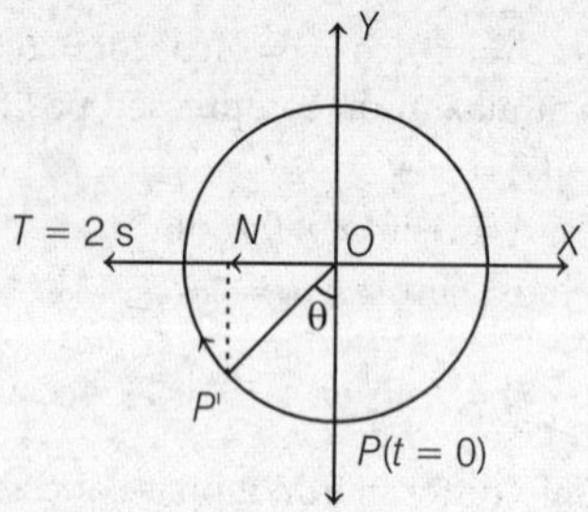

Displacement suffered by the particle

$$ON = OP' \cos\left(\frac{\pi}{2} - \theta\right) = OP' \sin\theta$$

But $\quad ON = -x(t)$

As it is left to mean position O hence, negative sign.

$\Rightarrow \quad -x(t) = 3\sin\theta \quad (\because OP = 3 \text{ cm})$

or $\quad x(t) = -3\sin\theta$

or $\quad x(t) = -3\sin \pi t$

as $\quad \theta = \pi t$

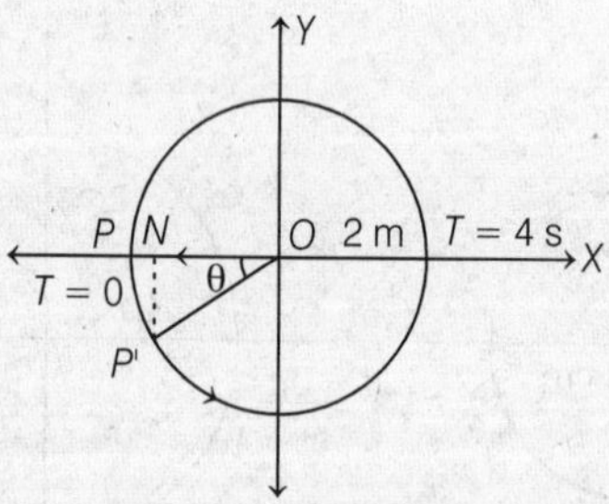

If the particle moves from P to P' in the time-interval t.

Angle swept by radius vector

$$\theta = \omega t = \frac{2\pi}{T} t = \frac{2\pi}{4} t = \frac{\pi t}{2} \text{ rad}$$

Displacement, $\quad ON = OP' \cos\theta$ or $-x(t) = 2\cos\frac{\pi t}{2}$

Negative sign to indicate left to mean position.

$$\Rightarrow \qquad x(t) = -2\cos\left(\frac{\pi t}{2}\right)$$

Note Pay attention to the direction of motion of the particle, clockwise or anti-clockwise to get the correct sign in the final result.

Question 12 Plot the corresponding reference circle for each of the following simple harmonic motions. Indicate the initial ($t = 0$) position of the particle, the radius of the circle and the angular speed of the rotating particle. For simplicity, the sense of rotation may be fixed to be anti-clockwise in every case :
(x is in cm and t is in second).

(a) $x = -2\sin\left(3t + \frac{\pi}{3}\right)$ (b) $x = \cos\left(\frac{\pi}{6} - t\right)$

(c) $x = 3\sin\left(2\pi t + \frac{\pi}{4}\right)$ (d) $x = 2\cos \pi t$

Thinking Process The given functions are first converted into cosine functions through manipulation and then compared with standard SHM equation to get the parameter values. The same is depicted graphically.

Sol.

(a)
$$x = -2\sin\left(3t + \frac{\pi}{3}\right)$$
$$= 2\cos\left(3t + \frac{\pi}{3} + \frac{\pi}{2}\right) = 2\cos\left(3t + \frac{5\pi}{6}\right)$$

On comparing to standard equation for SHM, $x = A\cos\left[\frac{2\pi}{T}t + \phi\right]$, we get

amplitude $A = 2$ cm

Phase angle $\phi = \frac{5\pi}{6} = 150°$

Angular velocity $\omega = \frac{2\pi}{T} = 3$ rad/s

This corresponding reference circle is plotted as below

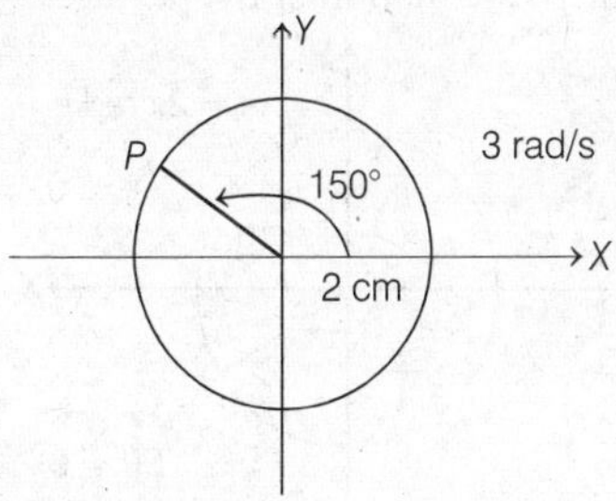

(b) $x = A\cos\left(\frac{2\pi}{T}t + \phi\right)$ is the standard SHM equation.

The given equation, $x = \cos\left(\frac{\pi}{6} - t\right)$

$= \cos\left(t - \frac{\pi}{6}\right)$ [As $\cos(-\theta) = \cos\theta$]]

On comparison, amplitude $A = 1\,\text{cm}$

Phase angle $\phi = -\frac{\pi}{6} = -30°$

Angular velocity $\omega = \frac{2\pi}{T} = 1\,\text{rad/s}$

The reference circle is plotted below

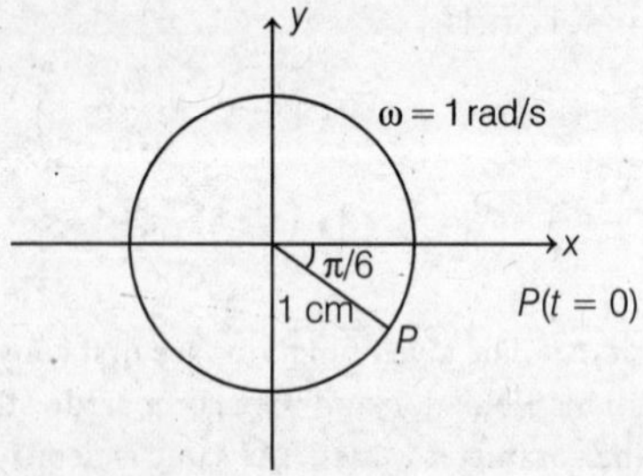

(c) Given equation

$$x = 3\sin\left(2\pi t + \frac{\pi}{4}\right)$$

$$= -3\cos\left[\left(2\pi t + \frac{\pi}{4}\right) + \frac{\pi}{2}\right] \quad \left[\because \cos\left(\frac{\pi}{2} + \theta\right) = -\sin\theta\right]$$

or $$x = -3\cos\left(2\pi t + \frac{3\pi}{4}\right)$$

On comparing with standard SHM equation

$$x = A\cos\left(\frac{2\pi}{T}t + \phi\right)$$

We get, $A = 3\,\text{cm}$

Phase angle $\phi = \frac{3\pi}{4} = 135° \Rightarrow \omega = \frac{2\pi}{T} = 2\pi\,\text{rad/s}$

The reference circle of the motion of the particle is plotted below.

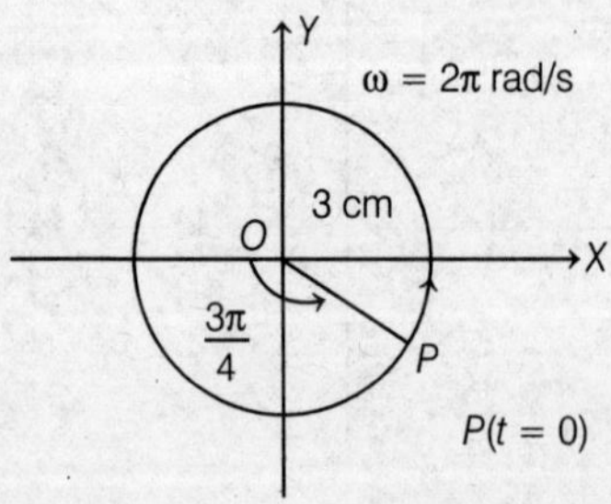

(d) Given, $x = 2\cos\pi t$

Standard SHM equation

$$x = A\cos\left(\frac{2\pi}{T}t + \phi\right)$$

Then, we get amplitude $A = 2$ cm

Phase angle $\phi = 0$

Angular velocity $\omega = \pi$ rad/s

The reference circle of the motion is plotted bleow.

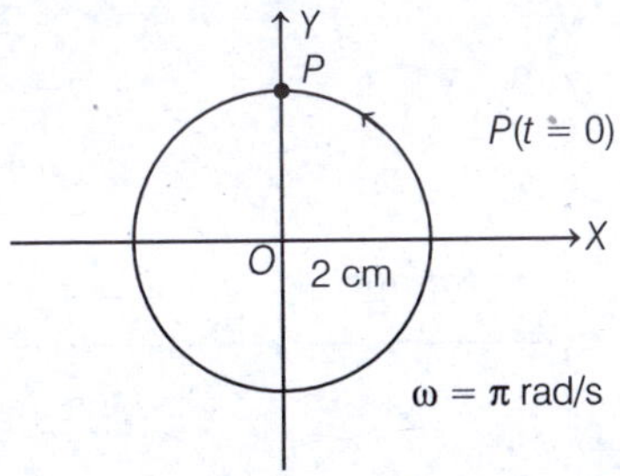

Note On X-axis, the foot of the perpendicular of the particle rotating with constant angular velocity the SHM equation follows the cosine function whereas on the Y-axis it is also SHM but follows with sine law and the two situations are not different except in initial phase.

Mistake Alert Student may use the wrong trigonometric identity of making errors in the conversion position.

Question 13 Fig. (a) shows a spring of force constant k clamped rigidly at one end and a mass m attached to its free end. A force F applied at the free end stretches the spring. Fig. (b) shows the same spring with both ends free and attached to a mass m at either end. Each end of the spring in Fig. (b) is stretched by the same force F.

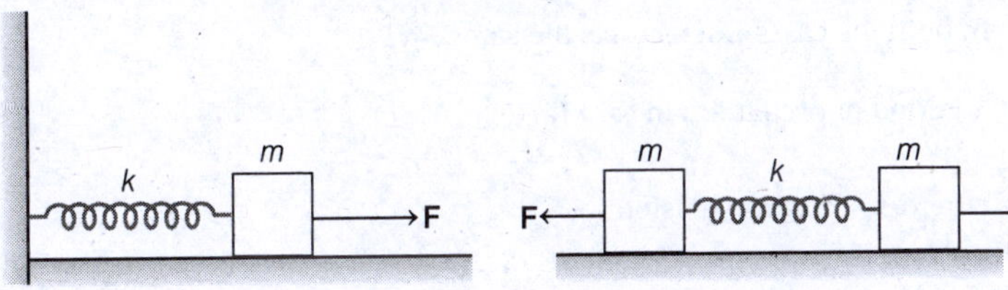

(a) (b)

(i) What is the maximum extension of the spring in both the cases?

(ii) If the mass in Fig. (a) and the two masses in Fig. (b) are released, what is the period of oscillation in each case?

◎ Thinking Process

- Draw the free body diagram to find the extension in the spring in two cases.
- In both cases the system would perform SHM. In the first the mean position will be the position of mass for unstretched case of the spring whereas in second case it will be centre of mass of the spring block system which will be the mean position for oscillation.

Sol.

(i) **Case (a)** $F = -kx$

$\Rightarrow |F| = kx$

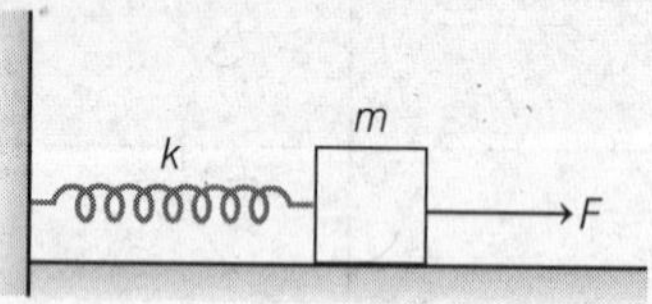

$\therefore$ $$x = \frac{F}{k}$$

Case (b),

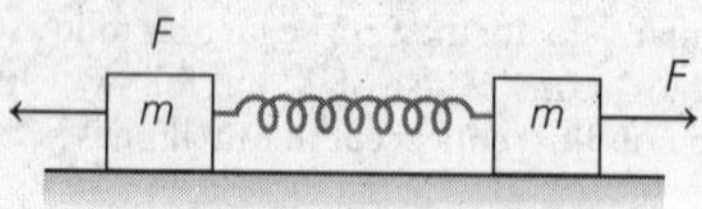

If x' is the extension in the spring then, drawing free body diagram of either mass (as the system under applied force is under equilibrium).

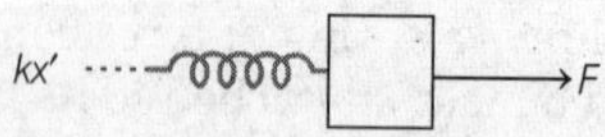

$$kx' = F$$

$\therefore$ $$x' = \frac{F}{k}$$

In both the cases extension is the same $\left(\frac{F}{k}\right)$.

(ii) $\therefore$ Period of oscillation in **case (a),**

$$F = -kx$$

where, x = given extension

But $$F = ma$$

$\therefore$ $$ma = -kx$$

$\Rightarrow$ $$a = -\left(\frac{k}{m}\right)x \quad \text{...(i)}$$

$$a \propto -x \quad \left(\text{As } \frac{k}{m} \text{ is a constant}\right)$$

On comparing Eq. (i) with $a = -\omega^2 x$, we get

$$\therefore \quad \omega = \sqrt{\frac{k}{m}}$$

Period of oscillation,

$$T = \frac{2\pi}{\omega} = 2\pi\sqrt{\frac{m}{k}}$$

Case (b),

The system is divided into two similar systems with spring divided in two equal halves. $k' = 2k$

Hence, $F = -k'x$

$k' = 2k$ (on cutting a spring in two halves its k doubles)

$\Rightarrow \quad F = -2kx$

But $\quad F = ma$

$\therefore \quad ma = -2kx$

$$\Rightarrow \quad a = -\left(\frac{2k}{m}\right)x \quad \text{...(ii)}$$

$\Rightarrow \quad a \propto -$ displacement $\quad$ (As $\frac{2k}{m}$ is a constant)

On comparing Eq. (ii) with $a = -\omega^2 x$, we get

$$\omega = \sqrt{\frac{2k}{m}}$$

Period of oscillation,

$$T = \frac{2\pi}{\omega} = 2\pi\sqrt{\frac{m}{2k}}$$

Note Had the masses in case (b) been different still we would have got a single period of oscillation and not two different value.

Question 14 The piston in the cylinder head of a locomotive has a stroke (twice the amplitude) of 1.0 m. If the piston moves with simple harmonic motion with an angular frequency of 200 rad/min, what is its maximum speed?

◎ ***Thinking Process*** In SHM maximum speed is at the mean position when acceleration is minimum (= 0) whereas maximum acceleration is at either of extreme positions where speed is minimum (= 0).

Sol. Given, angular frequency of the piston, $\omega = 200$ rad/min

Stroke length = 1 m

$\therefore$ Amplitude of SHM, $\quad A = \frac{\text{Stroke length}}{2} = \frac{1}{2} = 0.5$ m

Now, $v_{max} = \omega A$

$$= 200 \times 0.5 = 100 \text{ m/min}$$

$$= \frac{100 \text{ m}}{60 \text{ s}} = 1.67 \text{ m/s}$$

Mistake Alert Student can incorrectly relate the stroke length and amplitude. Forgetting that the stroke length is twice of the amplitude.

Question 15 The acceleration due to gravity on the surface of moon is 1.7 m/s^2. What is the time period of a simple pendulum on the surface of moon, if its time period on the surface of earth is 3.5 s? (g on the surface of earth is 9.8 m/s^2.)

Thinking Process Consider the two time periods separately. Then, get the ratio and put the given values to get the result.

Sol. Given, acceleration due to gravity on moon (g_m) = 1.7 m/s^2

Acceleration due to gravity on earth (g_e) = 9.8 m/s^2

Time period on earth T_e = 3.5 s

Time period on moon T_m = ?

On the surface of the earth, time period = T_e

$$\therefore \quad T_e = 2\pi\sqrt{\frac{l}{g_e}} \quad \text{...(i)}$$

On the surface of the moon, time period = T_m

$$\therefore \quad T_m = 2\pi\sqrt{\frac{l}{g_m}} \quad \text{...(ii)}$$

g_e, g_m are acceleration due to gravity on the earth and moon surface respectively.

On dividing Eq. (i) by Eq. (ii),

$$\frac{T_e}{T_m} = \frac{2\pi}{2\pi}\sqrt{\frac{l}{l} \times \frac{g_m}{g_e}}$$

$$\Rightarrow \quad \frac{T_e}{T_m} = \sqrt{\frac{g_m}{g_e}}$$

$$\Rightarrow \quad T_m = \left(\sqrt{\frac{g_e}{g_m}}\right) T_e$$

Putting the values, we get

$$T_m = \sqrt{\frac{9.8}{1.7}} \times 3.5 = 8.4 \text{ s}$$

Note Don't first find the length of the simple pendulum to same time and avoid lengthy calculation. While comparing the two time periods make sure that similar quantities must have same units, not necessarily SI unit, as being ratio they cancel out.

Question 16 A simple pendulum of length l and having a bob of mass M is suspended in a car. The car is moving on a circular track of radius R with a uniform speed v. If the pendulum makes small oscillations in a radial direction about its equilibrium position, what will be its time period?

◎ *Thinking Process* For a simple pendulum $T = 2\pi\sqrt{\frac{l}{g_{eff}}}$; so you should always find the g_{eff} in the situation; the pendulum is oscillating and then calculate the time period.

Sol. The bob is subjected to two simultaneous, accelerations perpendicular to each other *viz* acceleration due to gravity g and radial acceleration $a_R = \frac{v^2}{R}$ towards the centre of the circular path.

$\therefore$ Effective acceleration $a_{eff} = \sqrt{g^2 + \left(\frac{v^2}{R}\right)^2}$

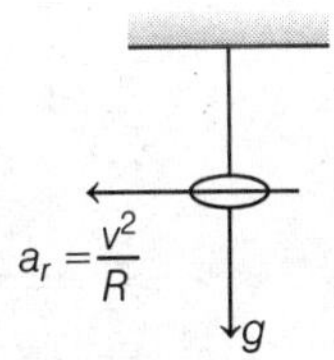

$\therefore$ Time period of the simple pendulum $T = 2\pi\sqrt{\frac{l}{a_{eff}}}$

$$= 2\pi\sqrt{\frac{l}{\sqrt{g^2 + \left(\frac{v^2}{R}\right)^2}}}$$

$$= 2\pi\sqrt{\frac{l}{\sqrt{g^2 + \frac{v^4}{R^2}}}}$$

Note Acceleration is a vector quantity. Hence, while finding the resultant of two accelerations, add them vectorially and not algebraically. Now, you consider the magnitude of resultant acceleration for further calculations.

Question 17 A cylindrical piece of cork of density ρ of base area A and height h floats in a liquid of density ρ_l. The cork is depressed slightly and then released. Show that the cork oscillates up and down simple harmonically with a period

$$T = 2\pi\sqrt{\frac{h\rho}{\rho_l g}}$$

where ρ is the density of cork. (Ignore damping due to viscosity of the liquid).

◎ *Thinking Process* Whenever we have to find an expression for time-period of an oscillating system, then first of all find restoring force and then go step by step following the basic principle.

Sol. Mass of the cylindrical cork (m) = Volume × Density

$$= Ah\rho$$

In floating condition the weight of the cylinder is just balanced by the upthrust of the liquid.

When cylindrical cork is displaced down by a depth x further and then released it oscillates about its mean position.

Restoring force acting on it = Weight of extra liquid displaced

$$F = -\text{(Volume} \times \text{Density of liquid)} \times g$$

$$= -(Ax\rho_l)g$$

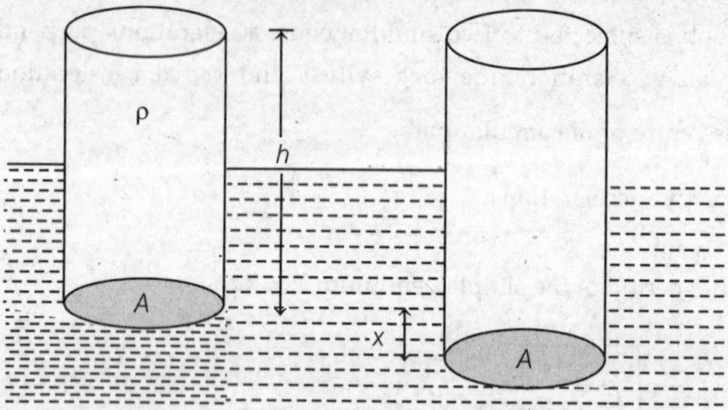

Acceleration of the cylinder

$$a = \frac{F}{m} = -\frac{Ax\rho_l g}{m}$$

Substituting value of m, we get

$$a = \frac{-Ax\rho_l g}{Ah\rho} = \frac{-\rho_l g}{\rho h} x \qquad \ldots\text{(i)}$$

As $\frac{\rho_l g}{\rho h}$ = constant

∴ Acceleration $(a) \propto -$ displacement (x)

Therefore motion of the cylindrical cork is SHM.

On comparing Eq. (i) with $a = -\omega^2 x$, we get

$$\omega = \sqrt{\frac{\rho_l g}{\rho h}}$$

Time period $T = \frac{2\pi}{\omega}$

$$T = 2\pi\sqrt{\frac{\rho h}{\rho_l g}}$$

Note Time period of the oscillation does not depend upon the amount of push given to the cylinder. It depends on the length of the cylinder. But the extent of push decides the amplitude of oscillation.

Question 18 One end of a U-tube containing mercury is connected to a suction pump and the other end to atmosphere. A small pressure difference is maintained between the two columns. Show that when the suction pump is removed, the column of mercury in the U-tube executes simple harmonic motion.

◎ *Thinking Process* Start from the beginning, find the restoration force and then apply the rule to determine time period in typical SHM.

Sol. Let area of cross-section of each arm of the U-tube be A.

When a small pressure difference be maintained between two columns then liquid column falls through height h in one arm. Now difference in liquid column in two arms = $2h$

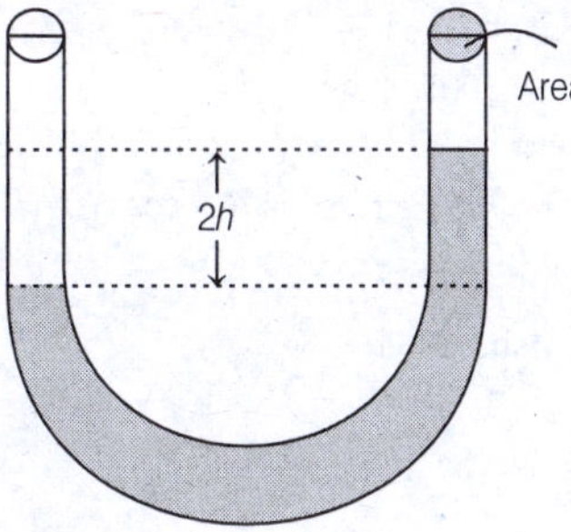

Density of mercury column = ρ

Accleration due to gravity = g

Restoring force

$$F = -\text{Weight of mercury column in excess of one arm}$$
$$= -(\text{Volume} \times \text{Density} \times g) = -(A \times 2h \times \rho \times g)$$
$$= -2A\rho g h = -k \times \text{Displacement in one arm } (h)$$

Clearly, $2A\rho g$ = constant = k (say) (As $F = -kx$)

$$F \propto -h$$

Hence, motion is SHM, $k = 2A\rho g$

$\therefore$ Time period, $T = 2\pi\sqrt{\frac{m}{k}} = 2\pi\sqrt{\frac{m}{2A\rho g}}$

where, m = mass of the mercury column of length $2l$

If ρ_{Hg} is density of mercury,

then $m = Al\rho$

$$\therefore \quad T = 2\pi\sqrt{\frac{Al\rho}{2A\rho g}} = 2\pi\sqrt{\frac{l}{2g}}$$

Note It should be noted that the SHM in U-tube is independent of cross-sectional area of the limb, density of the liquid and total mass/volume present. But it does depend on total length of the liquid column in it.

DIKSHA APP Questions

☐ Multiple Choice Questions

Q.1 The equation describing SHM of a particle along X-axis with symbols having their usual meaning is $x = 4\sin\left[100\,\pi t + \frac{\pi}{6}\right]$.

The equation can be rewritten as

(a) $x = 2\sqrt{3}\sin(100\pi t) + 2\cos(100\pi t)$
(b) $x = 2\sqrt{3}\sin(100\pi t) - 2\cos(100\pi t)$
(c) $x = 2\sin(100\pi t) + 2\sqrt{3}\cos(100\pi t)$
(d) $x = 2\sqrt{3}\cos(100\pi t) - 2\sin(100\pi t)$

Sol. (a) Since we know that, $\sin(A + B) = \sin A\cos B + \cos A\sin B$

On comparing with given equation

$$x = 4\sin\left[100\pi t + \frac{\pi}{6}\right]$$

Here, $A = 100\pi t$

$B = \frac{\pi}{6}$

So, equation can be rewritten as

$$x = 4\sin(100\pi t)\cos\frac{\pi}{6} + 4\cos(100\pi t)\sin\frac{\pi}{6}$$
$$= 2\sqrt{3}\sin(100\pi t) + 2\cos(100\pi t)$$

Q.2 The instantaneous displacement, x (in cm) of a particle moving along X axis is $x = 8\sin 10\pi t\cos 10\pi t$

Which of the following statements is correct ?

(a) Motion is not simple harmonic
(b) Motion is simple harmonic with $A = 8$ cm, $\nu = 5$ Hz.
(c) Motion is simple harmonic with $A = 4$ cm, $\nu = 10$ Hz
(d) Motion is simple harmonic with $A = 8$ cm, $\nu = 10$ Hz

Sol. (c) The given equation can be written as

$$x = 4\sin 20\pi t \qquad \ldots(i)$$

(using trigonometric identity $\sin 2\theta = 2\sin\theta\cos\theta$)

Comparing equation 1 with standard equation of SHM

$x = A\sin(\omega t + \phi_0)$ we have

$A = 4$ cm, $\omega = 2\pi\nu = 20\pi$

$\Rightarrow \quad \omega = 10$ Hz.

$\phi_c = 0$

Q.3 Two particles execute SHM of same amplitude A and same frequency ν along X axis. The maximum separation between the two particles during their motion is $\sqrt{3}$ A. The intial phase difference ϕ_0 between the two SHMs is

(a) $\frac{\pi}{3}$ (b) $\frac{2\pi}{3}$ (c) $\frac{\pi}{6}$ (d) $\frac{\pi}{4}$

Sol. (b) Let instantaneous displacement of two SHM are A_1 and A_2 then

$$A_1 = A\sin 2\pi\nu t$$

and $$A_2 = A\sin(2\pi\nu t + \phi_0)$$

The separation between two particles at any instant is

$$A_2 - A_1 = A[sin(2\pi\nu t + \phi_0) - \sin 2\pi\nu t]$$

$$\sqrt{3}A = 2A\cos\left(\frac{2\pi\nu t + \phi_0 + 2\pi\nu t}{2}\right)\sin\left(\frac{2\pi\nu t + \phi_0 - 2\pi\nu t}{2}\right)$$

$$\sqrt{3} = 2\cos\left(2\pi\nu t + \frac{\phi_0}{2}\right)\sin\frac{\phi_0}{2}$$

the maximum value of $\cos\left(2\pi\nu t + \frac{\phi_0}{2}\right)$ is ± 1

so $$\sqrt{3} = 2\sin\frac{\phi_0}{2}$$

$$\frac{\sqrt{3}}{2} = \sin\frac{\phi_0}{2}$$

$$\frac{\pi}{3} = \frac{\phi_0}{2} \Rightarrow \frac{2\pi}{3} = \phi_0$$

Q.4 The momentum *versus* position curve for a particle of mass 'm' executing SHM, of force constant K is a circle. Then the numerical value of m is equal to

(a) k (b) $\frac{1}{k}$ (c) k^2 (d) $\frac{1}{k^2}$

Sol. (b) By energy conservation principle

$$\frac{1}{2}mv^2 + \frac{1}{2}kx^2 = E \text{ (constant)}$$

$$\frac{m^2v^2}{2m} + \frac{1}{2}kx^2 = E$$

$$\frac{p^2}{2mE} + \frac{x^2}{\frac{2E}{k}} = 1$$

Comparing equation with equation of circle we have

$$\frac{x^2}{a^2} + \frac{y^2}{b^2} = 1$$

$$2mE = \frac{2E}{k} \Rightarrow m = \frac{1}{k}.$$

Q.5 A particle executes SHM of amplitude A and total energy E. When the instantaneous displacement of the particle is $\pm\frac{A}{\sqrt{2}}$, k and u denote the kinetic and potential energy of the particle. What is (i) $\frac{u}{k}$ and (ii) $\frac{E}{u}$?

(a) $\frac{u}{k}=1; \frac{E}{u}=2$ (b) $\frac{u}{k}=1; \frac{E}{u}=1$

(c) $\frac{u}{k}=2; \frac{E}{u}=\frac{3}{2}$ (d) $\frac{u}{k}=\frac{1}{2}; \frac{E}{u}=\frac{2}{3}$

Sol. (a) As $x=\pm\frac{A}{\sqrt{2}}$. The potential energy at any instant is

$$u=\frac{1}{2}kx^2=\frac{1}{4}kA^2 \quad \text{...(i)}$$

Total energy of SHM $E=u_{max}=\frac{1}{2}kA^2$ ...(ii)

So, KE is given by $K=E-u=\frac{1}{4}KA^2$

$$\frac{u}{K}=1 \text{ and } \frac{E}{u}=2$$

Q.6 $u=\alpha+\beta x^2$ is the relation between the instantaneous potential (u) and instantaneous displacement (x) of a particle of mass m. α and β are constants. Which of the following statements is correct?

(a) Motion is periodic but not simple harmonic.

(b) Motion is simple harmonic of time period $2\pi\sqrt{\frac{m}{\beta}}$.

(c) Motion is simple harmonic of time period $2\pi\sqrt{\frac{m}{2\beta}}$.

(d) Motion is neither periodic nor simple harmonic.

Sol. (c) In general, potential energy and displacement at any instant u and x in SHM satisfy the relation

$$u=u_0+\frac{1}{2}kx^2$$

but we have $u=\alpha+\beta x^2$

On comparing equation we have $\frac{k}{2}=\beta$ or $k=2\beta$.

The time period of SHM is given by

$$T=2\pi\sqrt{\frac{m}{2\beta}}$$

Q.7 A mass M attached to a spring of spring constant k_1 executes vertical oscillations of time period T_1. The mass is reduced by 25% and attached to another spring of spring constant k_2. The time period of vertical oscillations is 50% more than T_1. $\frac{k_2}{k_1}$ is

(a) $\frac{2}{3}$ (b) $\frac{1}{3}$

(c) $\frac{9}{4}$ (d) $\frac{4}{9}$

Sol. (b) Initially $T_1 = 2\pi\sqrt{\frac{M}{k_1}}$

Second time

$$T_2 = 2\pi\sqrt{\frac{M'}{k_2}} = 2\pi\sqrt{\frac{M-\frac{M}{4}}{k_2}} = 2\pi\sqrt{\frac{3M}{4k_2}}$$

$$\therefore \quad \frac{T_1}{T_2} = \sqrt{\frac{M}{k_1} \times \frac{4k_2}{3M}} \Rightarrow \frac{T_1^2}{T_2^2} = \frac{4k_2}{3k_1}$$

$$\left(\frac{2}{3}\right)^2 = \frac{4k_2}{3k_1} \Rightarrow \frac{k_2}{k_1} = \frac{1}{3}.$$

Q.8 A mass M attached to the free end of a vertical spring executes SHM of time period T. The mass is immersed completely in a non-viscous liquid as shown in figure. What change; if any is observed in the oscillations of mass M?

(The mass remains inside liquid throughout the motion)

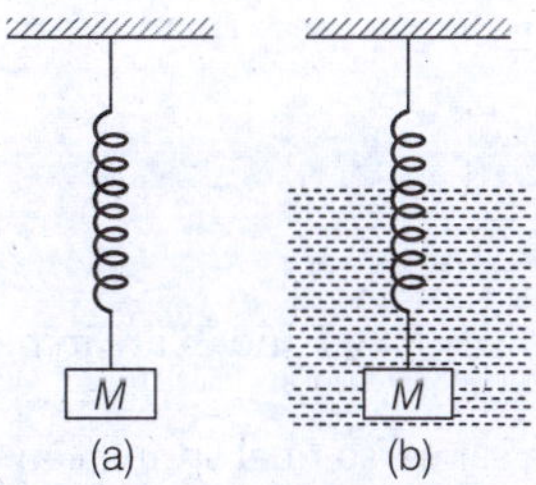

(a) There is no change.
(b) Time period increase.
(c) The mean (or equilibrium) position move upwards. Time period remains the same mean (or equilibrium) position move downwards.
(d) Time period remains the same.

Sol. (c) When mass is immersed completely in liquid, its effective acceleration decreases. As a result mean equilibrium position moves vertically upwards.

Now time period (T) of oscillations is $T = 2\pi\sqrt{\frac{M}{k}}$.

since mass M and k remains same so the time period of oscillations remains same.

Q.9 A second pendulum has a bob of a material of density ρ. The bob is immersed completely in a non-viscous liquid of density $\sigma = \frac{\rho}{2}$. The time period of oscillation is

(a) 2 s (b) $2\sqrt{2}$ s (c) $\sqrt{2}$ s (d) 1 s

Sol. (b) The time period of second pendulum is 2 s having length 'l'

So, $$T = 2\pi\sqrt{\frac{l}{g}} = 2 \quad \text{...(i)}$$

When bob is immersed completely in liquid the effective value of g is

$$g_{\text{eff}} = g\left(1 - \frac{\sigma}{\rho}\right)2 = g\left(1 - \frac{1}{2}\right) = \frac{g}{2} \quad \text{...(ii)}$$

The new time period T' of oscillation is

$$T' = 2\pi\sqrt{\frac{l}{g_{\text{eff}}}} = 2\pi\sqrt{\frac{2l}{g}} = 2\sqrt{2}\text{ S.}$$

Q.10 For the arrangement as shown in figure; the time period of oscillations of mass M is

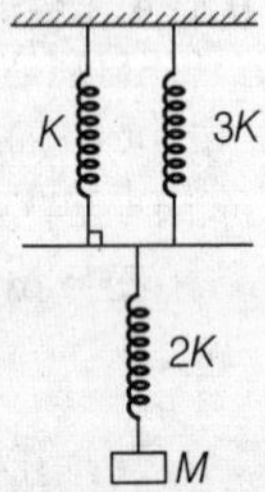

(a) $2\pi\sqrt{\frac{M}{6k}}$

(b) $2\pi\sqrt{\frac{2M}{k}}$

(c) $\pi\sqrt{\frac{3M}{k}}$

(d) $2\pi\sqrt{\frac{2M}{3k}}$

Sol. (c) In figure springs of constant k and $3k$ are in parallel. So, effective spring constant is $k' = k + 3k = 4k$.

Now k' and 2 k are in series, so final spring constant is

$$\frac{1}{k'} = \frac{1}{k'} + \frac{1}{2k}, \frac{1}{k'} = \frac{1}{4k} + \frac{1}{2k}$$

$$\frac{1}{k'} = \frac{1+2}{4k} \Rightarrow k' = \frac{4k}{3}.$$

So, effective time period is

$$T = 2\pi\sqrt{\frac{M}{k'}} = 2\pi\sqrt{\frac{3M}{4k}} = \pi\sqrt{\frac{3M}{k}}.$$

Waves

CHAPTER 14

Important Points

01 A wave is a disturbance that travels through a medium, carrying energy, without transporting matter.

02 There are two types of waves

(i) **Transverse Wave** When a transverse wave propagates in a medium its particles vibrate normal to the direction of motion of wave. These waves travels in the form of crests and troughs.

(ii) **Longitudinal Wave** When a longitudinal wave propagates in a medium, its particles vibrate parallel to the direction of motion of wave. These waves travels in the form of compressions and rarefactions.

03 Speed of longitudinal wave in a long rod

$$v = \sqrt{Y/\rho}$$

where, Y = Young's modulus of the material of rod and

ρ = density of the material of rod.

04 Speed of longitudinal wave in a gas

$$v = \sqrt{\frac{\gamma p}{\rho}}$$

where, p = pressure, ρ = density and $\gamma = \frac{C_p}{C_V}$

05 Speed of transverse wave in a string

$$v = \sqrt{\frac{T}{\mu}} = \sqrt{\frac{T}{\pi r^2 \rho}}$$

where, T = tension in the string

μ = mass per unit length of the string

06 Equation of a plane progressive wave

$$y = a \sin \frac{2\pi}{\lambda}(vt - x)$$

or $$y = a \sin 2\pi\left(\frac{t}{T} - \frac{x}{\lambda}\right)$$

where, λ = wavelength, a = amplitude

T = time period, x = distance from the origin

07 Modes of vibrations in a stretched string

First (fundamental) Mode of Vibration

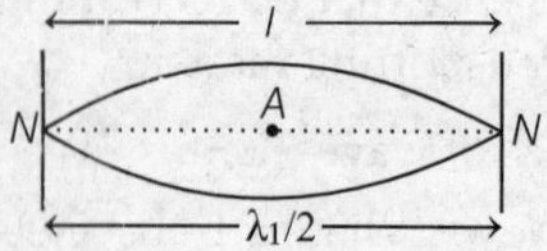

$$l = \frac{\lambda_1}{2} \Rightarrow \lambda_1 = 2l$$

Fundamental frequency $\nu_1 = \frac{v}{\lambda_1} = \frac{v}{2l} = \frac{1}{2l}\sqrt{\frac{T}{\mu}}$

Second Mode of Vibration

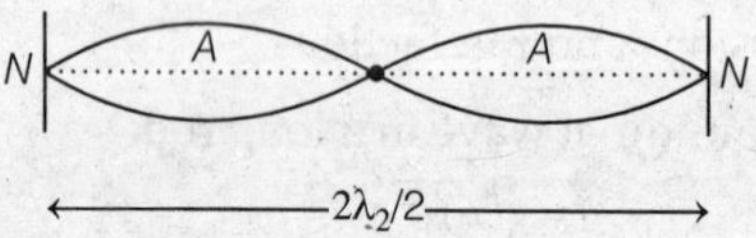

$$\lambda_2 = l$$

and $$v_2 = \frac{v}{l} = \frac{1}{l}\sqrt{\frac{T}{\mu}} = 2\nu_1$$

Third Mode of Vibration

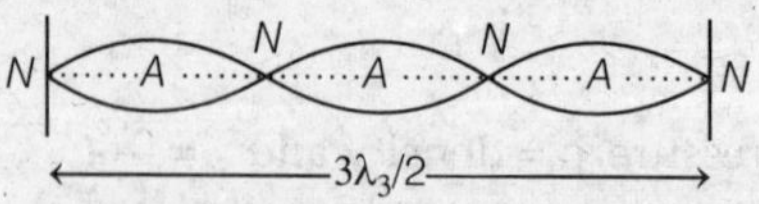

$$l = \frac{3\lambda_3}{2} \Rightarrow \lambda_3 = \frac{2l}{3}$$

and $\quad \nu_3 = \dfrac{v}{\lambda_3} = \dfrac{3v}{2l} = 3\nu_1$

$\therefore \quad \nu_1 : \nu_2 : \nu_3 : .... = 1 : 2 : 3 : ...$

08 In closed organ pipe, only odd harmonics are produced.

$\therefore \quad \nu_1 : \nu_2 : \nu_3 : ... = 1 : 3 : 5 : ...$

where, $\quad \nu_1 = \dfrac{v}{4l}, \nu_2 = \dfrac{3v}{4l}, \nu_3 = \dfrac{5v}{4l}$

09 In open organ pipe, even and odd both types of harmonics are produced.

$\therefore \quad \nu_1 : \nu_2 : \nu_3 : ... = 1 : 2 : 3 : ...$

where $\quad \nu_1 = \dfrac{v}{2l}, \nu_2 = 2\dfrac{v}{2l}, \nu_3 = 3\dfrac{v}{2l}$

10 When two sound waves of slightly different frequencies interfere, they produce periodic variations in amplitude known as beats. This results in a regular rise and fall in intensity of sound.

On beat consists of one minimum and maximum in sound intensity.

$$\text{Beat} = |F_1 - F_2|$$

Where F_1 and F_2 are frequencies of the two source.

11 **Doppler's Effect** When there is a relative motion between a source of sound and the observer, then the frequency observed by the observer is different from real frequency of the source. This phenomena of a apparent change in frequency is called Doppler's effect.

When an observer travels with speed v_L away from source, which is at rest, then apparent frequency

$$\nu' = \nu\left(\frac{v - v_L}{v}\right)$$

where, v = speed of sound in air

12 When a source is moving with speed v_S, towards the observer which is at rest, then apparent frequency

$$\nu' = \nu\left(\frac{v}{v - v_S}\right)$$

13 When observer and source both are moving in same direction (in the direction of sound), then apparent frequency

$$\nu' = \nu\left(\frac{v - v_L}{v - v_S}\right)$$

14 In general apparent frequency

$$\nu' = \nu\left[\frac{\text{Relative velocity of sound with respect to observer}}{\text{Relative velocity of sound with respect to source}}\right]$$

Exercises

Question 1 Astring of mass 2.50 kg is under a tension of 200 N. The length of the stretched string is 20.0 m. If the transverse jerk is struck at one end of the string, how long does the disturbance take to reach the other end?

◎ ***Thinking Process*** Velocity of a transverse wave on the string is given by $v = \sqrt{\frac{T}{\mu}}$ · Where, T = tension in the string, μ = mass per unit length of the string.

Sol. Velocity of transverse wave

$$v = \sqrt{\frac{T}{\mu}}$$

where, T = tension in the string = 200 N

μ = mass per unit length

$$= \frac{\text{Mass}}{\text{Length}} = \frac{2.50}{20} = 0.125 \text{ kg/m}$$

$$\therefore \quad v = \sqrt{\frac{200}{0.125}} = \sqrt{1600} = 40 \text{ m/s}$$

Time taken by the disturbance to reach the other end

$$t = \frac{l}{v} = \frac{20}{40} = 0.50 \text{ s}$$

Note Take all relevant data in SI unit and calculate the required quantity at last to avoid lengthy calculations.

Question 2 A stone dropped from the top of a tower of height 300 m high splashes into the water of a pond near the base of the tower. When is the splash heard at the top given that the speed of sound in air is 340 m/s? ($g = 9.8 \text{ m/s}^2$)

◎ *Thinking Process* Time taken by the stone to reach the surface of the water after drop is equal to time of free falling plus time taken by the sound wave to reach the ear is the total time.

Sol. Height of the tower (h) = 300 m

Initial velocity $u = 0$

Acceleration due to gravity $g = 9.8 \text{ m/s}^2$

Speed of sound in air = 340 m/s

Time taken by stone to reach the pond = t_1

Using equation of motion,

$$h = ut + \frac{1}{2}gt_1^2$$

$$\Rightarrow \quad 300 = 0 + \frac{1}{2} \times 9.8 t_1^2$$

$$\Rightarrow \quad t_1 = \sqrt{\frac{300 \times 2}{9.8}} = 7.82 \text{ s}$$

Time taken by the sound to reach the top of the tower

$$t_2 = \frac{h}{v} = \frac{300}{340} = 0.88 \text{ s}$$

$\therefore$ Total time $\quad t = t_1 + t_2$

$$= 7.82 + 0.88 = 8.7 \text{ s}$$

Note Note that the stone suffers a uniformly accelerated motion from the top of the tower to water surface and hence takes a different time to that when the sound of splash travels with a single constant speed to the observer.

Question 3 A steel wire has a length of 12.0 m and a mass of 2.10 kg. What should be the tension in the wire so that speed of a transverse wave on the wire equals the speed of sound in dry air at 20°C = 343 m/s?

Sol. Given, velocity of the wave $v = 343$ m/s

Required tension $T = ?$

$$\text{Mass density } \mu = \frac{m}{l} = \frac{2.10}{12}$$

$$= 0.175 \text{ kg/m}$$

Speed of transverse wave in wire

$$v = \sqrt{\frac{T}{\mu}} \Rightarrow T = v^2\mu = (343)^2 \times 0.175$$
$$= 20588.575 \text{ N}$$
$$\approx 2.06 \times 10^4 \text{ N}$$

Note Put the data in the final expression and take care of the units (they must be coherent, preferably SI) and than calculate in the minimum steps to get an accurate result.

Question 4 Use the formula $v = \sqrt{\frac{\gamma p}{\rho}}$ to explain why the speed of sound in air

(a) is independent of pressure?

(b) increases with temperature?

(c) increases with humidity?

◎ *Thinking Process* Using the formula given, going for manipulation to get the result required.

Sol.

(a) Given, speed of sound $v = \sqrt{\frac{\gamma p}{\rho}} = \sqrt{\gamma\left(\frac{p}{\rho}\right)}$ ...(i)

where, p = pressure

ρ = density

From ideal gas equation,

$$pV = nRT$$
$$\Rightarrow pV = \frac{m}{M}RT \quad \left(\because \text{Number of moles } (n) = \frac{m}{M}\right)$$
$$\Rightarrow p = \left(\frac{m}{V}\right)\frac{RT}{M}$$
$$\Rightarrow p = \rho\frac{RT}{M} \quad \left(\because \text{Density } \rho = \frac{\text{Mass } (m)}{\text{Volume } (V)}\right)$$
$$\Rightarrow \frac{p}{\rho} = \frac{RT}{M}$$

Putting the above value in Eq. (i), we have

$$v = \sqrt{\left(\frac{\gamma RT}{M}\right)}$$

where, R, T and M are universal gas constant, absolute temperature and molecular mass respectively which are constant, hence the expression actually is independent of pressure.

(b) Speed of sound in air $v = \sqrt{\gamma \frac{RT}{M}}$,

where, γ, R and M remaining constant.

$\therefore v \propto \sqrt{T}$, hence as temperature increases velocity also increases.

(c) The molecular mass of water is 18 which is less than that of $N_2(28)$ and $O_2(32)$.

(Therefore, as humidity increases in the air, it becomes less and less in mass or density of air decreases).

Now, $$v = \sqrt{\gamma \frac{RT}{M}}$$

$$v \propto \sqrt{\frac{1}{M}}$$

As M decreases, velocity increases.

Quick Solution

$$v = \sqrt{\frac{\gamma p}{\rho}} \Rightarrow v \propto \frac{1}{\sqrt{\rho}}$$

As density of humid air is less than normal air so velocity of sound in air increases.

Note Actually when pressure is increased, then volume is reduced such that mass/volume $= \rho$ also increases and (p/ρ) remains constant. But when temperature is increased pressure and volume both increases hence affecting the sound velocity.

Question 5 You have learnt that a travelling wave in one dimension is represented by a function $y = f(x, t)$, where x and t must appear in the combination $x - vt$ or $x + vt$, i.e., $y = f(x \pm vt)$. Is the converse true? Examine if the following functions for y can possibly represent a travelling wave :

(a) $(x - vt)^2$

(b) $\log\left(\frac{(x + vt)}{x_0}\right)$

(c) $\frac{1}{(x + vt)}$.

◎ ***Thinking Process*** Conceptual question based on fundamentals of characteristics of a travelling wave.

Sol. The converse is not true means if the function can be represented in the form $y = f(x \pm vt)$, it does not necessarily express a travelling wave. As the essential condition for a travelling wave is that the vibrating particle must have finite displacement value for all x and t.

(a) For $x = 0$

If $t \to 0$, then $(x - vt)^2 \to 0$ which is finite, hence not is a wave as it passes the two tests.

(b) $\log\left(\dfrac{x + vt}{x_0}\right)$

At $x = 0$ and $t = 0$

$$f(x, t) = \log\left(\frac{0 + 0}{x_0}\right)$$

$$= \log 0 \to \infty$$

Hence, it is not a wave.

(c) $\dfrac{1}{x + vt}$

For $x = 0, t = 0$

$$f(x) \to \infty$$

Though the function is of $(x \pm vt)$ type still at $x = 0$, it is infinite, hence it is not a wave.

Note A wave could be either in form of a single propagating wave or a continuous travelling wave. It should not be always thought of a continuous travelling wave. The third category of waves is stationary wave, which though is a wave but not travelling, the energy in such waves is confined locally. While testing a function for a wave you should always check for all the possibilities.

Question 6 A bat emits ultrasonic sound of frequency 1000 kHz in air. If the sound meets a water surface, what is the wavelength of (a) the reflected sound, (b) the transmitted sound? Speed of sound in air is 340 m/s and in water 1486 m/s.

◎ ***Thinking Process*** Whenever a medium through which a wave travels, changes the frequency does not change but the wave velocity changes. Hence, use the basic relation $v = \nu\lambda$ and calculate the new wavelength.

Sol.

(a) The reflected sound travels in the air, so

speed of sound in air $v = 340$ m/s, frequency $\nu = 1000 \times 10^3$ Hz

Wavelength of sound $\lambda = \dfrac{v}{\nu} = \dfrac{340}{10^6} = 3.4 \times 10^{-4}$ m

(b) Speed of the sound wave in water, $v_w = 1486$ m/s

$\therefore$ Wavelength of transmitted wave $= \lambda_t = \dfrac{v_w}{\nu} = \dfrac{1486}{10^6}$

$$= 1.49 \times 10^{-3} \text{ m}$$

Mistake Alert Student can forget to convert unit to SI unit *i.e.*, (meters, hertz, sounds).

Question 7 A hospital uses an ultrasonic scanner to locate tumours in a tissue. What is the wavelength of sound in the tissue in which the speed of sound is 1.7 km/s? The operating frequency of the scanner is 4.2 MHz.

◎ ***Thinking Process*** Direct application of the relation $v = \nu\lambda$.

Sol. Speed of the wave $v = 1.7 \text{ km/s} = 1.7 \times 10^3 \text{ m/s}$

Operating frequency of the scanner $\nu = 4.2 \text{ MHz}$
$$= 4.2 \times 10^6 \text{ Hz}$$

$\therefore$ Wavelength of sound in the tissue

$$\lambda = \frac{v}{\nu} = \frac{1.7 \times 10^3}{4.2 \times 10^6}$$
$$\approx 4.0 \times 10^{-4} \text{ m}$$

Note Ultrasonic waves are the sound waves of frequencies higher than audible range. They travel through human tissue differently depending upon the density of the soft or hard tissues.

Question 8 A transverse harmonic wave on a string is described by

$$y(x, t) = 3.0 \sin(36\,t + 0.018\,x + \pi/4)$$

where, x and y are in cm and t in second. The positive direction of x is from left to right.

(a) Is this a travelling wave or a stationary wave?
If it is travelling, what are the speed and direction of its propagation?

(b) What are its amplitude and frequency?

(c) What is the initial phase at the origin?

(d) What is the least distance between two successive crests in the wave?

◎ ***Thinking Process*** The given equation can be compared with $y(x, t) = a \sin(\omega t + kx + \phi)$ and the parameters asked can be found out.

Sol.

(a) Given equation

$$y(x, t) = 3.0\sin\left(36t + 0.018x + \frac{\pi}{4}\right)$$

Comparing this with standard form

$$y(x, t) = a\sin(\omega t + kx + \phi)$$

Hence, the given equation represents travelling wave from right to left.

We have

$$\omega = 36 \text{ rad/s}, k = 0.018 \text{ cm}^{-1}$$

Now, frequency $\nu = \frac{\omega}{2\pi}$ and wave length $\lambda = \frac{2\pi}{k}$

Speed of wave $\quad v = \nu\lambda$

$$\therefore \quad v = \left(\frac{\omega}{2\pi}\right)\left(\frac{2\pi}{k}\right) = \frac{\omega}{k}$$

$$= \frac{36}{0.018} = 2000 \text{ cm/s}$$

$$= 20 \text{ m/s}$$

(b) Frequency of the given wave

$$\nu = \frac{\omega}{2\pi} = \frac{36}{2 \times 3.14} = 5.73 \text{ Hz}$$

(c) Phase angle $\phi = \frac{\pi}{4}$

(d) The least distance between two successive crest or trough is equal to the wavelength λ of the wave.

As $\quad k = \frac{2\pi}{\lambda}$

$$\Rightarrow \quad \lambda = \frac{2\pi}{k}$$

$$= \frac{2 \times 3.14}{0.018} = 348.88 \text{ cm}$$

$$= 3.49 \text{ m}$$

Note There are no crest and trough formation in stationary waves. Therefore, we get nodes and antinodes. It is the property of travelling waves.

Question 9 For the wave described in Q. 8, plot the displacement (y) *versus* (t) graphs for $x = 0$, 2 and 4 cm. What are the shapes of these graphs? In which aspects does the oscillatory motion in travelling wave differ from one point to another : amplitude, frequency or phase?

◎ ***Thinking Process*** To draw the displacement y-time (t) graphs for various x, we would find the value of y at given x-values and for one complete cycle to get the points.

Sol. For $x = 0$, the equation reduces to

$$y(0, t) = 3.0 \sin\left(36t + \frac{\pi}{4}\right)$$

Also, $\quad \omega = \frac{2\pi}{T} = 36 \text{ rad/s}$

$$\therefore \qquad T = \frac{2\pi}{\omega} = \frac{2\pi}{36} = \frac{\pi}{18}\text{ s}$$

$t(s)$	0	$\frac{T}{8}$	$\frac{2T}{8}$	$\frac{3T}{8}$	$\frac{4T}{8}$	$\frac{5T}{8}$	$\frac{6T}{8}$	$\frac{7T}{8}$
y(cm)	$\frac{3}{\sqrt{2}}$	3	$\frac{3}{\sqrt{2}}$	0	$\frac{-3}{\sqrt{2}}$	−3	$\frac{-3}{\sqrt{2}}$	0

For other values of $x = 2$ and 4, $(y)_{t=0}$ will be more than $x = 0$. They will lead in the order $x = 4$, $x = 2$, $x = 0$. All will be sinusoidal in nature. They do not differ in amplitude or frequency. They differ in initial phase.

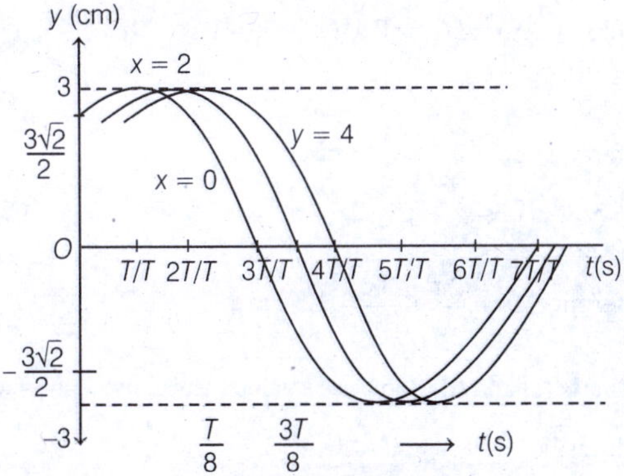

Note The graphs just have initial phase differences so, you need not find the values once you decide the initial phases correctly. Just draw the other graphs similarly differing by the phase calculated.

Question 10 For the travelling harmonic wave

$$y(x, t) = 2.0\cos 2\pi(10t - 0.0080\,x + 0.35)$$

where, x and y are in cm and t in second. Calculate the phase difference between oscillatory motion of two points separated by a distance of

(a) 4 m (b) 0.5 m (c) $\lambda/2$ (d) $3\lambda/4$

◎ *Thinking Process* Compare the given equation to the standard equation and then use the fundamentals.

Sol. Given wave equation

$$y(x, t) = 2.0\cos 2\pi(10t - 0.0080x + 0.35)$$
$$= 2.0\cos(20\pi t - 0.016\pi x + 0.70\pi)$$

On comparing with standard equation

$$y(x, t) = a\cos(\omega t - kx + \phi)$$

We get, $k = 0.016\pi$

$a = 2$ cm

$\omega = 20\pi$ rad/s

Phase difference

$$\Delta\phi = \frac{2\pi}{\lambda}\Delta x \text{; where } \Delta x = \text{path difference}$$

Now,

(a) For $\Delta x = 4\,\text{m} = 400\,\text{cm}$

Phase difference $\Delta\phi = \frac{2\pi}{\lambda}\Delta x = k\Delta x$

$$= 0.016\pi \times 400 = 6.4\pi \text{ rad}$$

(b) For $0.5\text{ m} = 50\text{ cm}$

Path difference $\Delta\phi = k\Delta x = 0.016\pi \times 50 = 0.8\pi$ rad

(c) For $\Delta x = \frac{\lambda}{2}$

Path difference $\Delta\phi = \frac{2\pi}{\lambda} \times \frac{\lambda}{2} = \pi$ rad

(d) For $\Delta x = \frac{3\lambda}{4}$

Path difference $\Delta\phi = \frac{2\pi}{\lambda} \times \frac{3\lambda}{4} = 1.5\pi$ rad

Note For parts (c) and (d) don't use k value instead use $k = \frac{2\pi}{\lambda}$ to get the result easily.

Question 11 The transverse displacement of a string (clamped at its both ends) is given by

$$y(x, t) = 0.06 \sin\frac{2}{3}x \cos(120\pi t)$$

where, x and y are in metre and t in second. The length of the string is 1.5 m and its mass is 3.0×10^{-2} kg.

Answer the following

(a) Does the function represent a travelling wave or a stationary wave?

(b) Interpret the wave as a superposition of two waves travelling in opposite directions. What is the wavelength, frequency and speed of each wave?

(c) Determine the tension in the string.

◎ ***Thinking Process*** Standing waves are characterised by fixed locations of zero displacements called nodes and fixed locations of maximum displacements called antinodes. In such wave equations, x and t factors does not appear as one phase rather they appear separate.

Sol.

(a) The given equation $y(x, t) = 0.06\sin\left(\frac{2\pi}{3}x\right)\cos(120\pi t)$ is of the form

$$y(x, t) = 2a\sin kx\cos\omega t$$

Hence, it represents a stationary wave.

(b) The two waves producing the standing wave

$$y(x, t) = 2a\sin kx\cos\omega t$$

are due to superposition of these waves,

$$y_1(x, t) = a\sin(\omega t - kx)$$
$$y_2(x, t) = a\sin(\omega t + kx)$$

We have

$$y(x, t) = 0.06\sin\left(\frac{2\pi}{3}\right)x\cos(120\pi t)$$

$\Rightarrow$ $$k = \frac{2\pi}{\lambda} = \frac{2\pi}{3} \Rightarrow \lambda = 3\text{ m}$$

Also, $\omega = 120\pi$ rad/s

Angular frequency $\omega = 2\pi\nu \Rightarrow \nu = \frac{\omega}{2\pi} = \frac{120\pi}{2\pi}$

$$\nu = 60\text{ Hz}$$

Wave speed $v = \nu\lambda$

$= 60 \times 3$

$= 180$ m/s

and $$y_1 = 0.03\sin\left(120\pi t - \frac{2\pi}{3}x\right)$$

$$y_2 = 0.03\sin\left(120\pi t + \frac{2\pi}{3}x\right)$$

(c) Speed of wave $v = \sqrt{\frac{T}{\mu}}$

Mass per unit length μ = Mass/Length $= \frac{3.0}{1.5} \times 10^{-2}$

$= 2 \times 10^{-2}$ kg/m

$\therefore$ $$T = v^2\mu$$

where, $v = 180$ m/s

$= (180)^2 \times 2 \times 10^{-2}$

$= 648$ N

Note A travelling wave has a speed but a standing wave has no velocity of propagation so has zero velocity. But in part (c) we have used the velocity to be non-zero. This is the velocity of the component waves which produce the standing wave and not that of the standing wave.

Question 12 (i) For the wave on a string described in Q. 11, do all the points on the string oscillate with the same (a) frequency, (b) phase, (c) amplitude? Explain your answers. (ii) What is the amplitude of a point 0.375 m away from one end?

◎ *Thinking Process* One of the characteristic properties of a stationary or standing wave is that. different points on the string have different frequency of vibration.

Sol.

(i) (a) All the points on the string vibrate with the same frequency, except at the node where frequency is zero.

(b) All the point on the oscillating string have the same phase, except at the nodes.

(c) All the point on the oscillating string have different amplitudes of vibration.

(ii) $y(x, t) = 0.06\sin\left(\frac{2\pi}{3}x\right)\cos 120\pi t$

Amplitude for the point at $x = 0.375$ m is $|y(0.375, t)|_{max}$

This is for maximum value of $\cos(120\pi t)$ factor which for $t = 0$

$$\cos 0 = 1$$

Now,
$$A = 0.06\sin\left(\frac{2\pi}{3} \times 0.375\right)$$
$$= 0.06\sin\left(\frac{2\pi}{3} \times \frac{3}{8}\right) = 0.06\sin\left(\frac{2\pi}{8}\right) = 0.06\sin\left(\frac{\pi}{4}\right)$$
$$= 0.06 \times \frac{1}{\sqrt{2}} = 0.042 \text{ m}$$

Note Amplitude varies only in case of stationary waves; it does not vary in case of travelling waves.

Question 13 Given below are some functions of x and t to represent the displacement (transverse or longitudinal) of an elastic wave. State which of these represent (i) a travelling wave, (ii) a stationary wave or (iii) none at all?

(a) $y = 2\cos(3x)\sin(10t)$ (b) $y = 2\sqrt{x - vt}$

(c) $y = 3\sin(5x - 0.5t) + 4\cos(5x - 0.5t)$

(d) $y = \cos x \sin t + \cos 2x \sin 2t$

◎ *Thinking Process* Typical forms of travelling and standing waves are

$$y(x, t) = a\sin(kx \pm \omega t \pm \phi)$$

and

$$y(x, t) = (2a\sin kx)\cos\omega t$$

A wave represents a travelling wave if (x, t) appear in the combination $(x - vt)$ or $(x + vt)$ and it should be finite every where and at all times.

Sol.

(a) As harmonic term ωt and kx appear separately hence represent stationary wave.

(b) $y = 2(x - vt)^{1/2}$ represent a function in x and vt terms but since power 1/2 changes the linear nature of the function hence it does not represent any wave.

(c) It represents a travelling wave as the terms kx and ωt are in combination of $(kx - \omega t)$.

(d) $y = \cos x \sin t + \cos 2x \sin 2t$ first term $\cos x \sin t$ is a stationary wave second term $\cos 2x \sin 2t$ is another stationary wave hence the combination is represented by y, which is a harmonic wave.

Note Combination of two stationary waves does not necessarily gives rise to a stationary wave.

Question 14 A wire stretched between two rigid supports vibrates in its fundamental mode with a frequency of 45 Hz. The mass of the wire is 3.5×10^{-2} kg and its linear mass density is 4.0×10^{-2} kg/m. What is (a) the speed of a transverse wave on the string and (b) the tension in the string?

◎ ***Thinking Process*** Fundamental mode of (stretched wire) vibration corresponds to a situation when the entire wire vibrates in one single loop, supports as nodes and mid-point as antinodes.

Sol.

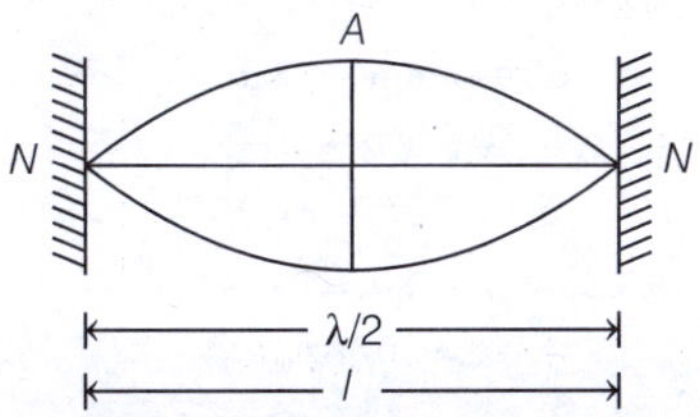

In fundamental mode of vibration,

$$\frac{\lambda}{2} = l \text{ or } \lambda = 2l$$

$$\nu = 45 \text{ Hz}$$

As $$\mu = \frac{m}{l} = 4 \times 10^{-2} \text{ kg/m}$$

$$m = 3.5 \times 10^{-2} \text{ kg}$$

$\therefore$ $$l = \frac{m}{\mu} = \frac{3.5 \times 10^{-2}}{4 \times 10^{-2}} = 0.875 \text{ m}$$

Now, from Eq. (i),

(a) $v = \nu\lambda = 2l\nu$

$v = 45 \times 2 \times 0.875 = 78.75$ m/s $\quad [\because \lambda = 2l]$

(b) As $v = \sqrt{\dfrac{T}{\mu}}$

$$\Rightarrow \quad T = v^2(\mu)$$
$$= (78.75)^2 \times 4.0 \times 10^{-2}$$
$$= 248.06 \text{ N}$$

Mistake Alert Student can misunderstand the relationship between wavelength and length of the wire in the fundamental mode.

Question 15 A metre-long tube open at one end, with a movable piston at the other end, shows resonance with a fixed frequency source (a tuning fork of frequency 340 Hz) when the tube length is 25.5 cm or 79.3 cm. Estimate the speed of sound in air at the temperature of the experiment. The edge effects may be neglected.

Thinking Process Whenever the successive resonance frequencies are given we consider the double of the length differences at which these occur to be the value of wavelength of the waves. Now, applying $v = \nu\lambda$, we can calculate the velocity.

Sol. Length at which first resonance occurs

$$l_1 = 25.5 \text{ cm}$$

Length at which second resonance occurs $l_2 = 79.3$ cm

$$\therefore \quad \text{wavelength } \lambda = 2(l_2 - l_1)$$
$$= 2(79.3 - 25.5)$$
$$= 2 \times 53.8$$
$$= 107.6 \text{ cm}$$
$$= 1.076 \text{ m}$$

Using $v = \nu\lambda$, $\nu = 340$ Hz

$\therefore$ Speed of sound in air $v = 340 \times 1.076$

$$= 365.84 \text{ m/s}$$

Note This method of calculating velocity of sound removes the edge effects thereby eliminating the end correction needs. In this question, as edge effects are to be ignored, so don't calculate the velocity taking the lower value of length of the column.

Question 16 A steel rod 100 cm long is clamped at its middle. The fundamental frequency of longitudinal vibrations of the rod are given to be 2.53 kHz. What is the speed of sound in steel?

Thinking Process Any metallic rod clamped at the middle will produce node at the centre and antinodes at open ends in fundamental and higher modes for fundamental mode length of the rod $l = \lambda / 2$.

Sol. In fundamental mode, $l = 2\left(\frac{\lambda}{4}\right) = \frac{\lambda}{2}$

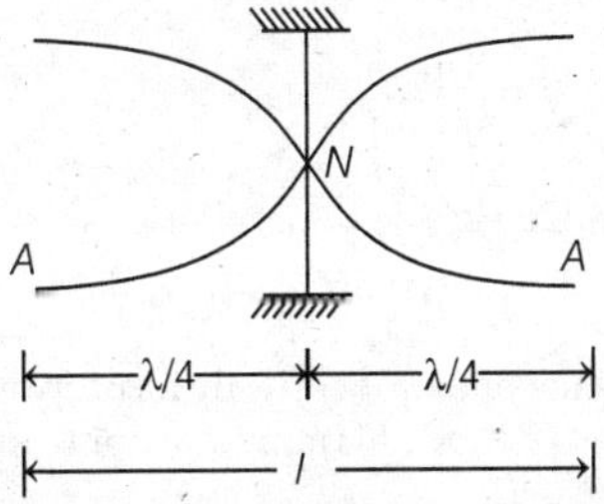

$\Rightarrow \quad \lambda = 2l$

Given $\quad l = 100$ cm, $\nu = 2.53$ kHz

Using $\quad v = \nu\lambda$

$$\Rightarrow \quad v = 2.53 \times 10^3 \times 2 \times 100 \times 10^{-2}$$

$$= 5.06 \times 10^3 \text{ m/s}$$

$$= 5.06 \text{ km/s}$$

Note Clamped ends in strings are always formed a node and free ends an antinode. The distance between two successive nodes or antinodes is half the wavelength and not the wavelength.

Question 17 A pipe 20 cm long is closed at one end. Which harmonic mode of the pipe is resonantly excited by a 430 Hz source? Will the same source be in resonance with the pipe if both ends are open? (speed of sound in air is 340 m/s).

Thinking Process In a closed pipe only odd harmonics are produced; whereas in case of an open pipe, all harmonic, even and odd are produced. Fundamental frequency is the minimum frequency of vibration.

Sol. Given, length of the pipe $l = 20$ cm

$$= 20 \times 10^{-2} \text{ m}$$

Frequency $\nu = 430$ Hz (source)

Speed of sound $v = 340$ m/s

Calculating fundamental frequency

$$\nu_{closed} = \frac{v}{4l} = \frac{340}{4 \times 20 \times 10^{-2}}$$

$$= 4.25 \times 10^2$$

$$= 425 \text{ Hz}$$

Hence, the fundamental frequency will resonate with the source.

For open pipe (fundamental frequency)

$$\nu_{open} = \frac{v}{2l}$$

$$= \frac{340}{2 \times 20 \times 10^{-2}}$$

$$= 850 \text{ Hz}$$

and then there will be no resonance.

Mistake Alert Student may incorrectly identify the harmonics for a closed pipe. May forget that only odd harmonics are present in a closed pipe.

Question 18 Two sitar strings *A* and *B* playing the note 'Ga' are slightly out of tune and produce beats of frequency 6 Hz. The tension in the string *A* is slightly reduced and the beat frequency is found to reduce to 3 Hz. If the original frequency of *A* is 324 Hz, what is the frequency of *B*?

Thinking Process The difference in frequencies is the number of beats. If tension in the wire is increased the frequency is also increased and *vice-versa*.

$$\left[\nu = \frac{1}{2l}\sqrt{\frac{T}{\mu}}\right]$$

Sol. Given, frequency of *A*, $f_A = 324$ Hz

Now, frequency of *B*, $f_B = f_A \pm$ beat frequency

$$= 324 \pm 6$$

or $f_B = 330$ or 318 Hz

Now, if tension in the string is slightly reduced its frequency will also reduce from 324 Hz.

Now, if $f_B = 330$ and f_A reduces, then beat frequency should increase which is not the case but if $f_B = 318$ Hz and f_A decreases the beat frequency should decrease, which is the case and hence $f_B = 318$ Hz.

Note Had the tension been reduced of *B* in the above case the beat frequency would have increased and not decreased.

Question 19 Explain why (or how)

(a) in a sound wave, a displacement node is a pressure antinode and *vice versa*?

(b) bats can ascertain distances, directions, nature and sizes of the obstacles without any "eyes"?

(c) a violin note and sitar note may have the same frequency, yet we can distinguish between the two notes?

(d) solids can support both longitudinal and transverse waves but only longitudinal waves can propagate in gases?

(e) the shape of a pulse gets distorted during propagation in a dispersive medium?

◎ ***Thinking Process*** Theoretical concept should be carefully applied to decide the result or reasoning.

Sol.

(a) At node, displacement is zero so the pressure is maximum whereas at an antinodes the displacement is mximum and pressure is minimum. Thus a displacement node is a pressure antinode and vice versa.

(b) Bats produce and detect ultrasonic waves. They have a developed 'Echo location' system. They emit sound of frequencies ranging between 20-100 kHz for this purpose. From the received echo signal and due to the sensitivity of their ears they get the information about the distance of the obstacle as well as the nature of reflecting surface.

(c) This is because the nature of waveforms and presence of overtones are different in the two cases *i.e.*, quality of both instrument are different.

(d) For transverse wave propagation the medium must have the property of sustaining shear or shearing stress. Solid passess this property and hence can support both longitudinal and transverse wave. However Gases cannot sustain shearing stress. So, they cannot support transverse wave propagation.

(e) A pulse is a combination of waves having different wavelengths. These waves travel in a dispersive medium with different velocities, depending on the nature of the medium. This results in the distortion.

Note At a point where compression and rarefaction meet the displacement is minimum. At this point pressure difference is maximum. Solids posses both volume and shear elasticity. Gases have volume elasticity but no shear elasticity.

DIKSHA APP Questions

☐ Multiple Choice Questions

Q.1 In the path of a progressive wave two points are 14 cm apart. What is the phase difference between these two points if the wavelength is 28 cm?

(a) $\frac{\pi}{2}$ (b) π

(c) 2π (d) $\frac{\pi}{4}$

Sol. (b) We know phase difference $= \frac{2\pi}{\lambda} \times$ path difference

$$\therefore \quad \phi = \frac{2\pi}{28} \times 14 = \pi \text{ radian}$$

Q.2 In the case of a plane progressive wave, if the maximum possible particle velocity is twice the wave velocity, then the magnitude of the amplitude of the wave in terms of its wavelength λ is

(a) $\frac{\lambda}{2\pi}$ (b) $\frac{2\lambda}{\pi}$

(c) 2λ (d) $\frac{\lambda}{\pi}$

Sol. (d) The equation of plane progressive wave is

$$y = a\sin\frac{2\pi}{\lambda}(vt - x)$$

Particle velcoity, $v_p = \frac{dy}{dt} = \frac{2\pi va}{\lambda} 2\cos\frac{2\pi}{\lambda}(vt - x)$

So maximum particle velocity is

$$\frac{2\pi va}{\lambda} = 2v$$

$$a = \frac{\lambda}{\pi}$$

Q.3 Which one among the following statements is correct with respect to reflection of waves ?

(P) when reflection takes place from a denser to a rarer medium, the longitudinal waves are reflected in the same phase but move in opposite direction.

(Q) When reflection takes place from a denser to a rarer medium, the longitudinal waves are reflected in the opposite phase and move in opposite directions.

(R) On reflection from a rarer to a denser medium, a longitudinal wave is reflected back with a change in phase.

(S) On reflection from a rarer to a denser medium a longitudinal wave is reflected back with no change in phase.

(a) (P) and (Q) (b) (Q) and (R)

(c) (P) and (R) (d) (Q) and (S)

Sol. (c) The reflected wave always travels in opposite direction to that of incident wave. When reflection takes place from denser to rarer medium no change in phase takes place but during reflection from rarer to denser medium a phase change of 180° (π) takes place.

Q.4 Given below statements are regarding transfer of energy in progressive and stationary waves.

(P) Continuous transfer of energy takes place from particle to particle in progressive wave.

(Q) Transfer of energy takes place from a particle to another particle provided they are in same phase during the propagation of progressive wave.

(R) In a stationary wave no transfer of energy takes place across the 'node' points.

(S) In a stationary wave no transfer of energy takes place across the 'antinode' points.

Example the above statements and identify which among them are correct.

(a) (P) and (Q) (b) (P) and (R)

(c) (P) and (S) (d) (R) and (S)

Sol. (b) In progressive waves there is continuous transfer of energy from particle to particle while in stationary waves nodes and and antinodes are permanent points. Since nodes are the points of zero displacement so, no transfer of energy across.

Q.5 Identity the correct statements among the following for a stationary wave.

(a) No change of density takes place at the nodes.

(b) Maximum change of density takes place at antinodes.

(c) Velocity of particles is zero at antinodes.

(d) Velcoity of particles is maximum at antinodes.

Sol. (d) In stationary waves nodes are the points of zero displacement so maximum change of density takes place at nodes and velocity of particle at nodes is zero. Antinodes are the points of maximum displacement so, no change in density take place but velocity is maximum as displacement is maximum.

Q.6 The equation of stationary wave is given by $y = 2\cos 4x \sin 20t$

Where x, y are in cm and t is in seconds.

find the value of the velocity of wave in cm/s.

(a) 2 (b) 4

(c) 5 (d) 10

Sol. (c) The given equation of stationary wave is

$$y = 2\cos 4x \sin 20t$$

Comapring the equation with standard equation of statioanry wave $y = 2a\cos kx \sin wt$

We have $k = \frac{2\pi}{\lambda} = 4\ \text{cm}^{-1}$ and $\omega = 2\pi\nu = 20$ rad/sec.

Now velocity of wave, $v = \frac{\omega}{k} = \nu\lambda = \frac{20}{4} = 5$ cm/s.

Q.7 A string of length 120 cm fixed at its two ends is undergoing stationary vibration. Considering the fundamental to be first harmonic, the positions (in cm) of maximum change in pressure in the third harmonic are

(a) 0, 40, 80, 120 (b) 20, 60, 100

(c) 0, 120, 60, 100 ,120 (d) 40, 80

Sol. (a) Nodes are the points of maximum change in pressure.

The diagram of third harmonic is

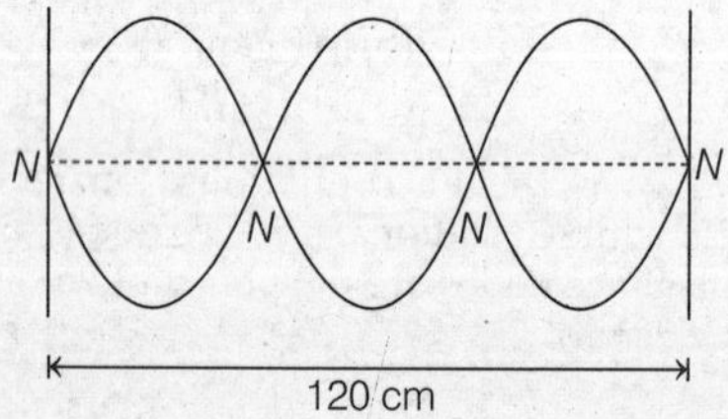

Length of each segment is $\frac{120}{3} = 40$ cm.

So, nodes are at points

$$0, 40, 80, 120 \text{ cm.}$$

Q.8 The second harmonic of a stationary vibration in an organ pipe of length 68 cm and one end closed is in unison with the vibration of a tuning fork. If the velocity of sound is 340 m/s, what is the frequency of tunning fork ?

(a) 300 Hz (b) 1350 Hz

(c) 375 Hz (d) 400 Hz

Sol. (c) The diagram of second harmonic for an organ pipe closed at one end is as shown in figure. From figure

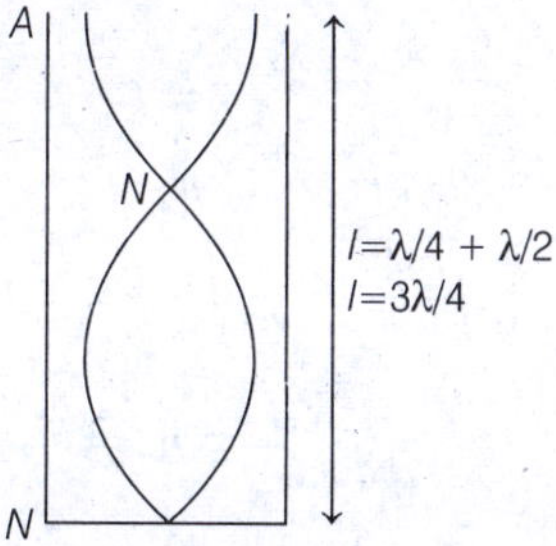

$$\frac{3\lambda}{4} = l = 68$$

$$\lambda = \frac{68 \times 4}{3}\text{ cm} = \frac{68 \times 4}{3 \times 100}\text{ m.}$$

The frequency of tuning fork, $\nu = \frac{v}{\lambda} = \frac{340 \times 3 \times 100}{68 \times 4}$

$$\nu = 375\text{ Hz.}$$

Q.9 Closed organ pipes of same length 'l' when sounded respectively in their fundamental and the second harmonic respectively produce four beats per second. Then the velocity of sound is

(a) $2l$ (b) $4l$

(c) $8l$ (d) $9l$

Sol. (c) According to questions

$$\frac{3v}{4l} - \frac{v}{4l} = 4.$$

$$\frac{2v}{4l} = 4$$

$$v = 8l.$$

Q.10 Two sonometers when sounded together produce two beats per second. They are made of wire of the same material and their length are equal. The tension in the second sonometer is 44% more than the first. The frequency of the fundamental of the first sonometer is

(a) 5 Hz (b) 10 Hz

(c) 20 Hz (d) 40 Hz

Sol. (b) According to question

$$\nu_2 - \nu_1 = 2.$$

$$\frac{1}{2l}\sqrt{\frac{T_2}{m}} - \frac{1}{2l}\sqrt{\frac{T_1}{m}} = 2 \qquad \left[T_2 = \frac{144T_1}{100}\right]$$

$$\frac{1}{2l}\sqrt{\frac{1.44T_1}{m}} - \frac{1}{2l}\sqrt{\frac{T_1}{m}} = 2$$

$$\frac{1}{2l}\sqrt{\frac{T_1}{m}}[1.2 - 1] = 2$$

$$\frac{1}{2l}\sqrt{\frac{T_1}{m}} = \frac{2}{0.2} = 10 \text{ Hz}$$

It is the frequency of first sonometer in fundamental mode.